Frontiers of Freedom

Ohio University Press Series on
Law, Society, and Politics in the Midwest

SERIES EDITOR: PAUL FINKELMAN

The History of Ohio Law, edited by Michael Les Benedict
and John F. Winkler

Frontiers of Freedom: Cincinnati's Black Community, 1802–1868,
by Nikki M. Taylor

NIKKI M. TAYLOR

Frontiers of Freedom

Cincinnati's Black Community,

1802–1868

Ohio University Press – Athens

Ohio University Press, Athens, Ohio 45701

© 2005 by Ohio University Press
www.ohiou.edu/oupress

13 12 11 10 09 08 07   5 4 3 2

Jacket/cover art: Cincinnati Wharf, 1869. Reproduced courtesy of HarpWeek.

Library of Congress Cataloging-in-Publication Data
Taylor, Nikki Marie, 1972-
    Frontiers of freedom : Cincinnati's Black community, 1802-1868 / Nikki M. Taylor.
        p. cm. — (Ohio University Press series on law, society, and politics in the Midwest)
    Includes bibliographical references and index.
    ISBN 0-8214-1579-4 (cloth : alk. paper) — ISBN 0-8214-1580-8 (pbk. : alk. paper)
    1. African Americans—Ohio—Cincinnati—History—19th century. 2. African Americans—Ohio—Cincinnati—Social conditions—19th century. 3. African Americans—Civil rights—Ohio—Cincinnati—History—19th century. 4. Cincinnati (Ohio)—Race relations. 5. Cincinnati (Ohio)—History—19th century. I. Title. II Series.
    F499.C59N428 2005
    305.896'073077178—dc22

                                                                        2004023115

To Kaia,

My sweet sunshine

CONTENTS

ILLUSTRATIONS

TABLES

ACKNOWLEDGMENTS

I cannot begin to acknowledge anyone until I thank my Creator, Savior, and Provider, the Great I AM. Thanks for your many blessings in the form of talents, opportunities, and friends to sustain my spirit. God has placed me in a special place to share this story with the world, and I am humbled by the opportunity. Of all the many lessons and blessings I have gained, the greatest of these is Faith. This book is the substance and evidence of that Faith.

I must begin by thanking my daughter, inspirational spirit, and biggest cheerleader, Kaia. She fills my days with laughter, my afternoons with joy, and my nights with meaning and purpose. On this long intellectual and personal journey, Kaia has demonstrated grace, understanding, and patience beyond her years. She exhibits the deepest pride and adoration of me and the work that I do. When my spirit was deflated because the project seemed endless or too burdensome, she restored me with soft words of encouragement: "Mommy, I know you can do it because mommies can do everything!" Although she thinks I can fly, I actually ride on her wings.

I would like to thank my mother and friend, Ladonna Taylor, for her investment in me. She planted the seeds of success into my soul when I was just a child. Her lessons of perseverance, focus, and mental toughness prepared me for this journey and others. The part of my spirit that embodies integrity, justice, and dignity, this part, I inherited from my mother. I love and appreciate her for all that she is and does.

Words alone cannot convey the depths of my gratitude to my adviser and mentor, Sydney Nathans. I acknowledge and appreciate the amount of time, attention, and dedication he spent building the scholarly foundation on which I now stand. He taught me so many of the skills upon which I draw as a scholar and historian: an infectious love for nineteenth-century history, the ability to find, extract, and amplify black voices in the most unlikely sources, and an approach to writing as an art unto itself. A gifted listener in a world of talkers, Professor Nathans respected my voice and ideas. If I could be half the scholar, writer, and mentor he is, I would consider myself blessed.

The idea for this book was hatched seven years ago in a graduate seminar with Peter Wood at Duke University, and he has been a steady source of support ever since. His greatest contribution to my intellectual growth was making me keenly aware of class in my research. It is from Professor Wood that I got the idea for the most innovative and original chapter in this book, "The Shadows." I dedicate that chapter to him. Ray Gavins, a master teacher, took me under his wing and walked me through the literature on African American history. It is from him that I developed the interest in black educational history that shaped the chapter "Palladium of Their Liberty."

I am deeply indebted to Paul Finkelman, my editor and mentor, for believing in *Frontiers of Freedom* when it was still a glorified dissertation. His enthusiastic endorsement, unwavering support, and praise for my research and writing have both inspired and uplifted me. I am fortunate to have a healthy list of other colleagues who have given of themselves at various stages of this project. Many of them read drafts of the manuscript, discussed ideas with me, or pointed me to sources. I am forever indebted to all of them. Roy Finkenbine pointed me to a treasure trove of sources at the University of Detroit Mercy. Peter Linebaugh and I have spent countless hours—"from the Maumee to the Hudson rivers"—discussing eighteenth- and nineteenth-century maritime laborers and the world they created. Adah Ward Randolph and I have found common ground in our interests in black educational history and African American community growth in nineteenth-century Ohio. Ruth Herndon and I had fruitful conversations about the warning-out system in the colonial Northeast. Abdul Alkalimat and I had several conversations about black Ohio and the Underground Railroad. I owe a great deal of thanks to Michael Washington for organizing a meeting with David Calkins early on in the project. That conversation convinced me that Cincinnati would make a compelling community study. And they were right. Others who read drafts, listened to my ideas, or offered thoughtful suggestions include Julius Scott, Michael Kay, Bob Korstad, John Thompson, Wilma King, and Christopher Phillips.

A long list of colleagues has provided an additional layer of sanity and support. They include Margo Crawford, Kathryn Dungy, Adah Ward Randolph, Ismail Rashid, Peter Linebaugh, Chouki El-Hamel, Darrick Hamilton, Dave Canton, Scot Brown, Hasan Jeffries, Khalil Muhammad, Fanon Che Wilkins, Luke Harris, Oscar Williams, Felix Armfield, Richard

Pierce, Rebecca Edwards, Joyce Bickerstaff, Tiffany Lightbourne, Norma Torney, Marla Frederick, and Deidre Hill Butler.

I want to extend my thanks and gratitude to my colleagues in the Vassar History Department for creating a supportive and collegial community in the halls of Swift. I have benefited immensely from the empathy and encouragement that we all give each other. It is refreshing to have colleagues who genuinely want to see me succeed and who go out of their way to make my environment conducive to success. I wish to give particular thanks to David Schalk for his mentorship and also to Jim Merrell and Bob Brigham for their leadership and commitment to my personal and professional happiness. I would also like to thank the faculty in Vassar's Africana Studies Program, the Center for African and Afroamerican Studies at the University of Michigan, and the Department of History at the University of Toledo.

Vassar College has been the primary source of financial support for this project. I am deeply appreciative of the grants and other research assistance my employer has provided. I also would like to acknowledge the Woodrow Wilson National Fellowship Foundation for the dissertation grant I received in the early stages of this project.

I began this project before the Ohio Historical Society had placed many of its materials on line, so I logged in hundreds of hours of old-fashioned research using the card catalogs. I was very dependent on the librarians and archivists for their knowledge of the collections. Tom Rieder and John Haas at the Ohio Historical Society are masters at their craft. Thomas Starbuck and Duryea Kemp have also been very helpful. I am also indebted to the staff at the Cincinnati Historical Society Library, particularly Anne Shephard and Laura Chace. The staffs at the Public Library of Cincinnati and Hamilton County's Rare Book Room and the University of Cincinnati Archives and Rare Books Department in Blegan Hall have been tremendously helpful.

I must, with all humility, acknowledge my project editor, Rick Huard. I have given him a far greater burden than he deserved, yet he took it in stride. His editorial skills are impeccable; I still marvel at how he transformed this book into a product of which I am now proud. Special thanks go to Gill Berchowitz, as well, for her vision and belief in this book and series at Ohio University Press.

I would like to express my deepest gratitude to my research assistants, Erica Weiner, Katherine Greenberg, Elizabeth Ghunney, and Andrew Ulrich. Erica's assistance in extracting data from the census and compiling profiles of the community was invaluable. Without a doubt, her careful work moved this project into its final stage. Katherine has also enriched my project in numerous ways, and I am forever indebted to her for that.

I began to envision writing the acknowledgments for this book more than ten years ago, when I was still an undergraduate at the University of Pennsylvania. It was at Penn that I developed a thirst for history and a desire to be a professor. I owe that to one man, Lee Cassanelli. Professor Cassanelli introduced me to a career option I had never imagined for myself. He taught me how to conduct historical research and helped me improve my writing. I am eternally grateful to him. I also benefited from the guidance of Robert Engs, Thomas Sugrue, and Drew Faust. Penn's Mellon Minority Undergraduate Fellowship Program provided the critical resources I needed to explore my research interests and to prepare for graduate school. I am extremely indebted to Valarie Swain Cade McCollum for her devotion and mentorship and to Pat Ravenell for her management of the program.

Writing a book is one of the most intellectually, spiritually, physically, and financially challenging endeavors one can undertake. In the course of getting this book to press, I have used all of my own resources ten times over and tapped the resources of those close to me. I thank my family and family of friends for being reserves of strength, motivation, and support. Anthony Allen, Gregory Allen, Malik Allen, and Jamie Cox have all made me proud to be their big sister. I also would like to thank my unusually long list of family members, particularly, Christy for all her hours of baby-sitting and encouragement. Special thanks, as well, go to the spirit of my late grandmother Harlene Duhart. Colleen Bonnicklewis and Ayanna Taylor, my friends, linesisters and fellow activists, have given me two reasons to believe in the pledge we made so long ago. I deeply treasure my friendships with Stacia Parker and Kathryn Dungy, which have been the most enduring I have. They have both shown me the meaning of sisterhood on so many levels. The bonds between us have been glued with genuine sisterhood—one forged in our youth—and reinforced by our mutual respect and admiration for one another. These are women who have stood on foundations of integrity, conviction, and purpose and never have compromised any of it. I am happy to have grown into the fullness of my womanhood with such strong and courageous peers beside me. John Owusu and David Donahue have been extraordinarily important to me. These pillars of strength have held me together in the worst of times and celebrated with me in the best of them. Soror Phyllis Wadley is a source of my deepest respect and admiration. I am indebted to her for keeping me centered on the Word. I am also thankful for friendships with John Dawson, Micheala

Brennan, Debbie Johnson, Karen Getter, Anifa and Isatu Rashid, Julie Fitzwilliam, Shenna Keane, Barbara Stubbs, Safiyya Shabazz, Raqiba Sealy-Bourne, Tanya Nelson, and Nikki McCoy. All of you have renewed me at different times with your words of encouragement, pride, and prayers. I wish to acknowledge the students who have inspired me along the way: Lori Boozer, Jade Keith, Chris Johnson, Elizabeth Ghunney, Will Sugerman, Tammie Carroll, Allen Thomas, and Eboné Dansby. Finally, I want to thank my father, James A. Taylor. My father occupies a special place in my heart. When I was a little girl he was my superhero. In many ways he still is. His unconquerable spirit has taught me to make huge leaps forward in life, without looking back, and without regrets or fears. I would also like to acknowledge my stepmother, Sylvia Taylor, who has been my father's source of support and stability over the years. Much of the joy, warmth, and sensitivity in his heart is owed directly to her presence in his life. Finally, I send love and gratitude to Peter Griffith (my completion). All of this is so much sweeter with his presence in my life.

Last, but not least, I would like to thank nineteenth-century black Cincinnati. The spirits of that community have waited far too long to tell their stories and take their rightful place in history. I hope I prove myself a worthy griot and historian of their struggle.

Introduction

"I THOUGHT UPON coming to a free State like Ohio, that I would find every door thrown open to receive me, but from the treatment I received by the people generally, I found it little better than in Virginia."[1] In fact, "I found every door closed against the colored man in a free State, excepting jails and penitentiaries, the doors of which were thrown wide open to receive him."[2] These are the words of John Malvin, the only African American to leave an extant record of his life experiences in Cincinnati in the 1820s. He had been born free in Virginia and settled in Cincinnati in 1827, at the height of its transition from a frontier town to a city. Like so many other Americans, Malvin undoubtedly was drawn to Cincinnati by job opportunities and hopes of social and economic freedom.

Located on the Ohio River at the nexus of the North, the South, and the West, Cincinnati presented a wealth of opportunity in the nineteenth century. The city emerged as a force in manufacturing and became the national leader in pork packing and steamboat construction in the mid-1820s. Cincinnati became the leading supplier of manufactured goods for most of the South and the West, earning the reputation of "Queen City of the West."[3] People seeking jobs and other economic opportunities left the Northeast and upper South and flocked to Cincinnati in this era of prosperity. In less than fifty years, Cincinnati transformed itself from a village to a booming city, rivaling older, more established cities in population growth. By 1850, Cincinnati was the sixth-largest city in the United States, having a population of more than 115,000.[4] The black population was 3,237, making it one of the ten largest free black communities in antebellum America.[5]

Cincinnati was a city full of promise, but for African Americans that promise was betrayed. For most of the nineteenth century, African American settlers must have quickly sobered to the fact that, although Cincinnati was in a free state, they would enjoy only limited freedom and citizenship. The framers of the Ohio state constitution prohibited slavery in 1802, but not out of compassion for African Americans; that same body restricted suffrage to white men. If that were not sufficient ammunition against the state's black population, the notorious Black Laws that followed shortly thereafter in 1804 and 1807 ended any doubts about whether white lawmakers wanted blacks—fugitive or legitimately free— living in the state. These laws severely proscribed black immigration into the state and excluded African Americans from several rights of citizenship. In the ensuing decades, a series of additional legislative assaults denied blacks civil rights—including the right to testify against whites or to serve on juries—and relegated them to an inferior status. In addition to these legal disabilities, black Cincinnatians were plagued by frequent acts of racial violence. From 1829 through the late 1840s, there were four major mob attacks directed against African Americans in the Queen City. Only Philadelphia rivals this figure in the antebellum period. Mobs were so frequent and virulent in antebellum Cincinnati that the city was called "Queen City of Mobs."[6]

Given such a racial climate, John Malvin's initial optimism quickly turned to disappointment and disillusionment. Within two years of his arrival in Cincinnati, he followed the course of scores of African Americans who had found the city too hostile and migrated to another part of the state. Malvin's residence in Cincinnati, although brief, underscores the limits of African American freedom in the nineteenth century.

Rather than simply revisiting how *unfree* African Americans were in Cincinnati, this book charts the emergence and maturation of the black community in this particular urban context. Specifically, it examines the process by which a transient population of former slaves developed into a self-conscious black community. This study follows black Cincinnati as it moved from alienation and vulnerability in the 1820s toward collective consciousness and, eventually, political self-respect and self-determination by the 1840s. History demonstrates that racism and discrimination never prevented African Americans from imagining and demanding freedom in words or action. Black Cincinnatians used various strategies to expand the frontiers of freedom, including assisting fugitive slaves to freedom, emigrating to cooperative settlements, and agitating for access to public schools and the repeal of repressive laws. This community expanded its boundaries beyond Cincinnati, forged coalitions with other black communities in the state and nation, and built alliances with local abolitionists.

This book is framed between two legislative moments that settled the question of black citizenship at the state and federal levels. The Ohio constitution laid the legal foundation that denied black Ohioans the privileges of citizenship throughout the antebellum era, while the Fourteenth Amendment to the U.S. Constitution conferred those rights upon all African Americans. *Frontiers of Freedom: Cincinnati's Black Community, 1802–1868* chronicles alternating moments of triumph and tribulation, courage and fear, pride and pain in the history of this black community. It tells the story of collective consciousness and moments of collective accommodation. It speaks of a vision of freedom that was constantly being redefined. More than anything, it chronicles the resilience of Cincinnati's black community from 1802 through 1868.

African Americans' definition of freedom is born and shaped by a specific set of local circumstances. In *The Story of American Freedom*, Eric Foner posits that "freedom has been used to convey and claim legitimacy for all kinds of grievances and hopes, fears about the present and visions of the future."[7] Hence, freedom is a symbol of American aspiration closely connected to notions of equality, justice, and even democracy. But freedom does not have a fixed definition because its meaning changes with its context. The sociopolitical and racial-economic climate determines how African Americans imagine, define, articulate, and pursue freedom in a given moment or context. Because the nature and extent of racism and oppression differ from one generation to the next and from one community to the next, black freedom in antebellum Cincinnati did not have the same meaning as it did in Charleston or New York. Place is, indeed, a critical lens through which to understand the African American freedom experience. And Cincinnati was certainly no typical nineteenth-century city, by any means.

Historian Henry Louis Taylor Jr. contends that nineteenth-century Cincinnati had a "dual personality, a schizophrenic northern and southern personality occupying the same urban body."[8] Although such a dual personality was typical of other border towns that stood between slave

and free states, Cincinnati was different. It also had a third personality—
a western one. Cincinnati assumed three intersecting identities: northern in its geography, southern in its economics and politics, and western
in its commercial aspirations.

Cincinnati was a northern city not simply because it was located above
the Mason-Dixon Line, but because the majority of its early settlers hailed
from the Northeast.[9] These settlers brought values and institutions with
them, contributing to the northern character of the city. Yet with a river
only half a mile wide separating it from the South, Cincinnati also assumed a southern character. Although "Cincinnati was located on the
'Frontiers of Freedom,' . . . the dark ramparts of slavery, with towering
walls and stormy battlements, overshadowed the 'Queen.'"[10] Cincinnati's
economy was dependent on the peculiar institution. The city's merchants
and manufacturers supplied southern slaveholders with food and goods
for their enslaved workforce. This trading relationship was so critical to
the city's economy that the business and merchant classes that governed
Cincinnati went to great lengths to ensure that southern economic interests were protected in the city by routinely returning fugitive slaves to
their owners and by arresting those who harbored them. Additionally,
they tolerated and sometimes even encouraged antiabolitionist mobs.
The city's dependence on trade with the slaveholding South made it the
northernmost southern city.

Just as surely as Cincinnati was the northernmost southern city, it was
the easternmost westward-*looking* city. In the nineteenth century, the West
symbolized boundless, uncharted economic opportunity.[11] Cincinnati's
business leaders aimed to make it the premier western commercial city, a
goal that was not difficult to achieve because it was the transportation
gateway to the West. In the first half of the nineteenth century, most
people traveling to the far West had to travel through Cincinnati via the
Ohio River. By 1848 Cincinnati boasted several roads, canals, and railroads that linked the city to St. Louis, Memphis, Lake Erie, Indiana,
Lexington, and Pittsburgh, facilitating commerce.[12] In many ways, the
Queen City of the West lived up to its name. One contemporary person
writing in 1848 observed, "In truth, with the exception of Pittsburgh,
there is no city in the West or South that, in its manufacturing capabili-
ties, bears any approach to Cincinnati."[13] Cincinnati's leading citizens
also hoped the city would craft a distinct western identity and culture.
One woman encouraged Cincinnatians to mold a regional cultural identity: "We should foster Western genius, encourage Western writers, pa-
tronize Western publishers, augment the number of Western readers,

and create a Western heart."[14] In many ways a western identity was forged in Cincinnati.

Although some might argue that Cincinnati's personalities were at odds with one another, Cincinnati was not a city at war with itself—its southern identity fighting against the northern one.[15] In fact, all three of its identities coalesced, forging a unique urban culture and a wealth of opportunities for white citizens from all walks of life. Nineteenth-century Cincinnati was a crossroad of opportunity for whites, but for African Americans it was the crossroad of the worst aspects of northern, southern, and western culture. In Cincinnati, a southern racial code, northern segregation and discrimination,[16] and western frontier mob violence[17] combined, with dire results for African Americans. They endured economic repression, racial segregation and exclusion, and the denial of civil rights compounded by extreme and frequent mob violence.

Cincinnati's distinct geographical location and sociopolitical and racial-economic conditions created an urban culture that profoundly affected the process of community-building among African Americans. Conditions there determined how quickly African American residents moved from a population of transients to a self-conscious community with stable institutions. Although the black population grew steadily, community-building was a slow and difficult process. Racist economic and social conditions, the constant threat of kidnappers or slave catchers, and mob violence led to a period of transience and instability, which delayed community cohesion and stability. Cincinnati's distinct urban culture also influenced black communal organization. The organization of this community differed from that of other nineteenth-century free black communities. For example, in other black communities of that period, the church typically was the most important black institution—it was not only a spiritual, social, and educational space but it was also the breeding ground of protest and activism. Historians of antebellum free black communities have assumed that every black community followed the same pattern, with the church at the center, but African American communities were shaped and organized according to their specific social and political needs and conditions. The situation in antebellum Cincinnati fostered an alternate model of community organization, with the black school at the center. Black public schools not only provided the community with a political, social, and educational space, but also were centers of protest and activism between 1849 and 1873. This book does not necessarily de-center the black church from its historical importance in Cincinnati or any other community; certainly, black schools could never fill the role of the black church. But it does suggest that the black church in Cincinnati could not completely satisfy this community's deepest yearning between 1849 and 1873: intellectual enlightenment, equality, citizenship, and educational self-determination.

Black Cincinnatians lived at the dangerous intersection of several American frontiers, including the frontiers of slavery and freedom. This book examines what the meeting of these frontiers at this peculiar junction meant for them and for the quality of their freedom. Cincinnati, Ohio, was an unusually tough soil on which to build a community, but African Americans slowly planted themselves in it and refused to be uprooted. Although the essential themes in this book are the ways in which African Americans defined and claimed freedom and asserted citizenship, there are other lessons about resilience, self-determination and collective dignity. If nineteenth-century black Cincinnatians teach us nothing else, they should teach us that freedom is not just a state of being, but a state of striving.

This book is an attempt to amplify voices that have long been muted, to put flesh around census data, to weave a story out of traveler's observations, to illuminate agency from public notices, and to resurrect a community from singular voices. When this project began as a graduate study at Duke in the late 1990s, several people warned of the immeasurable difficulties of retracing the footsteps and rediscovering the experiences of black Cincinnatians in the nineteenth century. With limited formal education and few public forums for self-expression, black Cincinnatians either did not produce or did not leave many written records of their community. Autobiographical voices like John Malvin's must, then, ring out in thunder tones. Despite the scarcity of sources written by or about African Americans, other records demonstrate that black Cincinnati was every bit as resolute and conscientious as other free black communities, if not more so.

A dearth of a broad base of black institutional records has also hampered efforts to get inside Cincinnati's black community. Few of the black churches or mutual aid organizations preserved institutional records in this period. Much of the evidence relating to these institutions came through the careful statistical records of the Ohio Anti-Slavery Society (OAS). Other bits and pieces of data were gleaned from travelers' accounts.

Cincinnati government did not fare any better at preserving the historical record of African Americans. Cincinnati municipal and criminal court records, the staple of any historian of nineteenth-century America, burned in a courthouse fire in 1884. Although some volumes of county registers or other log books survived, entries that include African Americans were few and far between. Institutional records of city infirmaries or orphanages are usually good sources to find African Americans, but in Cincinnati they were excluded from such places. Census takers routinely undercounted and misrepresented black residents; city directory compilers were even worse. There are moments of deafening silence in this text that are a function of the dearth of sources. This book, therefore, depends very heavily on the legislative record in its depiction of the sociopolitical climate in which African Americans lived, and in gleaning bits of social history from legal cases.

In order to resurrect this community, institution by institution, person by person, this book relies heavily on sources of autobiographical memory. Autobiographies by John Malvin, John Mercer Langston, Austin Steward, Levi Coffin, Eliza Potter, and several slave narratives were indispensable. With the exception of Eliza Potter, all of these authors wrote one or two decades after they lived in Cincinnati. Although the limitations posed by memory are obvious, the benefits of such sources are that these writers often fixed their autobiographical memories on moments that had historical significance for the larger community. John Malvin, for example, recounts living in Cincinnati during the 1829 riot; Langston recalls the 1841 riot; and Levi Coffin frames his autobiography after the 1850 Fugitive Slave Act.

This study also relies on community memory, or a history that is collectively shared and preserved through oral tradition. Peter Clark, Benjamin Arnett, and William Parham all relied on oral testimonies to reconstruct the histories of the Black Brigade, the African Methodist Episcopal (AME) Church, and the Masonic lodges, respectively. For example, although Rev. Benjamin Arnett, an AME minister who wrote the history of the Cincinnati church in 1874, did not personally witness the emergence of the AME Church, he learned this history from elder church members and previous ministers who did. Essentially, such people were the treasure-keepers of the church history. Each of their accounts of the early history of the AME Church becomes part of the community's collective memory.[18]

Any history of free blacks living, as black Cincinnatians did, on the edge of slavery would not be complete without a discussion of the Underground Railroad. Because assisting fugitive slaves was illegal and sometimes elicited mob violence, those who helped were naturally reluctant to leave records of their activism. Consequently, it becomes very difficult to reconstruct the inner workings of this activity. The chapter on the Underground Railroad relies heavily on fugitive slave narratives, the autobiographies of white abolitionists, and the letters, news clippings, and interviews in the Wilbur H. Siebert Collection. Ohio State University professor Wilbur Siebert collected oral testimonies from participants and their descendants in the 1890s—more than twenty-five years after emancipation ended its necessity. Although the passage of time made people feel less vulnerable about acknowledging their involvement in the system, time also had a detrimental effect on the memories of many Underground Railroad agents. Despite its shortcomings, the Siebert Collection is indispensable.

Nineteenth-century community studies tend to be histories of the black elite. Historians are bound by records, and literacy gave the black elite the advantage of being able to construct and preserve the historical record. Although much of this study covers that segment of the African American community, some space is devoted to the black lower classes. Lafcadio Hearn, who wrote extensively on this class in Cincinnati in the 1870s, left rich ethnographic editorials based on his observations. The chapter entitled "The Shadows" is a synthesis of that body of evidence. Naming this chapter "The Shadows" and placing it at the end of the book was not an oversight, but a deliberate, symbolic attempt to relegate these people to the same place they historically occupied in society. It is not the place of the historian to provide a corrective to history by integrating the shadow people into the narrative more fully than reality allows. Also, because the book is organized chronologically and because the evidence for that chapter comes from the 1870s, it is only natural that this chapter should be the last. Nonetheless, it is only fitting that the shadow people should have the last word.

Finding black women's voices, however, proved to be more difficult.[19] Most historical records exclude them altogether; others privilege black men. For example, black Cincinnati's institutional records predominantly reflect a male leadership corps in the community. Black men acted as ministers of churches, officers of the colored orphanage, trustees of the colored school board, teachers at black schools, editors of the black press, and presidents of emigration societies, school funds, and mutual aid organizations. In such positions, black men were the keepers and shapers of the historical record—a record that largely obscures the work and contributions by black women. Because institution-building is such an important element in community growth, black women's absence from the record might lead to misguided conclusions about their contribution in building communities. Even in the extant municipal and government documents, it is hard to rescue women from the record. City directories include names, ages, places of birth, and occupations of the "heads of household." In antebellum American society, head of household was a designation reserved almost exclusively for men. For census takers, women could not be heads of household, even when it was clear that there was no man in the home or when women were the primary breadwinners. Consequently, it was not until the 1860 U.S. Census that the occupations of female heads of household were recorded somewhat consistently.

For the most part, this is a chronological study, yet certain themes are dominant in some chapters. The organizational thesis is that 1841 is a watershed moment for this community. The rest of the story is shaped around that moment. Before 1841 black Cincinnati was a fragile, unstable community that was struggling to find its voice. Then, a major rupture nearly devastated and divested this community of its resources, but it slowly regained its confidence, facilitated with the help of allies. After that defining moment in 1841, the black Cincinnati community matured internally and began to articulate a vision of freedom that was linked to equality, self-determination, citizenship, and the elective franchise.

ONE

A City of Promise

The Emergence of the "Queen City of the West"

The West was another name for Opportunity.

—Frederick Jackson Turner, *The Frontier in American History*

"OYO THE GREAT," the "Beautiful River," and "La Belle Rivière" were names early settlers gave to the Ohio River.[1] Formed from melting glaciers thirty-five thousand years ago, the Ohio is fed by the Allegheny and Monongahela rivers near Pittsburgh, Pennsylvania, and flows toward the southwest more than one thousand miles to Cairo, Illinois. Along the way, the Beautiful River joins several lesser rivers, including the Scioto, Muskingum, Licking, and Wabash rivers. The Ohio River is characterized by sharp twists and turns, bends and dips. Its most dramatic feature is a twenty-two-foot drop: the Falls, in Louisville, Kentucky.[2] The river's swift and foaming currents made the water appear very white to nineteenth-century observers.

In the nineteenth century, the valleys along the Ohio River seemed to pay homage to it. Alexis de Tocqueville, who traveled extensively throughout the United States in 1831 and 1832, asserted that "the River that the Indians had named for its excellence the Ohio, or Beautiful River, waters one of the most magnificent valleys in which man has ever made his stay."[3] Dense poplar, swamp oak, and maple trees overhung the river, casting their shadows on the water. Towering trees, thick shrubs, and other vegetation covered tall hills.[4] The Ohio and its valley confirmed that this was, indeed, a "Beautiful River."

A biography of the Ohio River illustrates that communities were formed and destroyed in its valleys; lives were sustained and lost in its waters. Before 1500, the Hopewell, Adena, and Mississippian societies occupied the Ohio Valley region.[5] By 1700, the Shawnee, Mingo, Miami, Delaware, and Wyandot Indians—most of whom fell under the authority of the Iroquois Council of Pennsylvania—were inhabiting southwestern Ohio.[6] By the mid-eighteenth century, Ohio Indians were involved in a fierce three-way struggle with the French and British for control of the Ohio River and its valleys. The French wished to protect their lucrative trade routes linking Quebec to Louisiana; the British wished to expand its empire into the region; and Native Americans were determined not to allow the French or the British to displace them from the land.[7] In 1753, the Seneca "Half King" who had been appointed by the Iroquois to govern Ohio Indians declared to the French: "If you had come in a peaceable Manner, like our Brothers the English, we should not have been against your trading with us . . . but to come . . . and build houses upon our Land, and to take it by force, is what we cannot submit to."[8] At the time it served the Native Americans' interests to ally themselves with the British against the French during the Seven Years' War. After losing the war, France was forced to relinquish its claims to land in the Ohio valley under the Treaty of Paris in 1763. All land east of the Mississippi River was ceded to Britain. After the American Revolution, the U.S. Congress made these lands available to American settlers in the 1780s.[9]

In 1788, speculator John Cleves Symmes purchased one million acres of the Northwest Territory north of the Ohio River and between the Great and Little Miami rivers.[10] Symmes's purchase was located on a tract of land in southwestern Ohio referred to as the Virginia Military District, which was intended to be a settlement for Virginian veterans of the American Revolution. By 1789, three villages had been established on Symmes's purchase. One of the settlements, Losantiville, was established at the Ohio River, opposite the mouth of Kentucky's Licking River.[11] Losantiville settlers hoped the settlement's strategic location near the Ohio and Licking rivers would make the settlement a commercial entrepôt.[12] But before those dreams could be realized, Native Americans asserted their ownership of the land by bloodshed.

The tiny settlement was not secure from incursions. A powerful confederation of Native Americans led by the Shawnee constantly terrorized Losantiville settlers. The settlers were no match for the Ohio Indians, who were, at the time, the "dominant military power in the valley."[13] The Shawnee Indians and their allies were such fierce opponents of white settlements that the area earned the name "Miami Slaughter House."[14]

In an effort to protect the lives and property of the white settlers, the U.S. government built a fortress—Fort Washington—around Losantiville in 1792. Yet even this could not deter Native Americans' resolve to contest white settlers' claims on the land. Settlers were so afraid to leave that Losantiville became a community confined behind the walls of Fort Washington. And even that did not secure the safety of white settlers.[15]

Several significant battles took place between Ohio Indians and white settlers before Losantiville and her sister settlements became secure. Generals Josiah Hamar and Arthur St. Clair were soundly whipped after they led troops into battle against the Ohio Indians in 1790 and 1791, respectively.[16] It was only after General Anthony Wayne defeated the Ohio Indians at the Battle of Fallen Timbers in 1794 that the walls of Fort Washington came down, signaling the end of all significant challenges to white settlement on the land. The name of the village was then changed from Losantiville to Cincinnati—after the society of former Revolutionary War officers.[17] With the new name came a new destiny. What had begun as a humble garrison settlement in 1788 had become, by the mid-1820s, a symbol of American aspirations.

———

Cincinnati, the seat of Hamilton County, was situated in a six-square-mile plain in the southwest corner of Ohio.[18] A terrace of hills overlooked the city to the north. The dense rolling green sharply cascaded toward the Ohio River valley. Its wonder was captured in the words of one traveler: "Hill beyond hill, clothed with the rich verdure of an almost tropical clime . . . . [E]verywhere foliage so luxuriant that it looked as if autumn and decay could never come."[19] Cincinnati was bounded on the east by Deer Creek, and on the west by Mill Creek. The Ohio River, just one-half mile wide, lay to the south of the city. The river separated the city from the South geographically, yet linked the city to the South economically and socially, through a vibrant Mississippi River trade. Just opposite Cincinnati, on the other side of the river in Kentucky, was the Licking River.

The city was situated on two levels. The first tier, extending from Deer Creek to Mill Creek, was only seven feet above the level of the Ohio River. The "bottom" frequently became a swampy den of filth and disease when the water level of the river rose.[20] When the water dried, the streets were left covered with a thick layer of mud and debris. The city's second level "rose sharply fifty feet above the first bank, forming a mile-wide table. . . . From the river, early Cincinnati looked like a green and open theater carved out of the hills."[21] Extending northward from Front

Street at the shore of the Ohio River, the streets were numbered in a grid pattern. Those running east to west were named after trees—Sycamore, Walnut, Vine, Elm, and Plum; cross streets were numbered from south to north. Many of the streets were connected with dark alleys—some with names, and some without.

By 1830, Cincinnati was a city of brick houses looking out onto cobblestone streets and paved sidewalks. One traveler remarked that Cincinnati in 1856 looked like "[a] second Glasgow in appearance, the houses built substantially of red brick, six stories high." Evidence of Cincinnati's prosperity filled the streets. On any given day, drays, stacked with goods, rumbled along the streets to and from the numerous warehouses and stores. Cincinnati's shops were filled with clothing and jewelry from as far away as Paris and London.[22] The walkways were filled with "a perfect throng of foot passengers" and "the roadways crowded with light carriages, horsemen with Palmetto hats and high-peaked saddles, galloping about on the magnificent horses of Kentucky."[23] Certainly, the image of covered carriages, pulled by teams of thoroughbred Kentucky horses and moving along cobblestone streets, is a romantic one. But such romanticism is misleading when applied to nineteenth-century Cincinnati.

Although Cincinnati was a city of brick houses, it was also a city of tenements and makeshift homes. The thoroughbred Kentucky horses that walked the streets were not alone; chickens and pigs freely roamed them as well. Before Cincinnati developed a system of garbage collection, residents were required to place their trash in the middle of the road so that the pigs could dispose of it.[24] The presence of the pork-packing industry made hog carcasses scattered throughout the city a common sight. Residents near Deer Creek suffered with the unbearable stench of pigs' blood from slaughterhouses flowing through the creek. To one woman, Deer Creek was "little more than the channel through which their [pigs'] blood runs away."[25] In 1828, English traveler Frances Trollope vividly recorded this other side of Cincinnati: "We found the brook we had to cross, at its foot, red with the stream from a pig slaughterhouse; while our noses, instead of meeting 'the thyme that loves the green hill's breast,' were greeted by odours that I will not describe . . . . [O]n leaving the city [we] had expected to press the flowery sod, [but] literally got entangled in pigs' tails and jawbones."[26] Certainly, Cincinnati was a city full of contradictions—where luxury and want occupied the same streets, where the peaceful quiet of the Ohio River was flanked by bloody creeks, where culture and refinement frequently gave way to mobocracy. And just across the river, slavery stood in the shadows of freedom. As one resident remarked, "Cincinnati was located on the 'Frontiers of Freedom,' and the dark ramparts of slavery, with towering walls and stormy battlements, overshadowed the 'Queen,' and cast a gloom over her mental prosperity."[27] These contradictions would certainly play a role in the development of the city's culture.

———

Cincinnati was located at a crossroad: a border town. Here, North met South, and East met West. The city was strategically situated north of the Ohio River and between the Great and Little Miami rivers, which provided access to other settlements within Ohio, while the Ohio River was a natural bridge between the eastern and western United States. In fact, the Ohio River was the primary access route to the West. It fed into the Mississippi River, which connected northern towns to southern ports and increased the prospects for trade. The markets that lay north, south, east, and west of Cincinnati were a wellspring of commercial potential. The intersection of these commercial highways in Cincinnati created a wealth of opportunity for merchants and capitalists.

Before the 1820s, however, Cincinnati could not access those markets for want of efficient roadways and transportation. Travel by land was slow and difficult. Roads often flooded, making them virtually impassable, and crossing mountains with freight was also very difficult. Consequently, rivers seemed to be the best option for transporting goods.[28] Among the earliest means of water transportation used in trade were ferries. However, ferries were not suited for longer distances; they also could not weather the rough waters of the Mississippi River. Consequently, ferries moved only small quantities of goods between northern Kentucky and southern Ohio on the Ohio River.[29]

Most goods were carried down the Mississippi River on tugboats or rigged barges with sails. These vessels were cumbersome and costly, as James Hall, a contemporary Cincinnati statistician, observed: "Under the best circumstances, these boats were slow and difficult to manage; the cost of freight was enormous and the means of communication uncertain."[30] Round-trip trade was hampered by the nearly impossible task of ascending the Mississippi with cargo in tow. To move goods between New Orleans and Cincinnati round-trip took more than one hundred days on a rigged barge.[31] Consequently, the majority of the vessels traveling on the Mississippi River headed downstream toward New Orleans. For example, more than eighteen hundred boats arrived in New Orleans in 1807, but only eleven went upstream.[32] Many of these barges were built for just one trip down the river. Once they arrived in the port of New Orleans, the vessels were dismantled, and the wood was sold for lumber.[33] After 1815, keelboats and flatboats replaced rigged barges and traveled regularly between Pittsburgh and points south.[34] Propelled by poles, keelboats were faster than barges; but a trip from Cincinnati to Pittsburgh could still take sixty days or more. Despite the slight improvement in time efficiency for the voyage to Pittsburgh, voyagers made these trips only three times a year.[35] Traveling by keelboat up the Mississippi was another matter altogether; the trip was slow and difficult, and the cost of freight was quite high. Consequently, Cincinnati rarely imported goods from the South in the Keelboat Era.

It was not until the invention of the steamboat and its expanded use after 1811 that time- and cost-efficient water transportation became a possibility. The steamboat dramatically shortened the journey between northern ports and New Orleans, ushering in a transportation revolution. The journey from Cincinnati to New Orleans by steamboat took only two weeks. The sixty-day trip from Cincinnati to Pittsburgh by keelboat was reduced to a mere twenty-seven hours by steamer.[36] Steam navigation also dramatically reduced the time up the Mississippi River; the journey from New Orleans to Cincinnati fell to thirty days, which, in turn, reduced freight rates and facilitated trade.[37]

Hence, steam navigation awakened the once-sleeping waters of the Ohio River; goods from near and far filled Cincinnati's wharves, waiting to be shipped to distant areas east, south, and west. Cincinnati was a leading exporter of hogs, cattle, and flour. Although there is no record of the extent of Cincinnati's commercial activity before the advent of the steamboat, in 1826 the city exported 55,000 barrels of flour, worth $165,000; 14,500 barrels of whiskey, worth $101,500; and 17,000 barrels of pork, worth $102,000.[38] In that same year, the city imported 1,450 tons of iron and 5,000,000 board feet of lumber.[39] Cincinnati became the "immediate place of shipment for the produce of nearly the whole Miami Country, and a small district of Indiana." It was also "the point of importation and distribution for most of the goods which supply that part of Ohio west of the Muskingum, nearly the whole of Indiana, large portions of Kentucky and Missouri, and even still more distant regions. . . . Cincinnati promises to become the *depot* of supply, to nearly all the West."[40] By 1830, the "Queen City of the West" was, as one contemporary source noted, "undoubtedly the largest provision market in the world."[41] Although an obvious exaggeration, this comment underscores Cincinnati's prominence in the western commercial scene.

With the increased access to other markets that steam navigation provided, Cincinnati quickly became a leading supplier of several products. Her chief manufacturing export after 1820 was pork: lard, ham, and bacon. In 1826, Cincinnati exported 17,000 barrels of pork, 1,280,000 pounds of lard, and 1,425,000 pounds of ham and bacon.[42] In the seven years between 1833 and 1840, the number of hogs packed in the city rose from 85,000 to 200,000, making pork packing the most important manufacturing industry in Ohio and, perhaps, in "the entire west."[43] The compilers of the 1826 city directory proclaimed that the pork-packing business in Cincinnati was "not exceeded by any place in the world."[44] Cincinnati's thriving pork-packing industry earned the city the nickname "Porkopolis."[45]

Steam navigation ushered in a commercial boom in Cincinnati. Drake and Mansfield, city directory compilers for 1826, observed, "Since its introduction here, it [the steamboat] has wrought a change in the appearance and nature of commercial transactions, which the most active fancy could, a few years since, have scarcely conceived; and this change is progressing with every addition to population and capital."[46] After 1820, there was a dramatic increase in manufacturing in the city. Manufactories popped up all over the city as merchant-capitalists vied to take advantage of the city's economic growth. By 1826, Cincinnati had scores of foundries and mills—including flour, lumber, paper, and powder mills. Local manufactories produced yarn, wool, white lead, and type. In addition, even a sugar refinery and a distillery were located in the city.[47] From 1825 onward, Cincinnati led all other American cities in steamboat production. That year, twenty-seven steamboats were produced in Cincinnati; the next year, that number rose to fifty-six.[48] Other products manufactured in Cincinnati included steam engines, castings, cabinets, furniture, and hats.

Although the transportation revolution inspired commercial and industrial growth, Cincinnati did not blossom into an industrial center overnight.[49] Before 1820, most manufacturing took place in private homes and was intended for private consumption. As market forces changed, the production of goods shifted from homes to private shops and mills. Although large manufacturing establishments were sprinkled throughout the city as early as 1819, individual craftsmen still produced most of the goods.[50] By the mid-1820s, master craftsmen and journeymen in private shops supported most of the manufacturing in Cincinnati. For example, the compiler of the 1819 city directory, Oliver Farnsworth, reported twenty-one blacksmith shops, three whitesmith shops, nine silversmith establishments, twenty-six shoemaker shops, and twenty-three tailors. The most common trade, by far, was carpentry. Farnsworth noted that there were between eighty and one hundred house carpenters and joiners and another four hundred journeymen and apprentices.[51] In 1826, Drake and Mansfield attested that "the artisans and manufactures of Cincinnati . . . constitute the bone and sinew of the community"; it was upon their work that "the prosperity of our city so materially depends."[52]

Manufacturing eventually moved from individual shops, where products were manually produced by artisans, to "factories." Factories—not yet the factories of the late nineteenth century—were establishments employing more than twenty workers. Although some mechanization was used, most of the labor was still manual. These factories essentially divided up craftwork. Each worker was assigned a task, and the product was passed on an assembly line. This type of factory began gaining ground by the 1840s. According to Charles Cist, publisher of the 1841 city annal, "Its [manufacturing] operations have grown up so silently and gradually, extending, in the course of twenty years, the workshop of the mechanic with his two or three apprentices, to a factory with from thirty to fifty hands."[53]

Despite Cincinnati's prominence as a manufacturing port, it had one shortcoming: it provided no direct water access to Lake Erie. By the early 1820s, there was growing support for a canal system to connect the Ohio River to Lake Erie. Supporters of the project envisioned Lake Erie as a waterway that could link Ohio to the northeastern states through the state of New York. New York's Erie Canal, completed in 1825, connected Lake Erie to the Hudson River through Buffalo, New York.[54] Advocates for an Ohio canal system hoped that linking the state to the Erie Canal would end the "West's isolation from Eastern states" and enhance commerce in both regions.[55] The canal system was also expected to improve intrastate commerce. Without it, farmers in the Lake Erie region were practically isolated from the rich Ohio-Mississippi River trade, forcing them to rely on the small, local markets for the goods they produced. Hence, it became increasingly clear that a canal system linking Lake Erie to the Ohio River would be immensely beneficial to the state.[56]

The construction for the Ohio and Miami & Erie canals began in 1825. The Ohio Canal began at the town of Portsmouth on the Ohio River and extended northward to a point south of Columbus. From there, it veered to the northeast through Newark and Akron before ending in Cleveland. The Miami & Erie Canal extended from Cincinnati, near Mill Creek, to the Great and Little Miami rivers near Dayton. Another section of the canal, the Miami Extension, ran from the Great Miami River through Dayton and Piqua, before joining the Wabash & Erie Canal near Defiance, Ohio.[57] When it was finally completed in 1845, the Miami & Erie Canal linked Cincinnati to Toledo. As expected, the Ohio canal system energized interstate commerce by making it much easier to convey goods between Ohio and eastern states. The canals also directly led to development in rural northern Ohio. The increase in trade sparked industrial development and population growth in areas like Toledo, which previously had been only sparsely populated.[58]

While steam navigation and the canal system ushered in a transportation and commercial revolution, the construction of the National Road in the 1830s and the building of railroads in the 1840s cemented it. These newer and more efficient forms of transportation made the canal system obsolete almost as soon as it was complete. The National Road, financed by Congress, was built with the aim of linking the East with the West. Paved roads replaced old dirt roads, making travel much easier and faster. The National Road extended from Wheeling, in present-day West Virginia, to Zanesville, Ohio. It was then extended from Zanesville through Columbus to the Indiana border.[59] The road had important intersecting turnpikes that linked it to cities like Cincinnati. Railroads did not sweep the state until the late 1840s, but, when they did, they replaced steam navigation as the primary means of transporting goods over long distances.

Despite a wealth of opportunities provided by development and a burgeoning economy, the labor pool was not sufficient to meet Cincinnati's manufacturing needs in the city's initial years of growth. The labor shortage was so acute that business owners were forced to think of incentives to compete with other burgeoning western towns for laborers. Thus, "western towns competed for these urban migrants, advertising openings for profitable enterprise and specific types of employment."[60] Emigration societies that offered assistance to migrants were another source of incentives for settlement. The Western Emigration Society, for example, connected emigrants to employment opportunities.[61] Of all the incentives to attract laborers, the most successful was money. Laborers in Cincinnati capitalized on the labor shortage by commanding high wages. In this period, unskilled laborers earned as much as one dollar per week, while journeymen earned two dollars per week—far higher than the wages paid in cities like New York.[62] Even with relatively high wages, skilled labor was particularly hard to come by. The apprenticeship system that produced skilled laborers required seven or more years of training, a period that was too long to meet the immediate needs for skilled labor in the city. Consequently, manufacturers developed several strategies to overcome the scarcity of skilled labor. The Apprentices' Library (1821) and the Ohio Mechanics' Institute (1828) were established to remedy the crisis by providing seminars, workshops, and other training to workers.[63] The labor shortage was finally resolved in the 1840s after the immigration of thousands of Germans and Irish into the Queen City.

Cincinnati's rapid economic growth and the availability of jobs made the city a Mecca of opportunity. Virtually every industry needed laborers of every skill level. Manufactories and mills sought trained hands to assist in the production of goods. Cincinnati desperately needed carpenters to build homes and businesses for a growing population. Teachers were needed to educate the population. Unskilled labor, too, was in high demand. Businesses needed strong men to lift freight on and off ships, to cart goods to and from the wharves, or to pack ham and bacon in the pork houses. Thousands of ditch-digging jobs became available with the construction of the canals. Settlers flocked to the city in search of economic opportunities. Some sought higher wages or steady employment, while others hoped to buy cheap land. Other settlers had visions of opening their own businesses or shops. Budding capitalists with the means to purchase equipment, labor, and raw materials hoped to make their fortunes by investing in enterprises like banks, manufactories, and mills. Most residents stood to profit from the market revolution. Gainful employment abounded in Cincinnati, especially during the 1820s. One visitor, Frances Trollope, noted that in two years of residence in the city she never saw a beggar, underscoring the near full employment laborers enjoyed.[64]

With such an abundance of economic opportunity, nothing could stem the tide of settlers. The population ballooned from 10,283 in 1819 to 24,148 in 1829—a 135 percent increase (see table 1.1).[65] Between 1840 and 1850, Cincinnati's population jumped from 46,338 to 115,434—a 149 percent increase. By 1860, Cincinnati was home to 161,044 people.[66] Cincinnati was, by far, the largest of the western cities throughout the antebellum era (see table 1.2). In 1840, Cincinnati's population was more than twice that of Pittsburgh, and almost three times that of St. Louis. In fact, Cincinnati was the sixth-largest city in the nation at the time.[67]

Migrants moved from every corner of the country to this western land of opportunity. Contrary to popular belief and despite Cincinnati's

Table I.I. Cincinnati Population Growth

Year	Blacks	Whites	Total	Blacks % of total
1810	82	2,458	2,540	3.2%
1815	200	5,800	6,000	3.3%
1818	367	8,763	9,120	3.9%
1819	410	9,873	10,283	4.0%
1820	433	9,381	9,841*	4.4%
1824	528	11,486	12,014	4.4%
1826	690	15,540	16,230	4.3%
1829	2,258	21,890	24,148	9.4%
1830	1,090	23,741	24,831	4.4%
1840	2,240	44,098	46,338	4.8%
1850	3,237	112,198	115,435	2.8%
1860	3,731	157,313	161,044	2.3%

Source: Daniel Drake, *Natural and Statistical View, or Picture of Cincinnati and the Miami Country* (Cincinnati: Looker and Wallace, 1815); Oliver Farnsworth, *The Cincinnati Directory* (Cincinnati: Morgan, Lodge, 1819); Harvey Hall, *The Cincinnati Directory for 1825* (Cincinnati: Samuel Browne, 1825); B. Drake and E. D. Mansfield, *Cincinnati in 1826* (Cincinnati: Morgan Lodge, and Fisher, 1827); Robinson and Fairbank, *The Cincinnati Directory for the Year 1829* (Cincinnati: Whetstone and Buxton, 1829); Henry Louis Taylor Jr. and Vicky Dula, "The Black Residential Experience and Community Formation in Antebellum Cincinnati," in *Race and the City: Work, Community, and Protest in Cincinnati, 1820–1970*, Henry Louis Taylor, ed. (Urbana: University of Illinois Press, 1993), 99; U.S. Census Bureau, *The Third Census of the United States 1810*, vol. I, ser. no. 3 (New York: Norman Ross Publishing, 1990), 62; *The Fourth Census of the United States 1820*, vol. I, ser. no. 5 (New York: Norman Ross Publishing, 1990); *The Fifth Census of the United States 1830*, vol. I, ser. no. 7 (New York: Norman Ross Publishing, 1990), 126–27; *The Sixth Census of the United States 1840*, vol. I, ser. no. 8 (New York: Norman Ross Publishing, 1990), 306; *The Seventh Census of the United States 1850*, vol. I (New York: Norman Ross Publishing, 1990); *The Eighth Census of the United States 1860*, vol. I, ser. no. 16 (New York: Norman Ross Publishing, 1990), 381; *The Ninth Census of the United States 1870*, vol. I, ser. no. 20 (New York: Norman Ross Publishing, 1990), 231.

* The census records a total population of 9,642. However, adding the total number of whites and blacks yields 9,841.

proximity to the South, relatively few of its settlers during its boom were southerners. The eastern states provided the biggest portion of its residents through the first half of the nineteenth century. In 1825, 394 heads of household were natives of Pennsylvania, 337 were from New Jersey, and 233 hailed from New York.[68] Virginia had the highest representation among southern states, with 113 heads of household; Kentucky, Cincinnati's closest southern neighbor, was the birthplace of only 42 heads of household. In 1841, 57 percent of Cincinnati's 12,232 native-born heads of household were from the eastern United States—largely from Pennsylvania.[69] Of Cincinnati's American-born heads of house-

Table 1.2. Population Growth of Western Cities 1830–1860

	1830	1840	1850	1860
Cincinnati	24,831	46,338	115,435	161,044
Chicago	—	4,470	29,963	109,260
Detroit	2,222	9,102	21,019	45,619
Lexington	6,026	6,997	—	9,521
Pittsburgh	12,568	21,115	46,601	49,217
St. Louis	14,125	16,469	77,860	160,773

Source: U.S. Census Bureau, *The Fifth Census of the United States 1830*, vol. 1, ser. no. 7 (New York: Norman Ross Publishing, 1990), 69, 113, 151, 153; *The Sixth Census of the United States 1840*, vol. 1, ser. no. 8 (New York: Norman Ross Publishing, 1990), 161, 279, 377, 413, 449; *The Seventh Census of the United States 1850*, vol. 1 (New York: Norman Ross Publishing, 1990), 158, 662, 705, 896; *The Eighth Census of the United States 1860*, vol. 1, ser. no. 16 (New York: Norman Ross Publishing, 1990), 90, 182, 246, 297, 414.

hold, 26 percent were southern-born, and only 18 percent hailed from Ohio and other western states. Of the tens of thousands who settled in Cincinnati during the antebellum era, many were African Americans. In 1800, there were only 337 African Americans in the entire Ohio Territory.[70] During the next thirty years, their population mushroomed. By 1830, there were 9,568 blacks living in the state, and by 1860, there were 36,673 black Ohioans.[71] Unlike the white population, the majority of Cincinnati's early black settlers were from the neighboring slave states of Kentucky and Virginia.[72] Not unlike other migrants who sought economic opportunity in Cincinnati, southern blacks, too, came with dreams. Undoubtedly, most sought jobs, and some probably endeavored to start their own businesses or even to buy land. Some may have simply wanted independent households after years of living in white homes. Others wanted to be treated with decency and equality. Some African American settlers probably hoped Cincinnati would offer them the chance to receive an education or religious instruction. On many levels, however, African Americans were not like other settlers: an indeterminate number were fugitive slaves. Yet, even for them, economic opportunities often outweighed the risk of discovery.

What is most striking about Cincinnati and probably best distinguishes it from other western cities in the nineteenth century is the number of foreigners who settled there. In 1840, 5,698 inhabitants, or more than 46 percent of the population, had been born abroad. Ten years later, at the height of the German and Irish immigration boom, that number swelled to 54,541, or more than 47 percent of the total population.[73]

Information about Cincinnati had been spread abroad through published travel journals. In Britain, prospective immigrants could read the journal of William Bullock, who had visited Cincinnati while on a tour through the western United States. Bullock had nothing but glowing praises for the city in his *Sketch of a Journey through the Western States*.[74] Like their American counterparts, many Europeans left their homes and headed for Cincinnati in search of economic opportunity. For example, Frances Trollope and her husband were on the brink of bankruptcy when they left England in the 1820s. Mr. Trollope's law firm had been failing, and the couple had a huge estate that they could no longer afford. The Trollopes, like so many other Europeans, hoped opening a bazaar in Cincinnati would reverse the decline of their fortunes.[75]

Germans were by far the largest immigrant group in Cincinnati between 1830 and 1870. In 1840, they comprised 28 percent of Cincinnati's total population; twenty years later, Germans made up more than 30 percent of the population.[76] The heavy German concentration in Cincinnati was not much different from that in other western cities. In Milwaukee, for example, German-born residents comprised 35 percent of the population in 1860.[77] It was inevitable that the heavy German

Table 1.3. Origins of Cincinnati's Heads of Household in 1841

A. NATIVE-BORN HEADS OF HOUSEHOLD

Origins	Total number	Percentage of native-born population
Pennsylvania	1,210	18.5%
Other eastern states	2,457	37.6%
Ohio	1,112	17.0%
Other western states (IN, IL, MI, MO)	83	1.3%
Upper South (VA, KY, TN, MD, DE, DC)	1,553	23.8%
Lower South (AL, MS, AK, GA, SC, NC, LA)	119	1.8%

B. FOREIGN-BORN HEADS OF HOUSEHOLD

Origins	Total number	Percentage of foreign-born population
Germany	3,440	60.0%
England	786	13.8%
Ireland	742	13.0%
Scotland	360	.6%

Source: Charles Cist, *Cincinnati in 1841: Its Early Annals and Future Prospects* (Cincinnati: Charles Cist, 1841), 39.

population would leave an indelible mark on Cincinnati society and culture for generations to come. As the German population increased, so did its influence on the political and social culture of the city. In 1856, one contemporary visitor observed, "Skilled, educated, and intellectual, they [Germans] are daily increasing in numbers, wealth, and political importance, and constitute an influence of which the Americans themselves are afraid."[78] This visitor was referring to German success in remaking Cincinnati throughout much of the nineteenth century. Germans dominated Cincinnati's city council and even the office of the mayor.[79] In addition, they achieved a great deal of financial success as merchants and manufacturers. So great was their influence that the German language was taught in many of Cincinnati's schools throughout the nineteenth century.

The first wave of German settlers arrived in Cincinnati in the 1820s and 1830s. Many were skilled and quickly found a niche in the city's economy as artisans. Some took jobs in the city's manufacturing or pork-packing establishments, and others dug ditches for the Miami & Erie Canal.[80] They quickly assimilated. According to one city official, "It may suffice to say that of all classes of foreigners, the Germans soonest assimilates to the great mass. It takes but one generation to obliterate all the distinctive marks of race—even of language, usually a most tenacious feature."[81] A second wave of Germans arrived in the Queen City in 1848, fleeing political revolutions in Germany.[82] This new wave of German immigrants—"Forty-Eighters" as they were called, was not as quick to assimilate. The Forty-Eighters retained their cultural heritage by establishing civic associations, clubs, newspapers, and elementary schools. Many congregated in the same neighborhoods, particularly in those north of the Miami & Erie Canal, east of Plum Street, and just south of the hills in an area called Over-the-Rhine.[83] Here, it was not uncommon to hear the German language spoken on city streets or in schools.

Although the Irish had been living in the Queen City for decades, the first significant wave of Irish immigration was precipitated by the potato famine in the 1840s. Between 1846 and 1854, nearly two million poor and starving farmers left Ireland, and many of them headed to America.[84] Despite the degree of desperation associated with their flight from famine, one cannot assume their decision to settle in Cincinnati was not informed. These migrants probably chose to settle in Cincinnati for the same reason others did before them: opportunity. After all, these Irish settlers had bypassed the usual stops of New York and Philadelphia and had scraped together additional fares for passage to Ohio. By 1851, Irish residents constituted almost 12 percent of the city's population.[85] Yet, the Irish never gained the political or economic power that Germans possessed in Cincinnati. It took a while before they were even regarded as citizens. Many had arrived in America impoverished and largely without skills. Many were Roman Catholics who came in the midst of a fervent revival of Protestantism in America.[86] Their seemingly strange accents and folkways bred much disdain and distrust among native-born whites in Cincinnati and beyond.[87]

It was not long before racial and ethnic hierarchies developed in Cincinnati. At the top of the hierarchy were native-born Protestant whites and English immigrants. Beneath them were the Germans, and even further down the ladder were the Irish. African Americans and Native Americans occupied the absolute bottom rung. These hierarchies were built on half-truths and ethnic stereotypes, which were accepted in the public imagination as absolute truths. Contemporaries perceived Germans as "a thinking, sceptical [sic], theorising [sic] people." The Irish were stereotyped as "a turbulent class, forever appealing to physical force" and prone to "influencing the elections and carrying out their 'clan feuds' and 'faction fights.'"[88] For many native-born whites, "Irish" also conjured up images of disease, pauperism, drunkenness, and crime. African Americans were considered a "thoughtless and good-humored community, garrulous and profligate."[89] They were also stereotyped as a lazy, criminal class that lacked sufficient intellect to be granted the rights and privileges of citizenship. For example, Daniel Drake asserted in the statistical record for the city that "a large proportion [of African Americans] are reputed and perhaps correctly, to practice petty thefts."[90]

These racial and ethnic stereotypes reinforced occupational stratification. In Cincinnati, the professional class of physicians, judges, merchants, legislators, and attorneys was predominantly composed of native-born whites, British, and Germans. Artisans were largely German: "Germans almost monopolise [sic] the handicrafts trades," whereas "the Irish are here, as everywhere, the hewers of wood and drawers of water; they can do nothing but dig, and seldom rise in the social scale."[91] The Irish, for example, had been recruited to dig ditches for the Miami & Erie Canal in the 1820s and for the National Road in the 1830s. Because they had few or no skills, the Irish were forced to compete with African Americans for unskilled, menial labor jobs as roustabouts and stevedores on Cincinnati's docks. Irish women competed with black women for positions as house servants. Struggling for acceptance in American society, the Irish tried to use their white skin as leverage over African

Americans. Irish women, for example, hoped to distinguish themselves from black female servants by emphasizing that they were "help," not "domestic servants."[92]

At the very bottom of the occupational ladder were African Americans, who almost exclusively worked in the cleaning and service fields as laborers, whitewashers, shoeblacks, porters, and stewards. Daniel Drake noticed in 1815 that African Americans were "prone to the performance of light and menial drudgery."[93] Such positions were seen as their appropriate lot. Some occupations were race *and* gender specific: washerwomen, for example, were almost always black women. Although most African Americans held positions as unskilled laborers, others found opportunities in the steamboat industry. In Cincinnati, as in other port cities like New York and Philadelphia, these jobs were a primary source of employment for blacks. People without skills could find work in various capacities on ships passing to and from the city. "Follow[ing] the river,"[94] a phrase that was generally used for all levels of unskilled labor on steamboats, was a common occupation for African American men. The steamboat industry provided lucrative opportunities in other positions as well. Black men secured jobs as cooks, barbers, and stewards on ships. Of the African American cooks listed in the 1836 city directory, most were "cook[s] on the river." A significant number of African American men worked as barbers on ships.[95] Although riverboat jobs were among the lowest on the occupational ladder, black men did not necessarily consider them as such; for them, these jobs afforded a measure of independence, the opportunity to travel, and, sometimes, decent wages.[96]

In terms of space and population, Cincinnati was a hypercongested city. "Business, industry, transportation, and residential space were jammed into six square miles."[97] The population stretched the city's resources to their limits. Land was scarce and expensive; finding housing was extremely difficult.[98] In fact, it was not uncommon for ten people to inhabit one home. The city was so congested that class could not determine where one lived; poor families might live on the same block as a wealthy ones. Because most workers resided within walking distance of their places of employment, laborers might live within yards of their employers. This congestion reduced the likelihood that any single racial or ethnic group would dominate any one area.[99] It also precluded ethnic or class isolation; most Cincinnatians came in daily contact with a diverse group of people. Still, certain residential patterns did develop. Most of Cincinnati's African Americans lived in the East End near Deer Creek or along the Ohio River. Because of their higher *relative* percentage of

African Americans and the presence of black institutions, these two areas earned the names "Bucktown" and "Little Africa," respectively. Yet, African Americans did not spatially dominate these areas.[100] At the neighborhood and street level, African Americans were not concentrated in ghettos, but lived in "residential clusters."[101]

The Irish and African Americans tended to occupy the same residential space. Some Irish resided in neighborhoods like Bucktown and Little Africa along the waterfront.[102] City directory compiler Charles Cist observed that, although most Irish lived near the Ohio River, by 1859 they comprised the largest percentage of foreign-born residents in wards one, three, four, thirteen, and seventeen—wards also heavily populated by African Americans.[103] As previously noted, until the 1860s Cincinnati was a "walking city,"[104] and most workers lived within walking distance of their places of employment. Because African Americans and Irish worked as unskilled labor on the river, it should not be surprising that their housing was in close proximity to the river. Because the Irish generally earned low wages, they, too, were forced to live in areas with cheap rents and compromised housing. Living and working in such close proximity, it is highly likely that Irish and black workers frequented the same taverns, grog shops, and brothels. Such extensive social and work interactions between the two groups undoubtedly made it hard for the Irish to distinguish themselves from African Americans. In fact, the Irish were called "niggers turned inside out"[105] by native-born whites in Philadelphia because they occupied the same social and work spaces. In periods of economic recession, fierce competition for jobs frequently set Irish and African Americans to blows. Labor competition alone cannot explain the depth of the animosity between Irish and blacks. Irish workers, feeling degraded by working alongside blacks, sometimes united against them to assert their higher caste status. Very likely embittered by their social standing in Cincinnati, Irish rowdies seized every opportunity to hurl insults at African Americans in the streets or in the taverns. Not wanting to stomach insults by *Irishmen,* African Americans frequently replied in kind, inciting physical clashes between the two groups.[106]

At times, the ethnic clashes in Cincinnati were between native and foreign-born whites. Sentiment against foreigners, or antialienism, rose in proportion to the increase in foreign migration in the 1840s.[107] The roots of antialienism were the massive social and economic upheavals of the day that fostered powerlessness, "fear, insecurity, and [even] paranoia."[108] When antialienism gave way to nativism in the 1840s, nativists determined who did and did not belong to the republic based on how

"American" they were.[109] They used religion, language, political ideas, and ethnicity as yardsticks to determine who should have access to citizenship. For example, many nativist organizations lobbied to exclude foreign-born people from holding public office.[110] Nativism was not directed against British immigrants. After all, they were English-speaking Protestants with belief and value systems that were consistent with those of Americans. It was quite ironic that religion, language, and culture were used to determine inclusion in (or exclusion from) the American republic. For English-speaking, native-born black Christians, nothing could grant them full citizenship in the republic. The nativist movement threatened to exclude and marginalize ethnic whites, but it created an additional layer of exclusion for African Americans. Although white skin did not automatically confer citizenship upon German and Irish immigrants, black skin was considered the antithesis of citizenship.

Despite the prejudices of nativist elements in society, foreign-born whites would not always be denied citizenship. Republican ideology, which centered on equality among white men, independence, industry, and citizenship, trumped those other elements in the long run. Even the Irish, as socially degraded as they were, eventually could, and did, become citizens. If they shed their accents and religious values and adopted white American cultural mores, foreign-born white men could eventually belong to the republic. The chances were even better for their children. Thus, in Cincinnati, citizenship was linked to whiteness; the union was a binding force that cut across ethnic, class, and social lines to anoint all white men loyal to the culture of the republic with the blessing of American citizenship.

The racial and ethnic tensions that began at Fort Washington and became an organic part of Cincinnati's cultural legacy were neither exceptional nor irrelevant. Perhaps the result of many varied groups of people coming together in a relatively short period of time and competing for resources, jobs, and living space, ethnic and racial tensions would play a significant role in defining the urban landscape that was Cincinnati. How Cincinnatians were changed by these forces would be the truest indicator of the city's promise.

TWO

A City of Persecution

The Emergence of a Community

Racial prejudice appears to me stronger in the states that
have abolished slavery than in those where slavery still exists,
and nowhere is it shown to be as intolerant as in states where
servitude has always been unknown.

Alexis de Tocqueville, *Democracy in America*

BLACK FREEDOM in the Ohio Territory had been secured in 1787,
when the Northwest Ordinance prohibited slavery east of the Mississippi
River and north of the Ohio River.[1] When Ohio drew up its constitution
in 1802, it followed the precedent of the Northwest Ordinance and
also prohibited slavery and indentured servitude. One year later, Ohio
joined the union as a free state. Although slavery was not practiced in
Ohio, the law did not automatically free fugitive slaves who settled there.
Nonetheless, Ohio's status as a free state offered an incentive for African
Americans—free and fugitive, alike—to settle there.

The majority of African Americans who migrated to the state in the
early to mid-nineteenth century settled in urban areas or in counties
along the Ohio River where they could most readily find jobs.[2] Not only
were there plenty of available jobs in Ohio, but free blacks did not have
to compete with slave labor. They were able to work to provide for themselves and even to save enough money to purchase enslaved loved ones.[3]
Of all Ohio's cities, Cincinnati had the largest African American population throughout most of the nineteenth century. In fact, in 1850, Cincinnati's African American population of 3,237 was the largest in the
entire Old Northwest.[4] One reason why blacks settled in the city was that

Cincinnati offered them greater economic opportunities than did other Ohio cities. If nothing else, African Americans could always find work in Cincinnati's steamboat industry.

Cincinnati *was* full of promise. For African Americans, economic opportunity was only part of that promise. Southern slaves were attracted to Cincinnati because it stood as a beacon of freedom. Sitting in the shadow of slavery, north of the Ohio River, Cincinnati was the destination of countless fugitive slaves. Cincinnati's abolitionist legacy after 1834 may have led some fugitives to believe the city was a refuge. They may have hoped that Cincinnati's powerful protectors would shield them from the threat of re-enslavement. Some fugitives may have been drawn to Cincinnati by the size of its black population, which provided a degree of anonymity and protection. In Cincinnati, African Americans were not as isolated as they were in less populated parts of Ohio. Many settled in Ohio with more idealistic objectives: some expected that social equality and freedom of opportunity would be extended to them. Some black settlers may have been seeking rights as citizens or relief from the oppressive laws that restricted their freedom in the South. Freeborn blacks and freed slaves even may have had the notion that northern whites were more benevolent and tolerant toward African Americans. Such beliefs impelled many to shed their slave status on a journey to the Promised Land north of the Ohio River.

African Americans may have settled in Ohio because of its promise of freedom, but by the end of the first three decades of statehood, the foundation had been laid for their exclusion from the republic. Nowhere was this legacy stronger than in Cincinnati. While Cincinnati blossomed as a city, its growth directly corresponded to the rise of racism against blacks. Instead of reaping the rewards of Cincinnati's economic prosperity—as did other citizens—African Americans met with political, social, legal, and economic oppression and repression. Just as the growth of the city shaped the black experience, Cincinnati's rise as a major urban center cannot be understood without acknowledging how African Americans contributed to it and how they were oppressed by it. Certainly, theirs is a story of promise *and* persecution.

—

The village of Cincinnati originally was inhabited by small farmers from Virginia and Kentucky, many of whom supported free labor on free soil for free (white) men. Some of these settlers were opposed to slavery, but not on moral grounds or because of a belief in racial equality. These yeomen wanted to be free from competition with slave labor and from the hegemony of the planter class.[5] They probably were just as resentful of African Americans as they were of the institution of slavery, the African American presence may have reminded the yeomen of their precarious position in the slave economy. Thus, many of them were, at once, antislavery *and* antiblack.

But in the early years of settlement, the African American population was too negligible to have caused concern. Records indicate that only 337 African Americans lived in what would later become Ohio in 1800, a number that comprised only 1 percent of the territory's total population.[6] Although the African American population was yet too low to create a significant concentration anywhere, delegates at the Ohio constitutional convention pondered how to curtail black settlement in the state as early as 1802. African American dreams of equality and citizenship became a nightmare of second-class status.

The 1802 Ohio constitutional convention met on November 1, 1802, to draw up a state constitution and to establish a bill of rights for Ohio citizens. Delegates at this convention raised six motions related to the status of African Americans.[7] Among the first of these motions was the issue of slavery. Convention delegates voted to prohibit not only slavery but indentured servitude for females over the age of eighteen and for males over the age of twenty-one, as well. This provision was intended to prevent individuals from enslaving blacks under the guise of indenture. Both measures solidly confirmed that Ohio was to be inhabited by free people. Having taken a firm position on slavery, delegates had to decide which rights would be extended to Ohio citizens. But first they had to resolve the question of who would receive the rights of citizenship.

The delegates debated whether to extend suffrage to African Americans. By a close vote, the convention decided to limit voter rights to "all white male inhabitants"—denying the franchise to men of color and to all women.[8] In a plea for universal male suffrage, one delegate motioned to amend the section by striking the word "white." However, this motion was narrowly defeated, by a vote of 19 to 14.[9] Another delegate put forward a motion to extend voting rights to "all male negroes and mulattoes, now residing in this territory, shall be entitled to the right of suffrage, if they shall within ___ months make a record of their citizenship."[10] Initially, this motion passed by a vote of 19 to 15, with nine of Hamilton County's ten delegates having voted for it.[11] Although this appeared to be a concession to African Americans, close consideration of the wording reveals that it extended suffrage to a very limited group of them. Only those black and mulatto men "now residing in the territory" were to enjoy the privilege of suffrage. Because the African American population of the state was only 337 in 1800, the measure would have enfranchised only a few dozen African American males of voting age. The careful phraseology raised some new questions. What would happen to black voting privileges when those men "now residing in the territory" left or died? Would their children inherit those privileges? Obviously cognizant of such questions, one delegate moved that "male descendants of such negroes as shall be recorded, shall be entitled to the same [voting] privilege."[12] The motion passed, guaranteeing voting privileges for at least *some* African Americans and their posterity.

These voting privileges did not last long. Later in the convention, another delegate motioned to rescind those privileges. Votes were recast, and some delegates reconsidered their earlier position. The new vote was tied at 17.[13] The president of the convention, Edward Tiffin of Ross County, cast the tie-breaking vote: he voted in favor of removing the section that extended suffrage to blacks. The specific wording limited suffrage to "white male" residents. This moment of schizophrenia—to grant voting rights to blacks, only later to remove them—was characteristic of the entire proceedings: legislators also vacillated on other civil rights for blacks.

The framers of the Ohio constitution initially denied blacks citizenship. The original provision read: "No negro or mulatto shall ever be eligible to hold any office, civil or military, or give their oath in any court of justice against a white person, be subject to military duty, or pay a poll tax in this state."[14] Although this provision initially passed by a vote of 19 to 16, it was later overturned when a delegate motioned to strike it. The final draft of Ohio's first constitution was silent on the issue of civil rights for African Americans—neither denying nor guaranteeing them. At the time, the black population in the state was negligible, so delegates felt confident enough to leave the issue open and to return to it at a later date.

The Ohio constitution was similar to other state constitutions: it was democratic in principle, but not always democratic in application. The framers of Ohio's constitution, perhaps, walked the line between rhetoric and application. Their indecisiveness suggests they were conflicted about framing a constitution that restricted citizenship to whites. According to historian Eugene Berwanger, these legislators feared that the U.S. Congress would reject antiblack legislation.[15]

The delegates of the Ohio constitutional convention undoubtedly operated under a mantle of white supremacy. It is highly likely that the framers of the constitution believed in inherent black inferiority. Perhaps some of them believed that blacks were unprepared to handle the responsibilities that came with citizenship and voting privileges; or, perhaps, they believed that blacks were not intelligent enough to understand political issues.[16] If the delegates had believed in full equality, neither race nor gender would have been factors in determining civil rights for Ohio residents, and there would have been no perceived need to limit suffrage to white males. At the close of the convention, the margin by which blacks had lost the right of suffrage did not matter as much as the fact that black Ohioans had been relegated to an inferior civil status from which they could not escape. The constitution's failure to address the issue paved the way for the future denial of civil rights for African Americans at state and local levels. Sadly, Ohio became the first state in the Old Northwest to legislate against African Americans, setting the precedent for how they would be treated throughout the West.[17]

Each successive legislative session more clearly defined the civil status of African Americans that had been left open in the constitution. In 1803, the Ohio General Assembly provided for the exclusion of blacks from the military.[18] The following year, the General Assembly passed the first of several oppressive laws—commonly referred to as Black Laws[19]—that stalked African Americans throughout most of the antebellum era.[20] (See the appendix for the text of the Black Laws of 1804 and 1807.) An Act to Regulate Black and Mulatto Persons, passed in 1804, required all African Americans living in the state to register their names and the names of their children at the local clerk's office. A fee of twelve and one-half cents was to be collected for each name entered. In addition to registering with the clerk, African Americans settling in the state after June 1, 1804, were required to produce a certificate of freedom issued from an U.S. court. The 1804 Black Law also prohibited anyone from employing any African American who could not produce a certificate of freedom. The fine for doing so was between ten and fifty dollars; if the African American was determined to be a fugitive slave, an additional fifty cents per day was to be paid to the owner.[21] The Ohio Black Law of 1804 reinforced the federal Fugitive Slave Act of 1793. The procedure for reclaiming fugitive slaves provided that slave owners or their agents could "apply, upon making satisfactory proof that such black or mulatto person or persons is [their] property." Furthermore, the local judge or justice of the peace was "empowered and required . . . to direct the sheriff or constable to arrest such black or mulatto person or persons and deliver the same" to the claimant.[22] Interestingly, the section does not define "satisfactory proof" of ownership. The implication is that *any* proof would have constituted "satisfactory proof" for a proslavery judge. The law mandated fines ranging from ten to fifty dollars for anyone who "harbored or secreted" a fugitive slave or "in any wise hinder[ed] or prevent[ed] the lawful owners from retaking" their slaves. Despite the severity of the law, it included an antikidnapping provision, which mandated a one-thousand-dollar fine for anyone "who shall aid and assist in removing" any black from the state.[23] This provision was aimed at protecting African Americans who were legitimately free from those who might kidnap and sell them into slavery.

The 1804 Black Law was intended to restrict the immigration of fugitive slaves into Ohio. The assembly feared that Ohio would be overrun by scores of indigent fugitive slaves who would need public support. Shortly after statehood, city directory compiler Daniel Drake asserted that the framers of the state's constitution had "predicted that we should be degraded by the free negroes of other states, and infested with their runaway slaves."[24] Legislators also may have feared that the state's commercial relationship with the slaveholding South would be jeopardized if Ohio was perceived as a refuge for fugitive slaves. At the time this law was passed, the state's black population was too small to warrant any real or immediate fears of being overrun by a black population. Yet the fear gained momentum.

Aiming to make the laws against black settlement even tougher, the Ohio legislature soon amended the 1804 act. An Act to Amend the Last Named Act, 'An Act to Regulate Black and Mulatto Persons,' passed in 1807, went a step beyond the Black Law of 1804 by discouraging not only fugitive slaves but *all* African Americans from settling in Ohio: "No negro or mulatto person shall be permitted to emigrate into, and settle within this state, unless such negro or mulatto person shall, within twenty days thereafter, enter into bond with two or more freehold sureties, in the penal sum of five hundred dollars." The bond was intended to guarantee good behavior and to provide for African Americans should they become unemployed or disabled. In the event that African Americans were determined not to be on good behavior (a standard subject to interpretation) or became unemployed, the sureties would be forced to pay a five-hundred-dollar penalty. Quite possibly, the Ohio General Assembly adopted these measures against black immigration because it feared African Americans would become an idle, criminal, and unproductive class. Thus, requiring black settlers to enter into bond with two sureties would safeguard the public from assuming the tax burden for the relief of black indigents.[25] Once the bond was recorded by the county clerk, the black settler was issued a certificate of settlement.[26] Like its predecessor, this act forbade anyone to "employ, harbor, or conceal" any African American who failed to meet the requirements for settlement; the fine for such an offense was one hundred dollars. Legislators outlined how this piece of legislation would be enforced: "[I]t shall be the duty of the overseer of the poor of the township where such negro or mulatto person may be found to remove immediately such black person, in the same manner as is required in the case of paupers."[27]

The requirements for black settlement under this legislation were unusually harsh and unrealistic. First, black settlers had only twenty days to find two citizens willing to guarantee the exorbitant bond, which amounted to more than a year's wages for a common laborer before 1830.[28] It was difficult for new settlers of any race—much less African Americans—to find two strangers willing to stand surety for them. Although employers were the most convenient and practical source for a freehold surety, many were deterred from hiring unsecured African Americans by the section of the law that levied a penalty against those who did so. Under such stringent conditions, it was a wonder that any African American could meet the requirements for settlement. David Grier, who moved to Ohio after being manumitted from bondage in Kentucky, stayed in the state just briefly before moving on to Colchester, Ontario, because he could not find two sureties: "From Ohio, I came here [Canada] on account of the oppressive laws demanding security for good behavior—I was a stranger and could not give it."[29] Many others probably followed his course and settled in more hospitable states or in Canada.

Ohio's Black Laws, intended to deter black settlement, were sometimes successful, as Grier demonstrated; however, they were not enforced for decades. Enforcement was impractical; only with great difficulty and diligence could local officials regulate black settlement. African Americans—fugitive and legitimately free—settled in the state without registering with the court or finding sureties, in some cases avoiding these requirements for decades. Lack of enforcement did not render the restrictive laws meaningless. In fact, the laws set a very dangerous precedent: antiblack sentiment codified by law. Although the Black Laws remained a dead letter in most Ohio cities, Cincinnati invoked them numerous times to deny jobs to African Americans or to get them off the pauper lists. When African Americans sought assistance during the depression of 1819, the overseers of the poor threatened to enforce the Black Laws to stop them from applying to the Poor Fund.[30]

The 1807 law also settled the question whether to grant African Americans citizenship rights. Section four of the law forbade African Americans from testifying against any white person.[31] This legislation extended even to cases in which a white person had committed a crime against an African American. Certainly, black Ohioans would have neither equal protection nor justice under this law. The web of legal oppression of African Americans in Ohio did not stop there. A series of additional legislative assaults denied blacks other civil rights, including the right to serve on juries,[32] or to attend public schools.[33] In fact, African Americans were not granted the right to a public education until 1849.[34]

Without the franchise, petitioning became the only way for blacks to participate in the body politic. Black Ohioans used the petition freely and without incident until 1839, when the General Assembly debated whether to deny them even that method of redress. Members of the General Assembly debated whether they had a duty to receive or consider the petitions of people who had no state constitutional rights. One element within the legislative body proposed that "[t]he blacks and mulattoes who may be residents within this state, [should] have no constitutional right to present their petitions to the General Assembly for any purpose whatsoever, and that any reception of such petitions on the part of the General Assembly is a mere act of privilege or policy, and not imposed by any expressed or implied power of the constitution."[35] Had the motion prevailed, any consideration of such petitions by the body would have been regarded as a gesture of grace or favor. One assemblyman had a paternalist recommendation: that African Americans present their petitions through white "protectors and guardians, who were capable of understanding and presenting their wants."[36] Without suffrage, the right of petition, or political parties to advance their interests, African Americans would have been rendered politically powerless in Ohio. Luckily for them, the motion did not succeed.

Not every part of Ohio enforced these repressive state laws equally. Whites in the Western Reserve area (Cleveland and Cuyahoga County in northeast Ohio), in particular, were not only less inclined to enforce the Black Laws but led the movement against this odious legislation. Unlike Cincinnati, the Western Reserve area had been populated largely by evangelical Christians from New England and Pennsylvania who tended to be more racially tolerant and socially progressive.[37] All of the Cuyahoga County delegates at the 1851 constitutional convention, for example, voted against the provisions that denied African Americans the rights of citizens. When the state extended suffrage to African Americans in 1867, Cuyahoga County voted in favor.[38] In addition, the Western

Reserve was one of the strongest abolitionist strongholds in the state.[39] The area also had elements that supported racial equality: Cleveland had integrated elementary schools by 1849—long before the rest of the state— and nearby Oberlin College was among the first colleges in the country to admit black students.[40] Perhaps the real evidence of the Western Reserve's racial tolerance and social progressivism is the number of African American leaders who quit Cincinnati and resettled there. Civil rights activists and leaders John Malvin, John Mercer Langston, and Charles Langston all lived in Cincinnati briefly before relocating to northeast Ohio.[41] Both Malvin and John Mercer Langston were drawn to the relatively progressive social and racial environment in the Western Reserve. After living in Cincinnati just five years, Malvin moved to Cleveland in 1832 and spent the rest of his life lobbying for rights for African Americans. He worked assiduously for the repeal of the Black Laws and helped organize the black state convention movement and black schools. John Mercer Langston relocated to Oberlin in 1844 after being educated in Cincinnati's high schools. He went on to build an illustrious career as the state's first black attorney, U.S. minister to Haiti, and member of the U.S. House of Representatives. Langston also served as a recruiter during the Civil War and as a Freedmen's Bureau agent.[42] Yet, despite the success these men found in the Western Reserve, it was no racial utopia. Cleveland, for example, had its share of racial animosity, but it was minor compared to what Cincinnati had to offer.[43]

Cincinnati's elected officials passed restrictive local legislation that added yet another layer to the oppression of African Americans. In 1804, Cincinnati's city council passed an ordinance prohibiting slaves from entering Cincinnati without their masters, an act intended to prevent Kentucky slaves from congregating in the city on their days off. Those who came into the city on business or for church services were required to carry a note from their masters indicating the specific duration of their visit.[44] In 1808, the city council passed an ordinance to eliminate, through increased policing, the menace of enslaved people "who resort to the town of Cincinnati under the pretext that they are free." Council members complained that these particular blacks lived "idle lives and [had] vicious habits" and tended to cause "riots, quarrels and disturbances."[45] In addition, Cincinnati excluded African Americans from the benefits of the Poor Fund and denied them admission to institutions like the city infirmary, hospitals, orphanages, house of refuge, and poor houses.[46]

As Cincinnati attempted to regulate the movement of Kentucky slaves when they were in the city, the Covington, Kentucky, city council passed its own ordinances regulating the movement of free blacks in that town. In 1839, the Covington council passed an ordinance that prohibited free blacks from "loitering" or walking around that city without "some good and plausible pretext and business calling."[47] City officials probably feared the influence free blacks might have on the slave population.

In addition to these legal impediments to the exercise of civil rights, black Cincinnatians also had to contend with customary efforts to strangle their freedoms. Custom, for example, prevented blacks from associating freely with whites. When white Lane Seminary students boarded with black families in 1833, there was public outrage. Sleeping in black homes suggested a degree of intimacy and social equality between the races, which was unsettling to most of white society.[48] The races were also subjected to de facto segregation within public institutions. If African Americans had access to public amenities at all, they were relegated to separate facilities, often in deplorable conditions. For example, in the 1850s, indigent and homeless African Americans were sent to the city Pest House, which housed people of both races with contagious diseases. As Cincinnati's population increased, the color line grew increasingly more rigid.

Before 1820, black Cincinnati was a largely dependent and transient population of free blacks, fugitives, and freed slaves.[49] Cincinnati's location on the edge of slavery meant that African Americans lived under the constant threat of kidnappers and slave catchers. Consequently, many African Americans lived in the city for just a short period of time before moving on. Those who did settle in Cincinnati found it difficult to establish independent households. In 1820, 65 percent of the black population lived in independent households, while 35 percent lived in white households. Live-in domestics more than likely made up most of that number.[50] African Americans who served in these homes performed work that was similar to the tasks of house slaves. They performed a variety of services in white homes like washing and ironing, cooking, dusting, cleaning, sewing, tending to children or pets, and serving as a personal assistants, drivers, or butlers. In exchange for their work, these live-in domestic servants might be provided with a room or a bed. Their work in white homes was physically demanding and time-consuming. Live-in domestics were subjected to constant scrutiny, had little privacy or free time, and were forced to abide by the rules of their employers. Live-ins were generally on call around the clock, and they usually received only one day off each week (or each month) to handle personal affairs and to socialize with family and friends.[51] In some cases, members of black families lived in different households: parents might be separated from their children, and husbands from their wives.[52] Such arrangements not only precluded stability and cohesion within black families but delayed the development of community.

By 1830, 80 percent of the black population of Cincinnati resided in independent households.[53] More than likely, it was the availability of jobs that enabled African Americans to make this transition to independent households so quickly. Even then, most did not own their homes, but rented them for terms of three to five years.[54] These rental properties consisted of wooden shanties, small and rickety frame dwellings, or battered buildings in run-down districts.[55] Property owners compromised the quality and safety of housing and sometimes charged higher rents than the property warranted.[56] Other, poorer, blacks who could not afford to lease housing inhabited dilapidated buildings, converted warehouses, or blacksmith shops. Regardless of whether the housing was cheap or compromised, it was, nevertheless, a step towards independence.

Those African Americans who lived in independent households tended to concentrate in neighborhoods in the Fourth Ward along the waterfront (levee), in an area known as Little Africa.[57] Another significant percentage of African Americans lived in the First Ward between Main and Broadway streets, just south of Sixth Street, in an area that was known as Bucktown. Largely drawn to these neighborhoods by low rents, African Americans probably also sought the fellowship and security of living near other African Americans. Levee residents, as poor as they were, sometimes resorted to illegal activity for survival. The area soon earned notoriety as a den of prostitution, gambling, drinking, violence, and other crime.[58] Whites editorialized about "night walkers, lewd persons, and those who lounge about without any visible means of support" in the black neighborhoods.[59] Although the white community had its share of prostitutes, gamblers, and thieves, as well, the vices (and crimes) of blacks received more attention. Nevertheless, this description of life on the levee is a reminder of what went wrong with black freedom in Cincinnati: it reflects the impact of unemployment and underemployment on Cincinnati's African American population.

The black population in Cincinnati did not become a community until African Americans began acting self-consciously for their own common good.[60] Historians James Oliver Horton and Lois E. Horton define community "as institutions (social, political, economic and religious) and sentiments based on shared experience and a sense of common destiny."[61] Racism—political, social, and economic oppression—was a powerful bonding force in Cincinnati and fostered mutual awareness. Mutual awareness, however, is more than just being aware of a common oppression; it hinges upon seeking solutions that are beneficial to the common good. Heightening mutual awareness proved to be an effective means of nurturing a sense of community and countering the effects of racism. Cincinnati's black community demonstrated its mutual awareness in many ways, including fostering racial consciousness among newcomers about the plight of African Americans in the city. When blacks arrived in the city, resident African Americans welcomed them with an orientation on the limits of their freedom in the city. When John Malvin arrived in Cincinnati in 1827, other African Americans informed him about the Black Laws.[62] This education not only softened the blow of disillusionment for new settlers but also safeguarded against the possibility that they might violate customary laws. This community proved it possessed mutual awareness in other ways, as well, but none was as critical in these early years as institution-building.

Because it is hard to document mutual awareness, historians often consider the presence of institutions as evidence of community formation.[63] The raising of a black church in 1810 is, therefore, the earliest evidence of the existence of a black community in Cincinnati. Although both the name and the denomination of the church are unknown, a man named William Allen was its first pastor.[64] This church was a potent symbol of black independence in Cincinnati—perhaps too potent a symbol, because it was burned three times. However, the black community rebuilt the church each time, and each effort to rebuild it sent a message about the black community's resolve not to be intimidated by violence.[65] Even more remarkable than its symbolic importance was this little church's initiation of the black church movement in Cincinnati.

Cincinnati's black church movement was part of a larger, national black church movement that had started two decades earlier in Philadelphia. In Philadelphia and in other northern cities, free black churchgoers had worshiped in white churches, where they were subjected to degrading treatment. As a rule, blacks had endured segregated seating in galleries, dark corners, or pews designated "Nigger Pews" at the back of the church.[66] During Sunday morning worship in St. George's Methodist Church in Philadelphia, for example, blacks routinely had been required to give up their seats to whites. Once whites had filled all of the available seats, African Americans were forced to stand along the wall.[67] Even after a larger church had been built, African Americans were relegated to the gallery of the new church, despite their significant contribution to the building fund.[68]

Generally, black churchgoers in the antebellum era were not able to participate in church rituals or functions on the basis of equality. Black preachers were not allowed to speak before white audiences and were excluded from formal ministerial education. African Americans were often prohibited from kneeling at the altar or taking communion until every white person had done so. Those who violated these social codes might find themselves humiliated in front of the church body, as was the case in St. George's. One day in 1792, as black ministers Richard Allen and Absalom Jones were praying at the altar, they were pulled from their knees because they had not waited until whites had finished praying.[69] Such treatment was a sobering reminder that white supremacy reigned even within the church. This incident catalyzed the efforts of Philadelphia's black community to establish its own churches. The community began raising funds to erect a building almost immediately.

Although discrimination was a major factor, it was not the only one that inspired blacks to form their own churches in Philadelphia. Many black Christians sought religious autonomy. They wanted to serve God as they wished—without the limitations or burdensome ritual of denominational affiliations. They desired a theology that rejected the myth of black inferiority. African Americans also sought the freedom to fellowship with other members of their race. Most importantly, blacks desired the ability to combine their religious work, with racial uplift—something they did not have the freedom to do in white churches.[70]

The Free African Society nurtured the black church movement in Philadelphia. Founded in Philadelphia in 1787 by Richard Allen and Absalom Jones, the Free African Society was essentially a mutual aid society designed to provide moral guidance and relief to its membership. It assumed other roles within the black community, as well; members pushed for temperance, establishment of a black burial ground, and abolition.[71] The society's most critical function was its religious meetings, which eventually became the basis for the first black churches in the city, Bethel Church and St. Thomas Episcopal, founded in 1794 by Allen and Jones, respectively.[72] By 1817, the Bethel Church had been incorporated as an independent African Methodist Episcopal church—the first independent black church in the nation—and Allen was appointed its first bishop.[73] The black church movement quickly spread from Philadelphia to other black communities throughout the nation.

The emergence of black churches in Cincinnati followed a similar pattern. Most of what is known about the Cincinnati black church movement comes from Rev. Benjamin Arnett, an AME minister and church historian. His book, *Proceedings of the Semi-centenary Celebration of the African Methodist Episcopal Church,* was commissioned as part of the church's fiftieth anniversary celebration. Although Arnett did not personally witness the emergence of the AME Church, he learned the history from elder church members and previous ministers who had witnessed it, the treasure keepers of the church history. Each of their accounts of the early history of the AME Church became part of the community's collective memory. Thus, *Proceedings of the Semi-centenary Celebration of the African Methodist Episcopal Church* is essentially oral history told from a collective community memory and passed from one generation to the next.[74]

According to this community's collective memory, the black church movement in Cincinnati was sparked in 1815 by the humiliations blacks suffered in Wesley Chapel, a white Methodist Episcopal church. There, African Americans were subjected to degrading seating arrangements. Every white church member was assigned a pew, but African Americans had no pews reserved for them, leaving them no place to sit during service.[75] It must have been painful to accept the fact that even within God's house, they were considered second-class Christian citizens. Quite weary of the racial insults they suffered at Wesley Chapel, they desired to worship in a place where "prejudice had no power to hurt"—a place where "the colored man could stand up in the full dignity of his manhood."[76]

Besides aspiring to worship with dignity, Cincinnati's African Americans also desired freedom in their form of worship. Those who attended Wesley Chapel felt their religious autonomy was being stifled. They desired the freedom to praise God with the emotional fervor—crying out, dancing, or leaping for joy—that had become a trademark of African American culture. In Wesley Chapel, blacks were forced to be reserved and sometimes were even "compelled to suppress their inclinations to leap and shout."[77] One day, an unidentified black man who was worshiping in Wesley Chapel was strongly moved to shout. He tried to prevent himself from making an outburst by stuffing a handkerchief in his mouth and, supposedly, burst a blood vessel in his efforts not to shout.[78] Regardless of its veracity, this anecdote reveals the dissatisfaction African Americans felt toward the conservative worship style of Wesley Chapel. They concluded that the only remedy was to establish their own church.

The black community elected Samuel Carrell, the first black member of Wesley Chapel, to "present a [financial] plea" to philanthropists Judge Henry Spencer and J. H. Piatt to help them in this endeavor.[79] Born and raised in Lancaster, Pennsylvania, after the passage of that state's Gradual Abolition Act of 1780, Carrell may have been born free.[80] Therefore, he would not have been as indoctrinated with the master-slave code that dictated that blacks speak to whites with deference and humility. In fact, Carrell tended to "speak up 'pert' before white folks."[81] He had an air of confidence that most freed blacks in Cincinnati had not yet acquired, and he was respected and admired for that. The community had full confidence that he was the best person to seek funds from white philanthropists. And they were right about Carrell—he convinced Spencer and Piatt to purchase a lot for the church near Deer Creek.

Once the lot was purchased, worshipers moved forward with their plans to raise the church. Joseph Dorcas, a black carpenter and architect, designed the church.[82] Using the skills of members of their own community, African Americans built the church with their own hands, brick by brick, in 1815.[83] Once the church—Deer Creek Methodist Episcopal— was raised, Dorcas and another African American, William Buck, acted as its ministers.[84] The two men shared ministerial duties, sometimes enlisting the assistance of other black exhorters, until they hired James King to preach.[85]

James King was a Kentucky slave whose master gave him permission to attend church in Cincinnati on Sundays. Because his master had consented to his entering a free state, King was a free man under an 1841 state supreme court decision that automatically freed slaves brought into the state with their owner's consent. Subsequently, King, with the help of Judge Spencer, petitioned for his liberty in court. Fearing that kidnappers would carry him back to Kentucky and re-enslave him, King was forced to go underground in Cincinnati for two years.[86]

Although the Deer Creek Church had its own ministers, lot, and building, it had retained its Methodist Episcopal theology and affiliation, which meant that Wesley Chapel was still its governing body. Essentially, black leaders could make no independent decisions, nor could the body assert its voice. Several members continued to be dissatisfied and hoped to end Deer Creek's affiliation with Wesley Chapel. The final break with the white Methodist Episcopal church came during a general camp meeting in 1823. When King and another black minister tried to take communion, white church elders told them to get up and wait until all the whites had partaken of the sacraments: "When all the whites had partaken of the holy Eucharist, then the minister, with a long face, invited the colored brethern [sic] and sisters to come forward and commemorate the death and suffering of their Savior."[87] But the "spirit of soul freedom was too strong," and the blacks refused to be humiliated any longer.[88] In an act of protest, they "would not go forward . . . because they were conscious that those who made the distinctions were wrong and were encouraging the spirit of caste and feeding the prejudices of the times."[89]

Led by King, a large group of African Americans severed all ties with the Methodist Episcopal, or ME, church and applied for admission into the *African* Methodist Episcopal, or AME, church. In 1824, the congregation was accepted into the fold of the AME with Phillip Brodie as its first pastor.[90] By joining the AME, this Cincinnati church had aligned itself with an influential national association of black Christians. The AME congregation in Cincinnati was no longer the stepchild of a white church, but part of a national network of independent black churches. Even with such prospects, not all African Americans joined the AME Church in Cincinnati: some remained in the Deer Creek Methodist Episcopal Church. Those who remained probably did not wish to sever their ties with Wesley Chapel.

For the first ten years, the AME congregation worked to secure a permanent building. Until then, the body met in the basement of Phillip Brodie's house and in other private homes.[91] They eventually secured space in an old blacksmith shop on North Street near New Street. The humble church was "made of rough boards set on end; the floor was of clab-boards; the seats were of the same, with the legs nailed on and no backs. The front [of the building] was painted red" and was known as the "Little Red Church on the Green" for years.[92] Despite the church's appearance, members prided themselves on having received no philanthropy for this building—it belonged wholly to them. Soon, however, the congregation outgrew the building and moved to a former carpenter's shop and lime house on Seventh Street, east of Broadway, which it occupied until 1834.[93] Despite its mobility, the AME Church always remained centrally located within the core of the black community in the First Ward near Sixth Street and Broadway: the church belonged to the black community, not to the city.

Independence from the white Methodists enabled the AME body to voice, in public, a critique of racism. Blacks had developed a critique of racism long *before* that moment, but the emergence of an independent black church provided African Americans in Cincinnati a space of their own in which to articulate this critique without fear of retribution. The AME Church also created a forum for dialogue and discourse about issues affecting the black community. As religious historian Eddie Glaude Jr. noted, "Black churches, then, were the sites for a public discourse critical of white supremacy and the American nation-state as well as the spaces for identity construction. Here African Americans engaged in public deliberation free of humiliation (at least by whites). They also spoke in a self-determining voice, defining a cultural identity through a particular idiom and style."[94] As its first political act, the Cincinnati AME congregation expressed its contempt for slavery by prohibiting slaveholders from membership in the church.[95] Although it was very unlikely that a slaveholder *would* join the AME Church, this prohibition was a way of publicly condemning slavery—a position black Christians in Cincinnati theretofore had been unable to do. The very existence of the church—created under such hostile conditions—was, itself, a potent symbol of resistance. Reflecting on the history of that church, Peter Clark, a black leader, stated to an AME congregation in 1874: "The existence of the African Methodist Church is a protest against prejudice and an assertion of the equal humanity of the African race, and there is a necessity for it to continue until that prejudice is dead, and that equality acknowledged."[96]

The church expressed its political voice in other ways, as well. AME ministers delivered politically charged sermons that denounced racial injustice. On any Sunday morning in the AME Church, one might hear a sermon about the evils of slavery or about how God had delivered Israel out of bondage in Egypt.[97] These sermons about the Exodus are telling: black Christians in Cincinnati had begun to draw parallels between Jewish bondage in Egypt and their own bondage in America. Just as deliverance had been divinely ordered for the chosen people in Egypt, African Americans believed the same would hold true for them. The biblical account of the Jewish Exodus had a liberating power for them: "The sacred history of God's deliverance of his chosen people was transformed into an account of black liberation."[98]

The Deer Creek Methodist Episcopal Church did not develop as strong a public critique of racism. Not surprisingly, the church's economic and political dependence on Wesley Chapel muted its political voice and decreased the likelihood that this congregation would challenge the status quo. In fact, when the AME body petitioned for a repeal of the Black Laws, the Deer Creek Church distanced itself. The latter submitted a public notice to that effect in the July 4, 1829, issue of the *Cincinnati Daily Gazette*: "We, the undersigned, members of the Methodist Episcopal Church, 200 in number, do certify that we form no part of that indefinite number that are asking a change in the laws of Ohio; all we ask is a continuation of the smiles of the white people as we have hitherto enjoyed them."[99] At the time this notice was submitted, whites were considering reviving the Black Laws, and the Deer Creek congregation was unwilling to take a controversial political position in such a climate. They may have been trying to stave off expulsion from the city. Sadly enough, this church won no friends by issuing its statement. In fact, this notice did not prevent authorities from invoking these laws at all.

While the Deer Creek congregation—dependent as it was on Wesley Chapel—may have been happy with the smiles of white people, the AME Church inspired and supported black political activism. Although denied the franchise and other citizenship rights, these black Cincinnatians found other ways to influence the political system. According to John Malvin, the AME Church led a petition campaign in 1829 to repeal the Black Laws. Recognizing that they had little power as nonvoters, AME Church members solicited the signatures of several of Cincinnati's most influential white citizens, including Nicholas Longworth, Jacob Wykoff Piatt, and John Clingman.[100] The black community hoped that these names would provide leverage in the struggle against the Black Laws. However, even with such powerful supporters, the legislature failed to heed this petition.[101]

The African American community strategically selected patrons—like Piatt and Longworth—who possessed both wealth and influence to champion civil rights, protect black freedom, and to otherwise assist in the struggle for equality. Seeking the patronage of men with property and standing was a good strategy in the 1820s in Cincinnati. In a climate in which one's freedom could be contested by any white who claimed that a black person was a fugitive slave, it was imperative that free and freed blacks align themselves with whites of means who were willing to attest to their free status. Patrons might advise slaves how to obtain their freedom by legal means. Judge Spencer, for example, was instrumental in advising Rev. James King in his suit for his freedom.[102] Blacks sometimes depended on their white sponsors for financial assistance. Employers, for example, might be enlisted to act as a surety for the five-hundred-dollar bond required under the Black Laws or to help buy a fugitive's freedom. Some patrons even funded black schools or churches. For example, Judge Spencer and J. H. Piatt purchased the land on which the Deer Creek Church was built.[103] Nicholas Longworth helped fund a black school and a movement by African Americans to relocate to Canada in 1829.[104]

Most patrons provided support only discreetly. Longworth, for example, was very generous with his philanthropy, but preferred to give to African Americans covertly. He quietly purchased the freedom of fugitive slaves and built schools for blacks.[105] Politically, he was a vehement critic of abolitionism and a strong supporter of colonization. Similarly, Charles Hammond, the editor of the *Cincinnati Daily Gazette,* often defended blacks in his paper and even provided them with the opportunity to submit articles and public notices in their own defense. Although Hammond provided a forum for African Americans to express themselves—which was far more than other editors of his day were willing to do—he never went so far as to publicly advocate racial equality. These sponsors were not willing to champion blacks' rights openly and thereby to risk public censure.

In sum, despite the relative independence of the AME congregation in its thought and actions, it still sought the patronage and support of powerful whites; yet, the strategic and fundamental desire to secure patrons did not negate the AME Church's role in fostering a black political voice. Not only did the AME Church provide a forum for political action in Cincinnati, but it also became a safe house for fugitive slaves. The church building was a hiding place for scores of fugitive slaves. In their own building and free of the control of whites, AME Church members were in a better position to assist fugitive slaves. They hid them in their homes and even conveyed them to points farther north. For their underground abolitionist activity, AME Church members earned a reputation as "so-called black abolitionists."[106]

Independent churches were not the only black institutions established before 1830; the community also opened schools. African Americans, like most Americans in the early nineteenth century, believed that education could break down the walls of discrimination, prepare them for citizenship, and improve their opportunities. Despite their yearning for education, African Americans were denied access to common schools until an 1825 legislative act provided for universal public education.[107] Sadly enough, that window of opportunity was slammed shut just four years later when the act was repealed, denying blacks access to public education for another twenty years. Because African Americans were denied a public education, white philanthropists, abolitionists, religious groups, and free blacks established private schools for them. These private schools occupied a central position in the institutional organization of Cincinnati's black community.

White Christians led the earliest efforts to educate African Americans in the Queen City. Cincinnati's Lancaster Seminary opened the first school for black youth in 1815.[108] Two years later, the Female Association for the Benefit of Africans was established to "bestow upon the Africans religious instruction and the rudiments of education."[109] In that same year, two other white women founded a Sunday school for blacks, which had an enrollment of between seventy and eighty students—20 percent of the entire black population—within three years.[110] In 1832, Lane Seminary students began organizing biweekly public lectures on scientific and literary subjects, which attracted African American audiences numbering in the hundreds.[111] Lane Seminary students also opened two schools in 1833 with approximately one hundred students.[112]

In these Sunday and religious schools, educators provided blacks with a combination of religious instruction and basic education.[113] Students were taught the fundamentals of reading and writing necessary to read the Bible. The objective of this education was to make blacks better Christians. To this end, teachers commissioned by the church or other religious groups may have approached their jobs as a mission to convert black "heathens."[114] This type of education was not liberating: it was not intended to prepare blacks to rise above their lot in life or even to enlighten them socially or politically. Nevertheless, Sunday schools laid the foundation for the development of regular black schools in Cincinnati.

By the 1820s, black education had moved from the domain of the church and religious groups into the hands of independent teachers. In 1820, a white man with the surname Wing began holding night classes for black children near Sixth and Vine streets, a practice which he continued off and on for years.[115] With secularization came the opportunity for blacks to open their own schools. As early as 1826, African Americans were educating themselves, often holding classes in abandoned buildings or converted pork houses. In 1826, a black man named Henry Collins established a school in an old pork house or carpenter's shop on Seventh Street between Broadway and Deer Creek. Henry McPherson established a school in 1826 on Sixth Street near Broadway. In 1827, Hugh Brown, a mulatto from Virginia, taught in a building on New Street.[116] Two more schools opened around the same time. One was run by a black man out of Glen's Old Pork House on Hopples Alley, near Sycamore Street; a black man named Mr. Cooly operated the other near Sixth Street and Broadway.[117] Children and adults alike flocked to the schoolhouses; one school established in 1834 overflowed with children and adults shortly after it opened.[118] According to an Ohio Anti-Slavery Society report, the demand from adults in their school was so high that it was necessary to open an evening school for them, which met three evenings a week.[119]

Despite this flurry of black school openings, none were permanent. As private schools, black schools were forced to rely on tuition for funding.

If students failed to pay their tuition, neither the teachers' salaries nor the building rent could be paid. Without the benefit of tax monies, it is highly unlikely that these schools had very many books or supplies. Teachers were hard to secure and, sometimes, too, were tuition receipts.[120] When many black families could barely afford decent housing, tuition was not as high a priority as the purchase of basic necessities. Lacking human and financial resources, black schools were extremely short-lived. In fact, most did not even survive a year, although this might partly be attributed to the transience of the population. Many African Americans did not remain in Cincinnati long enough to provide sustained support or leadership for these schools. Even the teachers moved into and out of the community.[121]

Vehement white opposition to black education also played a leading role in the schools' impermanence. In April 1830, black Ohioans sent a petition to the legislature praying to share in the benefits of the common school fund. The body responded that the fund was reserved for the exclusive purpose of free white citizens: "The common school fund is *not* the offspring of the offices of charity; but that the principal and interest is amply repaid by the exercise of those functions which the government itself imposes upon all her free white citizens" (emphasis added). With this declaration, the body confirmed that public education was reserved for free *white* citizens.[122] According to one Cincinnati teacher, John Wattles, those opposed to educating African Americans sometimes took their protests a bit further: "Those early schools were disturbed by the yells and the missiles of the mob, the teachers abused and the children scattered. For a time it was necessary, as their places of resort were discovered by the rabble, that the teachers should inform the children one day where they would meet the next."[123] Thus, the threat of mob violence, in part, led to the high degree of mobility and impermanence of these black schools. As a consequence of this repression, this education was—at best—irregular, short-lived, substandard, and terrorized. Despite these challenges, the seeds had been sown for black education in Cincinnati.

———

Cincinnati's social and economic ties to the South and its desire to become the commercial gateway to the West intersected with its repressive racial code. Yet African Americans had plenty of incentive to stay in Cincinnati. By 1829, Cincinnati's black community had laid a foundation of institutions, leadership, and activism. The AME Church provided a platform for political action, a site for fellowship, and place to fulfill the spiritual needs of the black community. Schools added another dimension to the freedom narrative by preparing blacks for citizenship. Black Cincinnati had begun to identify leaders, a group that consisted largely of ministers and others who would "speak up pert before white folks." Certainly this community was making strides toward self-determination by 1829. Yet, with the exception of the AME Church, black institutions were impermanent and underfunded. And despite the support of powerful patrons, the black political voice was still ineffective. The foundation that this community laid was neither strong nor secure. Little did African Americans know that even those seams would soon come undone.

A Place Called Freedom

The 1829 Riot and Emigration

> Citizens of our favoured Republic, but do not remove one
> step from your native state and mether [sic] country, rather
> become martyrs to the injustice, you have but once to die.
> But if you should be otherwise disposed and do emigrate
> from a home that has treated you so badly, we recommend
> you settle in Upper Canada.
>
> —*Rights of All*, August 14, 1829

IN LATE AUGUST 1829, whites determined to enforce old laws de-
terring black settlement in the state of Ohio provoked an exodus of more
than half the black population from the city of Cincinnati. Typically, antebellum mob action directed toward blacks was intended to punish or to
intimidate; rarely, if ever, was the goal to force the emigration of the entire black population. The mob action of 1829 was one of the earliest examples in American history of a white effort forcibly to cleanse society of
its black population. Although the 1829 mob action stands as an important benchmark in Cincinnati's history, the subsequent mass migration
of between eleven hundred and fifteen hundred African Americans from
the city was not an act of mass victimization. African Americans resisted
oppression, and they defined and pursued freedom on their own terms.
In fact, in an act of collective *self-determination*, a portion of the black community that quit Cincinnati in 1829 established an independent all-
black colony in Ontario, Canada, that they named Wilberforce.[1]

The decision to leave Cincinnati, the location of the colony, and the
process of settling it speak volumes about how these migrants from Cincinnati defined and pursued freedom and how they achieved their goals
in Canada.[2] Wilberforce's history, and ultimately the measure of its success, cannot be divorced from the history of black Cincinnati; after all,

it was the conditions in Cincinnati that led African Americans to seek a new home in Canada. Communities forged in Cincinnati and visions of freedom born in Cincinnati became transnational and planted themselves in Canadian soil. This is that story.

In 1820, no one could have predicted that by the end of the decade Cincinnati's black population would increase enough to become a nuisance to white society. In 1820, 433 African Americans comprised 3.9 percent of the city's population.[3] Between 1820 and 1829, however, the city's black population swelled by more than 400 percent—from 433 to 2,258.[4] This rate of growth amounted to 15 percent per year.[5] During the same period, the white population grew by only 100 percent. The largest increase in the black population came in the three-year period between 1826 and 1829, when it grew from about 700 to more than 2,250.[6] By 1829, blacks made up 9.4 percent of a total population of slightly more than 24,000.[7]

Many African Americans who arrived in the 1820s had been slaves and bore the badges of poverty. Most had little to no education, spoke poor English, lacked material possessions, and were poorly fed and clad. Having few resources and earning low wages, most African Americans were compelled to live in the least costly dwellings—usually in housing that was cheap and structurally compromised. They built small temporary shacks and shanties consisting of boards roughly nailed together. This ramshackle housing had no real floors, windows, or doors. Not all African Americans lived in makeshift homes; some blacks moved into abandoned buildings and shops, and others made their homes in houses that had been divided into several apartments. Despite the quality of this housing, it provided its inhabitants with some measure of privacy and protection from the elements. More importantly, it was a step toward independence for those who were making the transition from slavery or from life in white households.

Whites were not prepared for the sudden increase in the black population. Their anxiety about the African American presence grew at a rate proportional to their increase in the city. In less than ten years, Cincinnati had gone from a city with a few African American families sprinkled throughout, to one with a population that was nearly 10 percent black. That increase, coupled with Cincinnati's compact geographical size, made whites feel overrun by African Americans.

Each economic class of whites each had its own sources of anxiety about the growing black presence in Cincinnati. For the middle and upper classes, consisting of merchant capitalists, shopkeepers, and business professionals, the prospect of a large mass of *impoverished* blacks was particularly distressing. This specter of poverty stood in stark contrast to the city's image as Queen City of the West, "the seat of commerce, the arts, fashion, and literature—the place to which everyone reports for information upon the *manners and topics of the day*"[8] (emphasis in original). Cincinnati's docks along the Ohio River were lined with coffee shops, produce stores, wholesale merchants, clothiers, and grocers. Whenever a steamboat docked, its passengers and crew descended upon these shops in search of food, coffee, dry goods, clothing, or shoes. Southern planters frequently came ashore seeking to establish long-term trading partnerships with Cincinnati's wholesale merchants for the goods needed to sustain their enslaved workforce. The Cincinnati merchant class feared that a mass of impoverished African Americans residing in close proximity to their shops would hurt business.

Although fears of miscegenation were the usual justification whites provided for opposing black settlement in northern urban areas in the late antebellum era, these were not the fears voiced in Cincinnati in the 1820s.[9] At that time in Cincinnati, anxiety about the growing mass of African Americans was rooted partly in the perception of black immorality. White residents feared that black moral depravity negatively influenced society. As one resident expressed it, "We shall be overwhelmed by an emigration at once wretched in its character and destructive in its consequences."[10] Similarly, the editor of *Liberty Hall*, a local newspaper, lamented, "The rapid increase of our black population, to say nothing of slavery, is of itself a great evil," and complained of "night walkers, lewd persons, and those who lounge about without any visible means of support, and especially the negro house gamblers."[11] White leaders feared African Americans would become a tax burden. An editorial in a Columbus newspaper, *Ohio State Journal*, declared that African Americans were "an idle, intemperate and dissolute race . . . a burden on the resources of the State and to the energies of the laboring class of citizens."[12]

White laborers had their own reasons to resent the black presence. Many of them disliked the changes that were taking root in the Cincinnati labor market. To increase their profits, urban capitalists had long pushed for economic change. They began expanding credit and financing, regulating currency and banking, and encouraging newer, mass-producing manufacturing pursuits.[13] This market revolution, as it was called, hastened the destruction of the old artisanal system of manufacturing. Although the market revolution was not complete until much later, these tensions were being played out in Cincinnati as early as 1829.

In the dying artisanal system, tradesmen were a part of a "fluid hierarchy" of master craftsmen, journeymen, and apprentices.[14] At the bottom of the ladder were apprentices, who spent three to seven years learning their art from master craftsmen. Apprentices usually received only room and board. When the apprenticeship was over, the worker was given a suit of clothes and officially entered the trade as a journeyman, working for a small wage. Often, these journeymen aspired to become masters and saved their money so that they could eventually open their own shops.[15] Under this system, the craft took a lifetime to perfect. The skill and time that went into the craft usually kept prices high and output low.

For artisans, competition with technology and unskilled or semi-skilled workers was the worst part of this market revolution. Machines and nonmechanized assembly lines produced less expensive products in less time. Merchant capitalists began to divide the craft into a series of tasks, which were then parceled out to lower-paid workers—often women, children, and blacks. The division of labor among unskilled and poorly paid workers allowed investors to increase production and to lower costs. One way for the owner of a small business to make a profit was to the cut wages of journeymen, who could not hope to survive if other workers would do the same work for less pay. Goods could be produced without the experience of a master craftsman, and at much a lower price. Master craftsmen found themselves increasingly dispensable. While manufacturers and consumers profited from these changes in the market, artisans were being displaced. Consequently, many of them were forced into wage work simply to survive. Other displaced masters found themselves converting their trade into a series of "nonmechanized assembly lines" to remain competitive.[16] White artisans, probably already resentful that their crafts were being parceled out to unskilled and semiskilled labor, looked for someone to blame—who better than black workers, who were often perceived as the source of the changing labor market?

Although all black workers were held to the lowest levels of employment, their presence in the workforce caused concern for white laborers. Skilled blacks were especially threatening to white artisans. James C. Brown recalled that when he lived in Louisville, Kentucky, he was "an object of jealousy" to white artisans there because he was more successful in getting jobs. They threatened to "break every bone in his body unless he left the neighborhood."[17] The same was true in Cincinnati; white mechanics were unwilling to allow blacks into the trades. According to a report by the Ohio Anti-Slavery Society, "no colored boy could learn a trade or a colored journeyman find employment" in the city. In one case, white artisans threw down their tools and refused to work with a black cabinetmaker.[18]

Not only did many white Cincinnatians not want to work with African Americans, but they did not want to live near them either. On a very basic level, many white Cincinnatians simply did not want black neighbors. On August 29, 1827, white residents from the First Ward presented a petition to the city council complaining of "the dangers of fire to be apprehended from certain [indecipherable] all-board houses in that neighborhood tenanted by negroes."[19] The object of the complaint was "a frame or board building which has been erected for more than six years which was formerly occupied as a Blacksmith's shop and is now occupied by a negro grocery and another family." The petitioners also complained that "[w]ithin the period of a year there has been built directly contiguous to the corner tenement another board tenement of about the same dimensions with that on the corner not exceeding ten or twelve feet in height . . . . The whole neighborhood is covered with houses of a similar description built upon ground [indecipherable] for terms of from three to five years and inhabited by blacks."[20] This type of complaint was nothing new; blacks living in ramshackle housing in other cities attracted similar contempt from their city officials and reformers.[21]

The residential composition of the First Ward may explain why this complaint was initiated here. Artisans and unskilled laborers—the very people who most feared black labor competition—made up a significant portion of First Ward residents, and another significant, even disproportionate, number of its inhabitants were black. In 1826, 49 percent of the city's African American population resided in the First Ward, north of Sixth Street and east of Sycamore.[22] Although the 1829 city directory does not give exact population breakdowns for each of the four wards, an extrapolation from the 1826 directory suggests that some eleven hundred African Americans lived in the First Ward in 1829. They congregated there for a number of reasons, including the availability of unskilled work, low rents, and the presence of black institutions, such as the AME church.[23]

First Ward petitioners did not make any specific requests to the city council; they simply complained about the nature of black housing in the ward. Certainly, the black housing was a fire hazard, and, because of the frequency of fires in antebellum America, this was a valid concern.[24] And because Cincinnati had not yet established adequate municipal services (firefighters, police officers) to meet the needs of its growing population, any fire would have, rather quickly, destroyed a neighborhood. Because communicable diseases could easily spread through overcrowded structures, black housing also posed some health risks. Although the petitioners may have been genuinely concerned about the real threat of fires, the petition was more likely an indirect way to gain the city council's approval for a more sinister objective: removal of the African American population by leveling their homes.

When the petition was submitted, the city council opposed any action against the black population in the First Ward. Recognizing that poverty was the main obstacle to better housing for blacks, the council responded: "The committee think it highly improper to prostrate all those little tenements because the poverty of their tenants renders it improbable for them to build a more permanent dwelling. . . . We cannot drive the black population from the city in the summary way of pulling down the houses over their heads."[25] The city council's decision not to "drive the black population from the city in the summary way of pulling down the houses" made it neither friend nor ally of African Americans. Its class composition may have influenced the decision not to level black homes. The business class, consisting of wholesalers, large merchants, manufacturers, and large entrepreneurs, provided the economic, political, and social leadership in the city.[26] Some of Cincinnati's wealthiest merchants sat on the city council.[27] Many councilmen depended on black labor in their shops, factories, and homes.[28] Hence, they were disinclined to drive an entire population of workers from the city. The councilmen opposed the *forcible* removal of the black population. They may have favored a more discrete, humane, and voluntary means of removing the black population: colonization.

The American Colonization Society (ACS) was established in 1816 to settle free blacks in an African colony. Its founding members included some of the country's most influential men, such as Henry Clay, Andrew Jackson, and Daniel Webster. One hundred initial members, including many of Cincinnati's men of property and standing, established Cincinnati's chapter of the ACS in 1826.[29] Those who joined the ACS had a variety of motives. Some opposed slavery and hoped that colonization would influence slaveholders to emancipate their slaves and settle them in Africa. Others were certain that African Americans would never receive equality in America and that a return to Africa was the only alternative for them. Some ministers and other Christians joined the ACS because they hoped it would lead to an American Christian outpost in Africa, from which African Americans would lead the effort to Christianize Africa. Slaveholders also joined the ACS—hoping that a removal of free blacks would make slavery more secure.[30] They reasoned that the presence of free blacks planted notions of freedom in the minds of enslaved people, making them more anxious to secure freedom for themselves. Still others who joined the ACS were ardent racists who hoped colonization would ultimately rid America of its black population.

In its initial years, Ohio Colonization Society (OCS)—the state branch of the ACS—supported colonization largely for racist reasons. None of the Ohio Colonization Society's early records suggest that either emancipation or black equality was an objective—although the body did, in its first meeting, express its doubts that African Americans would ever be extended citizenship rights and equality in America.[31] The Ohio Colonization Society was guided by growing resentment that freed slaves from southern states were migrating to Ohio and contaminating the social landscape: "These miserable beings, with all the ignorance and degraded, habits of thinking and acting which pertain to slavery, are *flooded* upon us in Ohio and Indiana." The organization manipulated the public perception that African Americans flooded into the state on a daily basis. In 1827, the organization projected that in a few years the population of blacks in Ohio would equal that of whites. The OCS believed that the high rates of black migration to Ohio inevitably would result in a black uprising: "And in the fearful event of a *servile war,* it would not be in the slave holding states, and among slaves that those schemes of blood and ruin would be laid and ripened into maturity, but here, where they enjoy enough of freedom to feel their chains and to encourage them in an effort to break them off, and are not under the watchful restraints of a master."[32] This type of propaganda fostered public hysteria about the black presence in the state, and particularly in Cincinnati, where the black population was the largest.

Some of the Ohio citizenry expressed the same sentiments as did the Ohio Colonization Society. By the mid 1820s, some saw the organization purely as a deportation society and began demanding that the OCS remove the state's black population. One man editorialized that such an organization was needed because African Americans were "worse than drones to society, and they already swarm in our land like locusts." For this citizen, the solution to the problem was the removal of blacks by the OCS or some legislation prohibiting their settlement in the state.[33] A Cincinnati resident wrote: "We consider this class of people as a serious evil among us . . . . [T]he only remedy afforded is to colonize them in their mother country. Now is the time for the Colonization Societies 'to be up and doing.'"[34]

Although some hoped colonization would solve the perceived problem of the city's burgeoning black population, the colonization effort in

Ohio was ineffective. The expense of transporting blacks to Africa exceeded donations, making colonization a slow and impractical option. By far, the biggest obstacle the movement faced was the one presented by African Americans themselves. According to a report by the Ohio Colonization Society, "A great majority of the free people of colour, manifest a very great unwillingness to migrate to Africa."[35] By rejecting colonization, black Ohioans were not unlike their cohorts in other northern communities. In Philadelphia, more than three thousand African Americans met at Bethel AME Church in 1817 to draw up a resolution denouncing the American Colonization Society. As third- and fourth-generation Americans—some of whom had served in the American Revolution and the War of 1812—black Philadelphians believed they had earned their right to call the United States home. They felt they were as American as the members of ACS and resented efforts to banish them to far-off lands. This community also distrusted the motives of the American Colonization Society, believing that it was "a deportation society whose members believed in both black inferiority and in the necessity of ridding the country of its free black population in order to preserve the institution of slavery."[36] Black Cincinnatians, more than likely, resisted ACS colonization schemes for similar reasons. It seemed clear to white citizens that "whilst the Colonization Society rids us of a few, the Legislature ought to devise some mode to prevent the people of this state from suffering [because of the African American presence]."[37]

Despite the varying rationales among the different classes and sectors of whites in the city, by 1828 most supported an action that would prevent the further growth of the black population. Although the city council had been unwilling to take any steps to *remove* the existing black population, it did support measures to *check* further black migration into Cincinnati. In response to yet another citizen's petition in 1828, the Cincinnati City Council appointed a committee "to take measures to prevent the increase of the negro population within the city."[38] Unfortunately, there is no extant evidence of this committee's specific accomplishments. Meanwhile, the question of how best to arrest the growth of the black population continued to inspire debate. In March 1829, whites from the Third Ward met to discuss issues they deemed pertinent to the upcoming election for township trustees.[39] These residents desired an effective solution to the "problem" of blacks flooding the city. They resolved, "From the third ward no person shall be elected for Township Trustee who will not put in force the act of the Legislature relative to black and mulatto persons."[40]

Popularly referred to as the 1807 Black Law, this act compelled African Americans to find two freehold sureties to give a five-hundred-dollar bond guaranteeing their good behavior and their support before settling in the state.[41] Politicians committed to enforcing the Black Law carried the spring elections—not just in the Third Ward, but throughout the rest of the city, as well.[42] Besides this election, another development that spring played a critical role in reviving the 1807 Black Law. In March, the Ohio Supreme Court heard arguments challenging the constitutionality of the Black Laws. The court decided that the laws were, indeed, constitutional.[43] To many supporters of the restrictive legislation, this ruling opened the door to their enforcement in Cincinnati.

As a result of developments that spring, the public imperative shifted from preventing further black immigration to warning out those who had not met the settlement requirements of the statute. The impetus for removal emerged from the working classes; white artisans, journeymen, and unskilled laborers advocated this measure because it would rid them of the pool of black labor. When it became clear that the workers would elect only those candidates who supported the enforcement of the 1807 Black Law, city leaders and politicians probably decided it was in their best interest to sanction it, as well. Among the elite, this move was a compromise between their practical labor needs and their desire to rid the city of "idle" blacks who might become a burden. While profiting from the labor of industrious blacks, the white elite probably saw the black vagrant as dispensable. Some of these prominent whites were of the same mind as *Cincinnati Daily Gazette* editor Charles Hammond when he wrote, "That part of our coloured population who are free, who are honest, who are industrious and correct in their deportment have nothing to fear from the enforcement of the laws. It is only the runaway slaves and idle vagrants that have occasion for alarm."[44] Hammond supported enforcement of the law against fugitive slaves, but not against free blacks. Perhaps he was naïve for thinking that the law would be enforced in a way that distinguished among these groups. African Americans, on the other hand, understood that enforcement of the Black Law precluded any *just* differentiation between vagrant and industrious blacks, or between fugitive slaves and legitimately free blacks. Despite such reassuring editorials from Hammond, African Americans suspected that all classes would be ejected from the city—vagrants, fugitive slaves, and industrious blacks, alike.

———

That spring, at the same time that whites were considering enforcement of the Black Laws, African Americans were making plans of a different sort. Some segments of the black community began organizing an emigration society with plans to leave Cincinnati.[45] Certainly, the looming threat of the enforcement of the Black Laws precipitated plans to resettle elsewhere.

In the hearts and minds of many black leaders in the nineteenth century, emigration was entirely different from colonization. Unlike emigration, colonization was initiated largely by whites, who determined not only *where* African Americans would settle but also *when*, and *how*. The resulting colonies were not only organized but governed by whites, as well. Emigrationists, by contrast, were those African Americans who consciously and conscientiously rejected America's definition of freedom and equality and who tried to secure these goals on their own terms by migrating from the country and forming independent colonies elsewhere. Lewis Woodson, a Pittsburgh minister who advocated black emigration and separate black settlements, emphasized that emigration had to be a "voluntary and free" movement with the primary objective of benefiting migrants and their children. He further noted that, "The mode, time, and place, of emigration must be left wholly to their choice."[46] A key component in emigrationist ideology was an overwhelming desire for self-determination.[47] White-controlled colonies went against the core African American cultural values of freedom, resistance, and self-determination.[48] African Americans wanted to make the choice of migration for themselves and to determine the terms of their new freedom. It is not surprising, then, that many black leaders supported emigration but vehemently opposed colonization.

The black emigrationist tradition in the United States dates back as far as the Revolutionary War Era, when the first emigrationist societies were formed.[49] Early black emigrationists were motivated by the belief that racial oppression precluded the possibility of enjoying freedom or equality in the United States. Only by returning to Africa could African Americans be free from racism and have control over their own lives and destinies. Those who supported emigration to Africa also believed that African Americans would help "civilize" and Christianize Africa.[50] The African Union Society of Newport, Rhode Island, founded in 1780, was the first to formalize plans to establish a settlement of African Americans in Africa. The African Union Society even sent agents to Sierra Leone to survey land for the colony. That same society also attempted to nationalize the emigration movement by communicating with groups in Newport, Rhode Island, and Philadelphia and inviting them to assist in the efforts.[51] Unfortunately, these plans were hindered by the inability to locate and secure land in Africa and to win popular support among African Americans.[52] Nevertheless, these early emigrationists articulated a vision that would be continued in the nineteenth century by men like Paul Cuffe and James C. Brown.[53]

The Cincinnati events of 1829 took place in the context of this emigrationist and self-determinist tradition in a community that had a recent memory of emigration upon which to build. In 1824, a group African Americans had formed the Cincinnati Haytien Union to investigate the possibility of emigration to Haiti.[54] The Haytien Union was part of a larger, national movement of African Americans who were recruited by the Haitian government to settle on the island. Facing a critical shortage of skilled labor in early 1824, President Jean Pierre Boyer sent a warm invitation to black Americans to settle in Haiti. The government offered to pay for their passage and grant them land. Recruiting agents promoted the scheme in black communities nationwide. Haitian emigration societies were formed in several cities, including Cincinnati, to investigate the feasibility of settling in Haiti, which had become an important cultural symbol of black resistance and freedom following a successful slave revolt (1791–1804). Undoubtedly, many who left the United States for Haiti were seeking to live in a nation governed by black people. Perhaps some of those who left had grown pessimistic about the possibility of ever attaining equality in the United States. Although estimates indicate that more than six thousand African Americans left the United States for the black republic,[55] only a very small number left from Cincinnati.[56] But by 1829, more black Cincinnatians were receptive to the idea of forming a black colony elsewhere.

At least a few black emigrationists considered rural Ohio an ideal site for an all-black colony. Lewis Woodson, who had lived in Ohio in the 1820s, wholeheartedly supported the idea. In 1828, he applauded a philanthropist's offer to purchase one hundred acres of land in Guernsey County for a black colony, which was to be named "Africania." Woodson envisioned a black settlement that would "entirely alter our condition." He hoped that there African Americans would "be free from the looks of scorn and contempt—free from fraud—and in time, free from all the evils attendant on partial and unequal laws."[57] Although this idea was never realized, it does demonstrate that emigration to a separate colony was being discussed among some black Ohioans in the 1820s in a context other than that of racial violence.

James Charles Brown emerged as the leader of the Cincinnati emigration movement of 1829. Born a slave in Frederick County, Maryland, around 1796, Brown had been separated from his parents at a young age and taken to Kentucky by his owner. A mason by trade, Brown had hired out his time and purchased his freedom for eighteen hundred dollars in 1817. As a skilled freedman, he had endured physical threats from white mechanics who resented him in the workplace. Brown was an easy convert to the emigration movement. In 1819, acting as an agent for the American Colonization Society, Brown traveled to Texas to survey a potential site for a black colony. According to him, the Texas colony was never established because whites there were opposed to it.[58] Shortly after his return from Texas, Brown moved to Cincinnati. With his experience, he was a suitable leader for the Cincinnati emigration movement.

Near the end of June 1829, African Americans met to elect "two Representatives from among two thousand people, to explore some distant part of the globe for these people to emigrate to."[59] At that meeting, they chose two land agents, Israel Lewis and Thomas Crissup, to survey a site for a colony in Upper Canada. Very little information can be found about either of these two agents. Thomas Crissup had migrated to Cincinnati sometime before 1820.[60] Israel Lewis had lived most of his life as a slave until he escaped with his wife and settled in Cincinnati.[61] Although there is no historical record of where he escaped from or when he settled in the city, what is certain is that Lewis, like Brown and others, must have been disappointed by his freedom experience in Cincinnati and optimistic about finding a new one in Canada.

Upon their arrival in Upper Canada, Lewis and Crissup met with the lieutenant governor of Upper Canada, General John Colbourne, to discuss the prospects of settling in the area. Colbourne reportedly said, "Tell the Republicans on your side of the line that we Royalists do not know men by their color. Should you come to us you will be entitled to all the privileges of the rest of His Majesty's subjects."[62] Colbourne was referring to the fact that Canada made no legal distinctions between its white and black residents; African Americans were entitled to every benefit of citizenship, including suffrage. The prospect of equal treatment under the law was very attractive to those who had long been denied rights of citizenship. Without hesitation, the representatives accepted Colbourne's welcome.

Once their legal status had been guaranteed, the representatives sought to purchase land for the colony. Land ownership was important to the emigrants—part of how they defined freedom. They recognized that land ownership promoted autonomy and self-sufficiency. Lewis and Crissup entered into a contract with the Canada [Land] Company for the purchase of four thousand acres of land in Biddulph Township at $1.50 (U.S.) per acre.[63] The agents selected good land. It was covered with a "black vegetable mould"—a sign of fertile soil—and contemporary travelers reported that the land was "well situated."[64] The land was on the Au Sable River, less than twenty miles from Lake Huron and the Thames River and eight miles from the shores of Lake Erie. This location along major bodies of water seemed as promising for the prosperity of Wilberforce as the location on the Ohio and Miami rivers had been for that of Cincinnati. If nothing else, proximity to these bodies of water would allow its self-sufficient farmers to trade their produce in larger markets.

The rural location of the colony was also far enough from any city to shield its residents from the racism and threats of mob violence that had marked their experience in Cincinnati. The settlers believed that the urban environment, fraught with racism and discrimination, had hindered blacks from reaching optimum prosperity and self-sufficiency. Indeed, the urban environment in Cincinnati had brought only persecution without prosperity. According to Austin Steward, who later became a member of the board of managers for the colony, the urban environment had relegated blacks to menial labor and barred them from achieving real independence. He noted that "[o]ur people mostly flock to cities where they allow themselves to be made 'hewers of wood and drawers of water;' barbers and waiters." He believed if they could but "retire to the country and purchase a piece of land, cultivate and improve it, they would be far richer and happier than they can be in a crowded city."[65]

The proposal to relocate from cities to rural environments was rooted in the emigrationist ideology of agrarian economic independence and self-sufficiency. Lewis Woodson also urged African Americans to migrate from cities in favor of the countryside, where they would have "a more powerful means of changing our present dependent and precarious condition, into one of comfort and independence."[66] Consonant with these ideals, Wilberforce was intended to be an independent rural settlement populated by black farmers who raised cattle and grew crops. Farming was the means by which settlers remained independent.

These steps to plant the colony reveal a great deal about this community's vision of freedom. Yet, it was a vision that was constantly evolving: Cincinnati once had been the Promised Land to fugitive and freed slaves because of its promise of physical freedom and job opportunities. As the African American community matured, that type of freedom proved inadequate to meet its needs. Wilberforce, Ontario, became the new Promised Land because of its promise of freedom from oppression, social and legal equality, opportunities for land ownership, and self-sufficiency. One other benefit that the emigrationists did not explicitly articulate, but which was nonetheless valuable to them, was the opportunity to control their own institutions, culture, and destiny.

Back in Cincinnati, while the agents were away locating and negotiating land deals in Upper Canada, the overseers of the poor submitted a notice that appeared in the *Cincinnati Daily Gazette* on June 30, 1829. The notice warned African American residents in the city that "[t]he Undersigned, Trustees and Overseers of the Poor . . . hereby give notice that . . . the act to regulate black and mulatto persons, and the act amendatory thereto, will hereafter be rigidly enforced." The notice gave African Americans thirty days to enter into bond or to expect, "at the expiration of that time, the law rigidly enforced."[67] This was not the first time African Americans had received a public notice about the enforcement of the Black Laws. A similar notice had appeared in the papers on August 31, 1819—a time when the city had been feeling the sting of an economic depression— and had given African Americans just thirty days to enter into bond or be warned out by the overseers of the poor.[68] However, the tone of the 1819 notice was far less ominous than that of the 1829 notice.

African Americans interpreted "rigid enforcement" of the 1807 law to mean nothing short of mob violence. Although the community had already initiated an emigration scheme, these plans were hastened by the threat of a mob attack. Upon the return of the agents to Cincinnati, the community redoubled its efforts to leave before violence erupted. Realizing that it would be nearly impossible to prepare a mass migration of the entire population of 2,250 in thirty days, Brown appealed to the public for a three-month extension of the deadline: "withhold your mighty arms until our representatives return; we beg your sympathy until we find shelter."[69] An extension would have given time for agents to survey sites for a colony as well as to better prepare the black community for resettlement. African Americans certainly did not want to be ejected from the city by force; rather, they wanted to play a proactive role in their migration out of Cincinnati. They wanted to be emigrants, not refugees.[70] From July 30 to August 10, 1829, the Cincinnati emigrationists ran daily notices in the *Gazette* informing the public about the status of their effort.[71] They hoped to assure the white public that they had made significant progress in the effort to settle elsewhere. In spite of such acts of reassurance, some whites felt they were not moving quickly enough.

Working-class men, "animated by the prospect of high wages, which the sudden removal of some fifteen hundred laborers from the city might occasion," took the law into their own hands.[72] On several nights between August 15 and August 22, mobs of two to three hundred attacked the black section of the Fourth Ward, near Columbia Street and Western Row. Armed largely with huge stones, the mob destroyed black-owned or black-occupied buildings, homes, and shops.[73] According to one source, "The houses of the Blacks were attacked and demolished, and the inmates beat and driven through the streets till beyond the limits of the corporation."[74] While many of the rioters belonged to the laboring classes and had practical reasons to force the black population out of Cincinnati, "gentlemen of property and standing" supported them in spirit, if not in body. "Gentlemen of property and standing" participated in or winked at mob action because it preserved their political power.[75] Acting mayor William Green was slow to take any action against the mob and, despite appeals to authorities, African Americans received no police protection from this terrorism.[76] When the smoke cleared, between eleven hundred and fifteen hundred African Americans had left Cincinnati during the week of violence.[77]

Those who left Cincinnati that summer did not leave in one mass exodus. There were at least two major streams of out-migration that summer—the willing and organized emigrants and the refugees—and, therefore, at least two different rationales for leaving. Most of those who left had been forced out of the city by violence, fear, or the inability to find work.[78] These African Americans left Cincinnati not as an organized community but as individuals or family units in flight. Their migration, then, was an impetuous action precipitated by oppressive conditions in Cincinnati. Such people were unprepared or *ill-prepared* for their journey. It is possible that many lacked the financial resources to travel far from Cincinnati and consequently settled in nearby towns or villages.[79] Their destination was not as important as simply finding a refuge, a place where they could be safe from violence. They were not running *to* any particular place, but running *from* Cincinnati. Thus, for this group of African Americans, the exodus was an act of survival, and not an act toward self-determination.

The second, smaller group consisted of those who participated in the organized scheme of emigration to Canada. Violence, certainly, must have hastened the departure of the emigrationists, but the violence obscures the steps this group had taken to decide to leave Cincinnati, locate another home, and organize the migration and the colony. For this group, the denial of civil rights and social equality were factors precipitating their decision to leave Cincinnati. Neither of the only two existing African American perspectives of that summer, written by John Malvin and James C. Brown, mentions the violence at all, suggesting it played a minimal role in their decisions to leave.[80] In fact, both Malvin and Brown portrayed the exodus of 1829 as a voluntary emigration precipitated by the desire for social equality and civil rights. Malvin wrote, "I suggested to the meeting [of black men] the propriety of appointing a committee to go to some country with power to make arrangements for the purchase of some place to live free from the trammels of social and unequal laws."[81] James C. Brown recounted how the mayor of Cincinnati had tried to convince him to end his emigration scheme—even telling Brown that every person he led to Canada was "a sword drawn against the United States." Mayor Isaac Burnet may have been concerned that a mass exodus would create a labor shortage in the city. Regardless, Brown remained steadfast in his plans. Seeing that Brown was undaunted by threats, the mayor resorted to softer tones and promised to "take steps to have the [Black] law[s] repealed" if Brown abandoned his plans to take African Americans to Canada. Brown claimed that he "paid no attention" to the mayor's promises and continued with his emigration plans.[82] Brown may have rejected the proposition to quit his plans because the vision of freedom he imagined was in Canada, not Cincinnati. Those black Cincinnatians who participated in the emigration effort to Canada were not simply seeking refuge from the violence; they were in search of a new home—one free of racism and prejudice. Their exodus was, at once, a statement against Cincinnati's brand of black freedom and an act toward defining it for themselves.

More than likely, the emigrant group consisted of those who could afford not only the cost of the journey but the cost of land, as well. This community mobilized all its resources to make the nearly four-hundred-mile journey through Ohio, across Lake Erie, and into the Canadian frontier. The emigration society moved in family units; James C. Brown prepared eighteen families for the journey. Some families traveled by wagons or horse toward Sandusky, the point of embarkation to cross Lake Erie.[83] Theirs was a moving community, forged in Cincinnati by people who believed in a vision of freedom and who transported both this vision and their community to Canada.

Although between 460 and 2,000[84] emigrants landed in Canada, most never even made it to the new colony in Biddulph Township. Disembarking at Port Stanley, on the Canadian side of Lake Erie, the migrants were undoubtedly daunted by the frontier Canadian landscape, which was practically "one unbroken forest."[85] To reach Biddulph Township from Port Stanley, the migrants needed to make the thirty-five-mile journey through heavy forest. To a group of travel-weary migrants, this must have been a major deterrent to settlement.

The land had been cleared only minimally by scattered settlers.[86] Clearing land and planting crops required a great deal of time, effort, and resources. At the time, it cost twenty-five dollars per acre to have the land cleared, a heavy financial burden for those whose resources had been exhausted by the journey.[87] Perhaps the agents had failed to forewarn the migrants before they left Cincinnati of the arduous work of clearing the land, building homes, and planting crops that lay ahead of them. Would-be colonists must have weighed their options: should they settle in a new colony where they might starve to death before the first acre was cleared or in an established town where they could quickly find work to feed their families? One contemporary observer indicated that all but or "five or six" families abandoned the scheme on the shores of Lake Erie.[88] Most of the Cincinnati migrants settled in established towns where they could find work.[89]

There is no way to track the dispersal patterns of *all* the Cincinnati migrants once they abandoned the scheme; however, according to one contemporary source, "several hundred" of the Cincinnati migrants settled in Colchester Township, which was twelve miles from Amherstburg and opposite Detroit along Lake Erie.[90] With an uncanny resemblance to their counterparts in Cincinnati, white Colchester inhabitants prayed for the House of Assembly to legislate to "prevent their [blacks'] further emigration." Otherwise, "many of the white population will be induced to leave the Province, or take violent measures to rid themselves" of the African American settlers. Specifically, the petitioners demanded that the immigrants be required to pay a bond or produce letters attesting to "their good characters from the country they recently left." In addition, these whites requested that the assembly disfranchise blacks.[91] Although the assembly never responded to this petition, nothing could change local sentiment against African Americans. This conscious and deliberate attempt to prevent them from settling in Colchester mimicked the events in Cincinnati and certainly must have reopened some wounds for those black Cincinnatians who settled there. They had moved to Canada believing in its promise of equality between men. They also had expected to find a refuge—a place where they would not be plagued by proscriptive legislation, bonds, violence, or the denial of civil rights. Surely, they must have been disillusioned to learn that whites in Canada were willing to take the same measures against them as had the whites in Cincinnati. Given what African Americans faced in urban Canada, an independent colony seemed to be a better option.

Had it not been for the determination of those "five or six" families that proceeded onward to the intended settlement, the vision of an all-black independent colony crafted in Cincinnati would have died on the shores of Lake Erie. Subsequent recruiting efforts drew blacks from other northern cities into the colony, and, by 1832, there were thirty-two families residing in Wilberforce.[92] The growth of the colony was fraught with challenges from the beginning. The biggest obstacle came in trying to purchase the land on which the colony was to stand. Land ownership was the key to real freedom for these settlers. With it, they hoped to become self-sufficient farmers, no longer dependent on whites for their livelihoods. These settlers also expected that owning land would give them ownership of themselves and, ultimately, their destinies. A *community* of black landowners would insulate blacks from white hostilities such as those expressed in Colchester; it would also safeguard against the type of mob violence they endured in Cincinnati. With land ownership standing for so much, the success of the entire colony hinged upon the contract with the Canada Company.

Israel Lewis and Thomas Crissup, acting on behalf of the colony, had contracted with the Canada Company to buy four thousand acres of the Huron Tract of land for six thousand dollars, which was to be paid by November 1830.[93] Lewis and Crissup made some critical errors that jeopardized the contract with the Canada Company. First, they overestimated the number of colonists that would settle in Biddulph. These men had expected that the entire black population of Cincinnati would remove to the settlement and purchase all four thousand acres. The small group that actually settled in the colony was in no position to purchase all of the land. Second, they probably had not expected that most of those who did reach Canada would elect to settle elsewhere. Last, but most important, the agents had overestimated the financial resources of the colonists. Few were in a position to buy land immediately—especially after financing the journey. If the settlers failed to uphold their end of the contract with the Canada Company, they might lose the land altogether.

Realizing they could not buy all the land themselves, the colony's leaders appealed to several sources to help purchase the land. First, James C. Brown advertised for assistance in the *Cincinnati Daily Gazette*. When no contributors came forward, Brown and other leaders appealed to the Ohio state legislature, hoping it would donate funds to effect a black exodus from the state.[94] This effort, too, was in vain. Finally, the leaders appealed to the Quakers—a group that had been sympathetic to African Americans in the past. On September 20, 1830, James C. Brown and Stephen Dutton purchased eight hundred acres of land on four lots north of and four lots south of Proof Line Road with money donated by Quakers from Indiana and Ohio.[95]

Once they had land, settlers assumed the herculean task of clearing the forest and planting crops. Survival was difficult while waiting for the crops to harvest. According to one firsthand account, "there was a great deal of destitution and suffering before their harvest could ripen."[96] Colonists could not expect to find wage work because the colony was not located near any towns with a demand for wage labor. In fact, the most significant settlement near the new colony was London—little more than a village of only thirty homes—located fifteen miles away.[97] Consequently, Wilberforce settlers were forced to think of ingenious ways to put food on the table. Austin Steward, who wrote the only African American firsthand account of life in the colony, sold animal skins, hunted, and operated a tavern during his residence there.

After they had put crops in the ground, the settlers began to build the town. They built log homes—some even had "well-shingled roofs"—a far cry from the "loose-board shacks" some African Americans had inhabited in Cincinnati.[98] By 1832, the settlement boasted three sawmills— one of which was powered by water—a gristmill, several general stores, and taverns.[99] Patrick Shirreff, a Scottish critic of Upper Canada, declared in 1835 that the settlement was "in most respects equal, and in some, superior, to settlements of whites in the Huron Tract of the same standing."[100]

The first institution established in Wilberforce was a school.[101] When abolitionist William Lloyd Garrison visited the colony in November 1831, he noted that twenty to thirty children attended the school.[102] It was good that Wilberforce settlers did establish their own schools because provincial education was yet in its early stages in frontier Canada. In large townships, ministers typically operated small private "schools"; in smaller communities, residents "could usually find some old soldier or an itinerant American to give a scanty measure of training to their children."[103] The existing Canadian school system was not developed enough to meet the needs of the black settlers in Wilberforce: sporadic teachings by an unqualified itinerant were not consonant with their educational goals. Building on an educational tradition formed in Cincinnati and carried to Wilberforce, the settlers had established three schools by 1832.[104] Some of those who migrated to Wilberforce had received an education in the private schools in Cincinnati; others, like Israel Lewis and his wife, had been slaves and had never received a formal education.[105] Others probably had only a functional education—basic knowledge of how to read and write. The colonists' desire for education should be distinguished from a desire for mere *literacy*. Wilberforce colonists desired more than instruction in reading and writing; they wanted education on every level—elementary and Sunday schools, a seminary, and a manual labor college. Despite their limited educational backgrounds, many former slaves and fugitives recognized that education was essential to enjoying all the privileges of freedom, including equality.[106] Education provided the opportunity to rise above menial labor jobs, buy land, or become astute entrepreneurs. Wilberforce parents probably hoped that a quality education would guarantee that their children would be treated as equals. In any case, those three schools were more than what was available to most white Canadians. According to Benjamin Lundy, "a number of respectable white people send their children to [the Wilberforce schools] in preference to others that are conducted by white [itinerant] teachers."[107]

Elementary schools were not the only educational endeavor undertaken by the Wilberforce colonists: they also attempted to establish a manual labor college for boys.[108] The impetus for the college emerged at the First Annual Convention of the People of Colour held in Philadelphia in 1830. The convention delegates originally resolved to establish a college for African Americans in New Haven, Connecticut. However, after the mayor of New Haven vowed to do everything in his power to resist such a project in his city, the supporters of the scheme turned to Wilberforce as a potential site for the college.[109]

Wilberforce leaders welcomed the opportunity to have the college located in the colony. Leaders envisioned it as an international college for blacks from the United States and Canada. After New Haven rejected the original proposal for the school, however, national black leaders lost interest in the endeavor. Once Wilberforce agreed to host the college, the entire fundraising effort fell on its shoulders. The colony's board of managers began a subscription campaign in the United States and Britain to raise money. Although Nathaniel Paul did collect £107.42 for the college while he was in England,[110] this collection fell pitifully short of what was needed to make the vision a reality. Despite the outcome, this effort reflects the value that the black immigrants placed on higher education in an era when other Canadian settlers were content with rudimentary education.

While education was a primary objective of the settlers, they were also concerned with their spiritual and moral welfare. The settlers probably began having religious meetings soon after they arrived in the colony, although there is no concrete evidence of formal meetings until 1832. Then, Lundy reported that there were two churches—Methodist and Baptist—as well as a temperance society.[111] Enos Adams was the pastor of the Methodist body, and Rev. Nathaniel Paul served the First [African] Baptist Church until sent abroad as a fundraising agent for the colony. According to one historian, by 1835, the First Baptist Church, the more popular church in the colony, had a congregation of twenty and belonged to the Western Baptist Association.[112] Historian Donald Simpson noted that white settlers throughout the district were attracted to the colony's church revivals. In fact, Benjamin Paul had converted some Welsh families to the Baptist faith in Lobo Township.[113] Wilberforce's churches, like its schools, served whites throughout the district, as well.

But the colonists sought more than educational and spiritual enlightenment; they also sought to exercise political power. Provincial law dictated that each township elect commissioners, whose duties included transacting the business of the township. Wilberforce residents elected three commissioners from their own settlement in 1835.[114] Austin Steward was elected to the office of clerk for Biddulph Township, and his duties included holding "all moneys, books, and papers belonging to said town" and administering oaths.[115] Coming from states that denied them suffrage, most blacks in the colony probably never had voted in a state election. In this context, even this level of political participation was a step toward citizenship. For the first time, these African Americans had a voice in determining the affairs of their community.

———

The Cincinnati riots and the subsequent mass out-migration evoked an outpouring of sympathy for that community across black America. The *Rights of All,* a black newspaper edited by Samuel Cornish in New York City, covered the events in Cincinnati, including the emigration and riot. During its short existence, the *Rights of All* provided a national forum for a shared sympathy, understanding, and dialogue about the crisis.[116] On August 14, just one day before the violence erupted, an African American writing in the *Rights of All* defiantly advised black Ohioans, "Do not *remove one step from your native state and mether* [sic] *country, rather become martyrs to the injustice, you have but once to die.*" The editorial went on to recommend Upper Canada as a possible home, should they decide to leave.[117] Thus, emigration to Upper Canada had already been sanctioned in the national black press as a solution to local racism in Cincinnati even before the violence erupted. Many free blacks saw parallel oppressions in their own local communities. The events in Cincinnati solidified a national black consciousness among free blacks and initiated a national dialogue about the condition and future of the race.

Responding to an invitation, northern black leaders assembled in Mother Bethel Church in Philadelphia in September 1830 to discuss problems facing their communities on both local and national levels. African American leaders from other northern communities collectively searched for solutions to alleviate the suffering of black Cincinnatians in the short run and to empower all African Americans in the long run. The delegates discussed emigration to Canada as a remedy to racism. The assembly organized itself as the American Society of Free Persons of Colour "for the purpose of purchasing land, and locating a settlement in the Province of Upper Canada."[118] This 1830 convention was just the beginning of the black convention movement, which was an ongoing public discourse among African American leaders about problems facing their communities and possible solutions. The black convention movement was, in fact, the closest thing to a nineteenth-century civil rights organization.

The national black convention pledged itself to raise money and encourage settlement in the Cincinnati colony. The convention believed that by emigrating to Canada, African Americans would "have ample opportunity to reap the reward due to industry and perseverance" in a "land where the laws and prejudices of society will have no effect in retarding their advancement."[119] The body outlined the benefits of emigration to Canada: "1) Under that [the Canadian] government no invidious distinction of colour is recognised [sic], but there we shall be entitled to all the rights, privileges, and immunities of other citizens, 2) That the language, climate, soil, and productions are similar to those in this country, 3) That land of the best quality can be purchased at the moderate price of one dollar and fifty cents per acre, 4) The market for different kinds of produce raised in that colony, is such as to render a suitable reward to the industrious farmer."[120] The convention was confident that "[i]t will be much to the advantage of those who have large families and desire to see them happy and respected, to locate themselves in a land where the laws and prejudices of society will have no effect in retarding their advancement to the summit of civil and religious improvement."[121] The American Society of Free Persons of Colour articulated a definition of freedom that was consistent with the goals of the Cincinnati settlers: self-sufficiency, freedom from discrimination, and civil rights. Thus, the principles of the Wilberforce colony not only won the endorsement of the first black national convention but also became part of that organization's definition of freedom.

After attending the First Annual Convention of the People of Colour, colonizationists Arthur Tappan and Benjamin Lundy, and abolitionist William Lloyd Garrison all became supporters of the colony.[122] Colonizationists supported emancipation with the intent to immediately colonize the freed slaves in Liberia. They generally supported efforts to resettle freed blacks anywhere outside the United States, including Texas and Canada. Success at Wilberforce would expedite their objectives. Abolitionists, on the other hand, did not necessarily link abolition and colonization. Although opposed to any effort to colonize freed slaves or to making colonization a condition of freedom, abolitionists were generally supportive of blacks who desired voluntarily to emigrate to another country. A successful colony of willing black emigrants might advance the abolitionist agenda.

Abolitionists hoped that a self-sufficient and productive colony of free blacks would seriously challenge the proslavery argument that slaves, once freed, would degenerate into an immoral, lazy, unproductive lot without the discipline they had received through slavery. In 1833, William Lloyd Garrison declared, "As it [Wilberforce] increases in population, intelligence and power, it will render the prolongation of that accursed and bloody system more and more insecure, and increase more and more the necessity of abolishing it altogether and without delay."[123] Although some abolitionists hoped the success of Wilberforce would prove the advantages of abolition, others envisioned it as a refuge for fugitive slaves. One Wilberforce settler, Austin Steward, hoped the colony would become "an asylum for the oppressed, where our colored friends could obtain a home . . . besides providing a safe retreat for the weary fugitive from Slavery."[124] Garrison expected the colony to be not only an asylum for fugitive slaves but an *encouragement* for slaves to flee.[125] Similarly, abolitionist Charles Stuart envisioned the colony as "a vista of hope, always growing, for all the enslaved people, who may succeed in making their escape thither."[126] Although these goals differ from the original goals of the Wilberforce colonists, abolitionists and colonizationists also hoped to make Wilberforce a model colony.

Abolitionists publicly extolled the virtues of Wilberforce, hoping to attract more black settlers. Benjamin Lundy, an antislavery, antiracist supporter of black colonization, used his antislavery journal, *Genius of Universal Emancipation,* to illuminate the positive aspects of the colony, including the vegetation, climate, schools, and the industry of the settlers. Lundy also sold maps with directions to the colony to blacks throughout the United States.[127] Charles Stuart extolled the virtues of the Canadian colony in his pamphlet, *Remarks on the Colony of Liberia and the American Colonization Society with Some Account of the Settlement of Coloured People at Wilberforce, Upper Canada.* Stuart opposed involuntary colonization to Liberia, but supported the voluntary emigration to Upper Canada initiated by blacks from Cincinnati. William Lloyd Garrison also used his abolitionist journal, the *Liberator,* to publicize the colony. Thus, Wilberforce became an ornament of the abolitionist movement and was praised in abolitionist journals.

The publicity generated at the black conventions and sustained in abolitionist circles began to attract other settlers to the colony. Ironically, Cincinnati was no longer a major recruiting ground. Most of the African Americans who were willing to leave the city had already done so in 1829. Moreover, by 1830, the threat of violence in Cincinnati had receded, which led to the return of many who had left in 1829. Information about the Canadian colony circulated throughout northern free black communities in the black press, the black convention movement, black churches, public meetings, antislavery journals, the abolitionist movement, and by word of mouth. Austin Steward's life illuminates how free blacks from other cities were drawn to the colony in Biddulph Township. A former slave freed by New York's abolition of slavery in 1827, Steward was living in Rochester, New York, at the time the colony was planted. He had probably learned of the Cincinnati riot while he was an agent for the first black newspaper, *Freedom's Journal;* more than likely, he had learned of the colony while serving as a New York delegate at the first black national convention in 1830.[128]

The small colony that had begun with only "five or six families" grew quickly. Although Cincinnati blacks had planted the colony, later migrants hailed from other cities—largely from the eastern seaboard states. Within the first eighteen months, families from Boston, Rochester, Albany, New York, and Baltimore joined the Cincinnati group. Austin Steward, for example, left his successful grocery business in Rochester and removed to the Canadian colony in 1831. Three Pauls moved from different American cities: Nathaniel Paul migrated from Albany, New

York; Benjamin Paul moved from New York City; and Thomas Paul Jr. moved from Boston. Another colonist, Daniel Turner, hailed from Baltimore, as did Peter Butler, a former slave who had worked as a sailor and a caulker on ships docked at Port Stanley before settling in the colony in 1830.[129] By 1831, there were fourteen or fifteen families living there.[130] In 1832, there were thirty-two families in Wilberforce, with a total population of ninety-five.[131] By 1835, the township boasted 166 inhabitants.[132]

There was a striking difference between the Cincinnati group and blacks from other places: most of the latter had been leaders in free black communities in the United States before migrating. Austin Steward not only served as vice president of a national emigration society but was a well-respected member of the Rochester black community. He was an agent for *Freedom's Journal* and a delegate at the first black national convention. Steward explained that he had relocated to Wilberforce because he felt duty bound, as a conscientious activist, to assist in building the colony as a refuge for fugitive slaves.[133] The Pauls all had illustrious careers as ministers and leaders in northern free black communities. Brothers Nathaniel and Benjamin served as pastors of the First African Baptist Churches in Albany and New York City, respectively, while their nephew, Thomas Jr., was an apprentice with the abolitionist *Liberator* in Boston.[134] The Pauls, along with Steward, quickly rose to leadership of the colony—as managers, teachers, ministers and agents. Although the newcomers settled there a year or so after the Cincinnati group, they quickly began to shape the direction of the colony in conjunction with the abolitionist movement.

The newer settlers were instrumental in organizing the colony. When Steward arrived, the colony had neither name nor structure. He claims that it was he who named the colony Wilberforce, after the prominent British abolitionist, a decision that was probably a conscious effort by the newcomers to win support from antislavery communities in Britain and the United States.[135] After the colony was named, the newcomers created a board of managers to oversee the business of building institutions and soliciting funds.[136] The first board of managers consisted of Austin Steward (as president), Joseph Taylor, Phillip Harris, John Whitehead, Peter Butler, Samuel Peterson, and William Brown.[137] The newcomers replaced the old Cincinnati leaders—James C. Brown and Israel Lewis—relegating Lewis, the colony's organizer, land agent, and original leader, to a mere fund-raising agent.

The seeds of discontent between the old and new guards were sown during the fund-raising campaigns. The subscription campaign, an organized effort to raise money for the colony's schools, was mired in controversy from the beginning. In 1831, two fund-raising agents were chosen to solicit funds among the abolitionist circles: Israel Lewis was sent to the United States and Nathaniel Paul was sent to England. Wilberforce residents appointed Lewis as a fund-raising agent for the colony because they trusted and respected him as a leader. This appointment was reserved for individuals of character and accomplishment: who else would best represent the colony abroad? Agents were probably also chosen for their skills in public speaking and raising funds. Austin Steward described Lewis as "an eloquent speaker" with a "commanding manner."[138] As a minister, Nathaniel Paul certainly had experience both in raising money and in public speaking. Wilberforce colonists believed that they had chosen men of integrity who had a sincere interest in the prosperity of the colony.

Both agents failed to live up to the settlers' expectations. They took extended absences from the colony and failed to remit or satisfactorily account for any funds collected. Paul sporadically sent correspondence from England reporting on his activities, seldom mentioning the monies he had collected on behalf of the colony. When he failed to return to the colony and account for his activities or the money, the colony tapped into its meager resources to send another agent abroad to finish his work. But Paul was no thief—at least not according to the lieutenant governor of Upper Canada, John Colbourne, who had sent Paul to England with a letter of unwavering support for his mission. Several prominent British citizens also attested to Paul's respectability and good character.[139] While in England, he aligned himself with the British abolitionist movement and even became a spokesperson for it. Busy lecturing about the plight of blacks in the United States and meeting with prominent British abolitionists like Wilberforce and Thomas Clarkson,[140] Paul merely lost sight of his original mission and responsibility to Wilberforce.[141] Paul contributed to the abolitionist movement in England, but he did so at the expense of the Wilberforce colonists who had sent him to raise money. The colonists had anxiously awaited Paul's return, fully expecting him to remit a satisfactory amount to the colony's board of mangers. When he finally returned to Wilberforce four years later, Paul was empty-handed, claiming his expenditures had exceeded his receipts. The Wilberforce settlers "became excited well nigh to fury—so much that at one time we found it nearly impossible to restrain them from having recourse to Lynch law."[142] Paul left Wilberforce soon after he returned in 1835; Steward implied it was because he was no longer welcome there.

Frustrated by Paul's disappointing fund-raising effort abroad, Wilberforce's board of managers expected Lewis's campaign would be more fruitful. However, Lewis also had extended absences from the colony. He sent no money and failed to communicate any progress to the board of managers. Early in 1832, only months into his tenure as agent, Wilberforce's board of managers concluded that they disapproved of the job Lewis was doing. He resigned from his post shortly thereafter. The board's disappointment soon gave way to suspicions of wrongdoing: the board suspected Lewis had embezzled the funds he collected on behalf of the colony to live flamboyantly and to lavish his friends with gifts.

These suspicions became full-fledged accusations by December 1832. Then, the board of managers issued a circular in the *Liberator* charging Lewis with "practicing a deception upon our friends in the United States, by taking up donations, pretending that such gifts will faithfully be applied to our relief."[143] In a letter to a confidant, Steward recounted how he had been deceived: "Sir, we know that you are actuated by the purest motives, but you are deceived in the character of the man, (Lewis). When I was living in the States and only saw him there, collecting money for the poor, I thought him honest as you now do; but two or three years' residence in Wilberforce Colony, has abundantly satisfied me that his object is to get money, that he may live in a princely style, and not for the benefit of the poor as he pretends."[144] In March 1833, Arthur Tappan issued a "caution" against Lewis in the *Liberator*.[145] In 1839, Wilberforce colonists issued a "Caution against an Imposter" in the *Friend of Man:*

> Whereas, we the undersigned, have learned from authentic sources, that Israel Lewis (a man of color) has collected large sums of money in Upper Canada and the United States, during the last nine years, only a small part of which has ever reached the Wilberforce Settlement or has in any degree benefitted [sic] the settlers, while, on the other hand, as the effect of his base conduct, much distress has lately come upon some of us:—We, therefore, as citizens of said Wilberforce Settlement, in the township of Biddulph, London, District, U.C., feel again called upon to protest against the aforesaid Israel Lewis, whose perfidious conduct, under the cloak of religion and humanity, we heartily deprecate and abhor; and would hereby warn the Christian public against him as unworthy of confidence.[146]

These stunning public accusations of Lewis's alleged crimes became part of public abolitionist discourse. Abolitionists outside the colony joined in branding Lewis a swindler. In a letter to Steward, Samuel Cornish, the founder of *Freedom's Journal,* professed that Lewis was "one of the worst men living, whose deeds will yet come to light."[147] A scathing editorial by abolitionist Hiram Wilson, who had worked extensively to establish schools in black Canadian colonies, blasted Lewis: "It [Wilberforce] might have been more prosperous than it now is, had it not been for the agency of Israel Lewis. That notorious villain, who ought to have been colonized to Liberia, years ago, or in some penitentiary, has succeeded in collecting thousands from the public."[148] Wilson estimated that Lewis had collected thirty thousand dollars under false pretenses, of which "the board for the colony had not received the amount of one hundred dollars."[149]

Israel Lewis did have some supporters who publicly defended his character. The *Rochester Inquirer* stated that he had "ample credentials of good character."[150] Benjamin Paul published a "certificate" endorsing Lewis "in all his undertakings."[151] Francis Smith, another settler, expressed outrage at seeing "base and slanderous publications" in the *Liberator.*[152] The *Utica Recorder,* giving Lewis the benefit of the doubt, provided him with some good advice to prove his integrity: "The only course which is now honorable to himself, and safe to the community, must be to discontinue soliciting from the public for assistance, until his testimonials are renewed."[153]

Lewis defended his own reputation. He filed a ten-thousand-dollar lawsuit for slander against Arthur Tappan for the 1833 public caution against him.[154] Lewis also responded to Steward's accusations by writing letters to the press. According to Lewis, "a majority of the settlers," dissatisfied with the existing board of managers led by Steward, had voted it out in July 1832 and organized the Wilberforce Colonization Company—also referred to as the Wilberforce Colonization and High School Company—with a new board of managers and Lewis as president.[155] Lewis explained that he did not remit funds to Steward's board of managers because the colonists had voted the board out; therefore, it had no authority to receive funds from Lewis. In a letter to the public, Lewis asserted that he did not recognize any board of managers but the one he labored for.[156] Lewis claimed that all the funds he had collected were to benefit the Wilberforce Colonization Company—a "company formed by several white gentlemen" with "the patronage of upwards of 700 of the generous and noble citizens of Albany" to erect and operate a manual labor college.[157] Although no manual labor college was ever erected, according to Lewis, the company had the support of one-third of Wilberforce's colonists.[158]

Israel Lewis speculated that Austin Steward had initiated a campaign to defame his character because he had established a rival organization. He wrote, "A small minority were dissatisfied, as might be expected; and among other means employed by them to counteract our [the new board of managers'] influence, they have brought me before the public as a base impostor, unworthy of confidence."[159] At least one Wilberforce colonist—Francis Smith—corroborated Lewis's assertion in the April 13 issue of the *Liberator*.[160]

While it is difficult to determine which account is true, it is certain that there were serious schisms within this relatively small community. Israel Lewis and his supporters were on one side, and Austin Steward and his board of managers on the other. Underlying these tensions was a struggle for power. According to Israel Lewis, the volatility of the situation was heightened by differences in the agendas Lewis and Steward had for the colony.[161]

Many of the original Cincinnati leaders abandoned the colony within its first decade. James C. Brown, the president of the emigration society, briefly returned to Cincinnati after his wife "became dissatisfied" with life in Canada within the first year. However, his family returned to Canada shortly thereafter.[162] The Browns moved to Toronto and, finally, to another all-black Canadian settlement, Dawn, where Brown became a trustee of the settlement and its manual labor school, the British-American Institute.[163] Brown's departure from Wilberforce should not be interpreted as an abandonment of its vision of freedom: he simply pursued that vision elsewhere. Other officers of the emigration society, Thomas Crissup and Elijah Forte, were once again living in Cincinnati as early as 1830, suggesting that they only briefly stayed in Wilberforce. Israel Lewis spent most of his time away from Wilberforce and eventually moved to Montreal where he "died a pauper."[164]

By the time the Irish began moving into the area in the late 1840s, the black population was very small. The Canada Company, responding to pressure from white settlers, refused to sell any more land to blacks. Local whites intimidated the black settlers who remained. For example, in 1849, the property of three Wilberforce settlers, William Bell, Ephraim Taylor, and Rev. Daniel Turner, was destroyed by arson, acts that perhaps were intended to drive them away.[165] As the black population shrank, the Irish population grew. Irish settlers bought Wilberforce's land and even used its buildings—churches and schools. Eventually, the Irish community supplanted Wilberforce altogether. The town of Lucan (named after an Irishman) was erected on some of the land on which Wilberforce once had stood, and Wilberforce passed into the margins of history. The only memento to acknowledge this community is a plaque that erroneously states that Wilberforce was founded by a community of "fugitive slaves."

Before concluding that Wilberforce was a failure, it is important to revisit the goals of the original settlers from Cincinnati. The original objective of the emigration campaign was to find a place where blacks might enjoy citizenship rights and equality under the law. As they made plans to relocate, that definition of freedom evolved to include land ownership and self-sufficiency. Once the emigrants arrived in the colony, the community expanded its definition of freedom yet again to include education and political participation. The short history of this community suggests that freedom was not a state of being, but a state of striving.

Although Wilberforce passed so quietly and quickly into history, its settlers offered a compelling vision of freedom. In the face of the violent denial of social, political, and economic freedom in Cincinnati, this community had a vista of hope that freedom was obtainable elsewhere. Through land ownership, education, moral development, social and legal equality, and suffrage, these colonists—even if briefly, even if slightly—tasted freedom.

FOUR

Emerging from Fire

Rebirth and Renewal, 1829–1836

It is impossible to keep a people asunder for any time, who
are so strongly and peculiarly identified together, when
there is a vigorous effort made to unite them.

Frederick Douglass, *North Star*, October 26, 1849

MORE THAN ELEVEN hundred African Americans chose not to
migrate to Canada or to nearby towns in Ohio during the riots of 1829.
They chose to remain in Cincinnati in spite of the violence and the mass
exodus. These African Americans braved mob terrorism, the destruction of their homes and businesses, and placed themselves in a position
to endure more violence, as well as continued denials of justice, citizenship, and economic equality. And although their decision to stay might
seem less heroic and, perhaps, less political than the migrants' decision
to leave, those who remained in Cincinnati were no more resigned to live
under oppression than those who left; nor were they any less desiring of
social, economic, or political freedom.[1] This group that remained had
the same resolve to obtain the privileges of citizenship as had the group
that left.

These African Americans who stayed behind were faced with the tremendous challenge of restoring and rebuilding their community, almost
from scratch. The riots and the concomitant exodus ruptured community networks and threatened to obliterate the sense of mutual commitment among African Americans in Cincinnati. The looming threat
of additional mob violence slowed the momentum of black institution-

building that had developed before 1829. The magnitude of the population loss undermined the already fragile black institutions; schools and churches lost critical membership and leaders. Of all the challenges confronting the African American community, none was more critical than overcoming its sense of vulnerability and alienation.

Cincinnati's black community employed several strategies to emerge from the fire and to restore a sense of safety and community.[2] The first priorities were rebuilding and stabilizing community institutions and grooming new leaders. It was within these fledgling institutions that the black community focused on its own intellectual, spiritual, and moral improvement between 1829 and 1836, and it was from within them that the community regained its strength and forged a collective identity.

Who remained in Cincinnati after the 1829 exodus and riot? A demographic summary extracted from the 1830 census indicates that there were 562 females and 528 males. Black men averaged 23.3 years of age, and black women, 22.6 years. Of those who remained, 25 percent were under the age of ten.[3] This black population was young and dispersed throughout the city. The First Ward and Fourth Ward had the highest number of black residents, 429 each. In the First Ward, African Americans made up nearly 9 percent of the population; in the Fourth Ward, they comprised 10 percent of the population. The 110 blacks residing in the Third Ward comprised only 2.6 percent of the total population of the ward in 1830. Second Ward and Fifth Ward had the smallest number of black residents, 75 and 47, respectively.[4]

Many African Americans who decided to continue their residence in Cincinnati after 1829 were motivated by emotional or financial ties to the city—ties that tugged harder than the urge to leave. The largest percentage of those who remained were poor, bound to Cincinnati by a lack

Table 4.1. Population Breakdown by Ward, 1830

Ward	# African Americans	# Whites	Total	% African Americans
One	429	4,390	4,819	8.9
Two	75	5,957	6,032	1.2
Three	110	4,082	4,192	2.6
Four	429	3,861	4,290	10.0
Five	47	5,451	5,498	.85

Source: Lyle Koehler, *Cincinnati's Black Peoples: A Chronology and Bibliography, 1787–1982* (Cincinnati: Cincinnati Arts Consortium, 1986), 11.

of financial resources. Many of Cincinnati's African Americans—trying to survive on paltry wages as they were—did not have the means to finance a major move to another town. According to James C. Brown, the organizer of the exodus to Canada, "A large number of them [African Americans] are without the means to even commence their journey."[5] Consequently, a disproportionate number of those who were left behind were impoverished. *Cincinnati Daily Gazette* editor Charles Hammond observed, "The late attempt to enforce it [the Black Law of 1807] here has . . . driven away the sober, honest, industrious, and *useful* portion of the coloured population. The vagrant is unaffected by it."[6] In reality, the "honest and industrious" found themselves thrown out of jobs by the section of the Black Law that prohibited employers from employing those who had not complied with the 1804 settlement requirements. The consequence was that "it [the application of the Black Law] has reduced honest individuals to want and beggary, in the midst of plenty and of employment; because employers are afraid to engage them."[7] Despite the high number of impoverished blacks who remained, the exodus did not completely divest Cincinnati of all of its African Americans of wealth or industry.

There were several compelling reasons to stay in Cincinnati. A significant number of black Cincinnatians who remained in the city were working to purchase loved ones from slavery. In 1835, the Ohio Anti-Slavery Society reported that more than half of Cincinnati's black population formerly had been enslaved and that more than 30 percent of them had purchased their own freedom.[8] After securing their own liberty, many of these same people had worked assiduously to purchase relatives from bondage. Certainly, the availability of jobs helped facilitate these efforts. A British traveler estimated that as much as two-thirds of the city's black population was working to buy the freedom of friends and relatives in 1833.[9] Some individuals were able to purchase multiple loved ones from bondage. In one family, a man purchased himself, his wife, infant, and small child for $750. That same man offered $450 to purchase his two other enslaved sons; however, that buying price was rejected by the boys' owners. Another man paid $1,130 for his wife and children.[10] Henry Boyd not only bought his own freedom but saved enough to buy his brothers from bondage for $900. Another gentleman, Richard Keys, who had paid his owner $20 a month for twelve years, was forced to pay an additional $850 for his freedom. His wife managed to save $400 doing extra washing at night for several years, which she used toward her freedom price. Richard added another $192 to that sum, and she was set free.[11] Individuals like these may have been exceptions; most people worked as a part of a family effort to purchase relatives. Parents, for example, sometimes worked to buy the freedom of their children. Children also had to pitch in to help purchase their parents or siblings, as was the case of a ten-year-old girl who could not attend school because she was working to help buy her father from bondage.[12] Even on the paltry wages many received, these African Americans proved not only that they were industrious but that they had a tremendous degree of resolve.

Another reason why many African Americans found it difficult to leave Cincinnati was quite simple: jobs. Despite the virulent antiblack spirit in the city, it was still easier for blacks to get jobs in Cincinnati than in smaller towns, where job opportunities were few to none. Some who remained may have been immobilized by the fear of an uncertain future elsewhere. To settle in a new city with no assurance of finding employment was a dim prospect. In this vein, families with small children would have been less likely to leave. Some individuals may have been too old to try to reestablish themselves elsewhere. Individuals like Moses John, who worked as an unskilled laborer on the Ohio River for more than ten years, chose not to leave Cincinnati in 1829.[13] Costillo Jones, a cook, was living in Cincinnati as early as 1820 and remained there after the riot.[14] Skilled laborers like John Spinning, a plasterer and bricklayer, and ship carpenters Samuel and William Sizer also chose to stay.[15] Steady work and decent wages would have been an incentive to remain.

Black property owners and entrepreneurs also elected to remain in the city after 1829. Having achieved a measure of economic freedom and stability, such families had a lot to lose by packing up and leaving town. In addition, the looming threat to their homes and businesses motivated black property owners to remain to protect their investments. The Hatfield family, for example, remained in spite of the mob action. Self-employed barbers with their own shops, John and Joseph Hatfield settled in Cincinnati around 1820 and continued to live there throughout the antebellum era.[16] Even if the Hatfields had the financial means to emigrate, they may have been unwilling to leave their businesses. Among other property owners who stayed was an anonymous black man who had purchased his freedom for six hundred dollars before settling in Cincinnati. Although this man had come to Cincinnati without one dollar in his pocket, he worked hard and acquired property valued at three thousand dollars.[17] Like the Hatfields, this self-made man had every incentive to remain in Cincinnati. Some of these families may have complied with the 1807 Black Law and had posted bond.[18]

Capable leaders also remained in Cincinnati after 1829. James King, the minister who had helped organize the AME church was still in Cincinnati in 1830.[19] His successor, Wyle Reynolds, also remained through the crisis of 1829.[20] Secular leaders also chose to remain in the city after 1829. James C. Brown, the chief organizer of the emigration scheme to Canada, briefly returned to Cincinnati in 1830. Other leaders of that movement, Thomas Crissup (land scout) and Elijah Forte (secretary), also returned by 1830.[21]

In the final analysis, the black population that chose not to migrate included a diverse group of people: poor folks and property owners, skilled and unskilled laborers, entrepreneurs and ministers. Their reasons for staying were just as compelling as the reasons of those who left. Certainly, there was enough talent, dedication, and social capital among this population to rebuild the foundation that had been shaken by the exodus and the violence.

———

The AME church was one of the few black institutions that survived the upheaval of 1829. The church had endured by retaining its leadership and a critical membership base. Ministers James King and Wyle Reynolds did not emigrate; neither did many of the other members of the congregation. Church members were generally more likely to have remained in Cincinnati after 1829.[22]

The AME Church was a critical training ground for Cincinnati's new generation of black leaders.[23] African Americans gained leadership skills within the church and then implemented them in the wider community. For example, Joseph Fowler began his ministry in the AME Church shortly after his arrival in Cincinnati in 1826. He served as a steward, trustee, and class leader within the church.[24] Fowler's activities and service extended outside the church as well; he is remembered as an important educator in the black community.[25] Similarly, Owen T. B. Nickens joined the AME Church in December 1824, shortly after migrating to Cincinnati from Virginia. Soon thereafter, he became a lay minister for the church.[26]

Nickens quickly emerged as one of the most prominent leaders of the black community. He had the substance to lead black Cincinnati at a particularly low point in its history. Owen T. B. Nickens was confident, articulate, racially conscious, and unafraid to speak up, which was probably why he was invited to speak at the Cincinnati celebration of the abolition of slavery in New York in 1831. His only surviving speech, it provides some insight into his character. Nickens's address not only condemned slavery and celebrated black liberty, but it also promoted black racial pride. He preached about ancient African history: "That land of your fathers is the birth-place and cradle of arts and sciences. In that dark continent, was the light kindled that so conspicuously blazed in Greece and in Rome; that light which now beams with exuberant splendor and meridian brightness, on the auspicious shores of Europe and America. From our royal fathers in the land of Egypt, the nations of the earth have learned the policy and rules of political government."[27] In addition to reminding his audience of the grandeur of ancient African civilization, Nickens also preached about its heroes, like Hannibal and Cleopatra. He provided his audience with a black history that not only countered the history of slavery and degradation in this country but filled African Americans with racial pride. In 1831, few African Americans had this degree of racial consciousness or the courage to express it publicly.

People like Owen T. B. Nickens developed their leadership skills in black churches by serving as stewards, trustees, or even lay preachers. This experience in the black church prepared them to lead the larger black community. Leaders in the church had the moral authority to make the transition to secular leadership. It was not uncommon for black ministers also to be involved in other civic organizations, like temperance and moral reform societies. Nickens himself founded a school for African American youth in Cincinnati in 1834. The following year, he was instrumental in organizing a moral reform society. Nickens's leadership extended far beyond Cincinnati; he also served as a state representative for the national black convention movement.[28] Owen T. B. Nickens seems to be typical of black leaders in other antebellum communities, with his multiple leadership positions in religious and secular institutions.[29] It was dedicated people like Nickens who kept the AME Church afloat after the crisis.

By 1834, the AME congregation had outgrown the building at Seventh Street, east of Broadway. No longer content with worshipping in converted shops, the congregation commenced planning for the construction of a chapel. They purchased a lot that was just one block away on Sixth Street, also east of Broadway.[30] Soon thereafter, the congregation began raising money for the new house of worship. According to Rev. Benjamin Arnett, who presided during the church's fiftieth anniversary in 1874, the labor and expertise for raising the church had come from within the black community. Mr. Griffith provided the sills and lumber for the building from his lumberyard on Hunt Street. Peter Harbeson, a member of the congregation, was the architect and carpenter, and Dr. Commodore F. Buckner did the brickmasonry.[31] When the building was complete, it was christened "Bethel," which in Hebrew means "The house of God."[32] The biblical Bethel was a site of worship and sacrifice, as was Cincinnati's Bethel. The name also linked the Cincinnati church to the mother church of the same name in Philadelphia. "When it [the church] was sufficiently finished for occupancy, they went in; and everybody was glad, for the Lord had done a great thing for them . . . these people looked back to the times when a few of them met in the old red church and praised God."[33] In less than ten years, this congregation had gone from worshipping in basements and a carpenter's shop to its own chapel.

Bethel AME may have inspired a similar movement among black Baptists. The popularity of the Baptist faith among African Americans throughout the country can be attributed to the Second Great Awakening. Both Baptist and Methodist churches had a magnetic appeal for African Americans, who were attracted to the emotionally charged style of worship with the hand clapping, speaking in tongues, and holy dancing practiced in these churches. Another appealing aspect was their espousal of spiritual equality among blacks and whites. People worshiped and praised God together at revivals without regard to race. The churches' political message was also part of their appeal; they condemned slavery as a sin against God and man. Although the Methodist faith was initially more popular among Cincinnati's black population, by the mid-1830s the Baptists were gaining ground.

Before 1835, Cincinnati black Baptists worshiped in a white church, Enon Baptist Church. On July 21, 1831, a group of black congregants met to consider forming a separate and independent church. Although it is uncertain why black Baptists wanted to form a separate church, it is highly likely that discrimination within the white church and blacks' desire for autonomy were key factors.[34] Bethel AME Church provided a living example that such independence was possible. Many of those in attendance at that planning meeting had previous leadership experience in the black community. George Jones and Thomas Arnold, for example, were former leaders of the Deer Creek Methodist Episcopal Church.[35] Elijah Forte, who had served as the secretary of the emigration scheme to Wilberforce, was also in attendance at that July meeting of black Baptists. Thus, those leaders who conceived of this break had a certain degree of experience, vision, and confidence in the possibility of black autonomy.

The initial meeting did not bear any fruit, so the body decided to continue its affiliation with Enon Baptist Church until "such time as it may seem fit in the providence of God that we become a separate church."[36] There are several possible explanations why black Baptist leaders decided not to separate at this juncture. First, they may not have had the financial resources to break away at that time—after all, a complete separation from Enon Baptist would have required the black Baptists to have their own building or space. Perhaps they realized that they could not proceed without the philanthropy of white Baptists. Another possibility is that the leaders and body of Enon Baptist Church were opposed to an independent black Baptist church. Although the sentiment was there, the time was not yet ripe for a complete separation. Nevertheless, black Baptist leaders did take steps toward semiautonomy by establishing a separate branch of the Enon Church: the Colored Branch of the Enon Baptist Church. Elijah Forte was appointed as its leader, a position he held for several years. For four more years, the church maintained its affiliation with Enon Baptist Church.[37]

In February 1835, the Colored Branch of the Enon Baptist Church sought the approval of the three local white Baptist churches—Enon, Sixth Street, and Ninth Street Baptist churches—to become an independent body.[38] The black Baptists sought white approval even though Baptist churches, in general, had no centralized authority structure and functioned independently.[39] Baptists could form independent churches while maintaining control of their own affairs, including the ordination of ministers.[40] Consequently, Baptist churches formed independent confederations later than other churches. Even when they did, they were loose associations. The three white Baptist churches in Cincinnati were not an association, and, consequently, black Baptists did not *need* their approval to establish their own church. They may not have wished to alienate white church leaders by establishing a church without their nod of approval. Having secured the consent of the white churches, the black Baptists moved forward with their plans. The first independent black Baptist church in Cincinnati was established on the second Sunday in February 1835 with forty-five members. It was christened the "African Union Baptist Church of Cincinnati."[41] Like many other black churches around the country, Cincinnati's African Union Baptist assumed the name "African" as "a signal act of self-assertiveness" and pride in the congregants' African heritage.[42]

The African Union Baptist congregation purchased a brick house on the eastern side of Western Row, between Second and Third streets, for six hundred dollars.[43] The church was located in the heavily black-populated section of the Fourth Ward, near the western bank of the Ohio

River, otherwise known as the Levee. The congregation met at the Western Row location for just four years, until it built a chapel on Baker Street in 1839. Thereafter, the African Union Baptist Church was referred to as the Baker Street Chapel.[44] David Nickens, the brother of Owen T. B. Nickens, was selected to serve as the first pastor of the church. In the late 1820s, David, a freed slave, had migrated from Virginia to Chillicothe, Ohio, where he served as the pastor of a black Baptist church which was organized around the same time.[45] A respected leader in the larger black Chillicothe community, David Nickens was called on to speak at its 1831 July 5th celebration.[46] The main theme of Nickens's 1831 speech was racial unity, although he was also critical of the racist laws in the state. He boldly rejected the myth of black inferiority and promoted racial pride with references to a glorious African past. Nickens proclaimed that "All the now civilized world is indebted to sable Africa for the arts of civilization and learning."[47] His address also envisioned a Pan-African unity: "We shall soon be able to stretch our hands across an ocean . . . and there unite with our sable brethren in cultivating friendship and good feelings, till the whole race become enlightened."[48] The Nickens brothers articulated some of the earliest and strongest examples of black pride in Ohio, if not the nation. Certainly, this duo was exactly what black Cincinnati needed to hasten its rebirth. After David's move to Cincinnati, the Nickens brothers laid the foundation for the strongest black community in Ohio in that era, including significant contributions to the institutional life of Cincinnati's black community as ministers, teachers, and moral reformers. As the leader of the African Union Baptist Church, David Nickens surely must have addressed his congregation with the same fire for racial unity and racial pride that he did in his 1832 Chillicothe address. He served as the minister for the African Union Baptist Church until his premature death in 1838 at the age of forty-four,[49] and was succeeded by Rev. Charles Satchell.[50]

Cincinnati's three black churches reflected the theological, political, and demographic diversity of the black community. Bethel AME Church and the African Union Baptist Church were economically and politically independent of white churches—an independence that allowed these churches the freedom to exercise a stronger political voice without fear of white backlash. Deer Creek Church, as an affiliate church, compromised its political voice for the benefit of the patronage of the white parent church. Bethel and African Union Baptist churches were located in the First Ward and Fourth Ward, respectively—neighborhoods with a high concentration of African Americans. Although many African Americans simply attended the church closest to their homes, some class distinctions did emerge. In 1840, John Mercer Langston reported that the African Union Baptist Church was composed largely of the "better class" of blacks.[51] Swedish traveler Frederika Bremer, who visited Cincinnati's leading black churches, confirmed that the "negro aristocracy" attended the Baptist church. She further observed that the Baptists were led by a mulatto who had the "demeanor of the white race" as well as "good intellect and conversational power." Bremer described the Baptist service as "quiet," "very proper," and sparsely attended.[52]

The AME Church, by contrast, was representative of the black masses. Bremer reported that it was full of "African ardour and African life," and described a service that was neither proper nor quiet: "The singing ascended and poured forth like a melodious torrent, and the heads, feet, and elbows of the congregation moved all in unison with it, amid evident enchantment and delight." In stark contrast to the Baptist minister, Bremer described the AME minister as "very black . . . with a very retreating forehead, and the lower portion of the countenance protruding." In her opinion, he was "not at all good-looking."[53] What Bremer described were physical characteristics that were more common among the masses than among the black elite. And although Bremer did not ascribe to *this* minister the same inherent intelligence she had to the mulatto Baptist minister, she did acknowledge that he preached with "flowing eloquence" and that the congregation "hung upon his words."[54]

Class differences aside, all three black churches filled the spiritual needs of this community. They also provided the community with spiritual and education services, including Sunday schools, Bible study, prayer meetings, and literary societies.[55] Black churches also proved to be important social spaces for grooming leaders, mobilizing the masses, soliciting funds, disseminating information, and raising consciousness. More importantly, it was from within this exclusive racial and social space that the African American community was able to identify and coordinate strategies of uplift and mutuality.

The moral reform movement, a public extension of the black church, had gained momentum in Cincinnati by 1835. Moral reform initiatives generally were led by ministers and were rooted in Christian principles of morality. The moral reform movement urged individuals to work hard, pray hard, study hard, and to avoid alcohol, gambling, prostitution, and other vices. Following these tenets ensured that the individual's life would be consistent with the will of God.[56] The message was similar to what African Americans would have heard in church; the difference was that the efforts of the moral reform movement were not directed toward black Christians. The movement's goal was to reach the unconverted: those who normally lived outside the reach of the black church. Consequently, African Americans formed societies to carry the message of Christian morality from the church to the secular black community.

The moral reform movement was more than just a faith movement; it was also designed to elevate African Americans' social status. Realizing that society would use any immoral behavior to argue that African Americans were unworthy of citizenship rights and that slaves were unfit for freedom, antebellum black leaders strove to influence the rest of the community to become more virtuous and moral—to exhibit Christian principles.[57] Because white prejudice failed to differentiate between class and religious faith among African Americans, black leaders recognized that their social status could be only as high as the worst among them: if one African American was a thief, the entire race would be judged and stereotyped accordingly. Some leaders probably did feel that some African Americans, through their own immorality, helped poison the public mind against their race. Since they were partly responsible for public opinion about the race, many African Americans realized they would have to play a role in their own redemption through moral, respectable public behavior.[58] Thus, the moral reform movement was essentially a respectability campaign. As such, moral reform efforts were not about making white society feel that African Americans had assimilated or shed enough of their vices to belong to the republic. Rather, African Americans used respectability as a weapon of protest. The goal was to change popular public opinion about the race, thus "impelling whites to dismantle obstacles to black elevation [and equality] that not only degraded black life but perpetuated obstacles that fostered prejudice in the first place."[59] White society would then be forced to concede equality and support the extension of civil rights to African Americans. Hence, the moral reform movement was also a civil rights campaign.

The temperance society was an outgrowth of black Cincinnati's moral reform movement. Organized on April 1, 1835, with 225 members, the temperance society required members to pledge to abstain from all "intoxicating liquors, including wine, cider and all malt liquors." They also vowed to work to prevent the abuse of alcohol by others.[60] They considered drunkenness a sin because it provoked brawling, disorderliness, poverty, perverse moral judgment, and confusion of the mind.[61] Pushing abstinence may have been an attempt to improve the spiritual lives of blacks, but abstinence achieved another objective as well. African Americans had to be conscientious about the image they projected to the larger society. Alcoholism and public drunkenness could compromise the community's respectability: the entire community would be judged by the behavior of a few intoxicated people. Thus, free blacks "espoused temperance not because alcoholism or drunkenness was a race preoccupation, but because abstinence so well represented the moral uplift and social control which lay at the heart of much antebellum reform."[62] With so much on the line, the temperance society was uncompromising: members could be expelled for *any* consumption of alcohol. With the help of the Ohio Anti-Slavery Society, the message of temperance spread through the black community. The Cincinnati Anti-Slavery held lectures on temperance for the black community. Such efforts were fruitful; in an 1837 report, the president of the OAS boasted that in a six-month time period, not one black man had been intoxicated in Cincinnati. By 1837, the temperance society had three hundred members; two years later, it was reported that one-quarter of all of Cincinnati's 2,240 African Americans belonged to a temperance society.[63]

Although temperance societies encouraged African Americans to stop using alcohol, black leaders felt such organizations did not go far enough in discouraging other forms of vice. Consequently, in 1837, Rev. David Nickens and his brother, Owen T. B. Nickens, established the Moral Reform Society of the Colored Citizens of Ohio with David as the society's first president. According to its constitution, the society was created to encourage the "the suppression of intemperance, licentiousness, gambling, Sabbath-breaking, blasphemy, and all other vices"[64]—essentially, behaviors Christianity defines as sin. The Moral Reform Society's membership, then, consisted of the most pious of African Americans—those who were trying actively to live sin-free. The society resolved, "[W]e will not associate with [members of] either sex, until we have evidence of sincere repentance and abandonment of their sins."[65] The Moral Reform Society, like the temperance society, was an extension of the church into the secular realm. The Reverend David Nickens was an evangelical Baptist preacher who approached moral reform from a religious standpoint. For him, moral reform was necessary to cleanse black society of its sins. A resolution drawn up by Nickens confirmed this: "That the only firm basis on which the Moral Reform Society can stand securely, and effect the desired end, is the *benign principles of religion*" (emphasis in original).[66]

As the president of the Moral Reform Society, David Nickens governed the behavior of the membership. Both men and women were held to the same standard of moral virtue. The executive's charge was to "strictly watch over the affairs of the society and members admonishing them to maintain true principles of morality and integrity, 2) to impress on the minds . . . the importance of temperance, morality, virtue, and industry, 3) to urge upon parents the propriety of bringing up their children in conformity to the principles, 4) to admonish, discreetly, the youth . . . to refrain from immoral and vicious habits, 5) to . . . influence [the community] to roll back the inundating current of depravity and misery."[67] Thus, the president of this society was invested with the moral authority to govern the behaviors of members. Nickens had earned that moral authority through his leadership of the Baptist church, and his leadership of the Moral Reform Society was a natural extension of his position within that church.

By 1835, two black benefit societies existed in Cincinnati: the Female Benevolent Society and the Cincinnati Union Society. Whereas mutual aid societies typically provided relief to members and their families in the event of illness, injury, unemployment, or death, benefit societies were philanthropic associations designed to assist the less fortunate. Seeing the pressing needs of destitute African Americans who were denied the benefit of the city's Poor Fund, more privileged black women realized that the burden of feeding and clothing these families rested on the shoulders of their community. Consequently, they organized the Female Benevolent Society in 1835 to "help relieve the poor."[68] Most female benevolent societies were more than just charity societies; they also enriched the political lives of black women through lectures and discussions.[69] Through participation in these societies, black women found a community of like-minded women working to uplift their community. The Cincinnati Union Society was formed in a similar spirit to "relieve persons in distress," although it seemed to serve a broader purpose as well. The Union Society sponsored a community-wide celebration of British emancipation in 1838 that included a church service, speakers, a march, and a dinner.[70] Restricted to male members, the Cincinnati Union Society boasted one hundred members in 1835.[71]

The philanthropic efforts of benefit societies were part of a larger effort of racial uplift. The moral reform, self-help, and black church movements were part of a larger, three-pronged program of racial uplift through the mind, body, and soul. This "model of distinct, complementary, and yet unequal components of human character undergirded nearly every analysis of African Americans' plight."[72] African Americans worked for the elevation of the body through benefit societies and for the elevation of the soul through churches, Sunday schools, moral reform, and temperance societies. They worked to elevate the mind through all levels of schools, literary societies, and library associations. For the race to be elevated from its degraded social position, none of these three prongs of uplift could be ignored.

Although the impetus for black education in Cincinnati began with white philanthropy in 1815, by the mid-1820s, blacks were educating themselves in their own schools. Although the effort was sustained, the individual schools were impermanent. The upheaval of 1829 crippled blacks' educational initiatives in the city. Independent black schools disappeared from the historical record between 1829 and 1834; one plausible explanation is that they went underground as a protection against mob action. One resident observed that even in the years preceding the 1829 mob action, black schools had operated covertly to avoid trouble: "For a time it was necessary, as their places of resort were discovered by the rabble, that the teachers should inform the children one day where they would meet them the next."[73] This secret pursuit of education was reminiscent of black educational efforts in the slave South. African Americans may have continued this clandestine education after 1829 to avoid another mob attack.

The movement to educate blacks in Cincinnati was also complicated by a policy of exclusion from public schools. African Americans were denied admission to Cincinnati College (later the University of Cincinnati), the city's law school, the College of Teachers, the Academy of Natural Sciences, Farmer's College, Ohio Female College, the Medical College of Ohio, Lane Seminary, the Baptist Theological Institution, and all of the city's secondary schools.[74] They were also denied access to the common school fund, even for the purpose of establishing separate schools. In April 1830, African Americans from the First Ward sent a petition to the local Board of Trustees and Visitors praying to share the benefits of the common school fund.[75] The school trustees' response was: "The common school fund is *not* the offspring of the offices of charity; but that the principal and interest is amply repaid by the exercise of those functions which the government itself imposes upon all her free white citizens" (emphasis added).[76] With this declaration, the city's white leaders confirmed that public education was reserved for free *white* citizens.

The black community also faced the opposition of Charles McMicken, the founder of several of the city's educational institutions. Intent on removing free blacks from Cincinnati, McMicken, a colonizationist, purchased ten thousand acres of land north of Liberia in West Africa in

1830. McMicken hoped that Ohio's black population would settle the colony, dubbed "Ohio in Africa."[77] Apparently, the scheme never got off the ground: not one person left for the colony. McMicken inserted a clause in his will prohibiting black youth from attending any of the educational facilities he had founded in Cincinnati, including Cincinnati College. He concluded, "[T]hose who are not willing to go to [Ohio in Africa] . . . to acquire a knowledge of the duties of freedom, are not worthy of it."[78]

New allies stepped in to fill the educational void created by the riot of 1829. The allies were mostly young, white New Englanders who were students at Cincinnati's Lane Seminary. Led by Lyman Beecher, these reform-minded seminarians had come to Lane to be trained and to evangelize in the West. In 1832, Lane students began the task of educating the largely uneducated African American population of Cincinnati. Not only did they hold public lectures for African Americans,[79] but Lane seminarians sponsored Bible classes, a regular day school for adults and children, and an evening school.[80] The commitment of the Lane students invigorated other white reformers to educate blacks.

In the 1830s, educating African Americans became the primary racial uplift activity for whites in Cincinnati.[81] Because education was considered part of women's sphere, women were prominent figures in this uplift activity. In fact, the Ohio Female Anti-Slavery Association led the effort in Cincinnati, and several women operated schools at different intervals.[82] Male abolitionists were also involved in black education. Amzi Barber, the secretary of the Cincinnati Anti-Slavery Society (CAS), operated a school for black boys between the ages of ten and fifteen in 1836. Another CAS member, Augustus Wattles, also operated a school for black boys.[83]

Those who educated African Americans did so at the expense of their reputations, personal safety, and financial security. They received very little compensation for their work with black students. In the 1830s, teachers in black schools customarily worked for room and board, which averaged one dollar per week.[84] Some teachers received a salary funded by philanthropic donations or tuition receipts. Tuition of twelve and a half cents per week was paid directly to the teacher. Because tuition was too expensive for most black families to afford, teachers sometimes went unpaid for weeks. Even when they were paid, it was barely enough to cover living expenses. One teacher "worked night and morning to pay her board." Another teacher seriously considered teaching at a white school because the pay was higher: "I thought I could not earn money enough to clothe myself." Another teacher sometimes did not know from day to day how she would feed herself. At such times she would say to her scholars, "'Tell your parents that unless they send me some money to buy bread, I can keep a school no longer.'"[85]

These teachers not only faced financial difficulties but were treated with the "utmost scorn and contempt" by other whites. "People generally appeared to think that these teachers had . . . disgraced themselves by engaging in such an employment."[86] Consequently, few wanted to associate with them. These teachers had difficulty finding housing: "boarding-house keepers refused to entertain them, placing their trunks on the sidewalk, and telling them that they had no accommodation for 'teachers of niggers.'"[87] The uncertainty of the lodging was so great that one Ohio teacher expressed relief that they "were never compelled to lodge in the streets, or board in jail."[88] In addition, teachers of black children were sometimes insulted, stoned, and threatened, and their schoolhouses were mobbed.[89] Many of the teachers persisted with the profession because they believed they were doing God's work.[90]

Student teachers from Lane Seminary were among the most despised of these educators—largely because they associated with blacks on terms of equality. They caused public indignation by regularly boarding with black families in town. Even more incendiary was a visit to the seminary by several black women in a carriage to whom Lane students paid "marked attention." Another occasion that caused alarm was a Lane student's escorting of a black woman from her home to the seminary and back. Although the student had merely directed the woman to campus, "it was regarded by the community as part of a settled design to carry into effect the scheme of equalization."[91]

In 1834, African American efforts at self-education resurfaced in the public record when Owen T. B. Nickens, Baptist minister David Nickens, AME minister William Paul Quinn, and painter William M. Johnson organized an evening school with the help of Lane students.[92] Theirs was the first school operated by African Americans in nearly ten years. The tuition at the Nickenses' school was one dollar per month, although "none were turned away for lack of payment."[93]

Schools for blacks were usually physically located within the black community—either in or near the black churches or in private homes. African American families sometimes offered their homes as schoolhouses. Baker Jones allowed advanced and primary classes for boys in two of his homes on Sixth Street, east of Broadway.[94] Nickens operated the school in the Bethel AME Church on Sixth Street. The school remained inside the church until 1836, when it relocated to its own building on New Street, near Broadway.[95] Another school was located in a small room between Sixth and Harrison streets in the First Ward, very near Bethel AME Church. Another school operated out of Union Baptist Church on Western Row in the Fourth Ward.[96] The New Street Chapel on Sixth Street housed a school for girls.[97] Black churches often provided the facilities for these schools and, in some instances, provided most of the teacher base: many of those who taught in the schools also were ministers or church members. This sharing of social space and leadership reinforced cooperation and mutual dependence between black schools and churches.

Each school that opened quickly filled to capacity. A Sunday school that opened in September 1832 boasted 125 students within three years. The same level of intellectual interest was evident at biweekly public lectures on scientific and literary subjects organized by Lane students in 1832. African Americans flocked to the lectures in droves. Each lecture hosted an audience of 150 to 300.[98] In 1841, a Mr. Goodwin and a Mr. Denham opened a school in the Baker Street Church (African Union Baptist Church), which "was the largest of all the colored schools, having an enrollment of two or three hundred pupils."[99] It was not just the children who came seeking an education; adults also flocked to the schoolhouses. When a school for blacks opened in 1834, "it was immediately crowded to overflowing with children and adults." So many desired to learn that the schoolhouse was not large enough to accommodate adults and children at the same time, and so the school day was divided in half.[100] But even those arrangements did not satisfy the demand: "The clamor of the adults for admittance made it necessary to open an evening school for their benefit. This was held three evenings in a week, and [was] fully attended." In response to continued demands, another school and teacher were secured to hold classes for children and young women.[101]

All students, young and old, received more than just a rudimentary education; they were instructed in reading, spelling, history, arithmetic, geography, science, and grammar. Young black girls also learned homemaking skills such as needlework, which was deemed to be "a necessary part of their education, as before they had been known how to do little else than the most laborious kind of housework."[102] This curriculum was designed for more than just literacy; its purpose was to elevate the race through a broad-based enlightenment. Ultimately, this type of education was expected to prepare blacks for citizenship and self-sufficiency.

Black pupils eagerly attended classes and were excellent scholars. Invalidating popular assumptions that they were incapable of learning,

African Americans made significant progress in a short period of time. A report by the CAS boasts that one fifteen-year-old girl wrote a letter within ten days of her first lesson. It also claimed that boys aged seven and eight had learned their alphabet in two days and learned to spell three-syllable words and to read by the close of their first quarter of instruction.[103] Although this report was an obvious exaggeration by the OAS, other contemporary observers concurred that the students were making significant progress in a short period of time. Edward Abdy, a British citizen traveling throughout the country in 1833 and 1834, observed that black pupils were "so assiduous . . . in learning their lessons, that one of the instructors . . . assured me, that he had never witnessed such instances of rapid improvement."[104]

Despite blacks' eagerness to learn, their schools faced serious challenges. Many were forced to close for lack of teachers or schoolrooms.[105] Teachers also had to contend with irregular attendance by their pupils. A child might be in school one year and gone the next. Much of this instability arose because black children usually attended school only until they were old enough to work. Then, many were sent to work on the river.[106] Financial challenges also hurt black schools. Before 1835, philanthropy and the CAS wholly financed these schools. Members of the black community helped when they could, but before 1835 the total documented support from this source came to less than $150.[107]

On January 1, 1836, Cincinnati's black community organized a mutual aid educational society to shoulder most of the responsibility for financing its own schools. The Cincinnati Education Society—as it was named—was a cooperative effort to fund schools for black youth. Although mutual aid societies existed among free black communities throughout the country, an educational society of this sort was less common. Members of the society paid dues that were used to offset the cost of operating the city's black schools. Monthly membership dues were twenty-five cents for men and twelve and a half cents for women.[108] Most mutual aid societies existed to benefit the members exclusively; the Cincinnati Education Society was exceptional in that it aimed to benefit *all* African American children, regardless of their parents' ability to pay. The society's mission was to educate not only the children of its membership but orphaned and destitute black children as well.[109]

The Education Society sponsored Amzi Barber's school.[110] Barber, formerly a theological student at Oberlin College, was also a member of the Cincinnati Anti-Slavery Society and had a long career as a teacher and advocate of black education.[111] In 1837, he authored the report "Of the Present Condition of the Colored People in Cincinnati" and a series of articles in the local press about the condition of black education.[112] In its first year, the Education Society contributed $401 for the support of Barber's school. By April 1837, members of the society had raised a total of $794.33 for the support of the school; by 1839, they had contributed $889.03 toward the support of their schools.[113] Although it is difficult to determine how long the Education Society existed, it left a legacy of unprecedented mutual action and responsibility.

Despite the progress the black community had made in rebuilding its infrastructure after the riots, it still faced debilitating external assaults. The Black Laws of 1804 and 1807, still on the books, formed the backdrop of the black freedom experience in Cincinnati between 1829 and 1841, quietly mocking the gains African Americans were able to make. Black Cincinnatians were not naïve enough to think that they were secure: these laws might be enforced at any moment. To add further insult, other civil disabilities were enacted at the state and local levels with each passing year. After 1829, there was a two-year legislative quiet during which no new laws were enacted against African Americans. Then came the storm. In February 1831, the legislature passed "An Act Relating to Juries," which limited jury duty to white male inhabitants over the age of twenty-one.[114] Excluding blacks from serving as jurors had many implications, including making black defendants more vulnerable to a justice system that acted on the popular assumption that blacks were inherently criminal. The 1831 jury act, coupled with the section of the 1807 Black Law that prohibited African Americans from testifying in court against whites, meant that African Americans could not use the courts to secure justice for themselves and made them even less than second-class citizens.

Assailed legally without, African Americans were nearly divided internally along color lines. The complexity of the color issue itself was played out in Ohio courts. In 1829, Polly Gray, a woman of mixed ancestry, stood trial in Hamilton County Court of Common Pleas for robbery. When an African American who had witnessed Polly's crime was called to testify against her, her attorney objected to the admission of this witness on the grounds that the Black Law of 1807 prohibited blacks and mulattoes from testifying against whites. According to the attorney, his client was neither black nor mulatto, but "a shade of color between the mulatto and white." The judge overruled his objection, and the court heard the testimony of the witness. Although Gray was summarily convicted of the crime, she subsequently appealed on the ground that a black person had testified against her, when she herself was less than half black.[115] The case of *Gray v. State* went before the Ohio Supreme Court in 1831. Polly Gray had the burden of proving that she was neither black nor mulatto. Although the lower court had ruled that Polly was not white based on her color, her attorney argued that she could not legally be classified as mulatto or black because neither of her parents was black. The trace of African blood that could be seen in her skin was attributable not to her parents, but to a grandparent, making her a quadroon. In most southern states, Polly would have been considered a mulatto, which was "loosely defined to include someone with a black grandparent (quadroon) or great grandparent (octoroon)."[116] Ohio, however, strictly defined a mulatto as someone "begotten between a white and a black"; there was no classification for quadroons.[117] Thus, Ohio's narrow definition provided the legislative loophole Gray needed to win her appeal and to have her conviction overturned.

The opinion of the supreme court was that only three racial distinctions were mentioned in the law—white, black, and mulatto. Although recognizing that those classifications were ambiguous, the court ruled that it was "unwilling to extend the disabilities of the statute further that its letter requires" to include quadroons. The court was also concerned with the difficulty "defining and ascertaining the degree of duskiness which renders a person liable to such disabilities."[118] Being neither mulatto nor black by definition, Gray was extended the same civil rights as whites. In a similar case, *Thacker v. Hawk,* another quadroon brought suit after being denied the right to vote. Using the Gray case as a guide, the Ohio Supreme Court concluded in 1842 that anyone who was less than half black was entitled to vote.[119] In yet another case, *Williams v. School District of Greene County,* the Ohio Supreme Court decided to admit the "white" children of the quadroon plaintiff into public school in Greene County.[120]

Ohio was unique in how it addressed these cases based on color. Essentially, these cases challenged the court to consider degrees of *whiteness*. This was a radical departure from how mixed-race people were treated in the upper and lower South, where the "one-drop rule" applied. Ohio courts extended citizenship to quadroons; in the South, quadroons received no civil rights, although they might receive privileged social or economic status among those whites who believed them superior to darker-complexioned blacks.

The court's decisions threatened to construct a color caste within the black community in Cincinnati, with blacks and mulattoes at the bottom—completely disfranchised—while quadroons and octoroons enjoyed some of the liberties of citizens. These decisions illuminate a slippery social practice in Cincinnati and elsewhere that sometimes extended privileges to individuals with lighter skin. For example, in 1835 a white school at Sixth and Vine streets began admitting "colored children of a light hue."[121] This distinction was rooted not in parentage, but in visible appearance. Local officials had the power to determine when, whether, and which mixed race persons would receive such rights. In practice, officials sometimes extended rights to those with light skin rather arbitrarily and without investigating whether they were less than half black. For the most part, however, there was no extension of legal rights to light-complexioned blacks in any systematic way, and this precluded the development of a true caste system among black Americans in this period. Another important reason was black community resistance to such a system. In 1844, John I. Gaines advised city officials to make no attempts to establish separate schools for mulattoes. He proclaimed, "This I anticipate would be fraught with evil consequences. . . . It would not only divide the colored children, but create prejudices too intolerable to be borne."[122] Gaines, expressing the sentiment of the community, insisted that all children of African American heritage receive equal access to education, regardless of color.

———

African Americans' economic options continued to be stunted between 1829 and 1836. The city experienced tremendous economic growth in the 1830s, but African Americans did not reap many of its benefits. For white men, the trades allowed upward mobility; they could rise through the ranks from unskilled laborer to apprentice, journeyman, and master craftsman. For African Americans, such mobility was rarely possible. Racism negated the skills of black artisans and thwarted their hopes for upward mobility within craftwork. White employers, journeymen, and masters cooperated to keep African Americans from practicing trades in Cincinnati. White artisans created both informal and formal unions to lock African Americans out of the trades. According to an 1835 OAS report, after an African American cabinetmaker was hired in one cabinet shop, white journeymen threw down their tools and vowed that they would "never work with a Nigger." At a time when there was a shortage of skilled labor in the city, the Ohio Mechanics' Institute vowed to make certain that "no colored boy could learn a trade or find employment," and even held proceedings against its president for teaching a black man a trade.[123] African Americans were also systematically denied apprenticeships, the normal path for entrance into trades. The goal of such exclusions was to keep African Americans in servile or menial positions that reinforced the racial hierarchy. The 1836 city directory indicated that only 10 percent of the black heads of household were working in skilled positions.[124] Cincinnati resembled the economic culture of the upper South, where white artisans were aggressive in their efforts to keep free blacks out of the trades. There, they petitioned legislators and even formed labor unions to reach their objective. When those means were not effective, these southerners sometimes resorted to violence and intimidation.[125] Cincinnati emigrationist James C. Brown, for example, had been physically threatened by white mechanics when he lived in Kentucky in the early 1820s.[126]

Even when African Americans were not completely locked out of skilled work in Cincinnati, they suffered chronic underemployment. Those with skills were forced to take unskilled positions or seasonal jobs just to make ends meet. An enslaved silversmith from New Orleans, who had settled in Cincinnati after hiring himself out to pay for his freedom, found that "no one would encourage him in his business, or work with him; and he was compelled to subsist by the few jobs he could get, now and then, on board the steam-boats, or in the city."[127] Although he had practiced his trade freely and without incident as a New Orleans slave, he did not have such privileges as a free man in a free state. Generally, black artisans in Cincinnati were denied entry into even the most common trade practiced by African Americans: carpentry.[128] There were only four African Americans practicing the trade there in 1836. Similarly, there were just three African American blacksmiths and one silversmith.[129] It is also likely that many capable black artisans in Cincinnati worked jobs that allowed them to use only a small aspect of their craft. Masonry is a trade that encompasses several skills, including stonecutting, brickmaking, brickmoulding, bricklaying, plastering, and whitewashing.[130] In Cincinnati, there was only one black brickmason in 1836, but there were more blacks employed in the many subtrades of masonry, including a bricklayer, a plasterer, and six whitewashers. It is possible that some of these bricklayers, plasterers, and whitewashers were, in fact, masons who had been forced to work in the subtrades in order to survive. To white artisans, black bricklayers and whitewashers were far less threatening than black master brickmasons.

Professional opportunities were slim for African Americans. Not only did the few professional schools of the day refuse to admit them, but blacks were also denied opportunities to learn the professions by working under the tutelage of other professionals. In the early nineteenth century, many young men entered the professions of their fathers, who trained them. Professions, like trades, were passed from father to son. Outside of familial training, the only way to break into a professional career was through apprenticeship. For example, most aspiring attorneys learned the profession as law clerks, who studied and "read the law" under the supervision of a practicing attorney. But very few white attorneys accepted black law clerks. Even more difficult than finding a clerkship was gaining acceptance to the bar. By the eve of the Civil War, just one black attorney had been accepted to the Ohio bar.[131] Formal medical training consisted of learning to "prepare drugs, bleed, cup, extract teeth, and perform minor surgery, after which [the apprentice] commenced practical training, accompanying and assisting the doctor on his rounds."[132] But unlike the legal profession, the medical profession offered no real training for physicians, and licenses were not required to practice medicine. Hence, there was a wide range of skill in the practice of medicine, a field that included root doctors and healers. Even those African Americans in Cincinnati who managed to become physicians were considered "quacks"— a perception that probably arose from their less formal training.[133] Similarly, very few African Americans became teachers in the 1830s. Denied access to schools of higher education, many black teachers did not have much more education than their students.

Racism trapped African Americans in low-status, low-paying, and unskilled positions with little upward mobility. Cincinnati's African Americans disproportionately worked in service and cleaning positions as barbers, waiters, cooks, whitewashers, stewards, and washerwomen— occupations that were deemed appropriate for them. The most common occupations held by black heads of household in 1836 were riverworker (28), laborer (21), washerwoman (24), and barber (20)—all service or unskilled occupations.[134] Laborers might perform any kind of unskilled work from lifting freight unto ships, to removing trash.[135]

Washing and ironing clothes was a field occupied almost exclusively by black women in Cincinnati. Their race and gender predetermined their class position; doubly victimized by racism and sexism, black women had almost no occupational diversity and very little occupational mobility. Black men and white women had a few more occupational options than black women. Whereas white working women filled a range of positions as seamstresses, boarding house operators, carpet weavers, teachers, and tailors, black women essentially were confined to washing for a living. In fact, in 1836, 86 percent of black working women were washers.[136] Very few black women were able to escape this lot, although four were employed as a tailor, cook, barber, and steward.[137]

Barbering was the surest path to upward mobility for black men in the 1830s. In 1836, roughly 12 percent of the black heads of household were barbers.[138] Although barbering is often considered a service profession, in Cincinnati it carried a degree of prestige. Many of Cincinnati's black barbers owned their own shops and had a relative degree of independence. Barbering for prominent white clients granted black men access, when they accompanied their clients, to social gatherings and associations that otherwise would have been off limits. Barbering not only made the acquisition of wealth a possibility but also opened doors to enhanced class status.

In the 1830s, a significant portion of black workers were employed in the river industry, which broadly included all levels of unskilled work, including boatmen, deckhands, stewards, porters, and almost every other capacity on steamboats traveling to and from Cincinnati. Working in this industry had many advantages. Those who worked aboard ships had a greater degree of independence and mobility than did those with jobs ashore. Black river workers traveled extensively along the Ohio and Mississippi rivers—a freedom that very few African Americans enjoyed in the antebellum era. One major benefit of that mobility was the opportunity to escape the psychic, economic, and political sting of racism in Cincinnati, even if only temporarily. One drawback of this line of work was that mobility usually meant transience—something the fragile African American community could not afford. Many black boatmen were away from home for the majority of the year and moved from city to city in search of work in the winter season. Many of them were doomed to a lifetime of transience. In fact, those boatmen listed in the 1836 city directory were no longer in the city by 1842.[139]

At the other end of the occupational spectrum were the few African Americans who achieved a measure of economic success as entrepreneurs in the Queen City. A group of black men established a successful real estate firm, the Iron Chest Company, in 1838. Its members invested one dollar per week, which went to the construction of buildings. The Iron Chest Company's most noted accomplishment was the construction of three brick buildings that were leased to whites.[140] In the late 1830s, Robert Gordon, a former slave from Virginia, opened a very lucrative coal business that was worth $15,000 by 1847. Henry Boyd, a carpenter by trade, owned a business that manufactured corded bedsteads for which he owned the patent. By 1844, Boyd's company produced one thousand to twelve hundred bedsteads annually. In 1850, he owned real estate valued at $20,000.[141] By 1840, the black community owned property collectively valued at $209,000 and three churches worth $19,000.[142]

By the time John Mercer Langston arrived in the city in 1840, there were enough successful black families to constitute an aristocratic or elite class. Many of Cincinnati's black barbers fell into this category. Langston described these black "aristocrats" as a class of "good-looking, well-dressed and well-behaved" blacks of "considerable accomplishment . . . [and] a reasonable amount of means" who also exhibited a "consciousness of their personal dignity and social worth." According to Langston, William Watson's family was "the first family in colored society in Cincinnati." A barber of considerable means, Watson frequently received other members of the black elite into his "well-furnished" home with "pleasant rooms and parlors." A well-respected and influential member of the Baker Street Baptist Church, Watson also led Bible study and was the superintendent of the Sunday school.[143] Langston implied that membership in the black elite was about more than just financial success; it was also about respectability. Respectability included educational attainment, moral living, and dignified public deportment. Although this was the same standard of respectability associated with racial uplift, it also had another dimension. Not merely a concern with white society's perception of the race, respectability also included impressing other African Americans with conspicuous clothing and furnishings, as did William Watson.[144]

Diversity of wealth, occupation, and color existed within Cincinnati's black community between 1829 and 1836. Diversity sometimes even lent itself to distinctions, and nowhere is that more apparent than through the lens of color and class. Although class differences typically compromise internal unity within any community, among Cincinnati's African American community this was not so. The socioeconomic classes that had begun to form by 1840 were still too tenuous to be divisive. In a city in which their numbers were small, their financial stability precarious, and where proscriptive laws prevented them from being able to protect their investments, the black elite was neither a sizable nor stable class throughout the decade. Awareness of a common oppression helped to prevent the splintering of this community. Black Cincinnatians understood that they were still too vulnerable to allow superficial differences to divide them; they could not afford to. In short, the racial violence and political and social repression faced by all African Americans neutralized any class distinctions, bonding African Americans together in ways that transcended class.

Cincinnati's black community began its recovery between 1829 and 1836. The key to that recovery was its indigenous institutions, like the church. Black institutions fostered an environment that was conducive to identifying and grooming a new generation of leaders. Many of the community's leaders were trained in black churches and transitioned to secular leadership. From within black institutions the community was able to identify and coordinate strategies of racial uplift through mutuality. But this was still a tentative community; and with good reason.

FIVE

Building Strength Within

State and National Alliances, 1829–1841

In Union there is strength.

—Union Association of the Colored Men of New Richmond, Ohio

ALTHOUGH CINCINNATI'S African Americans had built an infrastructure for their community, they still faced challenging external obstacles in the 1830s. Racism refused to relinquish its chokehold on their freedom. African Americans had to contend with economic repression, debilitating legal setbacks, and, of course, mob violence. Local black leaders must have realized that as long as their community stood alone—without any allies—it would continue to be vulnerable to legislative assaults and mob violence. Consequently, in the 1830s this community made alliances with other African American communities throughout the state and nation, as well as with local white abolitionists. Having developed a strong group of committed and vocal allies, African Americans grew increasingly confident about asserting their right to be in the city. A political voice that had been timid and supplicatory in the 1820s resounded with increasing confidence each year before 1841.

The Cincinnati riot of 1829 inspired the black convention movement in the United States. News of the violence spread through free black communities throughout the country. African Americans were indignant and outraged about the violence and more conscious of their vulnerability to it. This is what prompted Baltimorean Hezekiah Grace to send a circular in the spring of 1830, inviting black leaders throughout the North and West to convene in Philadelphia the following September to discuss these concerns. Black Cincinnati was at the top of the agenda. From September 20 to September 24, 1830, twenty-six delegates representing several black communities met in Bethel Church in Philadelphia not only to discuss the events in Cincinnati but to consider whether to form a colony in Upper Canada "to afford a place of refuge to those who may be obliged to leave their homes, as well as to others inclined to emigrate with the view of improving their condition." Thus, Cincinnati *and* the Wilberforce colony were central to this historic moment. One of the outcomes of that initial meeting was the formation of the American Society of Free Persons of Colour. The objectives of this organization were to improve the conditions of blacks in the United States and to purchase land to establish a settlement in Upper Canada. Before the convention closed, delegates agreed to meet the following year.[1]

Although Cincinnati's black leaders do not appear to have attended this initial meeting, they did respond to an invitation to attend that body's first convention, held from June 6 to June 11, 1831. The First Annual Convention of the People of Colour convened in Philadelphia.[2] Representatives from states in the Northeast, upper South, and West were present. African Americans were so enthusiastic about the idea of coming together that some traveled from as far as Rhode Island. Black Cincinnati answered the summons and sent Charles Hatfield and John Liverpool as delegates.[3] Black Cincinnati's presence at this convention underscores its desire to connect to other black communities and collectivize its struggle. At the convention, leaders not only discussed problems confronting African Americans but also explored *solutions*. The representatives decided that education, temperance, and economy were the best means of elevating the race. They made plans to establish a manual labor college for African Americans in New Haven, Connecticut.[4] Subsequent meetings were held annually in Philadelphia for the next three years.[5]

Black conventions provided a forum for black communities across the nation to discuss their common plight. Although African Americans came from different localities, they all faced a similar set of challenges. The convention also provided a forum for African Americans to explore mutually beneficial solutions. The Cincinnati community became part of a national community that was united by its consciousness of a common struggle, a common objective, and solutions of general applicability.[6]

Black communities in several states, including Ohio, held their own conventions as well.

John Malvin claimed that he had conceived the idea of state conventions for black Ohioans. According to Malvin, he and a group of other black leaders appointed Cleveland teacher Molliston Madison Clarke (M. M. Clarke) "to canvass the State and lecture to the colored people on the propriety of calling a State convention."[7] In this capacity, Clarke likely would have spoken at black churches, which were the primary sites for mobilizing the community. The first state convention was held in Columbus in 1835. Like other blacks around the country, black Ohioans met annually to discuss the problems in their communities. Among the issues they discussed at these state conventions were their civil rights, the Black Laws, the right to a trial by jury for every resident in the state, and laws related to fugitive slaves. Black Ohioans also discussed strategies of uplift that mirrored those adopted by the black national convention movement, including moral reform, temperance, and education.[8]

The School Fund Institute of the Colored People of Ohio was born from the Ohio state conventions. The School Fund Institute was created at the meeting held in September 1837 to establish schools for black children throughout the state.[9] The institute was similar to Cincinnati's Education Society, but functioned at the state level. The School Fund Institute pooled funds collected from around the state and used them to operate black private schools. Molliston Madison Clarke was appointed the fundraising agent for the organization and he traveled the state soliciting funds for the support of these schools. The School Fund Institute established four schools in Cincinnati, Columbus, Cleveland, and Springfield, which operated for two years.[10] The institute is an example of how black communities in Ohio saw their destinies tied to the collective whole; they realized that the best way to establish and sustain schools was through mutuality and cooperation at the state level.

Black Cincinnati's alliances with other black communities in the state were still not strong enough to seriously challenge the status quo. African Americans, after all, had very little political power by themselves. Cincinnati's black community recognized that it needed allies with the political and economic power—and the white skin—to be heard and respected. The community needed allies who were not afraid to openly support its causes. Fortunately, blacks found those allies in the local white antislavery community.

The efforts of Lane Seminary students were the catalyst for the formation of a formal, organized antislavery movement in Cincinnati. In February 1834, Lane student Theodore Dwight Weld organized public debates on the question of abolition and colonization on campus. Over seventeen evenings, Lane students debated two questions: whether it was the duty of the people of slaveholding states to abolish slavery immediately and whether the American Colonization Society was worthy of the patronage of a Christian public. Arguing that slavery was a sin, Lane students concluded that it was the duty of the people in slave states to abolish slavery. They also felt the ACS was not worthy of the patronage of a Christian community.[11] These Lane debates converted many to abolitionism. The seminarians formed an abolition society—or an antislavery society—on campus and devoted themselves to the education of Cincinnati's black community. In addition to establishing a weekly science lyceum, Lane students also opened a Sunday school and held regular classes. In 1834, the students assisted local black leaders David and Owen T. B. Nickens with establishing an evening school for forty to fifty adult African Americans.[12] In addition to its educational thrust, the Lane abolition society supported social equality. Students boarded and dined in black homes and socialized with black families. Such social intercourse might have continued had the students not met with resistance from Lane Seminary's faculty, who condemned the students for interacting with blacks on the basis of equality. Yielding to public pressure, the faculty disbanded the antislavery society.[13] Refusing to submit, many "Lane Rebels" left Lane Seminary that summer in search of greener, more tolerant pastures at Oberlin College. Others, like Marcus Robinson, remained in Cincinnati and became active in the Ohio Anti-Slavery Society.[14]

Other abolitionists who were devoted to educating African Americans filled the void left by the Lane Rebels. Cincinnati Anti-Slavery Society agents Amzi Barber and Augustus Wattles diligently carried the torch. Women of the Female CAS also joined this effort. Like African Americans, these abolitionist teachers believed that education was the keystone to preparing blacks for freedom and citizenship. In conjunction with the black community, these abolitionists did much to educate African Americans, raise funds, lobby for a change in laws excluding blacks from public education, and support black efforts to educate themselves and operate their own schools.

In 1835, editor, attorney, and former slave owner James G. Birney moved his antislavery journal, the *Philanthropist,* from Danville, Kentucky, to New Richmond, Ohio, a village outside of Cincinnati. The *Philanthropist* was a godsend to Cincinnati's black community. In editorials Birney openly attacked slaveholders, the institution of slavery, and Christians who justified its continuation. He made it clear that African Americans were deserving of citizenship rights and equality. In a February 1836 article entitled "The African Mind," Birney turned the historical basis for white supremacy on its head: "But at more than one preceding period, they [Africans] have been for a length of time, at the head of civilization and political power, and must be regarded as the real authors of most of the arts and science. . . . While Greece and Rome were yet barbarous, we find light of learning and improving emanating from this . . . continent of Africa."[15] African Americans held Birney in high esteem. Here was a white man who had converted from his slaveholding ways, respected blacks' humanity, and was willing openly to support their cause. Here was an editor who respected their voice and their political views. The *Philanthropist* became a champion for African Americans, freed and enslaved. In addition to teaching whites about the glorious history of Africans, it also provided a forum for blacks to voice their concerns. Only in this journal were they fully free to express themselves.

Birney had removed the journal to the North because it was no longer safe for him to continue to print antislavery materials in the South. But Birney received no warm welcome on the other side of the Ohio River. In fact, the *Cincinnati Christian Journal* warned: "We have little doubt that his office will be torn down."[16] Threats came in from the South as well. A one-hundred-dollar reward was issued from Kentucky for the delivery of the body of Birney, "who in all his associations and feelings is black."[17]

Birney's scathing editorials against slaveholders infuriated Cincinnati's "men of property and standing." After all, many of them had secured their fortunes through commerce with the South. They were unwilling to allow Cincinnati's commercial interests be threatened by the rantings of an abolitionist. On January 22, 1836, a meeting was held to discuss how to arrest the encroachment of abolitionism in the city. Between five hundred and six hundred of Cincinnati's wealthiest and most powerful men attended, including senator and former Cincinnati mayor Jacob Burnett, financier Nicholas Longworth (the attorney and banker who had quietly donated money to help African Americans in the 1820s), and editor of the *Cincinnati Republican*, Charles Ramsay.[18] Because the *Philanthropist* was the voice of antislavery in the city, antiabolitionists felt it would be used to promulgate abolitionism. They determined to snuff the paper out by any means necessary.

Birney stood his ground and continued to print. In fact, he refused to censor himself or ease the tone of his editorials. As if to stoke the fires, on April 15, 1836, Birney disregarded the warnings of the city's stewards and moved the *Philanthropist* from New Richmond to Cincinnati, where the

OAS assumed control of the journal. With the move to the city, Birney both symbolically and literally catapulted abolitionism from Cincinnati's margins to its political center stage. But that move came at a price: three days later, a mob burned buildings in a black neighborhood and brutally beat the residents.[19] Although the mob was clearly prompted by the *Philanthropist's* move, the assailants took their out aggressions on the city's African American population and not on the white editor of the *Philanthropist.*

Tensions continued to mount as spring gave way to summer. July 5 was the day African Americans celebrated their own Independence Day, partly to dramatize the hypocrisy of celebrating American freedom when millions were yet enslaved. As they prepared to march through town, some African Americans were approached by a belligerent and confrontational group of whites. The whites shouted epithets and insults at the blacks. They accused them of "subsisting by pilfering and plundering and with enticing away the slaves of southern visitors." One African American "whose spirit had not been subdued into full submission" answered with "a firmness and fierceness of tone and language." Caught off guard by that response, the group of whites left the place in embarrassment.[20]

At midnight on the night of July 12, 1836, a mob of thirty to forty men broke into to the office of Achilles Pugh, printer of the *Philanthropist,* and proceeded to destroy the paper and the ink and dismantle the type.[21] So confident were they that their lawlessness would go unpunished that the next day antiabolitionists posted placards along street corners warning abolitionists that "[i]f an attempt is made to re-establish their press, it will be viewed as an act of defiance to an already outraged community, and on their own heads be the results which follow."[22]

Although the identities of many of these rioters remain a mystery, the mob was composed of at least three Kentuckians, some hired ruffians, several business owners, artisans, and some of the children of Cincinnati's men of wealth and standing. The makeup of this mob reflects an alliance among all classes of white society. Each class had different motivations, which included commercial interests and political ties (merchants and politicians), perceived threat to the institution of chattel slavery (Kentucky slave owners), and the fear of labor competition with blacks (artisans, laborers). What brought these classes of whites together that summer was their common objective—to cleanse Cincinnati of the threat of abolitionism and to terrorize blacks into resubmission to the racial order.

Because Birney refused to cease publication, the mob reassembled on July 30. Rioters broke into the office of the *Philanthropist,* "scattered the type into the streets, tore down the presses," and ransacked the building. The rioters decided against burning the building. This was not a typical mob driven by heated emotions; the rioters' actions were very deliberate and their victims clearly identified.[23] From the *Philanthropist* office, they moved to the home of Achilles Pugh, where they found neither him nor any printing materials. The band proceeded to Birney's home, intending to tar and feather him, but he could not be located. Returning to the *Philanthropist* office, the mob broke the presses and threw the pieces into the Ohio River. The rioters then turned their wrath toward the black community in Church Alley. They attacked black homes, brothels, and grog shops. Black residents returned the violence with gunfire, forcing the mob to retreat temporarily. After regrouping, the mob moved in for round two on this black neighborhood, but found that most residents had fled. Black homes and furnishings were ransacked and destroyed.[24]

Because abolitionism triggered such violent reprisals, men like Birney and printer Achilles Pugh risked their lives, fortunes, and personal reputations for the cause of abolition and equality each day that journal went to press. Neither Pugh, nor Birney, nor Birney's successor, Gamaliel Bailey, could have rested easy, knowing he might be murdered. Yet Bailey and Birney persisted in speaking for truth and writing for freedom.

The *Philanthropist* brought mixed benefits to the black community. This community bore the brunt of antiabolitionist contempt, as the 1836 riot illustrates. If anything, Birney's editorials in that press fomented existing antiblack sentiment and triggered renewed violence and antipathy against this community. African Americans suffered emotional and tangible losses after their homes were looted, their property was destroyed, and they themselves were driven from their neighborhoods. Even categorizing this mob violence as an "antiabolitionist mob riot" ignores the deliberate violence against the black community. James Birney was incapable of either shielding them from the violence or convincing city officials to do so. Allies like James Birney were willing to live and die by their commitment to help advance the cause for freedom and equality for African Americans. This was fact was not lost on African Americans. Such unwavering support from white abolitionists gave the African American community the courage to rally behind abolitionists—even against members of their own community.

Two black leaders who dared publicly to condemn abolitionism endured sharp criticism from their community. Dennis Hill, president of the Cincinnati Union Society, and M. M. Clarke, agent for the School Fund Institute, both issued public notices indicating that their respective organizations did not approve of the tactics of abolitionists. Their goal was to distance their organizations from abolitionists to avert any reprisals for such an association. Two days after the mob action of 1836, Hill issued a public notice on behalf of his organization: "We have, for the last few months, witnessed the efforts making [sic] by a few misguided and fanatical men amongst us, styled abolitionists, and headed by one Birney, and whereas, we have become convinced that the means they are using have a direct tendency to injure the interest of the colored population of the free states by exciting the passion of the white inhabitants, and we believe, to rivet more firmly, the chains of the slave."[25] The notice continued, "[W]e disclaim, in the most positive manner, all connection with the abolitionists, and hold in horror and contempt, their amalgamation doctrine in principle, as degrading, both to the white and colored population."[26] The notice concluded with a plea to abolitionists to "cease their misguided efforts here and leave us as they found us, to work out our own salvation." Hill and thirty-five members of the Cincinnati Union Society purportedly submitted the notice.[27]

However, the next day, the same thirty-five members issued a disclaimer insisting that Hill had used their names without their consent.[28] Perhaps Hill believed he had acted in the best interest of the community by consciously trying to make certain that his organization suffered no financial reprisals for associating with the despised and accursed abolitionists. And perhaps Hill even believed that such a notice would curb the mob violence directed at the black community. Regardless, Hill proved that his philosophy diverged so sharply from that of his constituents that it made him unfit for leadership: the membership of the Cincinnati Union Society removed him from office.[29] Union Society members were unwilling to forsake their allies who had risked so much on the behalf of African Americans. Nor were they willing to be conciliatory in order to gain the approval of powerful whites.

M. M. Clarke was also censured for trying to disassociate his organization from the abolitionists. Clarke disavowed the School Fund's association with abolitionists in a Columbus newspaper in 1839. In his capacity as agent of the School Fund Institute, Clarke was charged with raising money for black schools in the state. Because whites provided funds to support these schools, Clarke probably reasoned that it was best to reduce the risk of offending these potential benefactors. Like Hill, he was also reproached by Cincinnati's black community. The community issued a public notice charging Clarke with having "manifested a spirit of servility, unworthy the representative of a high-minded community of growing intelligence."[30] Judging by its response to Hill and Clarke, black Cincinnati no longer tolerated leaders of their stripe. This condemnation also reflects black Cincinnatians' rejection of riding on the backs of white patrons, because of the implicit dependence. However, this community still accepted assistance from those who respected them as equals.

Cincinnati's African Americans also had other assistance, in addition to that of journalist abolitionists like Birney, in attacking the disabling Black Laws. Without the elective franchise, petitioning had been the only means for African Americans to participate in the body politic. Yet Ohio's African Americans had rarely petitioned the Legislature before 1830. As they became educated and developed stronger, more stable communities throughout the state, African Americans began petitioning and memorializing. They realized that collective voices were more powerful than a solitary one. Consequently, between 1836 and 1841, the Ohio General Assembly was inundated with petitions and memorials by blacks and their allies throughout the state praying for the repeal of disabling laws.[31]

African Americans and their allies used memorializing and petitioning broadly—and not just for Ohio issues. They protested the annexation of Texas, the admission of slave states into the union, and the slave trade in the District of Columbia. Along with white citizens, African Americans flooded the legislature with memorials and petitions praying for the right to trial by jury for all residents, the right for blacks to testify in court against whites, and the right to a public education.[32] All efforts were futile; for the time being, the odious laws remained.

Locally, abolitionist attorneys also used their expertise to tear down the walls of legal repression in Ohio. Among them, none ranked higher in skill and importance than Salmon Portland Chase. In 1830, twenty-two-year-old Chase left Washington, D.C., headed for Cincinnati to begin his legal career. He settled into what had been a struggling practice, got married, and involved himself in a number of reform efforts. None of Chase's early reform efforts included helping to improve the condition of African Americans. In fact, Chase's racism led him to believe African Americans were inferior; he doubted the two races could ever live together peaceably. He, like many of the men of property and standing with whom he associated in Cincinnati, supported colonization as a solution to what they perceived to be the impassable race problem.[33] Nothing in Chase's professional or personal life foretold what he would become to the abolitionist community in Cincinnati.

Salmon Chase remained removed from the abolitionist movement in the city until 1836. Then the 1836 mob action against the *Philanthropist* pulled Chase into abolitionism rather suddenly and completely. During the mob action, Chase had bravely thrown himself in front of the angry mob and refused to allow them to enter an establishment to search for James Birney. That was, perhaps, a moment of epiphany for the young Chase, because from that moment forward, he was a decided abolitionist. Chase agreed to act as counsel for Birney and Achilles Pugh in suits against members of the mob for damages.[34] In 1837, Chase again came to the aid of James Birney, who had been charged with harboring a fugitive slave named Matilda. Matilda had been a slave in transit through Ohio with her owner when she decided to escape. She sought and obtained employment in the Birney home, where she was eventually detected. In Birney's defense, Chase argued that Matilda was a slave in transit who was knowingly brought into a free state by her owner. That, Chase declared, subjected Matilda to the laws of freedom in Ohio, where slavery was illegal, thereby proving Birney was not guilty of harboring a fugitive slave.[35] Chase was so committed to this line of work that he earned the nickname "Attorney General for Fugitive Slaves."[36]

Cincinnati's black community needed someone with Chase's legal expertise and abolitionist principles. He often represented them in freedom suits for a nominal fee or pro bono. The African American community routinely sought his counsel when slave catchers came to reclaim fugitive slaves. In a tribute to Chase at the African Union Baptist Church in May 1845, the black community of Cincinnati presented him with a silver pitcher as a token of its appreciation.[37] Another abolitionist attorney, John Jolliffe, joined Chase in this work in Cincinnati.

With such powerful allies, African Americans gradually developed political self-confidence. By the 1830s, the black community no longer tolerated the 1820s strategy of securing the *patronage* of powerful whites; in fact, this community had moved away from seeking the approval of powerful whites and was acting in its own interest. Those patrons, after all, had betrayed the black community by winking at the mob actions of 1829 and 1836. Instead, Black Cincinnati was moving toward building *alliances* with those who shared its commitment to ending slavery and racial discrimination.

Such alliances enabled this African American community to raise a stronger street voice of protest. In March 1839, the black community met at the New Chapel (formerly Deer Creek Methodist Episcopal) to protest white efforts to revive the Ohio chapter of the American Colonization Society. Black Cincinnati raised its voice in "unmitigated and unqualified opposition" to this organization. A resolution adopted at this meeting and published in the March 5, 1839, issue of the *Philanthropist,* charged the ACS with being "unjust," "unchristian," "anti-republican" and "unworthy [of] the patronage of Christian and republican people."[38] The contempt for this organization stemmed from African Americans' belief that colonization was antithetical to racial uplift. The notice charged that the ACS not only "fosters and sustains that prejudice, which they now declare to be invincible, by stigmatizing us as a worthless and inferior race" but "apologizes for the sin of slavery, and thereby so far as its influence operates, tends to the perpetuity of that accursed system."[39] This community concluded that, as free people, they would not "consent to become an instrument of slaveholders, and their co-adjutor [*sic*], the American Colonization Society, to fasten more permanently upon the necks of our brethren, the galling yoke of bondage."[40]

This proclamation echoes the words, if not the sentiment, of free black communities twenty years earlier. Black communities in Philadelphia and Boston had taken a similar public stand in 1817.[41] Black Cincinnati publicly opposed the ACS significantly later than these other communities because of the threat of mob violence and the enforcement of the Black Laws—both of which had made them afraid to do so earlier. Given such considerations, this 1839 notice is an even more important way to underscore the development of collective self-respect within this community. The same threat of violence that existed in 1839 had been there in 1829. The difference was that a community that had been terrorized and tentative ten years earlier now had more courage and political self-respect to condemn the ACS openly. This change is rooted in the developments of the 1830s: national alliances with other free black communities and the wide range of abolitionist support locally enabled black Cincinnati to challenge racism from a position of relative strength.

SIX

Standing Their Ground

A Community's Maturation, 1841–1861

> [T]o maintain in the future our liberties when won, we
> must learn to use arms; we must be a fighting people. Pre-
> sent to the world the picture of manhood; show yourselves
> lionhearted, be not afraid to die.
>
> —*Colored Citizen*, November 7, 1863

IN LATE AUGUST of 1841, Cincinnati's black community endured its third major mob attack in just twelve years. In a city where mob
violence was ingrained into the political, social, and economic culture, it
had become all too familiar. But this time, a number of African Americans refused to flee the city, as some had in 1829; some of them stood
their ground, armed themselves, and struck back in a united show of
self-defense. This act of self-defense was a watershed moment for the
black community. In that moment, African Americans chose to overcome decades of intimidation to defend their homes and families. This
decision to stand and fight signals that the black community had begun
to shed its sense of vulnerability and alienation and step beyond the veil
of fear. It also proves that this community had come to possess enough
confidence to lay claim to Cincinnati as home.

In the decades following this stand, black Cincinnati emerged as a far
more confident and vocal community. It asserted its permanence in the
city through a wave of institution-building that included a high school,
two newspapers, several mutual aid and benefit societies, Masonic lodges,
an orphanage, vigilance societies, and more churches. Not only did black
Cincinnati's institutional base broaden, but these new institutions served

a greater range of needs, suggesting that black Cincinnati had developed an articulation of what freedom was, understood how it had eluded them, and developed at least a provisional blueprint to obtain it.

In 1840, the birth of a certain newspaper exploited the resentment and hostility that had been building toward the black and abolitionist communities in Cincinnati. The *Enquirer*—a conservative, antiblack, antiabolitionist journal that followed the Democratic Party line—emerged then as the premiere instigator of hostility against these communities. The *Enquirer* manipulated existing seeds of antipathy, planted new ones, and articulated the resentment against the black community in pure and simple terms.

After nearly a decade of abolitionism in the city, tensions were already high. The 1841 *State v. Farr* decision, which automatically freed slaves who entered the state with their owner's consent, made matters worse. Abolitionists and Underground Railroad workers took full advantage of this decision by actively informing slaves in transit of the law, thus freeing dozens of slaves. The *Enquirer* editorialized that "a citizen of the slave States could not come to Cincinnati to trade—to spend the warm months, or pass the night in the course in traveling [*sic*], without having his negro servants decoyed or stolen away."[1] Cincinnati merchants, businessmen, and manufacturers had reason to be upset when southern slaveholders threatened to protest the decision through a boycott of Ohio goods.[2]

As a nationwide depression sent urban economies into a slump, the *Enquirer's* editors, John and Charles Brough, went as far as to blame the decline in Cincinnati's economy on abolitionist activity. They charged that abolitionism was the reason "Southrons [*sic*] . . . went elsewhere and threw the profits of their trade and travel to the hands of other communities." The editors claimed that "many a manufacture and many a laborer found practical evidence of its [abolitionism's] effects in diminished profits and decaying business."[3] The Broughs did not look beyond Cincinnati as a source for the city's economic problems. Rather than focusing on the real sources for the national depression—the collapse of the banking system, the credit system, speculation—the editors personalized the issues and found local scapegoats to convince the Cincinnati public that abolitionists had devastated the relations with the South and destroyed the city's economy.

Throughout the summer months of 1841, the *Enquirer's* editors used their propaganda machine to demonize African Americans, as well. Linking race and labor shortages, the editors complained that blacks were "constantly coming and squatting among us—crowding out white labor, when they worked at all, but more frequently living by plunder upon it."[4] The labor issue touched a nerve for those hardest hit by the economic slump and labor competition with blacks that summer. The paper also reported instances when African Americans broke racial codes of the day, which dictated that they should behave submissively in public. The editors charged that "[t]hese characterless vagabonds grew more impudent in impunity when they found themselves sustained by a faction of white fanatics, who lent them countenance."[5] Although some African Americans may have exhibited increasing confidence in their interactions with whites since the mid-1830s, the *Enquirer* portrayed this confidence as insolence. These charges were compounded by numerous rumors of African Americans attacking innocent white women, knifing hardworking German immigrants, and beating Irish lads. In light of these allegations of black aggression and defiance of the racial order, the *Enquirer* demanded strict enforcement of the Black Laws.[6]

Such scathing editorials, among other things, added to the mass of antiabolitionist and antiblack elements. The regular coalition of slaveholders, merchants, businessmen, and unskilled laborers was joined by an immigrant Irish population that exhibited antiabolitionist and antiblack feelings for different reasons. Although 1841 was yet early in the stream of Irish immigration, Irish and black workers had already begun to compete with each other for unskilled positions in a tough economy. Irish workers' grievances against abolitionists and blacks were rooted mostly in labor issues. For them, abolitionism shrank a job market that was already quite small because of African American laborers.

This hostility came to a head in the summer of 1841, after a confluence of events made the situation ripe for trouble. The scarcity of available jobs, decreasing profits for the city's manufacturers and businesses, the *State v. Farr* dictum, and the insecurities of lower-class whites and Irish immigrants about race and status in a changing labor market led to a series of racial clashes that summer.

On Tuesday, August 31, 1841, a fistfight ensued between Irish and black workers near Sixth and Broadway streets. Several of the Irish were severely beaten and decided to exact retribution from those who had bested them. The following day, a group of rowdy men, seeking to renew the conflict, armed themselves and walked over to the Dumas House, a black boarding house on MacAllister Street, and demanded that a man who had gone inside be handed over to them. When the residents refused, the group of instigators began attacking the boarding house and making threats to those within and to their neighbors in adjoining houses.[7] The black residents repulsed the attempted entry. Rumors of black resistance flowed through the city and across the river into neighboring Kentucky counties. By Thursday, bands of whites were roaming the city attacking innocent African Americans. According to one eyewitness, African Americans "were assaulted wherever found in the streets, and with such weapons and violence as to cause death."[8] In one instance, some African Americans decided to fight back and nearly stabbed their attackers to death. That act of self-defense further incensed antiblack elements. Facts were twisted into rumors that African Americans had been the aggressors. Officials ignored the unrest, but African Americans could read the signs of an impending mob attack quite well. Rumors, threats, and indiscriminate racial violence all foretold of what was soon to come.[9] Cincinnati's black citizens knew that in order to survive this attack, they would have to organize themselves in their own defense.

The only inside account of what the black community was thinking and feeling in those moments was recorded by John Mercer Langston, who was only eleven years old at the time. John Langston was born to Lucy Langston, a freed slave, and Ralph Quarles, the son of a wealthy white planter in Virginia in 1829. After his parents' deaths, the four-year-old John was sent to Chillicothe, Ohio, where he was raised by his father's friends.[10] In 1840, they sent Langston to Cincinnati to attend a school kept by Mr. Goodwin and Mr. Denham in the basement of the Baker Street Baptist Church. While he attended school, Langston lived with some of Cincinnati's most prominent black families. In 1841, the eleven-year-old John was living with a successful black barber, John Woodson, at Sixth and Broadway streets.[11] From the Woodsons' home, Langston had a perfect geographic and social vantage point from which to watch events unfold at the end of August 1841.

According to Langston, Major James Wilkerson organized the self-defense effort among African Americans at Sixth and Broadway.[12] Wilkerson had been born into slavery in 1813 in Virginia and was of mixed black, Native American, and white racial heritage. He had purchased his own freedom before migrating to Cincinnati, where he became an elder in the AME Church.[13] Langston described Wilkerson as a "champion of his people's cause" who was motivated by his desire to "maintain his own rights as well as those of the people whom he led." Although he was just twenty-eight years of age at the time of the violence, people had "full confidence in his ability, sincerity, courage, and devotion and were ready to follow him even to death." In preparation for self-defense, Wilkerson first made sure the women and children were forwarded to safety. He then organized the men into small groups, distributed arms, and assigned posts throughout the neighborhood.[14] On Friday, September 3, fifty armed black men waited on rooftops, in alleys, and behind buildings for their attackers to descend on their neighborhood.[15]

At the same time, there were preparations of a different sort at the Fifth Street Market. At about eight o'clock that same evening, a mob assembled. It was composed of Kentuckians, other "strangers . . . connected with the river navigation," and "boat hands of the lowest and most violent order," probably joined by elements of the Irish community.[16] Armed with clubs, sticks, and stones, the mob proceeded toward Sixth and Broadway, attracting recruits as it went. The mob moved toward the First Ward because 43 percent of the city's 2,240 African Americans lived there and many black institutions were located there.[17] By the time the mob arrived in the black neighborhood, eyewitnesses reported that it numbered seven or eight hundred people.[18] As the mob moved in, Wilkerson's men, garrisoned at different points in the neighborhood, fired into the crowd. The mob dispersed several times, regrouped, and advanced again. Several casualties later, the rioters retrieved an "iron sixpounder from near the river, loaded [it] with broiler punchings, &c. and hauled" it to the black neighborhood at Sixth and Broadway.[19] The mob discharged the cannon several times into black homes and other buildings as officials stood by. Despite the cannon fire, these African American men held their ground through most of the night. This band of warriors fought on, mortally wounding several of their assailants. Langston claimed that many of the white attackers were "carried directly from the fight to the grave."[20] But as the night grew old, the defenders could no longer sustain an effort against cannon fire and a mob of seven or eight hundred lawless whites.

African Americans probably expected that the militia's arrival at 2:00 AM would offer a reprieve from the attacks. Instead, the militia declared martial law against their community, treating the victims as villains.[21] The militia cordoned off several blocks of the black neighborhood at Sixth and Broadway streets and held those within captive. African Americans from other parts of the city were rounded up, marched to the restricted area in the First Ward, and detained until they paid bond.[22]

On Saturday morning, black leaders held an emergency community meeting at Bethel AME Church to discuss the recent events. Bethel AME minister Henry Adcrissan and educator Owen T. B. Nickens presided over this meeting and published the proceedings in the *Cincinnati Daily*

Chronicle.[23] Probably fearing that adverse public opinion might result in the expulsion of blacks from the city, this body decided that the wisest course was conciliatory compliance. They vowed to "strive in [the] future, as many of us have in the past, to conduct ourselves as [an] orderly, industrious, and peaceable people."[24] In order to reassure whites of its willingness to maintain law and order, the assembly expressed its disapproval of those who in a "peaceable community" carried "dirks, pistols, and other dangerous and deadly weapons." They volunteered to surrender all weapons in order to keep the peace. The group further vowed to comply with the Black Laws and "suppress any imprudent conduct among our population, and ferret out all violators of order and law,"[25] thereby trying to distinguish themselves—the "peaceable," respectable African Americans who had posted bond—from those who had defended themselves. The black elite rejected armed self-defense in favor of compliance with "order and law." Conciliatory compliance is reminiscent of Deer Creek Methodist Episcopal Church's strategy in 1829. That church had attempted to distance itself from the more radical elements of the black community that had demanded a repeal of the Black Laws. Like the Deer Creek congregation, this assembly at Bethel believed that compliance with the laws was the surest way to stay the violence. Also reminiscent of the 1829 strategy, African Americans at this Bethel meeting appealed to whites for protection from violence. Specifically, they sought the protection of the municipal authorities—the mayor, the city watch, and police officers.[26] Although a segment of the community did temporarily revert to the old strategies of compliance and intragroup distinction, this response should not overshadow the more militant, defensive efforts that arose in some parts of the community.

At approximately the same time as the Bethel meeting, Mayor Samuel Davies called a citizens' meeting at the courthouse to address the disturbance. The mayor, the sheriff, the township trustees, other city officials, and gentlemen of standing adopted ten resolutions—many of which were decidedly antiblack and antiabolitionist. The group placed the blame for the mob violence on the black community and adopted resolutions accordingly. First, the assembly resolved to enforce the law strictly and to suppress all violence. The citizens' meeting offered a harsh condemnation of abolitionists but also vowed not to tolerate mob violence—not even against them. Another resolution called for civil authorities to proceed immediately to the homes of African Americans, disarm them, and conduct "a vigorous search" for black offenders. In order to drive out undesirable elements of the black community, the authorities promised to enforce the 1807 Black Law and uphold the Fugitive Slave Act of 1793. Lastly, a "strong and sufficient patrol" was promised to protect African Americans and their property until they either gave bond or left the city.[27] These resolutions not only treated African Americans—and, to a lesser extent, abolitionists—as though they were the ones who had formed a mob and terrorized the city, but they also left them defenseless in a city where they were the hunted. The resolutions passed at the citizens' meeting suggest that the self-defense efforts among the black community were perceived as tantamount to insurgency.

To carry out the resolutions passed at the citizens' meeting, the militia and "swarms of improvised police officers"—some of whom may have been mob participants—were empowered to scour the city and arrest every black man they saw. John Mercer Langston reported that some black men hid to avoid arrest. Some hid in the chimneys of their homes while others stayed with their businesses. Langston's older brother Gideon, for example, closed his barber shop, fortified the doors and windows, and remained inside with five of his employees for more than fifteen hours.[28] Others simply fled to Walnut Hills above the city.[29] Approximately three hundred African American men were rounded up and marched off to jail. A mob followed the procession to the jail, hurling insults and threats at the captives.[30] The threats against the black prisoners were so great that the militia was forced to guard the jail. Some black men were charged with disturbing the peace, others were held until it could be determined whether they were fugitive slaves or until they gave bond. According to newspaper reports, Kentuckians had the freedom to visit the jail in search of runaway slaves.[31]

After the principal targets were in jail, the mob redirected its violence toward abolitionists on Saturday night. In what had become a mob ritual in Cincinnati, rioters broke into the office of the *Philanthropist* at Main and Walnut streets, removed the type and presses, broke them up, and, "in malignant Satanic triumph," threw them into the Ohio River.[32] Next, the mob leveled a confectionery and bakery shop on Fifth Street near Vine. An abolitionist bookstore on Main Street was also destroyed. After venting its fury there, the mob destroyed and looted several black homes throughout the city, and there were allegations that several black women were raped.[33] The militia and police seemed unable or unwilling to suppress the violence or to arrest rioters throughout the night. Early Sunday morning, after the arrests of a few rioters and the issuing of a condemnation by Thomas Corwin, the governor of Ohio, the mob finally lost its steam. The participants were probably also deterred by the hundreds of mounted police and militia that Corwin commissioned to ensure no further violence.[34] Despite the reign of the mobocracy for several days, only a dozen white rioters were arrested and tried for their crimes.[35]

The mob was, Langston declared, "the blackest and most detestable" moment in Cincinnati's history.[36] Certainly, African Americans' civil rights were violated in the aftermath. City officials' decision to enter black homes without warrants and seize their weapons of self-defense denied them the right to protect home and family. Declaring martial law in the black neighborhood and scouring the city to arrest every black male was yet another level of government-sponsored repression against African Americans who had committed no crimes. The response of the city officials underscores the way in which even basic rights and protections were denied to African Americans in Cincinnati.

White citizens transcended regional, class, and ethnic differences to unite against a common enemy. Many elements of society were complicit. The press had encouraged rioters to action, the Irish and lower-class white Kentuckians comprised the manpower behind the destruction and terror, and the militia rounded up black defenders. City officials had allowed the violence to go unchecked on Thursday and Friday, ignored black pleas for relief and protection, and ordered the militia to detain black residents. The mob was allowed to assemble and reassemble with impunity, while African Americans were treated like criminals. Cincinnati's ruling elite practically endorsed the mob's actions by passing resolutions that further encroached upon black freedoms.

The Cincinnati mob action of 1841 departs from typical mobs of the time in several critical ways. According to historian David Grimsted, southern mobs usually were directed at specific persons and generally fell into three main categories: punishing criminals, silencing abolitionists, and crushing slave revolts. Southern officials were less likely to suppress the violence or punish rioters. Northern mobs, Grimsted contends, usually were directed at the property—not the persons—of abolitionists and those who harbored fugitive slaves and were more likely to be suppressed by authorities.[37] The 1841 Cincinnati mob action was not strictly an antiabolitionist mob. Abolitionists were not the principal targets and were not singled out until the last day of violence—and then it was because a significant portion of the black population was either in hiding or in jail. What began as violence directed at a certain group of African Americans escalated to widespread violence against the entire race, coupled with (but not defined by) attacks on local white abolitionists. This mob action had elements of both northern and southern mobs, underscoring Cincinnati's border-town character. It followed neither the northern pattern of action against property nor the southern pattern of crimes against persons. In fact, the Cincinnati rioters targeted persons *and* property. Although the Cincinnati rioters stopped far short of the sadistic maiming, murder, lynching, or even burning alive that characterized efforts to suppress slave revolts in the South, they went far beyond what was common in the northern tradition in magnitude, virulence, and destruction. As in southern towns, city officials and the larger Cincinnati community allowed the mob to go unchecked in its initial phase. The editor of the *Cincinnati Daily Gazette* wrote that he believed "a determined corps of fifty or one hundred men would have dispersed the crowd."[38] Law and order gave way to a mobocracy in which the rioters respected neither power (leading attorney Jacob Wykoff Piatt's pleas for order were answered with yelling and stone-pelting) nor position (the mayor's call to order was met with yells of "Down with him!" and "Run him off!").[39] Although this mob action borrowed some elements from the northern tradition, it was largely a southern adaptation brought north.

The Cincinnati mob action of 1841 reached a new frontier in American history: race war. Never before had a racial contest of this magnitude happened between free people inside one of America's cities. The Cincinnati race war of 1841 happened in Cincinnati because it could—the conditions were ripe there. The mob action of 1841 has to be viewed against the backdrop of a long tradition of antiblack violence in the city, in which all manner of violence against African Americans—including forced exodus, the burning of black homes, personal violence, and murder—was legally and extralegally sanctioned.

Those who opted for self-defense chose a risky path, given the mob mentality that governed the city. These men chose to stand their ground and assert their manhood in an era when black men were denied the ability to provide for and protect their families. But they did more than merely defend their own homes and families that day; they also defended their community—the lives and property of their neighbors and the institutions within.[40] By challenging the infantilized, emasculated images of black men that colored the public imagination, these defenders proclaimed with resounding authority that they were indeed, *men*. Last, being the heroic defenders of family and community was an opportunity black men rarely had in nineteenth-century America, thereby making the act itself a version of freedom. Armed resistance was itself a manly act that expressed traits associated with masculinity, like bravery and strength.

Through their actions, these defenders sent a message to white Cincinnati society. The message was that there would be dire consequences for anyone who came into their communities wishing to do harm. These black men let Cincinnati know that theirs was not a community unprotected. It had protectors—armed with dirks, pistols, and muskets. Rather than live with the indignities of mob terrorism and the culture of victimization it created, African Americans chose to resist. Although this was not the first time black Cincinnatians had defended themselves with gunfire—individuals had done so in 1829—this was the first time self-defense had been organized and with the express aim of protecting the community. The courage that some members of the black community demonstrated in September 1841 was a long time in the making. When African Americans picked up those guns, they were defending more than their physical selves and their property; they were defending their spirits, freedom, and collective dignity. They fought for their community's survival, and for the right to claim Cincinnati as home. When the smoke cleared, this community firmly planted its feet in the Cincinnati soil.

In such a repressive and violent climate, Cincinnati's African American community could plant seeds of permanence and maturity only after it overcame its fear of that violence. The surge of institution-building in the years following the 1841 race-war is one indication of the maturation of this community. The number of black institutions and aid societies established in the post-1841 era was unparalleled. Some of the organizations gave African Americans a temporary retreat from the hostile climate in Cincinnati and the chance to fellowship with one another. Others reflected the desire for self-sufficiency: to provide for the community's sick, orphaned, and widowed. Schools and newspapers encouraged literacy and prepared black Cincinnatians for the advantages of citizenship. But the maturation of this community did not mean that social conditions had improved. In many ways, the path to economic freedom, citizenship, and social equality had contracted, making self-sufficiency even more important.

African Americans still could not apply for assistance from the Poor Fund, or be admitted to shelters, hospitals, or orphanages in the 1840s. John Malvin's observation in the late 1820s—"I found every door closed against the colored man in a free State, excepting jails and penitentiaries, the doors of which were thrown wide open to receive him"[41]—was still true twenty years later. African Americans were treated even worse than the immigrants who flooded the city that decade; for the immigrants, at least, had access to schools, hospitals, and orphanages. Rather than pressing the city government and state legislature for access to these institutions, the African American community drew inward and committed itself to providing its population with the services it needed. Mutual aid societies and benefit societies were central to this goal. Some of these societies purchased cemeteries where blacks could be buried with dignity; others paid the funeral expenses of members or provided death benefits to the member's family; and most of these associations provided financial assistance to sick or injured members. Finally, mutual aid societies were also social organizations, offering the opportunity for members to fellowship among themselves.

Cincinnati's black community established several of these organizations after 1841, including the United Colored Association (1844), the Sons of Enterprise (1851), and the Sons of Liberty (1852).[42] The Sons of Enterprise was formed for the purpose of "enhancing each other's interest, in rendering mutual aid and assistance." More specifically, the organization encouraged "the purchase of Real Estate, the erection of Public Halls, etc." and "industry, temperance and virtue among its members."[43] The Sons of Liberty probably linked property ownership to economic freedom and focused on economic development of its members by espousing hard work and good living. According to the organization's doctrine, these practices benefited the individual and uplifted the community.

Although there are no extant records from the other mutual aid societies in Cincinnati, they may have resembled the Union Association of the Colored Men of New Richmond, Ohio, a mutual aid and burial society located in a village outside of Cincinnati. The Union Association paid $1.50 per week in sick benefits to those members who were current in their dues. If the treasury were ever exhausted, members were expected to give additional monies to assist members in need.[44] This association, like many others, essentially acted like an insurance company. Because black Cincinnatians lacked access to public funds, such organizations were essential to the sustenance of black families. A couple of Black Cincinnati's mutual aid organizations aimed to raise money for churches.

Black women also formed their own mutual aid and benefit societies in this period. Their organizations included the Female American Association (1848), the Daughters of Union (1850), the Mount Moriah Lodge of the Daughters of Samaria (1853), the Dorcas Relief Society (1866), the United Sisters (1868), and the Independent Daughters of Hope (1873). The objective of the Daughters of Samaria was "to promote the cause of temperance and benevolence."[45] The city even boasted a Juvenile Daughters of Samaria organized for young girls between eight and sixteen years of age.[46] Such societies "spoke to the idea that women, while not abandoning their roles as wives and mothers, could also move into economic and political activities in ways that would support rather than conflict with family and community."[47] Mutual aid and benefit societies allowed black middle-class women to extend concerns of the family and home to the entire community.[48]

In 1844, Cincinnati's black elite, in collaboration with Lydia Mott and the Ladies' Benevolent Association founded the Colored Orphan Asylum "to provide an Asylum for the protection, care, and education of destitute orphan children of color."[49] Located in a house on Ninth Street, the institution accepted children whose parents were deceased, as well as those whose parents "orphaned" them because of their inability to provide for them.[50] The Colored Orphan Asylum was completely funded by philanthropy. The asylum raised money through members' subscriptions, donations from local businesses and churches, and festivals and bazaars.[51] Black youth at a local high school held benefit concerts to raise money for the orphanage, and the Ladies' Benevolent Association and the Young Ladies' Orphan Aid Society also helped by raising subscriptions, donating goods, and making clothes for the children.[52]

One of the main objectives of the Colored Orphan Asylum was to provide education for the youth and to equip them with the tools they needed to escape the lots cast for them. But because of financial strains, the managers of the Colored Orphan Asylum were unable to focus on education for the children until the mid-1850s.[53] Then the managers were forced to choose between a school and basic necessities for their wards. Consequently, the school at the orphanage failed "for the plain reason that food and clothing, absolute necessities, were with difficulty provided."[54]

Masonic lodges and fraternal orders also enabled the black community to become relatively self-sufficient. Functioning like mutual aid societies, Masonic lodges provided aid to their sick and disabled members and to deceased members' widows. In some cases the lodges also assisted with burial costs. Although they served functions similar to those of mutual aid societies, Masonic lodges are distinguished by their formal structure and secret ritual. Men were invited into membership and sworn to secrecy.

Black Masons had a rich tradition in America that began with Prince Hall and fourteen other black Bostonians in 1775. These fifteen men were initiated into Freemasonry by Irish Masons during the American Revolution. After futile attempts to gain a charter from the American order, Prince Hall and his cohorts were finally granted one by the British order on January 4, 1787. Hall was ordained provincial grand master of the First Independent African Grand Lodge of North America.[55] Commonly denied recognition by their local white counterparts, black Masonic lodges that wished to receive charters had to apply to the First Independent African Grand Lodge of North America in Boston. In 1797, Philadelphia's black community asked Hall to officiate the proceedings of their new lodge, the African Lodge of Pennsylvania. Between 1810 and 1814, three additional lodges were formed in Philadelphia.[56]

Although the Masonic Order grew increasingly popular among black men in eastern cities, more than thirty years passed before a black lodge was organized in Cincinnati. Because black Cincinnati was a younger community, its institutional development generally occurred much later than that of eastern cities. In any case, in 1847 black Freemasons in Cincinnati applied for admission to a white lodge.[57] Determined to never accept black Freemasons as their brothers, the white Columbia Masonic Lodge resolved that "it would be inexpedient and tend to mar the present harmony of the fraternity to admit any persons of color . . . into the fraternity."[58] According to historian William Hartwell Parham, Cincinnati's earliest black Freemasons had to travel to Pittsburgh to be initiated in St. Cyprian Lodge, a black lodge. They returned to Cincinnati and influenced others to join the organization. On March 3, 1847, William Darnes, John Johnson, and Joseph C. King traveled from Cincinnati to Pittsburgh for the initiation of Shelton Morris, George Peterson, Ashbury Young, and Lovell C. Flewellen. Upon their return to Cincinnati, the seven brothers petitioned St. Cyprian Lodge for a recommendation to be received into the First Independent African Grand Lodge of North America. They were so recommended on April 11, 1847, and the Corinthian Lodge was opened in January 1848.[59]

A group of black Freemasons who had received their Masonic degrees in eastern cities organized a second Cincinnati lodge, the True American Lodge, on March 18, 1848. The True American Lodge was not affiliated with the First Independent African Grand Lodge of North America, but with its rival, the Hiram Grand Lodge of Pennsylvania. The men who belonged to these two local lodges perpetuated a feud between their respective grand lodges. According to Parham, the two Cincinnati lodges "neither knelt at the same altars nor offered incense in the same temples," so great was their enmity toward one another.[60] A third Cincinnati lodge, St. John's, was established on May 20 of the same year under the auspices of First Independent African Grand Lodge of North America.

In the interest of opening a grand lodge, Cincinnati's black Freemasons put aside their differences and organized the first black grand lodge in Ohio in May 1849.[61]

In antebellum Cincinnati, black Freemasonry drew membership from the black elite. They were elite not because of their occupations, but because of their assets and standing in the community. A great many of Cincinnati's early black Freemasons made humble livings as common laborers. John Johnson was a whitewasher. George Peterson, Ashbury Young, and Lovell Flewellen were peddlers—although Flewellen also sometimes worked as a laborer. Even the officers of the grand lodge were employed as menial laborers: Preston Spottswood worked on the river, Prince Austin was a whitewasher, Samuel Hopes and Richard Phillips were peddlers, and Griffin T. Watson was a steamboat steward. What set these men apart from other common laborers was their property. Despite his menial and unskilled occupations, Flewellen had accumulated eighteen hundred dollars' worth of real estate by 1850, when he was only twenty-nine years old. George Peterson, a peddler, although unable to read or write, managed to acquire fifteen hundred dollars' worth of property. There were a few professionals among them, such as Owen T. B. Nickens (minister and teacher), William Darnes (barber), and William Easton (baker). William Darnes was born in Pennsylvania around 1809. By 1840, he had moved to Cincinnati, married a woman from Kentucky named Rebecca, and taken up barbering as a profession. Ten years later, Rebecca and William Darnes owned twenty-five hundred dollars in real estate.[62]

The Masonic lodges accepted men with high moral codes, who were also actively engaged in community uplift, and who were imbued with a sense of collective responsibility. Many of them also had leadership positions in other organizations. Owen T. B. Nickens was a minister, teacher, editor, and cofounder of the Moral Reform Society; Prince Austin was among those who established the African Union Baptist Church; William Darnes assisted fugitive slaves to freedom. George Petersen served as a trustee on the boards of the AME Church, the Colored Orphan Asylum, and the black school board in the 1850s. He was also the treasurer for the Colored American Association.[63] Lovell Flewellen served on the black school board in the 1850s.

Membership in the mutual aid societies and fraternal orders was also reserved to those with high moral character. The Union Association of the Colored Men of New Richmond, for example, had strict guidelines regarding respectability for its members. Any member convicted of a crime was expelled; members were also expelled for intoxication, gambling, or being in a house of ill-fame. Implicit in this connection is the idea that these mutual aid societies were willing to assist only those who proved themselves worthy of it.[64] Like the Masonic lodges, these mutual aid and benevolent societies drew their membership from the black middle class and elite. Reflecting bourgeois values and a Protestant work ethic and mores, this class of African Americans had practical concerns of their families' well-being in addition to idealist notions of racial uplift. It would have been difficult, if not impossible, to transfer these values to the black lower class, which, for pragmatic reasons, might choose survival by any means over Christian morality. For example, it would have been difficult to convince a single mother and prostitute to quit her occupation "for the good of the race." This class divide became even more complicated after the Civil War, when Cincinnati's black population was suddenly enlarged by a stream of freed slaves from the South, who arrived largely uneducated and unchurched. In fact, with the exception of the Colored Orphan Asylum and the by then defunct Cincinnati Education Society, there is no evidence that these organizations actually extended their arms to help the poorest of the poor.

Black Cincinnati's mutual aid societies, fraternal orders, and even the Colored Orphan Asylum were essentially racial uplift organizations. Mutuality lent itself to racial uplift because it was a striving for black self-sufficiency: the Union Association of the Colored Men of New Richmond, Ohio, indicated that it was "desirous of employing all the means in our power for the elevation of ourselves and community and race."[65] Within these organizations, African Americans assumed the responsibility of providing for their sick, orphaned, and widowed people, and essentially became less dependent on benevolent others to do it for them.

Also critical in the institutional life of this community was the black press. In 1844, black schoolteachers Owen T. B. Nickens and A.M. Sumner started publication of the *Disfranchised American*. The *Disfranchised American* was only the third black-run newspaper west of the Allegheny Mountains; only Pittsburgh's *Mystery* and Columbus's *Palladium of Liberty* preceded it. In 1863, barber William H. Yancy and the Reverend Thomas Woodson established another Cincinnati weekly, the *Colored Citizen*.[66] The mission statement of the *Colored Citizen*, dated November 7, 1863, read, "Feeling the stern necessity of a medium through which to speak, hear and be heard, to defend the right and denounce wrong, touching our interest more especially in this city, where colored citizens are shamefully wronged, we assume the responsibility of publishing the *Citizen*."[67]

By 1866, the *Colored Citizen* was being marketed as a regional paper for blacks in western cities, including Cincinnati, Louisville, Chicago, Columbus, and Indianapolis. Although there is only minimal evidence about the extent to which the journal *did* become a regional paper in terms of subscriptions, it did include communications from these and other western cities. The *Colored Citizen* primarily reported news and events within the local black community, but also carried mainstream national news related to the Civil War or politics, indicating that the community was looking outward to a world beyond Cincinnati.[68]

Both newspapers were short lived. Plagued by "limited subscriptions [and] unstable financing," black newspapers like the *Disfranchised American* and the *Colored Citizen* could not survive.[69] Only a few issues of the *Disfranchised American* were published; from what can be ascertained from contemporary sources, the *Colored Citizen* lasted at least three years before its demise. Although African Americans were making gains in literacy, the number of literate adults who could also afford the regular subscription—two dollars per year or five cents per issue—was probably still rather small.[70] Perhaps this is why editors of the *Colored Citizen* had broadened its target market to include other western cities.

In many ways, the names of the newspapers reflected the political and emotional tenor of black Cincinnati. The *Disfranchised American* was established on the heels of the 1841 antiblack mob after a decade filled with racial violence, legislative assaults, and a contracting path to citizenship. African Americans probably doubted that they would ever gain citizenship rights in the Queen City. But by the time the *Colored Citizen* was established two decades later, black "citizens" were more optimistic.

—

The black community also underwent an economic maturation after 1841, and class differentiations slowly evolved. By the early 1840s, there were enough successful black families to constitute an "aristocratic," or elite class in Cincinnati.[71] Many of those who belonged to this class had gained their wealth as entrepreneurs. Among the most notable of them was Robert Gordon, a former slave from Virginia who opened a very lucrative coal business in the 1830s. By 1847, his business was worth fifteen thousand dollars.[72] Samuel Wilcox, a merchant, also owned real estate valued at some twenty thousand dollars.[73]

A number of African Americans also earned their wealth through real estate development. In 1838, a group of black men established a successful real estate firm, the Iron Chest Company. Members of the Iron Chest

Company invested one dollar per week for the construction of buildings. The company's most noted accomplishment was the construction of three brick buildings that were then leased to whites. By 1840, the company owned nine thousand dollars' worth of property. Another unidentified African American owned seven houses in Cincinnati and four hundred acres of land in Indiana, and had a net worth of between twelve and fifteen thousand dollars in 1840.[74]

Some members of the black elite were part of a small but growing group of artists. James Ball earned a national reputation as a daguerreotype artist in the 1850s. Born and raised in Cincinnati, Ball had worked on a steamboat before going to Virginia to be a daguerreotype apprentice under John Bailey, a black man, in 1845. Upon his return to Cincinnati in 1849, Ball opened two daguerreotype galleries. Although the location of the first gallery is unknown, his second gallery was located on Fourth Street between Main and Walnut streets.[75] Ball's images reflected his respect for traditional African culture and life and his strong racial consciousness.[76] The success of his galleries and his career as a daguerreotypist granted Ball a degree of status within the black community. At the time, black daguerreotypists were still very rare. In 1860, for example, there were only six black men employed as daguerreotypists in Cincinnati.[77]

Although these entrepreneurs and artists were growing in number, it was barbers who swelled the ranks of Cincinnati's black elite. In many free black communities, artisans stood at the top of the occupational and social ladder. In Cincinnati, where access to the skilled crafts and trades was restricted, barbering filled the role that skilled labor did in other cities; it was the clearest path to upward mobility for black men. A semi-skilled service profession, barbering for prominent white clients was a very lucrative occupation in Cincinnati before the Civil War. In fact, many of Cincinnati's wealthiest African Americans were barbers. One of the most successful of these was William Watson, who had migrated to Cincinnati after being manumitted from slavery in Virginia in the early 1830s. Despite Watson's "limited education," John Mercer Langston observed that he had "vigorous mental parts," which enabled him to build a very lucrative business.[78] Watson established a barber and bathing house on the corner of Third and Walnut streets.[79] He was, by some accounts, "the leading colored barber" in Cincinnati; he was "possessed of considerable means, and conduct[ed] a profitable and prosperous business." By 1841, he owned two brick homes, several lots, and more than 560 acres of land in Mercer County. John Mercer Langston, who briefly resided with Watson, his wife Ellen, and their two children, wrote that the Watson home on Green Street between Race and Elm was "well furnished [with] pleasant rooms and parlors."[80] By 1850, the barber owned $5,500 worth of real estate. There are few such rich biographical portraits of other barbers, but the wealthiest of all was William Pilsoul, originally from South Carolina, who owned $10,000 worth of real estate in 1850. In that year, barbers were one of the wealthiest groups of black workers in Cincinnati; the combined real estate of the twenty-one barbers who owned property was $50,500.[81]

Barbering opened the door to social standing and upward mobility for African American men. Barbers were among the most prominent and influential members of Cincinnati's African American community, in which many of them also held leadership positions. William Watson, for example, was a prominent and wealthy member of the Baker Street Baptist Church, where he was a Sunday school teacher and superintendent.[82] William D. Goff and John Liverpool, both of whom represented the community at state conventions of colored men, were also barbers.[83] Cincinnati barbers were more likely than other black workers to own property and to send their children to school in 1850 and 1860. In the First Ward, which had one of the largest populations of black barbers in 1850, 83 percent of barbers' school-aged children attended school and were actually among the most educated of Cincinnati's black children.[84]

Barbering was an extremely attractive option for black men in Cincinnati. It had the fastest rate of occupational growth among all occupations between 1836 and 1850. In those years, the number of black men employed in the position increased nearly sevenfold—from 20 to 136.[85] So popular was barbering among black men that in 1850, it was the leading occupation for that entire population.[86] Because barbering was considered a black man's occupation, it was one of a few fields in which they did not have to compete with immigrant white labor. African American men had a niche in the city's economy and could set their own prices. Unlike other semiskilled occupations, it was not degrading, backbreaking, low-paying work, fraught with fierce labor tensions and instability. The prospect of financial and job stability, material gains, and social standing was enough to attract scores of black men to the field.

Although there were but few options open for black women to achieve financial independence, some did. In 1850, single black women were the wealthiest group among Cincinnati's black elite. The 1850 census indicates nine black women owned more than $2,000 worth of property each, and four of them owned more than $10,000 worth of real estate. The combined net worth of the nine wealthiest black women in 1850 was $61,500, making them wealthier than the entire population of black barbers![87] The 1850 census takers did not consistently record the occupations of women, so it is difficult to ascertain how these women gained their wealth—by inheritance, marriage, or work.[88] Because seven of the wealthiest nine had been born in the South, it is plausible that some of them were the daughters or mistresses of wealthy, southern white men. James C. Brown reported that, in the late 1820s, Cincinnati was full of unmarried women who had been the mistresses of planters in Louisiana, Mississippi, and Tennessee. After the planters married white women, they sent their "slave-wives and children to Cincinnati, and set them free."[89] It is likely that these men provided their mistresses or daughters with the means to survive as free women in Cincinnati—which might account for why these single women were so wealthy. Some of the wealthy women might have also been the widows of affluent black men.

There were some patterns that linked wealth and color among this group of women. Only three of the nine wealthiest African American women were listed as "black"; the rest were "mulattoes"—a classification that census takers associated with color, not parentage. The "mulattoes" were far wealthier than those designated "black."[90] Because many of these wealthy women in Cincinnati were classified as mulatto, it is possible that they were the beneficiaries of color privilege. According to historian James Oliver Horton, light-complexioned African American women were preferred marriage partners among skilled and propertied African American men.[91]

Eliza Potter's autobiography provides some insight into the lives of this emerging class of wealthy black women in Cincinnati. Potter, classified as a mulatto in the census, moved to Cincinnati from New York in the 1840s. Although she had worked as a domestic and child nurse, Potter followed her passion for styling hair when she settled in Cincinnati and became a hairdresser for elite white women. Her autobiography, *A Hairdresser's Experience in High Life,* published in 1859, is mostly about her service in that profession in Cincinnati in the 1850s.[92]

In 1860, Potter was one of only four black female hairdressers in Cincinnati.[93] In a city where the top three professions for black women in 1860 were washerwoman (46 percent), servant (17 percent), and seamstress (almost 13 percent), Potter was an exception. Potter also amassed a respectable amount of property. In 1860, she resided on Home Street in the upscale Fourteenth Ward and owned two thousand dollars' worth of real estate and four hundred dollars in personal property.[94] Certainly, her occupation was lucrative enough to allow her to raise two children by herself. Potter's two children, Kate and James, had been born in Pennsylvania in 1849 and 1851 respectively, possibly the offspring of a marriage toward which she harbored deep resentment. Potter did not write much about her children or her marriage. Reflecting on her marriage, Potter wrote, "I have seen other persons do the same thing [get married], and so, I suppose, I need not be ashamed to own having committed a weakness, which has from the beginning of time, numbered the most respectable of the earth among its *victims*" (emphasis in original).[95] Potter chose not to remarry, and her favorable financial position freed her from having to marry out of necessity.

Potter carved out a space for herself that allowed her entrée into the world of elite white women. Styling hair for this class exposed her to culture, refinement, leisure, and privilege. She traveled all over the country and world, attended exclusive social affairs, and vacationed at posh resorts with her clients. Potter was frequently away from home on extended trips and stayed out late at night to attend to her clients. Her work life spilled over into her social life so much that the two were nearly inextricably joined. Potter's occupation was, in many ways, similar to that of black barbers, who also labored in an exclusive white society. Unlike the barbers, Potter spent so much time working and socializing in that milieu that she was relatively socially isolated from Cincinnati's black community. For example, she attended the white St. Paul's Episcopal Church and lived outside the black residential core of the First, Fourth, and Ninth wards.[96] Despite Potter's immersion in white society, her commitments and responsibilities rested within her own race. She served as a trustee for the Colored Orphan Asylum and was arrested for assisting fugitive slaves to freedom. Potter also tried to use her influence among elite whites to persuade one of her slaveholding southern clients to manumit an enslaved woman and her child.[97]

Occupation, wealth, and status were not the only indicators of the elite class of African Americans: color was also a very salient class marker. Those designated mulattoes by census takers held 75 percent of the wealth in Cincinnati in 1860. Not only were "mulattoes" wealthier but they were also more likely to be educated.[98] Some segments of the black community privileged light skin in terms of aesthetics, advancement, and associations. James Oliver Horton's comparative study of color politics in Boston, Buffalo, and Cincinnati indicates that 92 percent of Cincinnati's mulatto men tended to marry mulatto women. In that same study, he found patterns of residential segregation by ward among lighter- and darker-complexioned African Americans.[99] These patterns of intraracial color preference and association did not necessarily mean that lighter-skinned blacks consciously distanced themselves *politically* from darker, poorer blacks as they did in Charleston and New Orleans. In fact, those designated mulattoes in Cincinnati were more likely to be linked politically with the black masses.[100] The same can be said of the black elite in general: they remained connected to and empathic toward the struggle of the larger black community. For example, although their children had the option of attending Cincinnati's private schools, the black elite led the fight for universal education.

A wider and stronger institutional base brought permanence and stability to black Cincinnati. These institutions advanced the intellectual, spiritual, and moral components of racial uplift. The result was a more confident African American population that was in a better position to argue for the extension of rights of citizenship and participation in the body politic. As John Mercer Langston observed, African Americans "were learning what their rights were, and how to advocate and defend them."[101] Nowhere was this community's maturity and confidence more evident than in the development of black schools in the 1850s.

SEVEN

Underground Activism

Fugitive Slave Resistance, 1841–1861

> "Now, Sam, tell us distinctly how the matter was," said Mr. Shelby. "Where is Eliza, if you know?"
>
> "Wal, Mas'r, I saw her, with my own eyes, a crossin' on the floatin' ice. She crossed most 'markably; it wasn't no less nor a miracle; and I saw a man help her up the 'Hio side, and then she was lost in the dusk."
>
> —Harriet Beecher Stowe, *Uncle Tom's Cabin*

ALTHOUGH PEOPLE HAD assisted slaves to freedom since the earliest days of black settlement in Ohio, most of them were not part of any organized network of assistance. Many of those who helped did so out of the kindness of their hearts—not because of any overarching political doctrine or objective. Included in this group were charitable Christians or Quakers, casual sympathizers, and good Samaritans who neither planned nor premeditated their assistance to runaway slaves. Such people offered one-time, or otherwise limited, assistance such as providing food, a warm bed, or a ride to the next town. This they did without cooperation or consultation with networks of other people. Spontaneous assistance was arguably the most common and indispensable aid fugitives might encounter on the road to freedom. Yet, cooperative, deliberate assistance to fugitive slaves can be used as a measure of a community's strength.

Cincinnati's history proves that the Underground Railroad was not built on the backs of individuals, but on the backs of communities. The Cincinnati Underground Railroad was characterized by communitywide networks and patterns of cooperative assistance to runaways. Although initially those networks were limited and perhaps minimally effective, by the mid-1840s the network was stronger and wider. It included people of different racial, class, and gender backgrounds whose religious, political, or social convictions inspired them to do this work. Individuals and families in these networks regularly made themselves available for a variety of tasks. No one person helped in the same way every time, although the same core of people did participate regularly. Cooperative assistance in Cincinnati included sewing clothes, sharing news or other information, transporting runaways from one home to the next, and raising money for rail tickets. Although this work was typical Underground Railroad work, some work was distinct to Cincinnati as a border and river town: rowing fugitives across the Ohio River, helping stowaways get off steamboats undetected, or informing slaves in transit about Ohio's laws of freedom. Time and time again, the cooperation of this entire Underground Railroad community was needed to forward even one slave to freedom.

The actual number of fugitives who passed through Cincinnati is unknown. That number is but one measurement of the effectiveness of the network; the quality of the assistance given to fugitives is another.[1] From the mid-1840s onward, few communities were as active, organized, or successful in forwarding slaves to freedom as was Cincinnati, Ohio. It was one of the most important cities on the western branch of the Underground Railroad. Cincinnati was a regional "union depot" for the Underground Railroad because several routes originated there[2] and diverged from the city toward Hamilton, Ripley, Lebanon, Palmyra, and Walnut Hills, Ohio, and Richmond, Indiana.[3] By the late 1840s, Cincinnati's network was connected to other networks extending throughout the state, as far east as Philadelphia and as far north as Canada.

Harboring and forwarding fugitives was an empowering form of antislavery activism. Unlike boycotting goods produced with slave labor or petitioning against the slave trade in the nation's capital, helping African Americans escape slavery was a direct and immediate blow to the institution. Underground Railroad activity was the predominant form of activism in Cincinnati's black community before 1865. The city's social climate strangled many public forms of resistance and protest with severe reprisals. Consequently, the black community took its abolitionist activism out of the public eye in the form of the Underground Railroad. The Underground Railroad was not only a form of black activist protest but is also central to understanding black community growth in Cincinnati.

Like the black community, the Underground Railroad reached its maturation in 1841, as well, but for different reasons. In 1841, a critical decision in Ohio courts, *State v. Farr,* opened the door for slaves in transit through Ohio to gain their liberty. *State v. Farr* was a state supreme court case that had overturned the convictions of seventeen abolitionists who had helped a group of Virginian slaves being transported through Ohio to escape from their masters. The convictions were reversed because the lower court had erred in the way it had submitted the case to the jury. When the supreme court chief justice issued the decision, he also took the opportunity to comment on the tangential issue of slaves in transit. He stated that any enslaved person brought into the state by an owner was automatically free because the U.S. Constitution only addressed fugitive slaves.[4] Although *State v. Farr* was tangential to the issue of slave in transit through a free state, this proclamation by Ohio's chief justice led most Ohioans to consider this dictum an official decision of the court.[5]

The dictum certainly vitalized the Underground Railroad community and changed the way rescues were made. In the decades that followed, the system evolved into an interracial community of committed activists. The conductors were important, but so were the abolitionist attorneys who fought for the liberty of fugitive slaves in courts and helped shape antislavery legislation. By the time the Fugitive Slave Act was passed in 1850, this community was prepared.

———

During his tour of the United States in 1831, Alexis de Tocqueville observed that the Ohio River was caught between two different worlds: one slave, one free. He found few redeeming qualities about slave society on "the left bank" of the river. In Kentucky, he observed, "Society is asleep; man seems idle." Slavery had stripped from white men the desire to be enterprising and industrious. Tocqueville observed that, by contrast, free labor had led to productivity and progress in Ohio.[6] Although the two banks had many differences, they also had one thing in common: the Ohio River. The river was both the "Frontier of Freedom" and the frontier of slavery.[7] It occupied a geographic middle ground. As a middle ground, the river was hardly neutral. For decades, the Ohio River was a corridor of freedom, ushering thousands of fugitive slaves to its northern banks.

To escaping slaves, the river must have seemed less like a corridor of freedom and more like a *barrier* to it.[8] Many runaways arrived at the southern bank of the Ohio River only to find that they had no way to cross it.[9] For those who were intimidated by the river's swift, foaming currents, the dream of freedom must have died right there. In the winter, the river was virtually impassable by boat because it usually was covered with a layer of ice. Sometimes not very far ahead of their owners, fugitive slaves had to make decisions on the safest, fastest, and most discreet way to cross the river. Those resourceful enough to find a way across the Ohio also had to wait for an opportune moment. Fugitives might hide in Kentucky brush and woods by day, while waiting for cover of night to cross.[10] In the summer months, desperate yet determined fugitive slaves sometimes took their chances trying to swim across the river; the more resourceful constructed makeshift rafts made of logs pinned together. A number of fleeing slaves found skiffs on the Kentucky or Virginia banks and rowed across the river themselves; others asked sympathetic fishermen or free blacks to carry them in their boats.[11]

Those fugitives who successfully crossed the Ohio River were those most familiar with it or those who had the human resources to help them. Prospective runaways who lived in the Kentucky counties that bordered the Ohio River had a better chance of crossing it. Naturally, they had more time to contemplate how and when to do so. They were more familiar with both the traffic patterns on the river and the river's character. Some chose to abscond in the winter by walking (or running) across the thin layer of ice that formed on the surface of the river. The character Eliza in *Uncle Tom's Cabin* is based on a real woman, Eliza Harris, who escaped across the Ohio River on drifting ice with her child in her arms.[12] Those slaves who lived close to the river knew when the ice was too fragile and when it was thick enough to support their weight. Deciding to flee in the winter was not always an act of desperation. Because the ice was stronger in the coldest months, those who contemplated escape had to weigh the costs and benefits of fleeing then, when the ice was the strongest but the temperature was dangerously low, or waiting until warmer weather when the natural footbridge was gone and there was more traffic on the river and docks. For those who used the iced-over river as a bridge, then, the most important conductor on the Cincinnati Underground Railroad was the Ohio River itself.

The river was not a complete barrier to the development of cross-community ties. In fact, the Ohio River connected the free black community of Cincinnati with the enslaved communities of Newport and Covington, Kentucky. Slaves in Newport and Covington, Kentucky, often knew the names of black Underground Railroad operators and even applied to them for assistance. Many slaves who ran away from neighboring Kentucky counties had loved ones and friends among the free black community in Cincinnati. These slaves were not only more determined to abscond but also had the most critical resource needed to escape: people to help execute the plan, harbor them, and put them in contact with others who could help.[13] A community of cooperating people on both sides of the river helped forward slaves across the Ohio River.

For example, when one woman, Sally, ran away from her master in Covington, a widow in her neighborhood hid her and then traveled to Cincinnati to consult with abolitionists about how to forward Sally to Ohio. They, in turn, coordinated a plan to disguise Sally as a man and to row her across the river. The widow's Kentucky friends supplied the disguise and walked Sally to the river, where William Casey, a free black Cincinnati man, was waiting to row her across.[14] These trans-river relationships were so threatening to the system of slavery that Covington officials tried to discourage them by passing ordinances that prohibited free blacks from loitering or traveling in the city without legal authority.[15] No ordinances, however, could stem the flow of slaves across the River of Freedom.

Innovations in transportation, particularly steamboats and railroads, facilitated and even encouraged flight from more distant southern states. Fugitives no longer had to travel on foot or on stolen horses and they could make the trip in a fraction of the time. Slaves who contemplated escape found a number of ways to secure passage on steamboats. Many stowed away, like the well-known fugitive slave William Wells Brown. Henry Bibb managed to walk right on board a steamer bound for Cincinnati and blend in with white citizens because he was so light in complexion.[16] Another small percentage of runaways were fortunate enough to find vessels owned by abolitionists who knowingly concealed them on board.[17] Other runaway slaves went aboard by posing as free people; others took jobs as laborers in return for passage.[18]

Black stevedores, boatmen, firemen, ship porters, cooks, and other river workers were often the first freedom agents slaves encountered. While their boats were docked in southern ports, black steamboat workers sometimes were approached by slaves asking for help in securing concealed passage aboard the vessels.[19] Empathetic black workers occasionally used refueling or loading time as an opportunity to sneak fugitives to and from the vessels. Once the fugitives were aboard, black workers hid them in their quarters and even brought them food for the duration of the journey up river.[20] They risked life, limb, and freedom to help the bondsmen: the punishment for helping a fugitive escape in some southern states was death or enslavement.[21] Once the vessel had docked in Cincinnati, these steamboat workers had to take great precautions getting the stowaways from the boat and into safe hands. Because black steamboat workers brought ideas of freedom and independence and possessed the willingness to help conceal fugitives, southern slaveholders considered them a dangerous class. Consequently, many southern states moved to legislate against these workers as they entered southern ports. After discovering that free blacks had played a critical role in planning a slave revolt in 1822, South Carolina legislators passed the Negro Seamen Act, which quarantined vessels with free blacks aboard and confined all out-of-state black maritime workers to jail while their vessels were docked in South Carolina ports.[22]

If river workers were a threat to slavery, so were the free blacks who came in contact with slaves on Cincinnati streets, on ships, on the docks, in the market, in churches, and in boarding homes. Before 1841, slaves were a very familiar sight in Cincinnati. According to black Cincinnati resident Andrew J. Gordon, "Before the promulgation of antislavery sentiment in this State, it was of common occurrence to witness at our public landing, in their transmigration to a Southern market, coffles of human beings, manacled and chained like beasts of burden and upon our principle [sic] streets and thoroughfares."[23] Slaveholders in the city on business or vacation routinely brought handmaids, nurses, and personal servants with them and boarded them at black-owned boarding homes.[24] Local Kentucky slaves were frequently sent into the city alone on errands or to buy dry goods, fruit, and other goods at the market. Some were granted passes to attend one of the black churches in the city or to work in various capacities.[25] It was inevitable that these slaves would have contact—even casual—with Cincinnati's free African Americans. That contact threatened slaveholders, because they exchanged more than mere greetings and pleasantries; free blacks shared ideas (or songs) of freedom, as the narrative of Kentucky bondsman, Allen Sydney, illustrates. Sydney had been hired out in 1840 to work as an engineer on a steamboat that docked in Cincinnati for weeks at a time. Working among free blacks made Sydney feel dissatisfied with his status: "[O]f course, I had enough to eat, and so had my wife . . . but I was dissatisfied, here was a man taking all my wages and giving me only board and clothes." After some time, Sydney developed relationships with African Americans who were willing to help him plan his escape from slavery. He met with Tom Dorum, a black Underground Railroad operator, who made the arrangements for the couple's escape to Canada.[26]

The most threatening piece of information that free blacks and abolitionists provided to slaves involved the Ohio supreme court's dictum in

State v. Farr (1842), which ostensibly freed those slaves brought into the state with their owners' consent.[27] *State v. Farr* created the perception that courts would no longer tolerate the transport of slaves through the state. And that perception was enough to encourage abolitionists to inform slaves of the prospect of freedom as soon as they arrived in the state. The perception was also enough to make slaveowners apprehensive about bringing their slaves into the state, even briefly. Some went to great lengths to avoid taking their bondsmen ashore—from boarding them in Covington, Kentucky, to changing boats before docking in Ohio.[28] Inasmuch as this dictum was customarily legitimized, it also set a precedent for other cases involving slaves in transit through Ohio, including *State v. Hoppess* (1845) and *Ex parte Robinson* [Rosetta Armstead Case] (1855).[29]

The *State v. Hoppess* case involved Henry Hoppess, who was traveling by steamboat from Arkansas to Virginia with his slave, Samuel Watson. Quite determined not to allow Watson to land on the Ohio shore, Hoppess attempted to transfer to another vessel midstream as theirs prepared to dock. Despite his best efforts, they were unable to change vessels before landing at the Cincinnati wharf. At some point during the day, Watson came ashore and, to his owner's dismay, was seen leaning against a post on the Cincinnati landing. Although he was "not a hundred yards from the boat," Hoppess immediately had him arrested as a fugitive slave. Salmon Portland Chase subsequently secured a writ of habeas corpus for Watson's release. During the hearing on the writ, both sides debated whether the docked steamboat technically had been in Ohio: specifically, whether the true boundary of Ohio was in the middle of the Ohio River or at the low-water mark near the shore. Judge Read, who presided over the hearing, concluded that "the right to use the shore for the purpose of navigation is incident to the right to navigate, and does not change the relation of master and slave." He ruled in favor of Hoppess, and Watson was subsequently returned to slavery. Nonetheless, Read's lengthy opinion reinforced the court's position on slaves in transit: "If a master bring his slave into the state of Ohio[,] he loses all power over him. The relation of master and slave is strictly territorial. If the master takes his slave beyond the influence of the law which creates the relation, it fails—there is nothing to support it, and they stand as man and man."[30]

The 1855 *Ex parte Robinson* case further tested Ohio's tolerance for the transport of slaves through its territory. That case involved Rosetta Armstead, a sixteen-year-old enslaved girl who was being transported by steamboat from Louisville, Kentucky, to Wheeling, Virginia, by her owner's agent when ice on the Ohio River impeded their journey. Miller, her owner's agent, decided to remove Rosetta from the vessel at Cincinnati and continue their trip by train; by so doing, he brought Rosetta under the jurisdiction of Ohio courts and was consequently served with a writ of habeas corpus for her release in Columbus. After the Franklin County court declared Rosetta free, Miller secured a warrant from a federal commissioner for her arrest under the 1850 Fugitive Slave Act. Rosetta was promptly arrested as a fugitive slave by U.S. marshal Hiram H. Robinson and taken back to Cincinnati. There, another writ of habeas corpus was presented to Marshal Robinson for Rosetta's release from illegal imprisonment. The county court judge declared Rosetta free because she had been brought into the state by her owner's agent; she was released. Rejecting the authority of the county court, Marshal Robinson seized Rosetta a second time under the same federal warrant. The county judge issued a warrant for Robinson's arrest for violating his ruling; he was arrested by the county sheriff and brought before a U.S. Supreme Court justice who eventually released him, positing that Robinson had had authority to execute his duties as a federal commissioner when he arrested Rosetta.[31] This case is significant because it brought the Ohio and federal courts into conflict over the issue of slaves in transit. As important as these cases were, they did not help fugitive slaves, who found no advocates in Ohio laws or courts. Fortunately for them, though, they had other advocates.

Free blacks were the first line of protection and assistance for fugitive slaves after they arrived in Cincinnati. Runaways stopped in cities with large black populations, like Cincinnati, to get assistance from free blacks.[32] Because trusting the wrong person could result in discovery and recovery, cautious fugitive slaves were not inclined to seek help from whites they did not know. Runaways may have viewed all whites as complicit in the system of slavery and therefore were reluctant to trust them. One white Underground Railroad operator in the city admitted that fugitives were "generally unwilling to tell their stories, or let us know what part of the South they came from . . . [or] give their names, or the names of their masters, correctly fearing that they would be betrayed."[33] Fugitive slaves naturally sought help from other African Americans because they felt they could trust them.[34] When fugitive slave Henry Bibb passed through Cincinnati, he did not feel comfortable asking a white person for assistance; instead, he asked a group of young African American boys who were playing in the street to direct him to an African American household. Bibb was directed to the home of Job Dundy, who was, more than likely, a member of the vigilance committee. Dundy informed Bibb about freedom in Canada, abolitionism, and the Underground Railroad. Dundy then put the grateful Bibb aboard the system in Cincinnati.[35]

Assisting fugitive slaves was dangerous work for everyone—especially in Cincinnati's turbulent, virulently antiblack, antiabolitionist climate. Although free black Cincinnatians were in a strategic geographic position to help slaves, they were also the most vulnerable segment of that society. Mob action was designed to discourage or repress all abolitionist activity: presses were thrown into the river, buildings were torn down, and abolitionists were hunted in the streets. No abolitionist activity aroused as much public hostility as assisting fugitives—"nigger stealing"—because it struck directly the city's economic relationship with the South.[36] Those who assisted fugitives were almost certain to be prosecuted to the fullest extent of the law. But it was the extralegal reaction to abolitionist activity that distinguished Cincinnati from other contemporary cities. Slaveholders and hired slave catchers were willing to go to great lengths to capture fugitives in this city, including mob violence—which they committed with impunity. It was rather easy for slaveholders to gather mobs in Cincinnati to reclaim their slaves. Henry Bibb's master had no trouble raising a mob of "ruffians" and "slavehunting petty constables" who were willing to be the "watch-dogs of slaveholders" for a few drinks or a few cents.[37] Another slaveholder quite easily rallied a mob from a tavern, which then proceeded to destroy the home of Englishman Cornelius Burnett after he refused to hand a nine-year-old child over to her owner. Fearing retribution, "penalty of the law [,] or the stigma on their reputation," many white abolitionists were unwilling to provide assistance to fugitive slaves. With a few exceptions, their involvement was largely tentative and limited to financial assistance through the mid-1830s.[38]

Given the social climate in Cincinnati, it is remarkable that *anyone* became involved in helping fugitives, much less African Americans. Without the privileges of citizenship or protection of the law, African Americans suspected of harboring fugitives might be subjected to home invasions and impromptu searches by authorities and private citizens alike.[39] They were extremely vulnerable, especially in the initial days of escape, when slave owners were most angry and most determined to find their slaves. The cost of reprisals in Cincinnati meant that few African American families were willing to commit themselves to this work on a regular basis. Noted Quaker abolitionist and Underground Railroad operator, Levi Coffin, commented that fugitive slaves were often captured and returned to slavery because African Americans were not "shrewd managers" of the system.[40] Coffin overstated the case about the incompetence of black managers; surely, what he detected was vulnerability, not incompetence.

The earliest evidence of organized, cooperative fugitive slave assistance in Cincinnati's black community comes from the late 1820s. John Malvin, for example, relates in his autobiography how he assisted several slaves during his brief tenure in Cincinnati. In the habit of going to the pier to watch the boats, Malvin once observed the docking of a ship with thirty slaves on board. While on deck, he had a conversation with a young pregnant enslaved woman, who was a friend of his family from his home county in Virginia. Malvin asked the woman if she would like to be free, to which she responded affirmatively. Malvin admitted, "[S]o great was my abhorrence of slavery, that I was willing to run any risk to accomplish the liberation of a slave."[41] That same evening, Malvin went aboard the vessel and helped the woman escape with her son. Once they were safely ashore, Malvin risked his own life and freedom by returning to the boat to help three other young slaves escape. He tapped into a network of unnamed people who helped him to conceal and forward everyone except the pregnant woman and her child to a safe house in Richmond, Indiana. He found a safe place for her in Cincinnati and paid her room and board until she was in a position to move on to Canada.[42]

Around the same time, members of Bethel AME Church reportedly also engaged in this work.[43] Fugitives were moved between black homes and churches before finally being spirited from the city by black conductors. What is certain is that most of the work of forwarding fugitives was carried out by African Americans until the late 1830s. Even James Birney observed in 1837 that "such matters are almost uniformly managed by the colored people. I know nothing of them [fugitive slaves] generally till they are past."[44] Anecdotal as they are, these examples provide evidence that the community was organized to resist slavery in what was one of the most racially oppressive decades in Cincinnati's history. Why did free African Americans risk their lives, property, and freedom to help fugitive slaves in such a climate? Although it was never publicly encouraged or articulated on any local or national black political agenda, assisting fugitive slaves was an implicit racial obligation. To be free and black in Cincinnati during the age of slavery was to be racially obligated to assist fugitive slaves.

The Cincinnati Underground Railroad matured as an institution in the 1840s, about the same time the black community reached its maturation. African Americans felt less vulnerable to mob violence and racial terrorism by then, which, in turn, made them more confident in their own abilities, more defiant in challenging the institution of slavery, and more daring in their activities. There was also a larger, dedicated network of black families who regularly provided shelter, food, and transportation for fugitive slaves. Members of the black community held regular vigilance committee meetings in which they coordinated their activities. African American agents sometimes traveled to Kentucky to meet with prospective fugitives and to coordinate the places and times of their departures. These agents loaded fugitives into skiffs or rowed them across the river. Agents also waited on the Ohio side to receive the runaways and escort them to their first place of refuge. Henry Young was a fourteen-year-old slave in Covington, Kentucky, in 1849 when he learned about Cincinnati's black Underground Railroad community. Two black operators, Tom Boswell and Jake Campbell, arranged for Young to be carried across the river by an Irish boy. From there, he was sent directly to Thomas Dorum's home on Main Street. According to Young, when he arrived at Dorum's home, Dorum and several other African American men—including John Hatfield and Mr. Oskins—were holding an Underground Railroad planning meeting. These men hid Young at several different locations in the city for three weeks before forwarding him to Hamilton, Ohio, and on to Newport, Indiana.[45] Young's account of this system reveals that black operators were diligent, committed, and organized, contradicting Levi Coffin's depiction of them as careless and untrustworthy.[46]

There were several black individuals and families who regularly provided assistance to runaways in Cincinnati. Two of black Cincinnati's most important and visible operators were Thomas and Jane ("Aunt Jane") Dorum. Tom Dorum was described as a "tall, heavy-set man with fair hair."[47] Originally from Kentucky, the Dorums probably had moved to Cincinnati during the massive influx of black migrants in the 1820s. A whitewasher by trade, Tom Dorum had accumulated real estate valued at three thousand dollars by 1850.[48] The Dorums were widely known throughout the free black community in Cincinnati and the slave communities of northern Kentucky. Black Cincinnatians often took runaways directly to the Dorums' home immediately upon their arrival in the city, as they had with Henry Young.[49] Although it is unclear when the Dorums began assisting fugitives, they harbored slaves from various locations throughout Little Africa over a period of two decades. This neighborhood along the river was an optimal location for assisting fugitives. In 1840, the Dorums lived on the southeast corner of Elm and Green streets in the Fourth Ward. Two years later, they moved to the corner of Third and Elm streets. By 1849, they were living on Main Street.[50] One possible explanation for their frequent moves was that remaining in the same house would have compromised their work and endangered the lives of the slaves they harbored.

William Casey was another black operator on Cincinnati's Underground Railroad and had the reputation of being a "shrewd Negro whose advise [sic] was sought by white operators."[51] Born in Virginia in 1804, Casey had moved to Cincinnati sometime in the 1830s. In 1836, he worked as a boatman, which may have been how he became active in the Underground Railroad. The earliest record of Casey in Cincinnati lists his home on Church Alley between Main and Walnut streets in the Fourth Ward. By 1840, he had moved to Post Office Alley and, by 1842, he lived on Masonic Alley—both homes were within blocks of the river. By 1846, Casey had moved again: this time to Bank Alley.[52] Casey's residential instability, like that of the Dorums, may have made his work more secure. William Casey was among the most daring of all of Cincinnati's conductors; he was known to row skiffs across the river to Kentucky to pick up slaves who had made previous arrangements to meet him there.[53] Venturing into slave states to help slaves to freedom was extremely risky. Even white abolitionists rarely went into slave territory to bring slaves out, and those who were apprehended were arrested and convicted. Calvin Fairbank, for example, was convicted of aiding a fugitive and sentenced to fifteen years in prison.[54]

John Hatfield and his family received fugitives at their home on Fifth Street between Race and Elm. Born in Pennsylvania in 1804, Hatfield was probably free when he and his brother, Joseph, migrated to Cincinnati during the population swell in the late 1820s.[55] John married a native Ohioan and had two children.[56] A barber by trade, he operated his own shop and was a well-respected member of the Cincinnati black community for decades. Although he never assumed traditional leadership positions in the black schools or churches, Hatfield was a leading member of the vigilance committee. Both Frances, his wife, and Sarah, his daughter, assisted with Underground Railroad activities, as well.[57]

The Hall and Burgess families also hid fugitive slaves in their homes on McAllister Street and Longworth Street, respectively.[58] William Watson, one of the more successful barbers, and Henry Boyd, a wealthy bedstead manufacturer, also harbored fugitives from time to time.[59]

Augustus R. Green, pastor of the Bethel AME Church between 1846 and 1850, was a faithful servant of God and a trusted and capable agent on the Underground Railroad.[60] Fugitive slaves were frequently brought directly to Rev. Green upon their arrival in the city. Green harbored them, moved them to safer places, and transported them to train stations. He was also a masterful fund-raiser in the black community, securing money to be used for fugitive slaves' room and board, clothing, and rail tickets.[61] Green was one of several black preachers who used their churches as stations and their members as operators on the Underground Railroad. In the 1820s, when the AME Church was yet in its infancy, its members concealed runaways and conveyed them farther north. The church continued to serve as a way station for runaway slaves through the end of the Civil War.[62] Members of another church, Zion Baptist, were called "Anti-Slavery Baptists" because of their work on the Underground Railroad. Located in a small house near the Ohio River on Third and Race streets, Zion was known as the "headquarters for the Underground Railroad" because slaves were commonly concealed in its basement.[63] Leading Underground Railroad workers William Casey and John Hatfield were both members of Zion Baptist Church. A third black church—a Wesleyan church—also served as a way station.[64]

Black Christians who participated in this activity may have felt it was part of their religious duty. The congregation at Bethel AME in the 1820s felt that the work would elevate the race and that God would protect them in the commission of their duties.[65] Other black Christians may have felt that assistance to slaves was a way of helping combat a great sin against humanity. Some even believed their assistance to runaways would help fulfill the Exodus story of Moses helping Israel out of an Egyptian bondage, across the waters of the Red Sea, through the wilderness, and into the Promised Land.[66] This biblical symbolism had many parallels in Cincinnati. African American fugitive slaves represented Israel; Underground Railroad operators represented Moses; the Ohio River was the modern version of the Red Sea; Cincinnati was the wilderness threatening to destroy Israel at every turn and the Promised Land was a place of relative safety—usually Canada. Thus, assistance to fugitives was divinely inspired spiritual work.

A way station more accessible than the black churches was the Dumas House, a black-owned boarding home located on McAllister Street (also known as "Eastern Row") between Fourth and Fifth streets in the First Ward.[67] Dumas House was a popular lodging place for African American visitors to the city—enslaved, or otherwise. Before *State v. Farr,* the guests included slaves who had accompanied their owners to the city. Other Dumas guests included black river workers who stayed at the house during the winter season. Many of Dumas's other guests could not find other housing in the congested city. Fugitive slaves sometimes stopped at the boarding house for lodging, food, or other assistance because it was a place of relative safety.[68] It is difficult to determine whether the owners of the boarding home actively or passively harbored these fugitives. Regardless, Dumas House was a prominent station on the Cincinnati Underground Railroad.

White abolitionists also harbored and forwarded fugitive slaves in the city. Prominent citizens like Salmon Portland Chase, James Birney, and Gamaliel Bailey all harbored slaves in the 1830s.[69] Birney was arrested, tried, and convicted of harboring a fugitive slave in 1837, although the Ohio Supreme Court eventually overturned the conviction. Among other white operators in Cincinnati was former U.S. president Rutherford B. Hayes. In an 1893 letter, Hayes exposed a network that had included Cincinnati's most powerful men, including himself, a justice of the peace, county prosecutor Joseph Cox, and Police Court attorney William Dickson.[70] Some of the important stations among white operators were College Hill, perched high in the hills six miles from the city, and the Walnut Hills district.[71]

Other notable white operators did not live in Cincinnati but nonetheless were involved in activities there. Laura Haviland and Delia Webster, both teachers, also conducted slaves to freedom. Laura Haviland was born in 1808 in Leeds County, Canada, into a Quaker family. Haviland and her family moved to Michigan in 1829 where she started the first antislavery society in the state. Religious tensions that arose during those antislavery society meetings led to her break with the Society of Friends, and she subsequently joined the Wesleyan Methodist Church. In 1837, Haviland opened the Raisin Institute, a school open to all children "regardless of color."[72] Her other legacy was her work the Underground Railroad network. Although based in Michigan and northwest Ohio, Haviland was known to travel as far south as Kentucky to accompany fugitives to freedom. She was also a close friend of Levi and Catherine Coffin and frequently spent time assisting with the system in Cincinnati.[73] Her activity demonstrates that the Underground Railroad did not necessarily have fixed stations and conductors and that people who assisted were quite mobile and interregional. As a woman, Haviland defied many gender conventions to pursue her work. So outraged were slave owners about the "sort of sisters they had in the North" that they put a three-thousand-dollar price for on her head at one point.[74]

Very few white agents were as brazen, fearless, and cunning as John Fairfield. Fairfield had been born into a slaveholding family in Virginia, where he not only developed deep antipathy toward slavery but decided to devote his life to helping slaves escape. Fairfield took his assistance to slaves a step further than most Underground Railroad agents. He went into the slave South, pretending to be a slaveholder, slave catcher, slave dealer, poultry dealer, or other character to gain slaveholders' trust.[75] Prospective fugitive slaves sometimes contracted Fairfield's services for a small fee. He ran his one-man seek-and-rescue operation as far south as Mississippi. No place was too far south, and no number of slaves was too many for him. Fairfield once brought twenty-eight slaves out of Kentucky, across the river, and into Cincinnati, where he turned them over to Cincinnati's conductors. Although Fairfield was never rooted in any particular community, Cincinnati was one of his primary bases of operation.[76]

But the work of one white abolitionist, Levi Coffin, transcended that of all others. Coffin, often called the "President of the Underground Railroad," was the most essential of Cincinnati's white operators.[77] Originally from North Carolina, Coffin had moved to Newport, Indiana, in 1826. Abolitionists and Quakers, Coffin and his wife Catherine ("Aunt Katy") managed the Underground Railroad in Newport for twenty years. Under their leadership and guidance, it became an important town on the freedom trail. In April 1847, the Indiana Society of Friends selected Levi Coffin to move to Cincinnati to open a wholesale depository of goods produced with free labor that supplied the small stores of those opposed to slave labor. Coffin mobilized and recruited many reluctant Cincinnatians into the clandestine system within months of his removal there.[78] From 1847 through the end of the Civil War, the Coffin home on the corner of Sixth and Elm streets was an important station. The Coffins hid fugitives in the basement and attic of the brick, three-story house, which reputedly had a tunnel that extended from the western side of the basement wall and into the basements of contiguous buildings.[79]

By the late 1840s, Cincinnati's Underground Railroad was an interracial cooperative as the networks between white and black workers merged. Although African Americans remained the first line of protection for runaways, when it became too dangerous for the fugitives to remain in the black community Levi Coffin or another white abolitionist was usually summoned for assistance. Runaways were then disguised and moved to safe houses among white abolitionists.

In one case, a black dockworker helped a slave woman who had traveled to Cincinnati with her owner to escape. The fugitive then was directed to the home of Tom and Jane Dorum at the southeast corner of Elm and Green. The Dorums, fearing the woman would be discovered in their home, sent an urgent message to the Coffins, indicating that the woman needed to be forwarded. Levi Coffin swiftly brought a disguise and put the woman on course to a depot in Indiana.[80] Another case involved the aforementioned John Fairfield, who rowed twenty-eight slaves across the Ohio River to Cincinnati. After he got across with the large party, Fairfield immediately went to the home of John Hatfield, seeking his advice and help. The party was simply too large to be quartered at Hatfield's house without being detected, so he sought Coffin's assistance. Fairfield, Hatfield, and Coffin moved the fugitives in covered wagons, as in a funeral procession, to hiding places among black families in College Hill and a white Presbyterian minister in the western section of town. White and blacks worked together to provide food, coffee, clothing, and shoes for the runaways. Soon thereafter, teams were hired and the party was conveyed farther north.[81]

White abolitionists contributed much-needed resources to the system. Harboring fugitives and safely conveying them to other towns was a costly endeavor which included food, clothing, housing, medicine, blankets, and transportation. Underground Railroad workers bore the expense of providing medicine or funerals for those fugitives who were ill or near death when they arrived. They usually paid fugitives' fares on ferries and trains, as well. The cost of hiring a driver and a two-horse team to transport larger parties thirty miles was ten dollars. Other expenses for fugitives included legal fees and the purchase price for their freedom.[82] Wealthy African Americans contributed funds as well, but generally Cincinnati's black community contributed only what it could, when it could, and was not in a position to finance the entire system by itself. Ultimately, white abolitionists, who were in a far better financial position to help, carried most of this burden. White Underground Railroad workers could more easily solicit donations from the white upper class. Levi Coffin, for example, went door to door in his neighborhood and openly encouraged merchants, grocers, and others to buy "stock" in the Underground Railroad.[83] White operators also had the advantage of owning homes or buildings big enough to hide fugitives: places with attics, cellars, or extra rooms.[84] They also owned wagons, carriages, horses, and other means of transportation and could provide other essential resources like extra clothing and bedding for the runaways.

Many duties in assisting fugitive slaves were both race and gender specific. Black men and women typically initiated contact with Kentucky slaves or with those traveling aboard steamers, and black men like William Casey rowed fugitives across the river. Females of both races were usually relegated to duties that were perceived to be within women's sphere. Black women cooked food for the fugitive slaves, and white women organized an Anti-Slavery Sewing Society that met weekly at Coffin's home to sew clothes for fugitive slaves.[85] Women also arranged many of the disguises—dressing women in dark veils or dressing men in women's clothing—that allowed fugitives to escape the city undetected. Men usually decided when the fugitives should leave each depot. White males usually made travel arrangements to put the runaways aboard rail cars, steamers, and carriages.[86] Consistent with gender and racial conventions at the time, white men also assumed the responsibility of speaking with persons of authority, like police officers, marshals, and slaveholders, as Levi Coffin often did. White male lawyers also performed the legal work of the operation. White and black men alike acted as drivers, concealing slaves in covered carriages and conducting them to the next station. All of this work on the Underground Railroad was essential, and every person was indispensable. Had it not been for the cooperative assistance of people of different backgrounds, the system may not have thrived in Cincinnati.

———

The Compromise of 1850 was intended to ease sectional tensions that had been growing between northern and southern states. To appease northern states, the compromise admitted California to the Union and ended the slave trade in the nation's capital. But it was concessions intended to placate southern states that ultimately destabilized northern free black communities. The Fugitive Slave Act of 1850—part of the Compromise of 1850—gave slaveholders more authority to retrieve their slaves from northern states. The law invested the federal government with jurisdiction over interstate claims by establishing federal commissioners to oversee cases involving alleged fugitive slaves. The burden of proof for the claimant was very low; all a person had to do to make a case was go before a federal commissioner with an affidavit from their home state describing the alleged fugitive slave. The person presumed to be the slave would then promptly be turned over to the said claimant. African Americans had no right to contest the claim; they were denied the right to a trial by jury and the right to testify in court on their own behalf. The law also nullified the writ of habeas corpus for them. Federal commissioners could be fined for failing to enforce the law, and they had a healthy incentive to rule in favor of the claimant: commissioners who remanded an African American to slavery were paid ten dollars, and those who ruled in favor of the alleged slave received only five dollars. Furthermore, the Fugitive Slave Act of 1850 gave federal marshals the power to compel "all good citizens" to assist in capturing runaway slaves. Those who interfered with the return of a fugitive slave could be fined one thousand dollars or subjected to a six-month jail sentence.[87]

The Fugitive Slave Act of 1850 threatened fugitive slaves, free blacks, and abolitionists alike. African Americans living in northern states no longer were protected by the presumption of freedom. Those who had been living as free people for decades had to look over their shoulders at every turn. Even those who were legitimately free had to worry about false claims against them. The threat to black freedom was especially potent in border cities like Cincinnati where proslavery sentiment made it easier to seize African Americans without due process.

The 1850 Fugitive Slave Act made it easier to kidnap free blacks with impunity. When two men wielding a knife and gun kidnapped George Jackson, a free African American, in broad daylight, none of the bystanders heeded his pleas for help. The bystanders did, however, follow Jackson and his kidnappers to the river and watched idly as they took him aboard a ferry bound for Kentucky. In a similar incident, Benjamin Chelsom was kidnapped from the Cincinnati wharves and carried back to Kentucky, where he had been manumitted years earlier.[88] Perhaps bystanders did not help because they feared prosecution under the Fugitive Slave Act or because there was a presumption that all African Americans were fugitive slaves.

Abolitionist communities throughout the nation waged a vigorous campaign against the Fugitive Slave Act. A wave of African Americans— many of whom were fugitive slaves—migrated to Canada after the enactment of this legislation. The risk of being re-enslaved was too great to remain in the United States. Black organizations issued proclamations condemning the legislation. Among the most vehement were those from the National Emigration Convention of Colored People held in Cleveland in 1854: "[we] abhor its existence, dispute its authority, refuse submission to its provisions, and hold it in a state of the most contemptuous abrogation."[89] Larger abolitionist communities also held meetings to voice their protests and to outline their course of action. Abolitionists in Chicago concluded the law was unconstitutional and vowed not to comply with the provision that compelled citizens to assist in the arrest of fugitives.[90] Black Ohioans joined the chorus of condemnation, and abolitionists in Cleveland and Dayton vowed to resist the Fugitive Slave Act.[91] Opponents of the law also protested by persisting in their efforts to harbor and conduct fugitive slaves to freedom. Some abolitionist communities were willing to do whatever was necessary to defend fugitives, as they did in Christiana, Pennsylvania, in 1851. There, African Americans responded with armed resistance to a Maryland slaveholder who was trying to reclaim his slave. The slaveholder was shot and killed, and his son was badly wounded.[92] The Christiana affair polarized the nation. Southerners were outraged that black men had taken the life of a white slaveholder. They felt that northerners were willing to stop at nothing to oppose slavery—even shedding the blood of white men. For northern abolitionists, the case illustrated just how far African Americans were willing to go to secure their freedom.

Of all U.S. abolitionist communities, Boston's was the most resolute in its resistance to the 1850 Fugitive Slave Act. In November of that year, Boston's African American and white abolitionists mobilized to prevent the capture of two fugitive slaves, William and Ellen Craft. The Crafts had escaped from slavery two years earlier and settled in Boston, where they became well-known speakers on the abolitionist circuit. The Crafts' national fame enabled their owner to track them down in Boston. When Boston's abolitionists got word that slave catchers had arrived to reclaim the Crafts, they posted signs throughout the city alerting sympathetic residents of the danger in their midst. The black community was also warned of the imminent danger from the pulpits of black churches. This community did everything in its power to protect the Crafts, including having the slave catchers arrested for a range of charges, such as conspiracy to kidnap. As the slave catchers closed in, armed black men retreated to the home of Lewis Hayden on Beacon Hill, where they barricaded the doors and vowed to die protecting the Crafts. Hayden had wired his house with explosives and threatened to blow up the entire house and everyone in it if anyone entered it to seize the Crafts. Discouraged by such dogged determination, the slave catchers gave up their quest.[93]

Just three months later, another case tested the resolve of this community. This time, one Shadrach Minkins was arrested as a fugitive from labor. On the day Minkins was scheduled to appear before a federal commissioner, more than fifty African Americans stormed the courthouse, seized Minkins, and whisked him away. Minkins was immediately put aboard the Underground Railroad and spirited onward to Canada.[94]

Perhaps that rescue by African Americans was proof that they were growing more militant and bold in their determination to resist the legislation. After Anthony Burns was arrested as a fugitive on May 24, 1854, Boston's black community attacked the federal courthouse where Burns was being held. Armed African Americans and whites broke down the

PLATE 1. Village of Cincinnati, 1800. *Reproduced with the permission of the Ohio Historical Society.*

PLATE 2. Broadway Street, just below black neighborhood at Sixth and Broadway, 1841. *Reproduced with the permission of the Ohio Historical Society.*

PLATE 3. Cincinnati Fifth Street Market, circa 1840: Point of assembly for the mob of 1841. *Reproduced with the permission of the Ohio Historical Society.*

PLATE 4. View of Cincinnati from the Ohio River, 1848. *From the collection of the Public Library of Cincinnati and Hamilton County.*

PLATE 5. Steamboats docked at the Cincinnati Wharf, 1848. *From the collection of the Public Library of Cincinnati and Hamilton County.*

PLATE 6. Cincinnati Wharf: Typical day's work for roustabouts and other levee workers, 1869. *Reproduced courtesy of HarpWeek.*

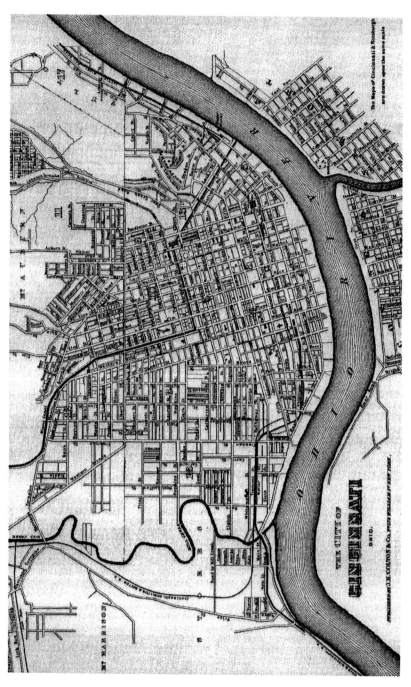

PLATE 7. Map of Cincinnati, 1862.

PLATE 8. Mob destroying the Cincinnati Courthouse, 1884. This scene typifies the spirit and destruction of mob action in Cincinnati. *Reproduced courtesy of HarpWeek.*

PLATE 9. Peter Clark, principal of Gaines High School. *Reproduced from Wendell P. Dabney*, Cincinnati's Colored Citizens: Historical, Sociological, and Biographical *(Cincinnati: Dabney Publishing, 1926).*

PLATE 10. Bucktown neighborhood, 1880s. *Reproduced with the permission of the Public Library of Cincinnati and Hamilton County.*

PLATE 11. John I. Gaines. *Reproduced from John Brough Shotwell,* A History of the Schools of Cincinnati *(Cincinnati: School Life Company, 1902).*

door with a battering ram, shattered windows, and entered the building, where they had a struggle with U.S marshals. After the melee, one marshal was dead, but Burns had not been rescued.[95]

Cincinnati's abolitionist community waged a campaign of resistance to the Fugitive Slave Act that resembled Boston's in tenor and tenacity. The community adopted many of the same strategies of resistance as had other northern communities, including migration, redoubling of efforts to aid runaways, and armed resistance. On at least one occasion, a black family refused to allow a slaveholder to enter their home to retrieve a family of fugitive slaves. After the owner threatened to break down the door and enter the home, the homeowner promised to shoot the first person who attempted to gain entrance without legal authority.[96]

The community's most effective response to this law, however, was the legal challenge. Several highly publicized local cases tested the application of the Fugitive Slave Act in Cincinnati. Eliza Potter, a black hairdresser who had settled in Cincinnati in 1840, was arrested under the law in the 1850s and charged with helping a man escape from bondage in Louisville, Kentucky. Prior to her arrest, Potter had traveled to Louisville with her employer, who owned several slaves there. By Potter's own account, when she was in Louisville she met a male slave who told her "a sad story of suffering" and asked if she "knew of a spot on this wide earth where he could be free." In her autobiography, Potter claimed she gave this man information about Canada without directions about how to find it. Apparently, the information Potter provided to this bondsman was not as benign as she claimed, because he absconded soon thereafter. Potter may have also helped the bondsman's sister escape a week earlier.[97]

After her return to Cincinnati, Potter was promptly arrested as an accessory under the 1850 legislation. She claimed that her arrest caused such a public stir that "thousands" of people, "some in sorrow and some in joy," followed her to the Ohio River, where she was handed over to Kentucky authorities.[98] Potter reported that many in the crowd believed that she had made her "final exit from Cincinnati." Without a confession or substantial evidence to prove her offense, Potter eventually was acquitted of all charges, but not before she served three months in prison awaiting trial.[99]

Another case concerned the freedom of George Washington McQuerry, who, along with three others, escaped from slavery in Washington County, Kentucky, in 1849. Whereas his compatriots wisely continued on to Canada, McQuerry settled in Miami County, Ohio. McQuerry married, fathered two children, and lived as a "sober industrious man, a good husband, a respected neighbor" for four years. McQuerry's owner found him in 1853, and had McQuerry arrested and taken to Cincinnati by a U.S. deputy marshal.[100]

When news of McQuerry's arrest reached in Cincinnati, the black community immediately mobilized to protest his return to slavery. That he had not been a member of the Cincinnati community was of little concern; he was a black man whose freedom hung in the balance, and that was reason enough for their involvement. Subsequently, a crowd of African American protesters gathered outside the hotel where McQuerry's owner was staying but was quickly dispersed by the police. Meanwhile, Peter Clark, a black civic leader and trustee of the Colored School Board, applied for a writ of habeas corpus to have the U.S. deputy marshal holding McQuerry show just cause why he had been deprived of his liberty. Had it not been for quick thinking by Clark, McQuerry would have been carried back to Kentucky without incident.[101] The writ of habeas corpus, which made provisions for a jury hearing, was the only way African Americans could secure a trial under the Fugitive Slave Act.

McQuerry had Cincinnati's best abolitionist attorneys, John Jolliffe and James Birney, working in his defense. They argued that McQuerry's four-year residence in the state had granted him de facto freedom. The heart of their defense, however, challenged the constitutionality of the 1850 Fugitive Slave Act. They argued that the U.S. Constitution gave states all power on the subject. Presiding judge McLean upheld the 1850 Fugitive Slave Act and remanded McQuerry back to slavery.[102] Although McQuerry lost his case, it was not because the abolitionist community had failed to mobilize many of its resources to secure his freedom.

In October 1853, another case tested both the law and the commitment of Cincinnati's abolitionist community. According to Levi Coffin, a slave known simply as Louis escaped from Kentucky and settled in Columbus, where he lived for a number of years until his owner found him. Louis was arrested under the 1850 Fugitive Slave Act and removed to Cincinnati. Louis's friends telegraphed Cincinnati's abolitionist attorneys, alerting them of the case. This time, the attorneys determined to challenge the slaveholder's claim by arguing that Louis was already free because his owner had previously brought him to Ohio. A trial was scheduled for the claimant to prove Louis was, indeed, his slave. On the day the case was to be tried, Louis decided not to take his chances with the American justice system. He inched his way backward in the crowded courtroom, ever so slightly, and received a series of encouraging nudges and taps from spectators as he went. The crowd slowly parted and quietly made room for Louis to escape, and someone in the crowd placed a "good hat" on his head to disguise him. Louis moved slowly through the black section of the courtroom and out the door of the courthouse. A few minutes passed before the court noticed he had absconded, but by then he was aboard the Underground Railroad and on his way out of the city.[103]

The most celebrated test case of all was that of Margaret Garner. On January 27, 1856, Margaret Garner and her husband, Robert, escaped from two plantations about sixteen miles from Covington, Kentucky, along with their four children and Robert's parents, Simon and Mary Garner. Upon their arrival in Cincinnati, the Garner family took refuge at the home of Margaret's uncle and cousin, Joseph and Elijah Kite, near Mill Creek in the western part of the city. Shortly thereafter, their whereabouts were discovered and federal marshals were dispatched to the Kite residence. The Garner men prepared for armed confrontation, determined not to return to slavery. As marshals battered in the door with a block of wood, Robert Garner fired a pistol at them. One of his bullets ripped through a marshal's finger and also shattered his jaw and teeth. As the marshals were gaining entrance, Margaret grabbed a knife and declared to her mother-in-law, "Before my children shall be taken back to Kentucky I will kill every one of them!" She then proceeded to slit the throat of her two-year-old daughter, Mary, nearly decapitating her. Margaret then attempted to cut the throats of her older children, who were found with bruises on their necks and heads. Before Margaret could be apprehended, she struck her infant child, Priscilla, in the head with a coal shovel but failed to kill her.[104]

The details of the horrific scene of bloodshed were burned into public memory for generations. Although Garner's actions might have become ammunition for the proslavery cause, they actually had the opposite effect. Abolitionists used this horrendous deed as a testament of how bad slavery was—that a mother would rather see her children dead than live as slaves.[105] Cincinnati's abolitionists interpreted Margaret Garner's actions not as child murder, but as the ultimate form of protest against slavery. Garner gained celebrity of mythic proportions. Locally, funds were raised for her legal fees.

Although they also faced state murder charges, the Garners first had to answer charges under the federal Fugitive Slave Act. John Jolliffe's defense against the charges focused on the fact that the Garners had been freed by Ohio laws because they had been to Cincinnati with their owner's consent on several prior occasions. However, the commissioner decided that the Garners' voluntary return to slavery after those visits had nullified their claims to freedom. Next, Jolliffe pushed to have the Garners released to state officials to answer charges for murder, hoping that an Ohio warrant would supersede one issued under the Fugitive Slave Act. Neither of these strategies was successful; the commissioner ultimately decided to send the Garners back to slavery.[106] In this case, federal law trumped state law, and the Garners never answered the murder charges. Judge McLean ruled that a "State Court cannot take from an officer of the United States, even on a criminal charge, the custody of a person in execution on a civil case."[107] The family was promptly "sold down the river" and placed on a steamer, the *Henry Lewis,* headed to New Orleans in March 1856. The *Henry Lewis* collided with another steamer in the Ohio River, sparking a fire aboard the vessel. After having miraculously survived her mother's blow to the head, little Priscilla drowned in the Ohio River.[108]

In the end, it was impossible to live in Cincinnati and not be affected by slavery or the underground or public resistance to it there. African Americans waged public protests, applied for writs of habeas corpus, helped fugitives escape crowded courtrooms, and continued to conceal and conduct fugitive slaves to freedom in spite of the law. White abolitionist attorneys developed defense strategies that either directly challenged the constitutionality of the law or invoked laws of freedom. In short, this community waged a multipronged attack on the law and its enforcement in Cincinnati. Resistance to the 1850 Fugitive Slave Act in Cincinnati thrust black underground activism onto the public stage.

EIGHT

"Palladium of Their Liberty"

Black Public Schools and the Road to
Self-Determination, 1849–1873

> Education is indeed the glory of any people. It is sure the
> palladium of their Liberty—the positive evidence of their
> permanent and growing elevation.
>
> —Proceedings of the Convention of the
> Colored Freemen of Ohio, January 14–18, 1852

Access to public schools was one of the most important civil rights issues for black Ohioans before 1849. After decades of protest and agitation, African Americans finally gained access to Ohio's public schools when the legislature repealed the laws of exclusion in 1849. But instead of allowing white and black children to attend the same schools, state legislators authorized an act to establish separate schools for the education of colored children.[1] Hence, racially segregated public schools emerged in Ohio long before Jim Crow was systematically codified at state levels and long before *Plessy v. Ferguson* sanctioned the rule "separate, but equal" at the national level.[2]

Racial segregation is never a positive value for society. Ohio's system of racially separate schools in a racist society resulted in inherent inequalities in the black public schools, including unequal financial resources, inferior facilities and materials, overcrowding, substandard curricula, ungraded classrooms, and underqualified teachers.[3] Yet even these inferior schools were better than the "forgotten alternative" of exclusion or impermanent and unstable private schools.[4] At the very least, because these segregated schools were state supported, all African Americans—not just a small minority—had the opportunity to receive an education.

In Cincinnati, public schools—even segregated ones—came as a relief to the black community. After decades of impermanent private schools, this was indeed a better alternative.

In Cincinnati, African Americans lobbied for and obtained the right to establish, administer, and manage their own school system, making the Colored School Board of Cincinnati among the first independent black school boards in the country. Elected by black male property owners, the board of directors—or trustees— directed and administered the day-to-day operations of the schools. The Colored School Board also hired teachers and regulated their salaries, set curricula and standards, maintained the school's property, and managed its own budget.[5] Black Cincinnati controlled the educational process, from policy to pedagogy, in an era when most African Americans were denied education and political power; this level of governance and management enabled the community to shape its own educational destiny.

By the time African Americans gained the right to attend public schools in the city, segments of their community had been attending private schools for more than thirty years. Churches, religious groups, itinerant teachers, and abolitionists all operated private schools for black Cincinnatians at various times between 1815 and 1849. The most significant private school for blacks was Gilmore High School for Negroes, the first high school for African Americans in the Queen City. The school was established in 1844 through the beneficence of a wealthy and generous New England Methodist Episcopal minister, Hiram S. Gilmore.[6] Classes were held initially in a converted carpenter's shop until Gilmore erected a large, five-room schoolhouse on Harrison Street.[7] He spared no expense, and even outfitted the schoolyard with gym equipment. Gilmore High did not immediately succumb to the same fate as other private schools in Cincinnati because of its extensive local and national fundraising efforts. The school held fairs and bazaars to raise money for scholarships for students who could not afford the tuition. The school choir frequently toured the country giving concerts, the proceeds of which were used to provide tuition and supplies for less fortunate students.[8] Gilmore's curriculum was designed to prepare its students for college and to teach them classical subjects, such as Latin, algebra, music, and art. Gilmore High employed only the finest teachers and earned such a fine reputation that young black scholars from all over the country moved to Cincinnati just for the opportunity to attend this school. Among Gilmore's most noteworthy graduates were the future Lieutenant

Governor of Louisiana, P. B. S. Pinchback, Congressman John Mercer Langston, renowned daguerreotypist Thomas Ball, and U.S. Recorder of Deeds Monroe Trotter. Talented local scholars—Peter H. Clark, John Isom Gaines, Joseph H. Perkins, Phillip Tolliver, and Dr. Commodore F. Buckner—also attended the school.[9] Despite its success and reputation, Gilmore closed its doors after just five years, when its founder and main benefactor moved to a utopian community.[10]

The most enduring legacy of Ohio's private schools was their success in educating and grooming a generation of leaders, teachers, and activists. By the early 1840s, there was a core group of black men and women who had been educated in these private schools and who, in turn, were educating other African Americans. This generation also led the struggle for access to common schools. Beginning in the early 1840s, delegates at African American state conventions shifted their focus from private schools to public schools. Philanthropy could not meet all of the operating expenses of private schools, and it was not feasible to increase tuition. In Cincinnati, the Education Society, although it had been a great example of mutuality, did not do enough. Even when benevolent whites completely funded private schools, as Hiram Gilmore had done, those efforts were short-term. Additionally, the schools could not meet the needs of a growing African American community. Black leaders realized that they would have to fight for publicly funded education.

Ohio's black leaders focused their challenge to laws denying them public education on the unjust tax system. An 1829 Ohio act mandated that black property holders pay a school tax and that their monies be appropriated by township trustees "for the education of said black and mulatto persons."[11] In practice, however, the state taxed black property owners for more a decade but did not provide education benefits or establish a separate school fund for African Americans. Although subsequent state legislation exempted African Americans from school taxes altogether, they continued to be taxed in practice, and their money used to support the very same public schools from which they were excluded.[12] Although African Americans in some communities requested a refund of their share of the local school fund so that they could start their own schools, they never received the funds owed to them.[13] The situation in Ohio was so outrageous that it circulated in the national black press. In an 1841 issue, the *Colored American* exposed these injustices and asked for public sympathy and action.

In Cincinnati, two Gilmore High graduates, John Isom Gaines and Peter Humphries Clark, led the battle for access to public schools. John

Isom Gaines was born November 6, 1821, to Isom and Elizabeth Gaines in Cincinnati. Although neither parent had been formally schooled, together they instilled in their son the value of education. Gaines attended a primary school operated by Lane Seminary students in the early 1830s and later attended Gilmore High. He worked for many years as a stevedore and a steamboat steward before opening a provisions shop near the river, where he sold goods to laborers and passengers traveling on steamboats.[14]

Although Gaines never pursued a college education, he was respected as one of black Cincinnati's foremost intellectuals. It is highly likely that his attendance at the school held by Lane students nurtured his political consciousness. Undoubtedly, instruction by abolitionist teachers must have helped him develop his critique of slavery and honed his oratory skills. Gaines attended a state black convention in 1838, which galvanized him to political action for his community.[15] An eloquent orator, Gaines frequently was invited to speak before African American and antislavery audiences. In 1841, at the age of twenty, he spoke publicly against the racial violence in the city that year.[16] Black citizens of Columbus invited him to deliver the keynote address at the anniversary celebration of emancipation in the West Indies on August 1, 1849.[17] Gaines served the black common schools as a clerk, member of the board of directors, and superintendent.

Gaines's nephew Peter Humphries Clark was born in March 1829 in Cincinnati. Clark also attended Gilmore High and then went on to attend Oberlin College.[18] At the time, Oberlin College was one of only a few colleges that accepted African Americans. After college, Clark moved back to Cincinnati and took a stereotyping apprenticeship.[19] Even more so than his uncle, Clark was fiercely uncompromising with white society on the issue of civil rights for African Americans. This dogged determination prompted historian Wendell Dabney to contend, "In his veins coursed no bootlicking blood."[20] Clark vehemently condemned colonization but supported voluntary emigration. Convinced that African Americans would never be treated equally in the United States, he made plans to emigrate to Africa in 1851.[21] Clark traveled as far as New Orleans, hoping to board a vessel headed to Africa, but when the ship was ready to sail, Clark was not on board.

Upon his return to Cincinnati, Clark committed himself to changing the racist system that had forced him to consider emigration. He became very active in the state colored conventions and even served in leadership positions within that organization.[22] He built his career and reputation as a teacher and principal in Cincinnati's black public schools. Clark had other interests as well, including the black press. In 1855, he published the *Herald of Freedom;* two years later he edited a Free Soil newspaper before moving on to work for Frederick Douglass's *North Star.*[23] In 1867, Clark established the Ohio State Auxiliary Equal Rights League, an organization that aimed to repeal all state and national laws that made racial distinctions.[24] Clark's contributions extend well beyond Cincinnati and well beyond the antebellum era: he was also a pioneer black socialist involved with party politics and workers' rights.[25]

In 1848 and 1849, a party struggle between Whigs and Democrats in the Ohio Legislature provided an opening for the Free Soil Party to propose the repeal of the Black Laws. In a deal that swung the balance of power, two Free Soil members offered their votes to the party that would support repeal of the Black Laws, the establishment of a public school system for African American children, and the election of Salmon Chase to the U.S. Senate. Democrats accepted the offer and, in exchange, won access to the open seat on the state supreme court. On February 10, 1849, the legislature enacted a statute that overturned the Black Laws and provided for a separate public school system for African American children paid for out of a proportionate share of each township's public funds allocated for common schools.[26] Although the repeal of the Black Laws did not end all denials of civil rights to African Americans, it ended some of the worst: the bond requirement and the exclusion from public schools.[27] The act also made provisions for a school board to be elected by black male property owners from each district. State legislators also extended limited voting privileges to black Ohioans.[28] Mobilized by a cadre of educated leaders like Gaines and Clark, Cincinnati's African American community quickly elected six trustees to manage its schools, with Gaines as the head of the board.

If black Cincinnati's educational gains took them to the frontier of freedom, city officials kept moving the border. In defiance of the 1849 legislation that had granted African Americans access to a public education, Cincinnati's city treasurer, William Disney, derailed the black school system by refusing to pay out monies from the general school fund to support black schools. Disney claimed that there was no law authorizing him to withdraw funds from the treasury for that purpose.[29] He also refused to acknowledge the authority of the black school board. Without funds, the black public schools were forced to close after just three months.[30]

African Americans refused to concede defeat after having waited so long for the right to attend public schools. John Gaines and Peter Clark accepted the challenge of organizing the community to action, raising money for legal representation to challenge the city's refusal to hand over the funds.[31] Subsequently, the black board of directors brought suit to force city officials to allocate money for their schools. In 1850, the state supreme court held in *State ex. rel. Directors of the Eastern and Western School Districts of Cincinnati v. City of Cincinnati,* that the black schools were entitled to their proportionate share of the school fund. The defense argued that the state constitution mandated that only white persons should hold power associated with government; hence, the 1849 act that authorized separate schools and provided for a separate black school board was unconstitutional on those grounds. The court concluded that there was "nothing . . . in the constitution prohibiting a colored person from holding such an office." In fact, the chief justice believed that "it was the intention of the framers of that law that colored persons might be elected directors."[32] African Americans reopened their schools shortly thereafter.

City leaders and school officials of the white schools requested that the legislature settle the issue by granting them authority over African American schools. Black educational autonomy in Cincinnati did not last long under such pressures. Beginning in 1853, a series of legislative acts stripped black Cincinnatians of the rights of school governance. This community lost the right to manage the budget for its own schools and to elect its own school trustees; the latter power was transferred to the white Board of Trustees and Visitors of Common Schools.[33] The Colored School Board that had been elected by the black community was dismantled. In 1854, Cincinnati's Board of Trustees and Visitors of Common Schools—the "White Board," as African Americans called it—handpicked black men to serve as the new Colored School Board, generally men whose politics were consistent with the ideas of the White Board.[34] These developments caused tension within the African American community. One faction, probably led by Gaines and Clark, felt that these "selected" trustees had "power to act . . . only at the nod of the Board of Trustees for the white schools." This faction feared that these selected trustees were "merely the *machines* in the hands of the 'White Board'" and therefore could not, or would not, act in the best interest of the black community.[35] The African American community felt it was being stripped of its autonomy on every level—from the classroom to the boardroom.

Furthermore, a white man, Stephen Massey, was appointed superintendent of the black schools. Under his supervision, white teachers systematically began to replace black teachers. Massey boasted that such a move was intended to usher in "a higher order of talent," but the racist implications of such a move were not lost on the African American community.[36] All of these moves were perceived as deliberate and direct attempts to thwart black desires for self-governance and self-determination. By 1855, several black leaders had expressed discontent with white teachers, Massey, and the token Colored School Board.[37] Additional calls for black-controlled schools came from other quarters, such as the Convention of the Colored Freemen of Ohio. The convention urged black citizens to petition the legislature for the right to elect black superintendents.[38] The White Board, rethinking whether it could manage the black schools as well as African Americans, recommended that the city council cede control of the schools back to that community.[39] Under this pressure, the legislature passed an act that handed control of the Colored School Board back to the African American community in 1856.[40] African Americans elected a new board in 1857, with John Gaines as superintendent.[41] Gaines never had time to fulfill his plans for the black public schools because he met an untimely death in 1859. The first black public high school was named in his honor in 1866.[42]

Cincinnati's black community learned several lessons between 1849 and 1856, and external challenges reinforced its commitment to self-governance and self-determination. Control of school administration, finances, curricula, and classroom instruction was essential to ensure that African American children would receive the best education possible.

Although the doors of public schools were opened for African Americans, there was no mad rush to fill the seats. Many years passed before the black community took full advantage of the schools. In 1856, 52 percent of the city's 1,190 school-aged black youth were enrolled in school. Five years later, only 30 percent of the city's black youth were enrolled.[43] Given the economic and social conditions that circumscribed African Americans' ability to attend schools, these statistics were respectable when compared to the figures for whites. For example, in 1854, the school enrollment rate for white children was only 44 percent.[44] Enrollment statistics worsened for African Americans after general emancipation and the subsequent migration of thousands of uneducated freed slaves into the city. In 1867, only 926 of the city's 5,364 black youth—or roughly 17 percent—had matriculated in school.[45]

Although the 1860 census by no means provides a complete account of the African American population in the city or of those who attended school, it reports that children of the black elite were more likely to attend school than were other black children. According to the census data for the Fourth Ward that year, 83 percent of the children of barbers and 75 percent of the children of seamstresses attended school. By contrast, in the same ward, only 48 percent of the children of washerwomen and 60 percent of the children of laborers attended school.[46] An extrapolation of that evidence indicates that barbers' children were the most educated group of black children in the city. These children came from homes in which education was emphasized and the family was less dependent on children's labor for survival.

Even for those who matriculated in school, regular attendance was problematic. Between 1858 and 1861, the daily attendance rates for African Americans were between 44 and 48 percent. Black school officials characterized this absenteeism as "truancy" and commented that "people seem to take an interest in everything save Public Instruction . . . At picnics and first of August celebrations they turn out by hundreds, but will not turn out at the annual examination of our Common Schools."[47] Officials observed that a portion of black children simply played in the streets.[48] While such observations may have been partly true, responsibilities to home and family also played a role in why so many children absented themselves from school on a regular basis. Black children usually attended school only until they were old enough to work. Then they were sent to do washing in households, to peddle on the streets, or to do odd jobs on the river.[49] School officials, as members of the black elite, initially could not easily empathize with this economic issue. The Colored School Board later struck a compromise between children's need to work and the importance of education, and established evening schools for youth over the age of ten who worked during the day.[50]

Furthermore, the schools lacked the resources to accommodate every pupil. The handful of qualified teachers who worked in this system was inadequate to meet the needs of the entire school-aged black population. Because there was no educational option beyond the sixth grade until 1866, youth who completed those grades could not continue in school. In sum, for the first twenty years of their existence, Cincinnati's black common schools were unable to meet all the needs of their community.

⎯

Educational capital is the range of resources that a community invests in its own education, including financial capital, experience, skills, leadership, support, and expectations. Black Cincinnati's educational capital included teachers and parents as well as the actual buildings that housed these schools.

Some of the most important assets Cincinnati's black community contributed to its schools were its teachers. Certain African Americans had opposed white teachers, not because of racial prejudice, but because they believed black teachers would have a more positive influence on black students. For children who rarely saw African Americans in professional positions, black teachers were, indeed, sources of inspiration. The mere presence of black teachers was enough to imbue these children with racial pride and optimism about their own futures. Given the racial and ethnic heritage they shared with their students, black teachers could certainly relate a little better to them than their white counterparts. Hence, these teachers could best prepare black children to navigate in a racist world. But qualified black teachers were yet rare in the late 1850s in Cincinnati.[51] Some, like Owen T. B. Nickens and A. M. Sumner, were seasoned veterans who had taught in private schools in the previous decade. Others, like Peter Clark, began their teaching careers in Cincinnati's colored public schools.[52] A number of black women assumed teaching positions in the girls' schools. Teachers were not the only examples of black leadership inside these schools. There were principals and teaching assistants, as well. Peter Clark, for example, served as the principal of several schools, including John Gaines High School.[53]

The Colored Public School system worked very hard to professionalize their teachers. In 1868, a normal school was established to train new teachers and to teach new skills to those who were already teaching.[54] The superintendent regularly urged teachers to use lesson plans and to establish pedagogical methods, and all teachers were required to meet regularly to discuss teaching methods.[55] All of these measures increased the overall occupational prestige of teaching. At the very least, teachers enjoyed higher incomes and more job stability than they had while working in private schools. The profession opened the door to middle-class wages and status. Despite the glaring wage disparities by gender, black teachers earned between twenty-three and thirty-five dollars per month in 1864; principals earned seventy-five dollars per month.[56]

Parents were another critical resource within the community—although not all black parents valued education to the same degree as did school leaders. Consequently, the Colored School Board tried to inculcate in them an appreciation for it. In an 1858 essay entitled "What Is the Duty of the Colored American Parent?" John Gaines bluntly urged mothers to consider the alternatives to education: "the penitentiary, the poor houses, and dens of infamy."[57] He tried to convince these parents that education safeguarded children against licentious and criminal habits. According to Gaines, education was the great equalizer of the races: "We must be their equals in human knowledge, improvements and inventions, and until we are, all schemes for equalizing the races upon the soil, are nothing but cob webs, to catch the weak and delude the weary." Gaines implored parents not to keep their children from school, but to become involved by "visiting the schools and attending our annual exams."[58]

The Colored School Board felt parental involvement was essential and that parental support would ultimately determine whether the schools failed or succeeded. The board realized that only collaboration between schools and parents could increase school attendance. In the late 1850s the board adopted a policy of sending teachers to visit the homes of students who were habitually absent. This policy was intended to increase communication between the school and parents, thereby discouraging truancy.[59] The Colored School Board treated parents as assets, and they were, indeed, a critical component of the community's educational capital.

Black Cincinnati's educational capital also included the rooms and buildings that housed black public schools. Before 1849, many private schools had been located in black-owned spaces, usually nothing more than rooms provided by African American families or churches.[60] The Cincinnati Colored Public School system provided its own school buildings, but financial constraints restricted them to inferior structures and, sometimes, mere rented rooms.[61] In the 1850s, African American children attended class in buildings that were generally unsanitary, unhealthy, and unsafe. The buildings were infested with vermin and insects and were located in neighborhoods plagued by crime. The girls' school was a "rat hole"; female students often had their lessons disrupted by rats scurrying across the floor. The classrooms themselves were "low, long, and dark with little or no ventilation." The walls had plaster peeling from them and had holes so big that the wind passed through them in the winter. Students in one school had to endure an "effluvia which . . . is enough to knock a man to pieces, and make him desire a brandy punch." One school official remarked that these buildings were "better suited for the repository of the dead."[62] It was difficult to learn with dignity under such conditions.

Stephen Massey had reported in his 1855 annual summary that the school buildings were a "disgrace to our city," yet his board did nothing about it. He felt the black community should assume responsibility for erecting new buildings: "Do not expect that the Trustees and Visitors of Common Schools will erect school-houses for you, when the laws under which they act, expressly provide to the contrary." Massey encouraged African Americans to unite for the benefit of the community and to erect their own schools: "Let every one work shoulder to shoulder, endeavoring to accomplish something that will elevate the present generation."[63] Surely Massey appreciated that there was a historical precedent of the African American community providing its own school buildings. Yet, when the two white high schools were valued at $80,000, Massey's call for self-sufficiency seemed more like accommodation to state-sponsored inequality.[64] Because its budget was pooled from a smaller and poorer tax base, the Colored Public School system would never have schools equal to those of the white system and simply did not have the supplemental funds needed for new buildings. The Colored School Board decided not to expend its budget on a capital building project and risk being left without funds for salaries or other operating costs. Determined that the city should bear the responsibility of providing decent schools, the Colored School Board lobbied for new buildings, where African American students could learn with dignity. In 1858, the city met its demands and leased a lot on Seventh Street between Broadway and Culvert, erecting a new school building for African Americans with four classrooms, two recitation rooms, a hall, and space for a playground outside.[65]

School libraries were other critical resources within these buildings. Although benevolent whites had established reading rooms and libraries for African Americans in the past, none had survived. The public school system gave rise to several of black Cincinnati's first permanent libraries. Black common school libraries were also open to the public, providing black families with access to books and learning.[66] Many of these libraries became centers of learning and intellectual inquiry and exploration.

As dilapidated as they were, Cincinnati's public schools were the only buildings outside of the black church that provided a social and cultural space in which to train a new generation of African American teachers, leaders, and administrators. The buildings also provided a space for the transmission of cultural knowledge and pride from teachers to students. Lastly, they were one of only a few public places where African Americans could be together as a community.

⎯

The Cincinnati Colored School Board acted as an educational broker, until state law dismantled separate school boards in 1873.[67] The Cincinnati board served as a buffer between white school officials and African American schoolchildren and their parents. This body negotiated the terms of African Americans' public education between 1857 and 1872 and represented their concerns and needs. The black school board was among the chief advocates of educational equality in Cincinnati after

1856. The Colored School Board also protected, cultivated, and contributed to that community's educational capital. In fact, as independent scholar David Calkins concludes, the "political aspects of the colored school system and the educator-politicians it supported [and groomed] were not only significant to the relationship to the black community [but] in the larger realm of municipal politics."[68]

Of the most important battles the Colored School Board waged was its advocacy of school equality. In 1854, the white common schools began offering classes beyond the sixth grade; white pupils had the advantage of Intermediate and High School education.[69] Such a move was intended to alleviate the overcrowding in the lower grades and to allow each student to progress according to his or her ability. The black common school system, by contrast, had no provisions beyond the sixth grade in the antebellum era. This lack of opportunity impeded black children's intellectual development in comparison to that of their white contemporaries. African American students who completed the sixth grade were "compelled to go over the same studies from year to year." Bright young scholars who wished to become teachers were left the schools and the city "because of the restricted course of study."[70]

Although the Colored School Board had requested a high school for the benefit of black youth as early as 1857, it was not until 1866 that Gaines High School was finally opened, named in honor of John Gaines.[71] Gaines High opened the doors of secondary education and the doors of opportunity. Secondary education was intended to enable African Americans to compete with their white peers for jobs and to prepare them for higher education. Most importantly, secondary education trained a new generation of African American teachers.

The Colored School Board lobbied for equality in other areas as well. In addition to trying to equalize black teachers' salaries with those of their white counterparts, it also focused on an accurate school census. Black common schools were funded based on the proportionate percentage of black youth to white youth in the city. An inaccurate enumeration meant that African American schools did not receive their fair share of the tax dollars. Before 1857, when the White Board still controlled the Colored School Board, there had been a woeful undercounting of African American youth in the city. Understanding the long-range implications of undercounting, the Colored School Board went to great lengths to ensure a more accurate accounting of the African American youth. For example, in 1856, 1,190 youth were counted; in 1858, the census counted 1,805 school-aged children.[72] Thus, the black public school system received a bigger slice of the tax pie between 1857 and 1859, an increase of $2,587.69.[73] By reclaiming its fair share, the Colored School Board had more financial resources for buildings and teachers' salaries.

Historians have yet to explain why Cincinnati's African American community did not wage a sustained struggle against separate schools. When black communities in Cleveland and Columbus moved toward a hard-line integrationist position in the 1870s, black Cincinnati remained relatively content with the dual school system. Historian David Gerber offers two explanations: 1) that Cincinnati's African Americans "were only too well aware, local white opinion was hardly favorable to racial mixing," and 2) that "blacks had pride in their long-established schools and confidence in their teachers, many of whom were trained under [Peter] Clark."[74]

In Cincinnati, black public schools were not necessarily bastions of inferiority and evidence of black degradation. In fact, Cincinnati's black public schools became important social and cultural spaces to develop and groom black leaders, develop a political ideology, formulate a social critique, articulate desires for freedom and equality, and strategize about how to obtain them. Cincinnati's African American community supported the dual system, despite its inherent inequalities, in part because of the history of the Colored School Board and the range of educational capital that this community possessed. The Cincinnati Colored School Board was a powerful advocate for educational access and equality for nearly two decades. Certainly, the community had pride in its schools, but what Gerber considers pride is something far greater: a legacy of self-determination and autonomy.

Although other free blacks believed that separate schools and churches "perpetuate[d] this wicked caste" which was "destructive to the peace and happiness of man," black Cincinnatians did not necessarily feel that way.[75] Integration was, at times, at odds with this community's larger objectives of equality, self-determination, and freedom from racism. The community opposed integrated schools because "[i]n a school of mixed races the colored children would be neglected by the teachers, who could not but be prejudiced against them in the interest of their own race."[76] Because separate schools provided advantages of self-determination and self-education, Cincinnati's black community was in no rush to push for integration and, in fact, was among the last in Ohio to do so. Autonomy was another influential factor: communities that had no independent black school boards pushed for integration much sooner than did

Cincinnati.[77] Black Cincinnati supported educational separation in part because the black schools were managed and taught by African Americans. As long as it had its own educational capital, black Cincinnati saw no reason to lobby for integration. In April 1872, Cincinnati's African American community mobilized to oppose a state bill designed to dismantle black school boards and to bring them all under the authority of the district boards.[78] An act to amend "an act for the reorganization and maintenance of common schools" was passed in May 1873 despite opposition in some quarters.[79] The Cincinnati black public school system was placed back in the hands of the Board of Trustees and Visitors for Common Schools (the White Board). Only then did it become painfully clear that that level of self-determination was no longer possible.

In Cincinnati between 1856 and 1872, the school eclipsed all other black institutions in importance as an agent for racial uplift—even the black church. Cincinnati's black leadership invested much of its time, energy, and resources in its public schools. Born out of the first extension of citizenship rights to African Americans by the state of Ohio, public schools represented decades of struggle for this community. The right to govern those schools and elect the trustees was a preparation for participation in the larger body politic. Black public schools also represented a viable opportunity to assert racial equality. Public schools did, in this period, what black churches had been doing for decades: they trained future generations of leaders and civil rights activists, provided the means for the social and economic elevation of both individuals and the race, and infused other institutions with an educated membership. In sum, the history of black Cincinnati summons a new interpretative understanding of black institutional life in the nineteenth-century city.

NINE

"Colored Citizen"

Defining and Asserting Citizenship, 1849–1868

> The liberty of a people is always insecure who have not ab-
> solute control of their own political destiny.
>
> —*Declaration of Sentiments*, National Emigration Convention of 1854

THE 1857 DRED SCOTT decision settled the looming question
of black citizenship at the federal level. In that case, Dred Scott, an enslaved African American, had sued for his freedom in federal courts on
grounds that he had lived in Missouri, a free state, with his previous
owner—making him a free man by the laws of that state. U.S. Supreme
Court Chief Justice Roger Taney held that Dred Scott, as a member of
the African race, was not a citizen and, therefore, had no right to sue in
federal court. The court's ruling was rooted in Taney's belief that the
framers of the U.S. Constitution did not consider people of African descent citizens and never had intended that they should reap the benefits
of citizenship—including access to the federal courts. Taney explained
that even if a state conferred citizenship upon someone and granted that
person all the rights of such, that act did not make that person a citizen
of the United States because states did not have the authority to grant
U.S. citizenship.[1] This decision was a devastating blow to African Americans throughout the nation, even more damning because it came from
the highest court in the land. Although African Americans had been
making economic and educational gains in many cities for decades and
were still striving toward respectability, these efforts counted for naught;

citizenship rights still eluded them. The Dred Scott decision sent waves of outrage and panic throughout free black America. It not only precipitated widespread public condemnation of the law in black communities but reinvigorated an emigration movement among those who felt hopeless about the prospect of equality in this country.[2]

The Convention of the Colored Men of Ohio joined the chorus of dissent.[3] At its 1858 convention, the organization proclaimed that the Dred Scott decision and Fugitive Slave Act of 1850 were "huge outrages" upon the laws of the land and humanity.[4] Similarly, at its first annual meeting in 1860, the all-black Ohio State Anti-Slavery Society issued a statement condemning both the Dred Scott decision and the Fugitive Slave Act.[5] Although these federally imposed disabilities were disheartening, black Ohio leaders focused their efforts and attention on attacking state-imposed barriers to citizenship. The Ohio State Anti-Slavery Society decried Ohio laws for providing neither protection of personal liberty nor rights of citizenship: "This state of our nativity or adoption affords us no protection for our personal liberty, and denies us almost every civil and political right."[6] Similarly, the 1858 Convention of the Colored Men of Ohio complained that the state "taxes a portion of its inhabitants without allowing them a representation, excludes them from offices of honor and trust, refuses them an impartial trial by Jury, refuses an equal education to their youth, disparages their patriotism by refusing to enroll them in her militia, allows them to be hunted through her cities, confined in her jails, and dragged thence to hopeless slavery, consigns their lunatics and paupers to the common jail."[7]

African Americans had waged a long and vigorous struggle for citizenship rights in Ohio, and the walls of exclusion began to crumble with the repeal of the odious Black Laws in 1849. The repeal not only removed barriers to black settlement and education in Ohio but also signaled a shift toward an expansion of citizenship for blacks.[8] For example, by then African Americans had gained the right to testify and sue in court and to enter into contract. They retained the right to present petitions and memorials to the legislature, a right they had exercised for decades. African Americans could invoke the writ of habeas corpus, which, as the last chapter demonstrated, was an important weapon in the battle against slavery. After 1842, some African Americans of mixed ancestry even were permitted to vote.[9] After 1849, black Ohioans were able to attend public schools, and in Cincinnati they managed those schools and elected their own school officials, exercising some measure of municipal power. They enjoyed the freedoms of speech, press, movement, and worship and the right to own and dispose of property as they wished. Laws protected free blacks against kidnapping.[10]

But the state continued to deny black Ohioans other critical citizenship rights. The 1851 Ohio constitutional convention refused to remove the words "white male" from the document, thereby also refusing to expand the definition of citizenship to include African Americans. In addition, they still could not serve on juries or in the military. They continued to be subjected to taxation without representation. The early stages of a de jure color line were extended into personal lives with the passage of laws prohibiting interracial marriage in 1861. Well into the mid-1860s, African Americans continued to live under the mantle of inequality, and with a compromised ability to enjoy or defend their right to be considered citizens by the state of Ohio. In short, although black Ohioans enjoyed some civil rights, others—perhaps the most crucial ones—eluded them. And because voting was the surest measure of citizenship status, disfranchisement trumped all other denials of citizenship to African Americans.

Although black Ohioans could not vote during most of the nineteenth century, those whose complexions were "nearer white than black" or who "held a larger portion of the blood of the white race" had enjoyed suffrage rights in the state since 1842. But many such persons were stripped of that privilege under an 1859 act to "preserve the purity of elections." True to its name, this act was an attempt to preserve the purity of the electorate by excluding those with any "visible admixture of African blood," which meant that any potential voter who appeared to be of African decent was excluded from the polls. Any judge of election convicted of extending voting rights to such persons could be fined between one hundred and five hundred dollars and sentenced to six months in the county jail.[11] Hence, under this new law, the only way a man of mixed ancestry could vote was to be undeniably white in complexion.

The 1859 act was strengthened in 1868 by the passage of the so-called Supplementary Act.[12] The Supplementary Act provided for judges of election to challenge the qualifications of any prospective voter with a "visible admixture of African blood." The voter in question was to be subjected to an interrogation about his background; sample questions included: "In the community in which you live are you classified and recognized as a white or colored person?" and "Do you associate with white or colored persons?" and "Were your parents married, and did they live together as man and wife?" After that examination, the prospective voter was required to produce two "credible" witnesses who could validate his racial background. The Supplementary Act also stated that visible appearance was not enough to classify someone as a white man; prospective voters of color, however fair in complexion, had to prove that they had more white blood than African.[13] This was a pernicious act that threatened to disenfranchise voters of color, and its meaning was not lost on the Ohio citizenry.

In a lawsuit related to the act, the state's supreme court justices concluded that the act's "manifest tendency and effect are to subvert instead of protect the right of suffrage, and to impede instead of facilitate its exercise, in a particular class of voters."[14] In what seemed to be more of a condemnation of the legislative branch of government than dictum, the court charged that "the act is calculated to impair and defeat the exercise of the colored man's constitutional right to vote [in Ohio]." Furthermore, because it had no other logical objective than to disenfranchise men of color, the court reasoned that the Supplementary Act seemed to be a "studied and cunningly devised scheme to effect that single object."[15] Hence, as the federal government marched toward an expansion of freedom under the Fourteenth and Fifteenth Amendments, Ohio seemed to be regressing in its extension of citizenship to African Americans. But African Americans did not stand by idly and wait for anyone to grant them their rights.

Between the repeal of the Black Laws in 1849 and the ratification of the Fourteenth Amendment in 1868, black communities throughout the state collectivized and institutionalized their efforts to secure citizenship rights for the race. The Convention of the Colored Men of Ohio was composed of representatives from black communities throughout the state who met annually to discuss the conditions and concerns of their local communities and how to address them collectively. In the 1850s, the organization became the primary civil rights organization for black Ohioans. No other organization at the local or national level was a better advocate for securing citizenship for black Ohioans.

The Convention of the Colored Men of Ohio argued that African Americans deserved the same privileges enjoyed by other citizens in the state. They based their arguments on issues of natural, human, and constitutional rights: "We possess the physical, the intellectual and the attributes common to humanity. As men then, we have rights, inherent rights, which civil society is bound to respect . . . protect and defend."[16] That specific argument had been a mainstay for free blacks for decades. Black Ohio leaders also supported their claims to citizenship by invoking the guarantees made by the Constitution and Declaration of Independence or by citing past examples of black patriotism in war.[17] Although those arguments may have been relevant at the federal level, they had little local specificity and did not compel Ohio to confer citizenship on African Americans.

Taxation without representation had been a major issue in the struggle for citizenship rights. The Convention of the Colored Men of Ohio argued that to levy taxes against African Americans but not to allow them the right to elect their representatives went against republican principles and created inherent inequalities within the state system. In an 1854 memorial, John Mercer Langston declared, "Since then, it is a cardinal, a fundamental maxim of your political faith, that taxation and representation are never to be saundered [sic], but always go together; and since we are taxed in common with all others to meet the expenditures of the government . . . we ought to have the advantages of a fair and impartial representation."[18] At its 1858 meeting, the Convention of the Colored Men of Ohio resolved that a state that taxed its residents without allowing representation and denied them the right to public office, an impartial jury, an equal education, or service in the militia "forfeits her claim to be called Christian or Republican."[19] The convention committed to "agitate this subject before the people, to circulate petitions on it among people, and memorialize the Legislature in regard to it, till our State government becomes a true democracy, conservative of equal and impartial liberty."[20] Despite this avowal, the convention was not successful; black Ohioans endured taxation without representation until 1870, when the Fifteenth Amendment granted them suffrage.

When agitation, appeals, and memorials to the legislature seemed futile, black men in Cincinnati tried another path to citizenship: military service. Shortly after the fall of Fort Sumter, they began mobilizing for military duty. They organized themselves into a company of "Home Guards" and prepared to defend Cincinnati in the event of an attack by southern troops. The Home Guards acted in the spirit of patriotism to the Union and loyalty to Cincinnati—an ironic loyalty because African Americans had no reason to prove themselves loyal to a city that had never been loyal to them. The Cincinnati Home Guards set up recruiting stations throughout the city and began drilling.[21]

Throughout free black northern communities, African Americans organized themselves into companies, practiced drills, and offered their services to their respective state militaries.[22] In New York, Providence, Washington, and Boston, black men and women volunteered a range of services to the military effort. African Americans in Cleveland and Albany,

Ohio, vowed to serve the same way African Americans had in the American Revolution and the War of 1812 and promptly organized themselves.[23] Blacks in Oberlin wrote to Secretary of War Simon Cameron, pleading for an opportunity to serve as soldiers in the Union war effort.[24] Initially, free blacks hoped that military service would prove they were deserving of citizenship rights; for black men, specifically, fighting in a war for freedom would prove them "Men."[25] Others joined the war effort to fight for the freedom of slaves. The primary objective of Cincinnati's Home Guards was "the defense of the city."[26] This manner of service suggests these men were willing to assume the responsibilities of citizens.

Throughout the nation, local police and white citizens initially rebuffed or repressed black military mobilization. Officials in Providence authorized local police to break up the drilling exercises, calling them "disorderly gatherings." The New York police chief intimated that he would be unable to stem the mob violence that would surely ensue should black men continue to drill.[27] In Cincinnati, officials tried at every turn to persuade the Home Guards to disband. According to Peter Clark, police seized the keys to their meetinghouse, forced them to take down the American flag hanging above the door of the recruiting station, and told the Home Guards, "We want you damned niggers to keep out of this; this is a white man's war." City officials and the local press repeatedly warned the Home Guards that "serious danger impended" should they continue their exercises.[28] The signs of an impending mob attack were undeniable to a community that could read them so well. To avoid conflict or retribution against the entire black community, Cincinnati's Home Guards agreed to issue a public disclaimer and to disband, ending the black voluntary effort to contribute to the city's defense.[29] Gone with it was the opportunity to prove, through loyal defense, that African Americans deserved citizenship rights—or so they thought.

In August 1862, Cincinnati city officials received word that a Confederate invasion of the Queen City was imminent. Because Cincinnati's location on the edge of the South made it extremely vulnerable to attack, concern quickly escalated to frenzy. After decades of economic and political identification with the slave South, Cincinnati's leading citizens and officials had to face the sobering reality that the war had polarized the nation along geographic and economic lines. The Queen City never felt more northern than it did then. State military leaders, stationed in Cincinnati, took steps to protect the city against the very states that had long been its life source.

On Tuesday, September 2, 1862, Cincinnati mayor George Hatch issued a public notice requesting all citizens to organize in defense of the city: "Every man, of every age, be he citizen or alien, who lives under the protection of our laws, is expected to take part in the organization." The call also commanded citizens to report at their regular places of voting.[30] With the reaction to the Home Guards still fresh in their minds, African Americans assumed that a call for *citizens* to organize for duty did not include them.[31] As disfranchised people, they had no regular place of voting, and at no time in Cincinnati's history had they been considered citizens. The denial of citizenship rights for African Americans had been written into the state constitution sixty years earlier and reinforced by subsequent laws, including the one that barred them from military service. Just a decade earlier, the Constitutional Convention of 1851 had upheld the framers' decision to restrict suffrage to white males.[32] African Americans were still excluded from orphanages, poor houses, and the militia, so they had good reason to ignore the calls for service.

When no black volunteers were forthcoming, Mayor Hatch established a special military police, which, according to one source, was composed of "a class too cowardly or too traitorous to aid, honestly and manfully," to round up all African American men and force them to help the war effort. This group of "brutal ruffians," masquerading as police, entered every black home between September 2 and September 4, 1862, abducted every able-bodied male inhabitant, and marched them all to the mule pen near the river. According to Peter Clark, who wrote the history of this experience, "Closets, cellars and garrets were searched; bayonets were thrust into beds and bedding; old and young, sick and well, were dragged out, and amidst shouts and jeers, marched like felons to the pen on Plum Street."[33] Without warning, explanation, or showing of just cause, black families were stripped of their fathers and sons and left defenseless in the midst of war. The same men who had eagerly volunteered to defend the city the previous year were now being compelled to do so.

Mayor Hatch had acted under the authority of General Lewis Wallace, an Ohio military leader charged with organizing the defense of Cincinnati.[34] Although state military leaders had authorized black military service in Cincinnati, local leaders had carried out the "recruitment." To fill wartime labor shortages when volunteers were not forthcoming, federal authorities sometimes resorted to impressing black men into labor.[35] It was neither a popular nor legal way of recruiting free men. Confederate officials and southern slaveholders routinely compelled the service of bondsmen for Confederate war efforts.[36] But for local northern authorities to abduct and impress an entire population of black male residents for local war efforts was not only quite unusual but practically unprecedented on free soil.[37] To add further insult, Cincinnati officials had no noble service in mind for these men, but marched them across the Ohio River into Covington, Kentucky, and to put them to work building fortifications, cooking, and serving white troops under conditions reminiscent of slavery. They were cursed at and otherwise subjected to degrading insults by their commanders.[38]

After considerable public outrage about their initial "recruitment," more compassionate leaders, like Judge William M. Dickson and Captain James Lupton, were obtained for these men. Dickson and Lupton organized these men into companies, chose black captains, and called them the "Black Brigade of Cincinnati." Although the Black Brigade was not recognized by the state (Ohio still barred blacks from the state military) or federal governments, Dickson and Lupton tried to create the semblance of a regular military unit for these men. African Americans were brought into duty with military formality, including patriotic speeches, symbols, and rhetoric. Lupton gave the brigade a U.S. flag inscribed with the name "Black Brigade" and encouraged his men to "Rally around it! Assert your manhood, [and] be loyal to duty." He also asserted that with the downfall of slavery there would be "one country, one flag, [and] one destiny."[39] Never before had black Cincinnatians been extended such an overt gesture of citizenship. By transforming the spirit of the work from the mundane to the patriotic, Captain Lupton offered them possibility, and effectively mobilized their hearts and bodies to serve the local Union war effort.

Despite Captain Lupton's grand and symbolic ceremonial gestures, the men of the Black Brigade were not recognized as soldiers. The only weapons they received were the spades needed to dig trenches. Instead of fighting, they performed the menial drudgery of military service: digging ditches, building fortifications, chopping trees, and making roads.[40] This degrading, heavy, dirty work was a far cry from the service they had been willing to render earlier as Home Guards. They received neither uniform nor arms, although they did receive two weeks' pay.[41] Although they had been compelled into service, relegated to menial labor, and placed on the front line of entry into the city without weapons, the men of the Black Brigade were expected to provide "willing and cheerful service."[42] The Black Brigade remained in service until the threat of a Confederate invasion of Cincinnati passed three weeks later. Contemporary sources indicate that more than 25 percent of the black population served.[43]

Rather than allow resentment to harden their hearts, these black men nobly labored in defense of their city. Although they did not engage in traditional defense, the men of the Black Brigade took great pride in knowing that they had contributed to the defense of the city through other means. They took what had begun as a harrowing and humiliating ordeal and redefined it. And although they never served in battle (save one that was only narrowly averted when a Union unit mistook them for Confederate forces), their white commanders extolled their virtue, courage and patriotism when they released from service on September 20, 1862. That day, the Black Brigade, in a ceremonious procession, marched through the streets of Covington and across a bridge into Cincinnati with banners flying and music playing.[44]

In many ways, the impressment of African American men into service for the defense of Cincinnati is ironic. African Americans were forced to defend a city that had never done the same for them. The very people who had been denied the chance to defend the city were forced to do so one year later. Although African Americans' volunteerism had been rejected, the responsibilities of citizenship were conferred on them instantly—by force, abduction, and impressment—a year later as a military expedient. Neither the members of the Black Brigade nor any other African Americans received citizenship rights as a direct effect of their service. Even after the formation of this brigade, Ohio proved intransigent toward allowing military service to become the path of citizenship for its black residents. State legislators resisted raising black regiments, even after the Emancipation Proclamation sanctioned it. The more than nine hundred black Ohioans who wished to serve as soldiers had to be mustered into the Massachusetts 54th Volunteers. Not until November 1863, several months after the federal government had authorized the enlistment of black soldiers, did Ohio begin organizing its own black regiments.[45]

Although the Black Brigade made only minimal progress in swaying legislators to extend citizenship, it inspired a great deal of collective self-respect, racial pride, and anticipation of the dawn of a new day for the black community of Cincinnati. Conscious of shaping and preserving its own history, the Black Brigade asked Peter H. Clark, lifelong educator and activist, to record its history for future generations. The history those men chose to remember was their designation as "[t]he first organization of colored people of the North actually employed for military purposes."[46] That designation is itself instructive; the black men of Cincinnati wanted to have an honorable place in history—not a pitiable one. Ignobly as the organization had begun, the members of the Black Brigade refashioned it into something honorable.

African American agitation for citizenship did not end after the war either. At the January 1865 meeting of the State Convention of Colored Men, delegates established the Ohio State Auxiliary Equal Rights League, which was designed to obtain "recognition of the rights of the colored people of Ohio as American citizens." The group chose Cincinnati as its permanent headquarters and elected Cincinnatian Peter Clark as president. The Ohio State Auxiliary Equal Rights League committed itself to fight for the repeal of state and national legislation that made racial distinctions.[47] The Ohio State Auxiliary Equal Rights League was part of a larger organization, the National Equal Rights League, which had been formed at the National Convention of Colored Men in October 1864 to secure full rights of citizenship for African Americans. The National Equal Rights League, one of the earliest national civil rights organizations, aimed at securing "full enjoyment of liberties, protection of our persons throughout the land, complete enfranchisement" and equality before the law.[48] By this time, black Ohioans were directing their struggle for citizenship at the federal level. It is not clear how long the Ohio branch of the Equal Rights League lasted, but black Ohioans finally won the full rights of citizens under the federal Civil Rights Acts of 1866 and the Fourteenth (1868) and Fifteenth (1870) Amendments to the U.S. Constitution.[49]

TEN

The Shadows

The Other Black Cincinnati, 1860s

> You and me, we sweat and strain,
> Body all aching and wracked with pain,
> Tote that barge, lift that bale,
> You show a little grit an' you lands in jail.
> I keeps laughin', instead of cryin',
> I must keep fightin', until I'm dyin',
> And Ol' Man River, he just keeps rollin' along.
>
> —Oscar Hammerstein II, "Old Man River" (modified by Paul Robeson)

THE OHIO RIVER shaped its own community and culture in nineteenth-century Cincinnati. This community included river workers, merchants, hotel operators, and others whose livelihoods were dependent on river commerce. The many prostitutes, hustlers, gamblers, and street thieves were just as dependent on the river trade and just as affected by its decline. Drawn to the river's edge at the height of Cincinnati's commercial boom, these people were united by hopes of personal economic success and reliance on the river. But just as the hopes for prosperity bound these residents together, so did the realities of destitution and dejection that set in as Cincinnati struggled to transition to a "manufacturing-based industrial center" in the 1860s.[1] Railroads began to replace steamers and dealt a death blow to the river economy that had catapulted the city to prominence just decades before. It became increasingly clear with each passing year that Cincinnati was no longer the preeminent commercial city in the West. The Queen City of the West relinquished her crown to other western cities, like Chicago and St. Louis.

These changes brought widespread job dislocation for those who directly or indirectly worked in the river industry. The rapid settlement of freed slaves in the mid- and late 1860s only exacerbated unemployment rates. White river workers shifted into the new industrial positions, and many of those who had previously occupied the lowest economic rungs— African Americans, women, and ethnic whites—fell off the regular occupational ladder altogether. Although the majority of them may have survived by taking odd jobs as day laborers, necessity forced others to engage in a sub-economy that included gambling, petty theft, counterfeiting, and prostitution. Many of the same people who occupied the lowest economic and social rungs of society also occupied the lowest moral rungs because of their involvement in illegal, illicit, or otherwise unsanctioned activity. And because many of them persisted in such activities, they were considered "Pariahs, Sudras, outcasts"[2] and inhabited the shadows of Cincinnati society.

Many of the same people who lived in the shadows of Cincinnati society also lived in the shadow of the river, on streets along the waterfront near the levee. The Cincinnati Levee was the waterfront area that extended from Broadway to Sycamore Street and included popular thoroughfares like Rat Row.[3] The Cincinnati Levee encompassed Little Africa, one of two significant concentrations of black homes and institutions in the nineteenth century.[4] Cincinnati's shadow community extended beyond the levee to include Bucktown, a predominantly black neighborhood concentrated east of Broadway between Sixth and Seventh streets, and Little Buck in the western part of the city at Sixth and Freeman streets.[5] The river neighborhoods gave birth to several shadow institutions, or institutions that sponsored illicit, illegal, or other underground activities: taverns, brothels, gambling dens, and boarding homes, for example.

This shadow community was strikingly different from the larger Cincinnati society. On the levee and in ships, taverns, shops, and other places of work and play, racial codes were broken and alternative social relations dominated. Levee residents and laborers collaborated for work and crime and convened for strikes and revelry, sometimes even without regard to race. Despite these many instances of interracial collaboration and cohabitation in the waterfront neighborhood, it was also the usual site for ethnic and racial conflict in the 1850s and 1860s.

The river experience also shaped a black community that differed from the larger black community. In contrast to the organized and institutional forms of resistance and self-determination that the larger black community employed before 1868, black shadow-dwellers used popular culture and crime to create an identity and to wage protest. They created folklore, folktales, and music as ways of protesting elite moral and social values. Gambling, prostitution, pimping, and thieving were not only means of survival but also means of defying social and racial norms established by the black and white elites.[6]

By nature, shadow communities prove difficult subjects for historians. Because members of these communities tended to be uneducated, they seldom produced written records of their lives or institutions. They rarely appear in records left by the elite, often because some of them participated in activities deemed unrespectable. And because many who inhabited the shadows participated in illegal activities, they consciously avoided the gaze of city officials, making it difficult to find them in the historical record.[7] Black shadow communities are even more of a historical unknown.

Much of what is known about Cincinnati's black shadow community in the post–Civil War era comes from journalist and ethnographer Lafcadio Hearn, who penned colorful depictions of this community in the 1870s.[8] Born on the Ionian Islands to a British father and a mother of mixed Greek and Moorish descent, Hearn endured a miserable childhood that included abandonment by both parents, rejection by his father's kin because of his swarthy complexion, banishment to a Catholic boarding school, expulsion from that same school, and survival in a workhouse for the poor. An accident disfigured his left eye and, compounded by a severe case of myopia, rendered the young Hearn practically blind.[9] Yet, his physical disabilities may have heightened his other senses and made him the skillful ethnographer that he later became. His writings are descriptive, full of sounds and movements. He had an ear for music and dialect. When Hearn settled in Cincinnati in 1871 at the age of twenty-one, his first job was as a reporter for the *Cincinnati Enquirer*. He took a job at the *Cincinnati Commercial* in 1875, and it was for this paper that Hearn penned his colorful depictions of black folklife and culture in Cincinnati.

Hearn successfully infiltrated the black shadow community. To provide the snapshots he did, he had to go inside the shadow places, inside brothels and taverns. He gained entrance into this community while accompanying police officers on their beat.[10] Hence, many of his sketches reveal that he viewed this community from a police officer's perspective, seeing more criminality than humanity in this community. For example, Hearn depicted Bucktown not as the institutional core of the black community but as a den for criminals and murderers. Hearn's love relationship with mulatto Althea Foley also gave him insider status in the black shadow community. African Americans recognized him as her lover and allowed him access to places from which white men otherwise were prohibited. Hearn never developed any real friendships with any African Americans other than Foley; they remained, to him, subjects of his work. Although some of his methods were flawed and many of his sentiments racist, Hearn's ethnographic sketches are the only glimpse into the life and culture of the Cincinnati black shadow community in the postbellum era. Because many of the same socioeconomic conditions he described in the mid 1870s were prevalent in the late 1860s, Hearn's writings can be used to extrapolate what this community was like then.

An examination of Cincinnati's shadow community and levee life from the vantage point of the Ohio River illuminates people, places, and institutions otherwise hidden in its shadows. The history of black Cincinnati is incomplete without following African Americans into those unworthy, dark, and dingy places in history: the docks, the bowels of the steamboats, the brothels, boarding homes, taverns, and places of unlawful activities. Lastly, there are people who made significant contributions to Cincinnati levee life in the nineteenth century—many of whom fall outside of traditional definitions of respectability. The history of black Cincinnati must begin and end at the Ohio River.

———

Right there, on the Ohio River in the 1860s, was the heart and soul of Cincinnati's shadow community: the river workers. They comprised the largest portion of that community and created much of its culture and moral economy. Generally, river workers were hardworking and upstanding people. Low wages and unsteady employment made them some of the most impoverished workers in Cincinnati after the Civil War. Thus, they moved between periods of employment and unemployment; and between making an honest living to occasionally resorting to unlawful activities to supplement their income and maintain their independence. This group also navigated between a riverine world and the one ashore, and all the spaces in between.

The river industry had been one of the leading employers in Cincinnati in the first half of the nineteenth century. Unskilled workers could find all types of jobs, from lifting freight onto ships to serving as steamboat cooks or firemen. The pay was good and the work was steady, until the river trade's decline. Before 1868, river work had been one of the most common occupations for African Americans in Cincinnati. In 1850, 20 percent of the black population worked in the industry; ten years later, that number had grown to 27 percent.[11] Most of those employed in the river industry worked as boat hands, a broad category that included unskilled work and odd jobs on board steamers. Boat hand was, in fact, the most common occupation among black working men in Cincinnati in 1860; nearly 19 percent of them were employed in this occupation.[12] The 1850s and 1860s were the golden age for black workers in this industry.

Although steamboat work previously had been a respectable profession, by the beginning of the river trade's decline in the late antebellum era, river work in Cincinnati had become synonymous with degradation.[13] Declining wages, a culture associated with filth, liquor, and roguery, and the menial nature of the work meant that few native white men assumed positions aboard vessels, except as captains or officers. Only 4 percent of native white men worked in the industry in 1860.[14] By then, the industry in Cincinnati had become the reserve of ethnic whites and African Americans. But the real degradation came from the nature of the work. River work was hard on the mind and body. With the backbreaking labor came low wages and little stability; there was always someone willing to work for less. Living and eating conditions on the vessels were insalubrious and unsanitary.[15] Those who accepted positions aboard were away from their home ports for eight months at a time, making it difficult to sustain home or family.[16]

The job was also filled with serious occupational hazards. Low water, snags, rocks, floating ice, collisions with other vessels, and the risk of explosion all threatened the steamers. On the Ohio River between 1831 and 1833, sixty-six vessels were lost: seven were destroyed by ice, fifteen by fire, twenty-four by snags, and five through accidents with other steamers.[17] Between 1817 and 1831, 256 persons lost their lives on these vessels, and another 104 were injured.[18] Sometimes it was human error that led to the loss of life aboard these vessels. The steamboat *Moselle*, a fairly new boat running between Cincinnati and St. Louis, exploded in April 1848. The captain of the vessel had been relatively inexperienced and "bent upon gaining for his boat, at all hazards, the distinction of being the fastest upon the river." The young captain took on more passengers than was advisable and proceeded to race another vessel. All four of the *Moselle*'s boilers exploded at once; the force of the explosion projected pieces of human bodies into the water for nearly one-quarter mile. More than 150 people lost their lives in that explosion.[19]

The working conditions were even worse for African Americans in this industry. The lowest, heaviest, dirtiest, and most dangerous river work was reserved for them. One contemporary source noted that it was not uncommon for the strongest black roustabouts to carry as much as five hundred pounds on their backs.[20] In 1860, African Americans also dominated the single most dangerous position aboard the steamboats: fireman. Steamboat firemen did not put out fires; their primary responsibilities were maintaining the ship's boilers and flues, monitoring the fuel levels, and adding lumber to the boilers when fuel was low—extremely dangerous work.[21] Many black firemen suffered serious burns, smoke inhalation, and loss of limbs, if not life, in fires, and the threat of a boiler explosion also loomed. Although fireman was the second-most-common profession for black men in 1860—employing 10 percent of that population—practically none remained by 1870.[22]

Black steamboat workers also endured a color line on board. Black and white boatmen ate separately and labored under different mates.[23] More than likely, they slept in segregated quarters as well. Long before Jim Crow was institutionalized in Cincinnati, black river workers were subjected to these conditions in the holds of ships. In addition, these floating workplaces largely duplicated the occupational discrimination of workplaces on shore. African Americans rarely had the opportunity to serve as captains, mates, pilots, or engineers but instead were relegated to service positions as steamboat waiters, barbers, stewards, or porters.[24] They generally earned less money than their native white and Irish counterparts. In 1862, black river workers earned thirty dollars per month, while Irish workers earned fifty dollars per month.[25] African American boatmen also had to deal with the "Negro Seamen Acts,"[26] which mandated that they be jailed while their vessels were in certain southern ports.[27] Despite the inequality and segregation aboard, the color line was not as rigid in the confined space of the vessels as it was on shore. The color line was set by the captain and observed by the crew, so its application and severity varied from vessel to vessel. But in this self-contained community where the work, living, and recreational places were the same, moments of interracial contact, fellowship, cooperation, and even interdependence could not be avoided. In fact, those moments were undoubtedly more common here than they were on the street.[28]

African American boat hands faced difficulty establishing stable families and love relationships. Some of the songs Lafcadio Hearn recorded, like "Let Her Go By," reflect the ritualized departure to which black boatmen became accustomed: "I'm going away to New Orleans! Good-bye, my lover, good-bye! I'm going away to New Orleans! Good-bye, my lover good-bye! Oh, let her go by!"[29] Because of the length of time they spent away from Cincinnati, boatmen suffered strained relationships with their spouses and children and had only fragile community ties.[30] Most of them had neither spouses nor children. Others laid roots in several ports cities by keeping multiple lovers or spouses. In general, however, these workers could not—or would not—commit themselves to any one person, a point reflected in the lyrics of the "Wandering Steamboatman":

> I am a wandering steamboatman,
> And far away from home;
> I fell in love with a pretty gal,
> And she in love with me.
> She took me to her parlor
> And cooled me with her fan;
> She whispered in her mother's ear:
> "I love the steamboatman."
> If I've a wife at New Orleans
> I'm neither tied nor bound;
> And I'll forsake my New Orleans wife
> If you'll be truly mine.[31]

For some black river workers, then, ideas of masculinity were grounded at least partly in infidelity and a roving eye. Certainly, black women were adversely affected by the occupational habits and cultural ethos of boatmen. A few even adopted the same culture of infidelity as their partners. Hearn suggested that "faithfulness to a roustabout husband [was] considered quite an impossible virtue on the levee."[32] Because their partners were away from home for extended periods of time, many mothers were forced into single parenthood.[33]

Steamboat workers' mobility also hampered their integration into and contribution to the black community on shore. It was hard for them to join churches, attend school, or otherwise participate in the civic and institutional life of the larger black community. Many of these boatmen were uneducated and unchurched. Reformers had doubts that boatmen could be redeemed: "Familiar, during eight months of the year, with all the vices of the river, it could not be expected that a four months residence on the shore, would mend their manners or morality."[34] Nonetheless, the Ohio Anti-Slavery Society had tried to establish a school for boatmen in June 1835, hoping that if they were "intelligent, industrious and sober, they would everywhere be letters of recommendation for all colored people."[35] Unfortunately, the school never opened. Along with weak personal and communal ties on shore, the work brought a degree of loneliness. In response, some black river workers developed deep, affectionate attachments to their vessels, which they reflected in verse.[36] In sum, river work created its own culture that celebrated physical strength, infidelity, and mobility. It also fostered a degree of rootlessness and familial and communal detachment. Very few black women worked in the industry, probably because the work was hard and heavy and kept them away from home too long.[37]

One way black steamboat workers were able to maintain attachments to both the community on the ships and the one on shore was through leisure and culture. Cincinnati's black river workers developed a distinct culture of phrases, songs, gestures, and identity: they were culture creators and carriers.[38] These workers created songs to maintain the pace of work on the vessels. Borrowing from the timing and rhythms of the old slave work songs, many were "half-[sung], half-chanted, in a call-response pattern"[39] and accompanied by "patting juba."[40] In addition, black boatmen sometimes took folk beliefs and superstitions crafted on shore down to the river and reshaped them. For example, levee residents generally had strong beliefs in the existence of spirits and ghosts, but roustabouts believed that the spirits could not cross water. For them, the steamboat was a sanctuary from these spirits.[41]

These steamboat workers also picked up cultural elements from various locations on the river, carried them onto steamers, and then transplanted them from the vessels to the streets and alleys of the Cincinnati Levee. Ethnographer and journalist Lafcadio Hearn recorded the lyrics of one steamboat work chant that reveals the work done and the places the crew had been:

> I wish I was in Mobile Bay,
> Rollin' cotton by de day,
>> Stow'n' sugar in de hull below,
>>> Below, belo-ow,
>> Stow'n' sugar in de hull below!
> De Natchez is a new boat; she's just in her prime,
> Beats any oder boat on de New Orleans line.
>> Stow'n' sugar in de hull below, &c.
> Engineer, t'rough de trumpet, gives de firemen news,
> Couldn' make steam for de fire in de lues.
>> Stow'n' sugar in de hull below, &c.
> Cap'n on de biler deck, a scratchin' of his head,
> Hollers to de deck hand to heave de larbo'rd lead.
>> Stow'n' sugar in de hull below, &c.[42]

Along with emancipated slaves, black boatmen may have been partly responsible for transplanting the Voodoo religion from New Orleans to Cincinnati. The religion, or at least one element of it, infused itself into the black shadow community in Cincinnati. According to Hearn, those seeking vengeance upon an enemy, love potions, and charms and amulets of protection against earthly enemies and disturbed spirits sought the services of Jot, the "obi-man,"—"the Voodoo of the Levee." Jot was a feared and respected religious leader within Cincinnati's black levee community despite the proliferation of black churches that dotted these neighborhoods. In fact, according to one contemporary, "levee folk stand much more in awe of Jot than they do the Almighty."[43] Jot's spiritual leadership suggests that Voodoo was a viable belief system for this segment of Cincinnati's black population. Although the religion may never have been considered an alternative to Christianity in Cincinnati, the two coexisted within the shadow community.

Cincinnati river culture—which was nearly inextricably linked to shadow culture—was shaped, in part, by leisure activities. How and where levee dwellers and river workers spent their leisure time provides some insight into how cultural values were constructed—and rejected—within this community. River workers spent much of their leisure time between trips on the river in Cincinnati's taverns, bars, saloons, dance halls, and other spots of popular entertainment. After a day's work on the waterfront, black stevedores, roustabouts, prostitutes, hustlers, and peddlers also spent their evenings dancing, drinking, eating, and socializing in these night spots. Known in Cincinnati as "ranches" or "cribs," these establishments were places of revelry and merriment, intimacy, and indecency. Homemade liquor, stogies, interracial sex, traffic in stolen goods, bar brawls, gambling, and other unsanctioned activity rendered these places shadow places, and their patrons shadow people. Only a certain class of African Americans frequented these locales. These were not places for the likes of Owen T. B. Nickens, Peter Clark, or other proponents of black racial uplift and respectability campaigns. Members of moral reform societies, temperance societies, or church groups (ostensibly) visited these places only to win the souls and commitments of those within.

Pickett's Tavern at 91 Front Street (also known as Rat Row) was among the most popular nightspots in the black shadow community in the postbellum era. Pickett's place was a tavern, bar, restaurant, ballroom, or theater, depending on the night or event. It was sometimes even a market for peddlers and thieves, who found ready customers in Pickett's patrons.[44]

The proprietor was an older black man, Henry Pickett, originally from Goochland County, Virginia. Pickett had been born a slave on a huge plantation. With fortitude of iron, Pickett had paid for his freedom twice. The first time, he hired his time as a waiter in Richmond and managed to save nine hundred dollars. His owner then took the money, reneged on his promise, and sold Pickett. The second time, Pickett hired his time as a steward on a steamboat and saved eighteen hundred dollars for his freedom. After also purchasing his wife and child for eight hundred dollars, Pickett moved his family to Cincinnati in 1854.[45] A very enterprising man, Pickett operated a grocery and a coffeehouse and tried land speculation before opening his Front Street tavern.[46]

Pickett's place comprised several rooms for eating and dancing and a ballroom with an elevated stage. This crib was located in space approximately sixty-five feet by twenty feet, and could hold between seventy and one hundred patrons. There were two entrances into the tavern, the first leading into the bar at the front of the building, off Front Street. The entrance from the river side opened into the ballroom. A saloon was located directly above the ballroom.[47] On most nights, Pickett's was a dance hall. In this and other dance halls, musicians played popular tunes on violins, banjos, guitars, fiddles, and bass viols. Amid the blasts from the instruments, the dance floors were filled with couples moving to the music. Musicians shouted instructions to "swing partners, forward and back, first fo' right and left" as patrons danced the "waltz, polka, lance, and quadrille."[48] As the music increased in tempo and volume, the dancing grew more animated. Dancers "leaped, shouted, and [swung] each other off the floor." "Men patted juba and shouted," and women's bodies curved, swayed, and twisted to the music as their limbs intertwined. The entire dance floor was a spectacle of bodies moving, feet stamping, shouting, laughing, and patting juba. The dance hall rang with a chorus of musicians and patrons singing or humming to tunes.[49]

On certain nights, Pickett's ballroom was transformed into a theater. The stage was outfitted with white muslin curtains, footlights, and a "green-room" or holding place for performers. Lafcadio Hearn described the ambiance of this theater rather vividly: "The dim light of trembling candle-flame, the blue wreaths of heavy tobacco smoke, the sound of vociferous laughter and the notes of wild music, all floated out together into the white moonlight." African Americans performed skits, dance routines, and comic shows on the ballroom stage. Black minstrels performed in blackface, using burned cork and paint to darken their skin and exaggerate their features.[50]

Pickett's clientele consisted of African Americans and Irish and native white women. According to Hearn, black skin was "a necessary passport into Pickett's," but many of these white women gained entrance because they were the wives or girlfriends of black men or by "feign[ing] to have colored blood in their veins."[51] Essentially, these white female patrons traded in their own racial and cultural identities for entrance into Pickett's and, ultimately, the black community. African Americans of every walk of life were allowed into Pickett's, but only a certain class of whites could enter: "White trash" rabble rousers were not permitted into the establishment.[52] Ironically, Pickett's policy of limited exclusion was more liberal than most. Cincinnati's saloons, dance halls, and taverns were generally segregated; whites patronized certain establishments, and blacks, others. Blazing Stump on Rat Row was reserved for whites, and Ryan's was frequented by black river workers.[53] The only people who seemed to have the freedom to cross that color line in Cincinnati's night life were white women.

The importance of these cribs to the secular black community cannot be overlooked. Taverns were central meeting places for the secular portion of the black community, just as the churches were for black Christians. But unlike the black church, taverns were social, not political spaces.[54] People met at cribs to be entertained, to eat, to drink, to dance, and to socialize. Here, African Americans gathered to escape racism, financial and domestic problems, and the harsh realities of their status. Over a glass of whisky or stale beer, they might commiserate about their jobs or relationships. Certainly, drinking together forged some friendships, but it led to brutal bar fights, as well.[55]

After a hard day's work and an even harder night's play, many of these shadow dwellers retired to boarding homes or hotels where they rented rooms on a nightly or weekly basis. Steamboat workers who were unable to find rooms or create stable residences on shore slept on the steamboats while they were in the port.[56] Although some African Americans boarded in integrated boarding houses or hotels, the majority stayed in all-black boarding homes.[57] The best-known black-owned boarding home in Cincinnati in the 1860s and 1870s was the Dumas House, which boasted three stories with spacious rooms and ballrooms.[58] Most of Cincinnati's black boarding homes were, however, humble tenements located along the waterfront area in the Fourth Ward. Nearly one-half of the black population in the Fourth Ward lived in boarding homes in 1860—a figure unmatched in any other ward.[59] The typical boarder was a male under the age of thirty who worked in the river industry.[60] The predominance of young men made these boarding homes centers of fraternity, or places where black men of this class could fellowship and spend their leisure time together. Many of these same men who boarded together on shore also worked together on the river, making their fraternal connections and allegiance to one another even stronger. Given their occupational and residential isolation from the rest of Cincinnati's black community, river workers crafted a distinct communal identity—one that celebrated masculinity, youth, and wanderlust, prided itself in womanizing and physical strength, and practiced drinking, fighting, and dancing.

Some of the boarding houses where the river workers lived hosted illicit, illegal, or otherwise unsanctioned activity. In the antebellum period, many, like the Dumas House, were stations on the Underground Railroad. In the postwar era, the Dumas House was the usual venue for poker and other forms of gambling.[61] Many of the larger boarding homes had bars inside that were open to the entire black community.[62] Boarding homes attracted prostitutes, who found an endless list of clients among the unattached young boatmen. Some of these places even doubled as brothels—another important institution within the shadow community. Prostitution itself was nothing new in black Cincinnati. In the 1840s and 1850s black career pimps like Luke Cord and Richard Gatewood—both of whom were arrested several times over—managed black prostitutes, but by the 1870s white madams like Mary Pearl, "Fatty Maria," and Mary Herron governed the industry.[63] Officials knew about some houses of prostitution, but the ones that concerned them most were those that sponsored interracial sex.[64] Inside these brothels and other houses of ill repute, an interracial corps of prostitutes served clients irrespective of race. Males of all races, ethnicities, and classes patronized these brothels, including "business men and people of respectability."[65] In the 1870s, madam Mary Pearl openly kept a brothel on 7 Rat Row, where black men patronized her white prostitutes.[66] The interracial sex inside violated an 1861 law prohibiting interracial marriage and sex between persons of "pure white blood" and persons with a "distinct and visible admixture of African blood."[67] According to historian Wendell Dabney, there were some efforts among Cincinnati officers to enforce the antimiscegenation law, which carried a fine of one hundred dollars and a jail sentence not exceeding three months. When Clara Coville, a white prostitute, kissed her black boyfriend in the street in the middle of the afternoon, she was promptly arrested and sentenced to a jail term. According to Dabney, white women were the ones usually punished for violating this law; white men were rarely punished for the same crime. To avoid arrest, some white women in interracial relationships claimed to be mulatto—passing for black—when questioned by authorities.[68] Mobs also checked interracial sex; two brothels were targeted by mobs in 1862.[69]

Life in these shadow places on the Cincinnati Levee in the postbellum era reveals a multiethnic community in which sexual and cultural intimacy was ubiquitous. Native Americans like "Indian Maria" and "Pocahontas" lived in the back bar rooms of white "desperados," and white women lived in buildings owned by African Americans.[70] Whether it was black singers who perfectly imitated the Irish accent and mannerisms or the Irish blood that "predominate[d] strongly in the veins of half the mulattoes of Bucktown," evidence of black-Irish relationships was readily apparent.[71] Native-born white women frequented black taverns, theaters, and dance halls, where they passed for black and absorbed black culture. Here, in the shadows, white women developed "strange attachments for black laborers," and white prostitutes worked for black pimps.[72] Biracial groups of thieves collaborated to steal and sell illgotten wares on the black market or were arrested together for counterfeiting.[73] Dabney observed that, among levee folks, "[c]rime rarely draws the color line."[74]

Although the river created opportunities for social and cultural intimacy among the races, it also created moments when these groups collided. The most serious racial conflicts between Irish and black levee workers resulted from a decline of the Ohio River trade that began in the 1850s, when railroads and national roads began replacing steamboats as the principal conveyers of goods.[75] The Civil War exacerbated this decline of the river trade. Nationwide, shipping on rivers declined by 21 percent in 1862; Cincinnati suffered a 27.5 percent decline.[76] Unemployment was high along the levee. In July 1862, competition for jobs between Irish and black stevedores on the Cincinnati waterfront came to a head. When Irish and German workers decided to strike for higher wages, blacks filled their jobs and for less pay. Upset about black strikebreaking, on Thursday, July 10, ethnic whites attacked black stevedores and roustabouts on the levee, shouting, "No damned niggers should work on the levee!"[77] African Americans along the levee were stripped naked and run out of their places of employment and homes by a vengeful mob. The violence continued through the weekend. Innocent African Americans were attacked and beaten as they strolled along the levee. Some African Americans hid on steamboats; others left the city; and some struck back. On Monday, July 14, a small mob of black men invaded an

Irish neighborhood in the Thirteenth Ward, "shot out windows" and invaded homes.[78] This was the first time African Americans actively had attacked whites in their neighborhoods.

In the days that followed, the white mob intensified in anger and destructiveness, moving beyond the levee toward Bucktown. There, it terrorized black citizens in their homes, broke up their property, and vandalized black institutions, like the AME Church and several brothels. In the spirit of 1841, blacks in that neighborhood fired at the advancing mob, and one white man was killed in the cross fire. Finally, on Wednesday, July 16, after seven days of riot, terror, and vandalism, the mayor called seventy-five volunteer guards, the Winfield Rifles, to suppress the violence and guard the city against future violence. The rioters were undeterred; that same night, violence against black levee workers resumed. The violence finally ended the following night when rioters had exhausted themselves and had succeeded in driving a significant portion of the black population into hiding, away from the central core of the city.[79] So ended the longest mob action in the city's history.

Although the violence had begun over the issue of strikebreaking on the levee, the spirit quickly transformed into an antiblack mob. The mob attacks against black homes and institutions reveal a deep level of contempt not only for the black levee worker but for the black community in general. The attacks suggest that the reasons for racial violence in nineteenth-century Cincinnati were never purely economic. The mob of lower-class, ethnic white immigrants resented the relatively equal social and economic relations that reigned in the shadow community. In fact, these relations within the shadows led to a loss of whiteness, or place in the racial and social order. Violence, then, was a way of reasserting whiteness and reminding both African Americans and themselves of their respective place and power in the racial and social order.

Regardless of the sources, the 1862 racial violence in Cincinnati illuminates the deep contradictions that existed within the shadow community. Even within an interracial community of people who lived, worked, and socialized together so intimately, racial enmity still could reach this magnitude. Hence, race never ceased to be relevant in Cincinnati. Even among the most disfranchised, disempowered class of all, race still mattered.

By the late 1860s, Cincinnati's levee community felt the sting of the river's decline. Tavern keepers, peddlers, small shopkeepers, prostitutes, and others who had previously profited from the river trade found themselves struggling to keep their businesses open.[80] Many steamers stopped running altogether or were forced to scale back on their workforce. No group of workers was more affected by the transition of the city's economy than river workers, who suffered severe job displacement. Because most African American and Irish river workers did not have the skills to transition into other fields, the competition for the few jobs that remained intensified. By 1870, the golden age for black workers in the river industry had nearly ended. Only seventy-nine African Americans were employed in Cincinnati as boat hands and only twenty-four as levee hands, underscoring the overall decline of the river trade.[81] The streets, bars, and taverns were filled with unemployed levee workers and boatmen. The decline of the Ohio River trade, unfortunately, coincided with the arrival of a large stream of freed slaves into Cincinnati following the Civil War, exacerbating an already tight job market. To make matters worse for Irish river workers, the freed slaves who settled in Cincinnati after emancipation were generally willing to work for less pay, forcing overall wages down. Between 1860 and 1870, the black population increased by 58 percent, swelling the black-dominated neighborhoods of Little Africa and Bucktown and spilling into other parts of the city.[82] Many of these freedmen had neither the skills nor the resources to make a quick or smooth transition to freedom. Many of them were impoverished, hungry, homeless, and desperately in need of income.

Rather than beg for handouts or assistance from whites, many suffering shadow dwellers survived as best they could, even if that meant occasionally stealing, gambling, or prostituting. This type of survival was nothing new; there had always been a class of African Americans who moved in the shadows and participated in the subeconomy. For example, the jail records from the 1840s and 1850s reveal a robust subeconomy in prostitution, larceny, gambling, and counterfeiting among this class.[83] But, by 1870, the number of those involved in such illicit activities drastically and tragically increased.

Signs of hardship were ubiquitous in the black shadow community following the Civil War. Some forty years after the poorest of the poor had inhabited loose-board shacks, living conditions had improved only marginally. Lafcadio Hearn painted a startling image of the Bucktown neighborhood as "a congregation of dingy and dilapidated frames, hideous huts, and shapeless dwellings."[84] There were signs of decay and abandonment: the early signs of an urban slum. Hearn added: "Bucktown by day is little more than a collection of shaky and soot-begrimed frames, blackened old brick dwellings, windowless and tenantless wooden cottages, all gathered about the great mouse-colored building where the congregation of Allen Temple [Bethel AME] once worshipped, but which has long since been unused, as its scores of shattered windows attests."[85] He described houses with roofs so far sunken in that they were near to street level and scores of "silent frames with nailed-up entrances, and roof[s] jagged with ruin." These homes lined broken brick streets flowing with "gurgling gutter-water [that] seems blacker than ink with the filth it is vainly attempting to carry away; the air is foul with the breath of nameless narrow alleys."[86] Although such descriptions are the poetic expressions of a reporter, they do capture the material conditions inside these black neighborhoods. The material and physical realities in which these people lived affected the black folklife that developed in Cincinnati.

Black shadow people took the physical and material realities of their marginality in stride. Many survived hard times through mutuality. Those who could not afford to maintain regular residences lived in boarding homes or hotels, which were still a far better alternative than residing in white households as live-in domestics. Some black families took in boarders, and others cohabitated with other families. Single mothers sometimes raised their children in households with other single mothers. Amelia Adams, her sister Josephine, and Mahalia Barber, for example, all lived in the same household in the Fourth Ward along with their children.[87] Struggling to make ends meet, these women probably found it easier to pool their resources and share the duties of parenting.

The shadow community also took care of its elderly and its orphaned children.[88] Maggie Sperlock, a "fat and kind-hearted old mulatto woman," took in and raised several children abandoned by their parents.[89] "Auntie Porter" did the same. Young women who wanted to be free of the responsibility of motherhood took their infants to Auntie Porter's house on Sixth and Culvert streets and promised to pay her twenty-five to fifty cents a week, although most never did. In her eighties by the time Hearn interviewed her, Auntie Porter had raised nineteen children from infancy to adulthood. She was widely known and respected throughout the community for her tremendous sacrifices. As she grew older and became less able to care for herself or the children she was raising, the shadow community pitched in to help. "Even the roughest and wickedest women in Bucktown will contribute a mite to help her, and if they lack the mite, will beg food for her and the children."[90] Not unlike women on plantations who raised other women's children, these women in Cincinnati did so despite the availability of the Colored Orphan Asylum. Sperlock's and Porter's mothering suggests that the black shadow community had not yet come to accept the idea of institutionalizing its orphaned children.

Along with these women, there were others who practiced mutuality and charity in the shadows. Henry Pickett, the owner of Pickett's Tavern, was also respected and appreciated for his charity among levee workers. He regularly provided unemployed workers with a warm meal, often on credit. For years, Pickett nominally charged steamboat men twenty-five cents for a meal and ten cents to sleep by his fire, but most were unable to pay even that small fee. Pickett extended this charity without expecting anything in return, and most of the time he received nothing.[91]

By the early 1870s, there were at least two black communities in Cincinnati with different, cultural values, institutions, and leadership. Shadow dwellers were most concerned with day-to-day survival, not respectability or racial uplift. While black leaders identified equal access to schools and the repeal of the Black Laws as critical issues facing the community, black levee dwellers did not identify easily with these issues. Survival had more immediate relevance. It was hard for the mainstream black community to find common ground with this class on certain issues, like education. After all, this was the class of parents about whom the trustees of the colored schools primarily complained in their annual reports. The children of this shadow class were among those who habitually absented themselves from school to work or play in the streets.[92] Practical survival won out over education for those families who so desperately needed their children's labor.

Shadow dwellers broke laws and social rules, flagrantly defying the color line by intimately interacting with whites in work, crime, and play. Women in this community did not subject themselves to middle-class models of womanhood. Some of them were loud, boisterous, smoked "great black, briar pipes," drank, chewed tobacco, and sometimes "squirted saliva" between their teeth.[93] Ironically, black women have more historical visibility in the shadow community than they do in the records of formal black institutions, suggesting that black women wielded more power in the shadows than they did in the larger black community—at least historically.

The black shadow community defined respectability differently too. According to Hearn's depiction of this community, respectability was a generosity of spirit, not a striving toward middle-class values. Auntie Porter was a noble and respectable character among these people because she took in children who were not her own and raised them. Respectability among this class was not tied to protestant morality, either. Despite the fact that he had once kept, in Hearn's opinion, "one of the lowest sinks in Cincinnati," Henry Pickett was respected because of his uncommon generosity feeding and housing the hungry and homeless.

Neither the black church nor the black school was the center of the shadow community, although some shadow dwellers did attend both. Taverns did as much to soothe the soul as church did for the larger community. Interestingly, as well, the black shadow class did not choose its leaders from among the educated, churched population. Because of the popularity of his nightspots, Henry Pickett was known as "the King of the Levee,"[94] respected by African Americans "from the junction of the Allegheny to the Mississippi."[95] Pickett wielded a great deal of power within the river community. Although he could neither read nor write, he was able to convert his reputation to real political power in the 1870s, when he acted as a recruiter for the Democratic Party. His political base was the very same river workers—now enfranchised voters—he once had fed.[96]

In many ways, the shadow dwellers were freer than most African Americans. The people in that community lived life fully and rarely subjected themselves to the mores—or laws—of the larger society. Crime was survival, and survival was a necessity. In the shadows, people made love to whomever they desired and danced with them too. People of this class were not much concerned with how white elites perceived them; they did not consume their time striving for respectability through temperance or moral reform societies. They did not institutionalize what was natural to them: helping their neighbors in need. And despite the hardship there in the shadows, despite the violence and the poverty, shadow people retained their dignity, humanity, and culture. As the Ohio River flowed on—and flowed freely on—so did the black shadow community of Cincinnati.

APPENDIX 1

The Black Laws of 1804 and 1807

5 OHIO LAWS 63 (1804)

An act, to regulate black and mulatto persons.

Sec. 1. *Be it enacted by the general assembly of the state of Ohio,* That from and after the first day of June next, no black or mulatto person, shall be permitted to settle or reside in this state, unless he or she shall first produce fair certificate from some court within the United States, of his or her actual freedom, which certificate shall be attested by the clerk of said court, and the seal thereof annexed thereto, by the said clerk.

Sec. 2. *And be it further enacted,* That every black or mulatto person residing within this state, on or before the first day of June, one thousand eight hundred and four, shall enter his or her name, together with the name or names of his or her children, in the clerk's office in the county in which he, she, or they reside, which shall be entered on record by said clerk, and thereafter the clerk's certificate of such record shall be sufficient evidence of his, her or their freedom; and for every entry and certificate, the person obtaining the same shall pay to the clerk twelve and a half cents: *Provided nevertheless,* That nothing in this act contained shall bar the lawful claim to any black or mulatto person.

Sec. 3. *And be it further enacted,* That no person or persons residents of this state, shall be permitted to hire, or in any way employ any black or mulatto person, unless such black or mulatto person shall have one of the certificates as aforesaid, under pain of forfeiting and paying any sum not less than ten nor more than fifty dollars, at the discretion of the court, for every such offense, one-half thereof for the use of the informer and the other half for the use of the state; and shall moreover pay to the owner, if any there be, of such black or mulatto person, the sum of fifty cents for every day he, she or they shall in any wise employ, harbor or secrete such black or mulatto person, which sum or sums shall be recoverable before any court having cognizance thereof.

Sec. 4. *And be it further enacted,* That if any person or persons shall harbor or secrete any black or mulatto person, the property of any person whatever, or shall in any wise hinder or prevent the lawful owner or owners from retaking and possessing his or her black or mulatto servant or servants, shall, upon conviction thereof, by indictment or information, be fined in any sum not less than ten nor more than fifty dollars, at the discretion of the court, one-half thereof for the use of the informer and the other half for the use of the state.

Sec. 5. *And be it further enacted,* That every black or mulatto person who shall come to reside in this state with such certificate as is required in the first section of this act, shall, within two years, have the same recorded in the clerk's office, in the county in which he or she means to reside, for which he or she shall pay to the clerk twelve and a half cents, and the clerk shall give him or her a certificate of such record.

Sec. 6. *And be it further enacted,* That in case any person or persons, his or their agent or agents, claiming any black or mulatto person that now are or hereafter may be in this state, may apply, upon making satisfactory proof that such black or mulatto person or persons is the property of him or her who applies, to any associate judge or justice of the peace within this state, the associate judge or justice is hereby empowered and required, by his precept, to direct the sheriff or constable to arrest such black or mulatto person or persons and deliver the same in the county or township where such officers shall reside, to the claimant or claimants or his or their agent or agents, for which service the sheriff or constable shall receive such compensation as they are entitled to receive in other cases for similar services.

Sec. 7. *And be it further enacted,* That any person or persons who shall attempt to remove, or shall remove from this state, or who shall aid and assist in removing, contrary to the provisions of this act, any black or mulatto person or persons, without first proving as hereinbefore directed, that he, she or they, is, or are legally entitled so to do, shall, on conviction thereof before any court having cognizance of the same, forfeit and pay the sum of one thousand dollars, one-half to the use of the informer and the other half to the use of the state, to be recovered by action of debt, *qui tam,* or indictment, and shall moreover be liable to the action of the party injured.

> ELIAS LANGHAM, Speaker of the house of representatives,
> NATH. MASSIE, Speaker of the senate.
> *January 5th, 1804.*

An act to amend the act, entitled "An act to regulating black and mulatto persons."

Sec. 1. *Be it enacted by the general assembly of the state of Ohio,* That no negro or mulatto person shall be permitted to emigrate into and settle within this state, unless such negro or mulatto person shall, within twenty days thereafter, enter into bond with two or more freehold sureties, in the penal sum of five hundred dollars, before the clerk of the court of common pleas of the county in which such negro or mulatto may wish to reside (to be approved of by the clerk) conditioned for the good behavior of such negro or mulatto, and moreover to pay for the support of such person, in case he, she or they should thereafter be found within any township in this state, unable to support themselves. And if any negro or mulatto person shall migrate into this state, and not comply with the provisions of this act, it shall be the duty of the overseers of the poor of the township where such negro or mulatto person may be found, to remove immediately, such black or mulatto person, in the same manner, as is required in the case of paupers.

Sec. 2. *Be it further enacted,* That it shall be the duty of the clerk, before whom such bond may be given as aforesaid, to file the same in his office, and give a certificate thereof to such negro or mulatto person; and the said clerk shall be entitled to receive the sum of one dollar for the bond and certificate aforesaid, on the delivery of the certificate.

Sec. 3. *Be it further enacted,* That if any person being a resident of this state, shall employ, harbor or conceal any such negro or mulatto person aforesaid, contrary to the provisions of the first section of this act, any person so offending, shall forfeit and pay, for every such offense, any sum not exceeding one hundred dollars, the one-half to the informer, and the other half for the use of the poor of the township in which such person may reside, to be recovered by action of debt, before any court having competent jurisdiction, and moreover be liable for the maintenance and support of such negro or mulatto, provided he, she or they, shall become unable to support themselves.

Sec. 4. *Be it further enacted,* That no black or mulatto person or persons, shall hereafter be permitted to be sworn or give evidence in any court of record, or elsewhere in the state, in any cause depending, or matter of controversy, where either party of the same is a white person, or in any prosecution, where shall be instituted in behalf of this state, against any white person.

Sec. 5. *And be it further enacted,* That so much of the act, entitled "An act to regulate black and mulatto persons," as is contrary to this act, together with the sixth section thereof be, and the same is hereby repealed.

This act shall take effect and be in force, from and after the first day of April next.

ABRAHAM SHEPHERD, Speaker of the house of representatives.
THOMAS KIRKER, Speaker of the senate.
January 25th, 1807.

Occupational Statistics for Cincinnati's African American Population

Table App.1. Occupations of Cincinnati's African American Population by Industry, 1850

Industry	Males employed	Females employed	Total employed	% of labor force
Steamboat	194	—	194	20.0%
Service	168	1	169	17.5%
Skilled/Semiskilled	317	6	323	33.5%
Unskilled	201	—	201	21.0%
Entrepreneurial	4	—	4	.4%
Professional	5	1	6	.6%
Unemployed	65	—	65	7.0%
Total	**954**	**8**	**962**	**100%**

Table App.2. Occupations of Cincinnati's African American Population by Industry, 1860

Industry	Males employed	Females employed	Total employed	% of labor force
Steamboat	494	16	510	27.0%
Service	191	123	314	17.0%
Skilled/Semiskilled	377	139	516	27.0%
Unskilled	137	360	497	26.0%
Entrepreneurial	2	5	7	.4%
Professional	22	13	35	2.0%
Unemployed/None	2	14	16	.8%
Total	**1,225**	**670**	**1,895**	**100%**

Table App.3. Industry Breakdown by Jobs as Listed in Census

Steamboat
Boat hand/Steamboat hand/
   Deck hand/River hand
Boatman/Steamboat man/River man
Cabin boy
Canal boat man
Fireman/Steamboat fireman
River basher
River character
River leader
River porter
Sailor
Steamboat barber
Steamboat berthmaker
Steamboat cook
Steamboat laborer
Steamboat pantry man
Steamboat steward
Steamboat waiter

Service
Artist
Baggage master
Barkeeper
Bartender
Bootblack
Butler
Carriage driver
Cash driver
Clerk
Coachman
Coffeehouse worker
Domestic
Driver
Dry good clerk
Eating house worker
Express driver
Grocer
Hack driver
Help
Hosier
Hostler

Hotel watchman
Huckster
Knife shiner
Market man
Messenger
Pantry man
Peddler
Porter
Restaurant help
Servant/Maidservant/Maid
Sexton
Shoe polisher
Stable hand
Steward
Trader
Waiter/Hotel waiter

Skilled/Semiskilled
Baker
Barber
Blacksmith
Bricklayer
Brickmason
Brickmoulder
Builder
Cabinetmaker
Camp roofer
Carpenter
Carriage maker
Caulker
Cigarmaker
Confectioner
Cook
Cooper
Daguerreotypist
Dressmaker
Drummer
Dyer
Engineer
Farmer
Furnituremaker
Hairdresser

Table App.3. (cont.)

Machinist
Mantuamaker
Moulder
Musician
Painter
Pastry cook
Plasterer
Picturemaker
Rectifier
Seamstress
Sewing shop worker
Shoemaker
Silver plater
Tailor
Tanner
Tobacconist
Turner
Wheelwright
Whitewasher
Wood cutter
Wood sawyer

Unskilled
Boiler cleaner
Car porter
Chambermaid
Cleans offices
Drayman
Hack driver
Hod carrier
Housecleaner/Housework/Housekeeper

Janitor
Laborer/Day laborer/Levee laborer
Rag picker
Washerwoman/Washer/Scourer of clothes
Water hauler
Wood guard

Entrepreneurial
Astrologist
Bedstead manufacturer
Boarding house keeper
Clothes dealer
Coal dealer
Fruit dealer
Landlord
Merchant
Saloon keeper
Speculator

Professional/Semiprofessional
Clergy
Druggist
Nurse
Physician/Doctor/Root doctor
Schoolteacher
Sister matron
Superintendent

Unemployed
None/Unknown/Thieving

Table App.4. Occupations for African American Women, 1850

Occupation	Number employed	Percent of reported working female population
Baker	2	25.0%
Dressmaker	2	25.0%
Mantuamaker	2	25.0%
Servant	1	12.5%
Teacher	1	12.5%
Total	**8**	**100%**

Table App.5. Occupations for African American Women, 1860

Occupation	Number employed	% of reported working female population
Barber	2	.3%
Boarding house keeper	4	.6%
Chambermaid (incl. steamboat chambermaid)	29	4.3%
Coffeehouse worker	2	.3%
Cook (incl. steamboat cook)	27	4.0%
Domestic	11	1.6%
Doubtful	13	1.9%
Dressmaker (incl. dressmaker's apprentice)	19	2.8%
Grocery store	1	.2%
Hairdresser	4	.6%
Help	1	.2%
Housekeeper	15	2.2%
Huckster	1	.2%
Janitor	1	.2%
Laborer (incl. steamboat laborer)	3	.4%
Mantuamaker	3	.4%
Nurse	4	.6%
Peddler	1	.2%
Porter	1	.2%
Rag picker	1	.2%
Restaurant help	1	.2%
Saloon keeper	1	.2%
Schoolteacher	7	1.0%
Seamstress	84	12.5%
Servant (incl. steamboat maid and maidservant)	116	17.3%
Sewing shop worker	2	.3%
Sexton	1	.2%
Sister matron	1	.2%
Stewardess (incl. steamboat stewardess)	2	.3%
Superintendent	1	.2%
Tailor	2	.3%
Waitress	2	.3%
Washerwoman	306	45.7%
Widow	1	.2%
Total	**670**	**100%**

Table App.6. Occupations for African American Men, 1850

Occupation	Number employed	% of reported working male population
Astrologist	1	.1%
Barber (incl. steamboat barber)	136	14.3%
Bedstead manufacturer	1	.1%
Blacksmith	12	1.2%
Bootblack (incl. shoeblack)	9	.9%
Bricklayer	3	.3%
Brickmason	1	.1%
Brickmoulder	1	.1%
Butler	2	.2%
Cabin boy	1	.1%
Cabinet maker	5	.5%
Carpenter	16	1.7%
Carriage driver	1	.1%
Caulker	1	.1%
Cigarmaker	1	.1%
Clergy	2	.2%
Clerk	1	.1%
Coachman	5	.5%
Coal dealer	1	.1%
Coffeehouse worker	3	.3%
Cook (incl. steamboat cook)	104	10.9%
Cooper	8	.8%
Drayman	18	1.9%
Drummer	1	.1%
Dyer	1	.1%
Eating house worker	1	.1%
Engineer	2	.2%
Farmer	2	.2%
Grocer	11	1.2%
Hosier	1	.1%
Hostler	1	.1%
Huckster	11	1.2%
Laborer	79	8.3%
Landlord	1	.1%
Merchant	1	.1%
Messenger	1	.1%
Painter	5	.5%
Physician	2	.2%
Picturemaker	1	.1%
Plasterer	5	.5%

Porter	29	3.0%
Rectifier	1	.1%
River basher	1	.1%
River character	1	.1%
River hand	7	.7%
River leader	1	.1%
Scourer of clothes	1	.1%
Servant	46	4.8%
Sexton	1	.1%
Shoemaker	5	.5%
Steamboat fireman	9	.9%
Steamboat pantry man	1	.1%
Steamboat worker	131	14.7%
Steward (incl. steamboat steward)	44	4.6%
Tailor	1	.1%
Tanner	1	.1%
Teacher	1	.1%
Thieving	1	.1%
Tobacconist	16	1.7%
Trader	3	.3%
Unknown	4	.4%
Waiter	71	7.4%
Water hauler	1	.1%
Wheelwright	1	.1%
Whitewasher	57	6.0%
Wood sawyer	1	.1%
None	59	6.2%
Total	**954**	**100%**

Table App.7. Occupations for African American Men, 1860

Occupation	Number employed	% of reported working male population
Artist	4	.3%
Baggage master	1	.1%
Baker	2	.2%
Bank messenger	1	.1%
Barber (incl. steamboat barber)	118	9.6%
Barkeeper (incl. bartender)	5	.4%
Blacksmith	5	.4%
Boat hand (incl. steamboat hand, river hand, and deckhand)	226	18.5%
Boatman (incl. steamboat man and river man)	40	3.3%
Boiler cleaner	1	.1%
Bricklayer	4	.3%
Builder	1	.1%
Cabin boy (incl. steamboat cabin boy)	6	.5%
Cabinetmaker	3	.3%
Camp roofer	1	.1%
Carpenter	20	1.6%
Car porter	2	.2%
Carriage driver	3	.3%
Carriagemaker	1	.1%
Cash driver	1	.1%
Cigarmaker	2	.2%
Chambermaid	3	.3%
Cleans offices	1	.1%
Clergy	6	.5%
Clerk (incl. hotel clerk)	5	.4%
Clothes dealer	1	.1%
Coachman	1	.1%
Coal dealer	1	.1%
Coffeehouse worker	3	.3%
Confectioner	1	.1%
Cook (incl. steamboat cook)	70	5.7%
Cooper	4	.3%
Daguerrotype artist	6	.5%
Doctor (incl. physician)	7	.6%
Domestic	1	.1%
Drayman	4	.3%
Driver	1	.1%
Druggist	1	.1%
Dry goods clerk	1	.1%
Engineer	1	.1%
Express driver	10	.8%
Farmer	3	.3%
Fireman (incl. steamboat fireman)	142	10.1%

Table App.7. (cont.)

Fruit dealer	2	.2%
Furnituremaker	1	.1%
Grocer	3	.3%
Hack driver	6	.5%
Hod carrier	4	.3%
Hotel watchman	1	.1%
Housekeeper	1	.1%
Huckster	7	.6%
Invalid	1	.1%
Janitor	4	.3%
Knife shiner	1	.1%
Laborer (incl. levee laborer, steamboat laborer and day laborer)	117	9.6%
Machinist	1	.1%
Market man	1	.1%
Moulder	1	.1%
Musician	1	.1%
Nurse	1	.1%
Painter	3	.3%
Pantry man (incl. boat pantry man)	2	.2%
Pastry cook	1	.1%
Peddler (incl. candy peddler)	2	.2%
Plasterer (incl. apprentice plasterer)	10	.8%
Porter (incl. bank porter, steamboat porter, and river porter)	53	4.3%
Root doctor	1	.1%
Sailor	1	.1%
Schoolteacher	5	.4%
Servant (incl. house servant)	42	3.4%
Sexton	1	.1%
Shoemaker	15	1.2%
Shoe polisher	3	.3%
Silver plater	1	.1%
Speculator	1	.1%
Stable hand	1	.1%
Steamboat berthmaker	2	.2%
Steward (incl. steamboat steward)	34	2.8%
Tailor	3	.3%
Tobacconist	25	2.0%
Turner	3	.3%
Unknown	1	.1%
Waiter (incl. hotel waiter and steamboat waiter)	58	4.7%
Washer	1	.1%
Whitewasher	78	6.4%
Wood cutter	1	.1%
Wood guard	1	.1%
Wood hauler	1	.1%
Wood sawyer	1	.1%
Total	**1,224**	**100%**

Table App.8. African American Occupations in Cincinnati, First Ward, 1850

Occupation	Males employed	Females employed
Astrologist	1	0
Baptist clergy	1	0
Barber	27	0
Blacksmith	2	0
Butler	2	0
Clerk	1	0
Coachman	1	0
Coal dealer	1	0
Coffeehouse keeper	1	0
Cook	7	0
Cooper	2	0
Drayman	2	0
Grocer	1	0
Huckster	1	0
Laborer	13	0
Landlord	1	0
Merchant	1	0
Painter	1	0
Plasterer	1	0
Porter	9	0
Rectifier	1	0
Servant	3	0
Shoemaker	1	0
Steamboat worker	19	0
Tanner	1	0
Tobacconist	1	0
Waiter	24	0
Wheelwright	1	0
Whitewasher	4	0
None	10	0
Total by gender	**141**	**0**

Total employed = 141

Table App.9. African American Occupations in Cincinnati, Second Ward, 1850

Occupation	Males employed	Females employed
Barber	11	0
Caulker	1	0
Coachman	2	0
Cook	13	0
Drayman	1	0
Grocer	1	0
Laborer	4	0
Physician	1	0
River hand	1	0
River character	1	0
Scourer of clothes	1	0
Servant	5	0
Steamboat cook	1	0
Steamboat worker	3	0
Steamboat steward	2	0
Waiter	3	0
Whitewasher	3	0
None	6	0
Total by gender	**60**	**0**

Total employed = 60

Table App.10. African American Occupations in Cincinnati, Third Ward, 1850

Occupation	Males employed	Females employed
Barber	8	0
Cook	9	0
Laborer	4	0
Picturemaker	1	0
Porter	7	0
Servant	1	0
Steamboat worker	6	0
Steward	1	0
Waiter	20	0
None	7	0
Total by gender	**64**	**0**

Total employed = 64

Table App.11. African American Occupations in Cincinnati, Fourth Ward, 1850

Occupation	Males employed	Females employed
Barber	35	0
Blacksmith	1	0
Bootblack	4	0
Bricklayer	1	0
Brickmoulder	1	0
Carpenter	6	0
Cook	20	0
Cooper	2	0
Drayman	4	0
Dressmaker	0	2
Engineer	1	0
Farmer	1	0
Grocer	3	0
Huckster	1	0
Laborer	7	0
Mantuamaker	0	2
Physician	1	0
Porter	2	0
Sexton	1	0
Shoemaker	1	0
Steamboat worker	49	0
Steward	5	0
Tobacconist	2	0
Trader	1	0
Waiter	11	0
Whitewasher	11	0
Wood sawyer	1	0
Total by gender	**172**	**4**
Total employed = 176		

Table App.12. African American Occupations in Cincinnati, Fifth Ward, 1850

Occupation	Males employed	Females employed
Barber	7	0
Blacksmith	1	0
Bootblack	1	0
Cook	4	0
Laborer	2	0
Porter	1	0
Servant	36	0
Trader	1	0
Unknown	2	0
Whitewasher	4	0
Total by gender	**59**	**0**

Total employed = 59

Table App.13. African American Occupations in Cincinnati, Sixth Ward, 1850

Occupation	Males employed	Females employed
Baker	0	1
Barber	7	0
Blacksmith	5	0
Brickmason	1	0
Carpenter	1	0
Cigarmaker	1	0
Coachman	1	0
Drayman	5	0
Laborer	18	0
Porter	1	0
Shoemaker	1	0
Steamboat worker	33	0
Tailor	1	0
Tobacconist	4	0
Whitewasher	8	0
None	12	0
Total by gender	**99**	**1**

Total employed = 100

Table App.14. African American Occupations in Cincinnati, Seventh Ward, 1850

Occupation	Males employed	Females employed
Baker	0	1
Barber	5	0
Cook	4	0
Hosier	1	0
Laborer	9	0
River basher	1	0
River hand	6	0
Servant	0	1
Steamboat worker	2	0
Steward	1	0
Tobacconist	5	0
Whitewasher	3	0
None	5	0
Total by gender	**42**	**2**
Total employed = 44		

Table App.15. African American Occupations in Cincinnati, Eighth Ward, 1850

Occupation	Males employed	Females employed
Barber	6	0
Cabinetmaker	2	0
Cook	1	0
Dyer	1	0
Laborer	3	0
Messenger	1	0
Methodist clergy	1	0
Plasterer	1	0
Shoeblack	1	0
Whitewasher	1	0
Total by gender	**18**	**0**
Total employed = 18		

Table App.16. African American Occupations in Cincinnati, Ninth Ward, 1850

Occupation	Males employed	Females employed
Barber	23	0
Bedstead manufacturer	1	0
Blacksmith	2	0
Bootblack	1	0
Bricklayer	2	0
Cabinetmaker	3	0
Carpenter	7	0
Carriage driver	1	0
Coachman	1	0
Coffeehouse worker	2	0
Cook	27	0
Cooper	4	0
Drayman	5	0
Drummer	1	0
Eating house worker	1	0
Engineer	1	0
Farmer	1	0
Grocer	5	0
Hostler	1	0
Huckster	9	0
Laborer	4	0
Painter	4	0
Porter	9	0
Servant	1	0
Shoeblack	1	0
Shoemaker	2	0
Steamboat barber	1	U
Steamboat cabin boy	1	0
Steamboat cook	12	0
Steamboat fireman	9	0
Steamboat pantry man	1	0
Steamboat river leader	1	0
Steamboat steward	26	0
Steamboat worker	16	0
Steward	8	0
Teacher	1	0
Thieving	1	0
Tobacconist	4	0
Trader	1	0
Unknown	1	0
Waiter	11	0
Water hauler	1	0
Whitewasher	18	0
None	7	0
Total by gender	**239**	**0**

Total employed = 239

Table App.17. African American Occupations in Cincinnati, Tenth, Eleventh, and Twelfth Wards, 1850

Occupation	Males employed	Females employed
Barber	6	0
Blacksmith	1	0
Carpenter	2	0
Cook	6	0
Drayman	1	0
Grocer	1	0
Laborer	15	0
Plasterer	3	0
Shoeblack	1	0
Steamboat worker	3	0
Steward	1	0
Teacher	0	1
Unknown	1	0
Waiter	2	0
Whitewasher	5	0
None	12	0
Total by gender	**60**	**1**

Total employed = 61

Table App.18. Property Held by Individuals Employed as Barbers, Cincinnati, 1860*

Name	Property value (real estate and personal property)	Name	Property value (real estate and personal property)
Cornelia Bartlet	$100	William Jones	$16,000
Richard Berry	$800	Fountain Lewis	$50
George Bourriss	$500	Lanford Lewis	$200
Rufus Broadie	$300	John Liverpool	$3,200
Samuel H. Brown	$100	Bend Payne	$300
William Carr	$50	Henry Porter	$300
Charles Clark	$12,000	William Royster	$75
Elliott Clark	$4,200	Edward Sanderlin	$400
Wiley Cousins	$25	Thomas Shipp	$50
William Darnes	$1,200	Basil Steele	$75
Theodore David	$300	James Stewart	$2,200
Daniel Davis	$75	Jerry Tailor	$300
William Dramery	$300	Samuel Taylor	$75
Dan Elliott	$700	John Thomas	$1,200
William Finley	$800	William Toney	$60
Elias Ford	$200	George Tospot	$300
Andrew Gordon	$500	Jonathan Tospot	$300
Jerry A. Hall	$100	Henry Tyler	$80
William Harrison	$255	Beverly Wilkinson	$100
Samuel G. Helton	$50	Charles Williams	$40
Henry Homan	200	George B. Williamson	$100
Moses Johnson	$25	**Toal**	**$48,185**

*Names of individuals employed as barbers but not holding property have been omitted.

Table App.19. Property Held by
African American Women, Cincinnati, 1860

Name	Occupation	Property value (real estate and personal property)
FIRST WARD		
Cornelia Bartlet	Barber	$100
Syche Bick (?)	Seamstress	$3,000
Esther Block	Washerwoman	$100
Mary Chase	Washerwoman	$50
Christania Everat	Restaurant help	$300
Mary Fox	—	$2,100
Matilda Green	Cook	$75
Sarah Harkins	Washerwoman	$100
Mary Jones	Washerwoman	$50
Mary Lee	—	$2,200
Eliza Moore	Washerwoman	$3,000
Lucy Porter	Washerwoman	$100
Tammy Preston	Nurse	$100
(?) Williams	Boarding house keeper	$100
May Wilson	—	$25,300
Mildred Wilson	Seamstress	$2,300
Martha Young	Washerwoman	$50
Total		**$39,025**
SECOND WARD		
Olivia Howard	Washerwoman	$50
Rebecca Stephenson	Washerwoman	$25
Total		**$75**
FOURTH WARD		
Eliza Bentley	Chambermaid	$500
Mary Liverpool	Washerwoman	$100
Kate London	Chambermaid	$1,000
Emily Williams	—	$1,500
Total		**$3,100**
FIFTH WARD		
Rachel Anderson	Washerwoman	$50
Susan Banks	Cook	$700
Maria Barlin	Washerwoman	$10
Elizabeth Cousins	Dressmaker	$200
Charity Ditcher	Chambermaid	$25
Jane Doram	Sister matron	$8,075
Elizabeth Fitzhugh	Washerwoman	$25
Emma Frye	Washerwoman	$75
Mary Goff	—	$10
Mary Harris	Washerwoman	$1,050

Harriet Johnson	Washerwoman	$25
Louisa Johnson	Washerwoman	$425
Maria McDonald	Washerwoman	$3,500
Charlotte Stith	Superintendent	$25
Total		**$14,195**

SIXTH WARD

Francis Blackburn	Dressmaker	$2,000
Maria Casey	Washerwoman	$2,050
Ann Leich	—	$2,000
Flora Omohundro	[7 years old]	$1,100
Total		**$7,150**

SEVENTH WARD

Margaret Brooks	Washerwoman	$25
Francis Freeman	—	$100
Martha Johnston	Seamstress	$200
Mary Jones	—	$50
Agnes Lewis	Seamstress	$400
Sarah Otrum	Cook	$50
Mary Rolls	Washerwoman	$30
Offidiah Sanderlin	[11 years old]	$1,000
Minnie Stringer	Seamstress	$200
Total		**$2,055**

EIGHTH WARD

Ann Epps	Washerwoman	$10
Martha Epps	Washerwoman	$80
Susan Hays	Seamstress	$15
Lotty Leavell	Washerwoman	$150
Eliza Mason	Washerwoman	$25
Harrietta O'Conner	Washerwoman	$20
Charlotte Weeks	Washerwoman	$10
Roda Wilkinson	Washerwoman	$50
Total		**$360**

TENTH WARD

Rachel Howler	Washerwoman	$55
Total		**$55**

TWELFTH WARD

Mary Parris	—	$5,000
Total		**$5,000**

THIRTEENTH WARD

Mary Bailey	Washerwoman	$75
Mary Baker	Washerwoman	$20
Annie Bell	Washerwoman	$140
Herietta Bell	Washerwoman	$60

Name	Occupation	Property value (real estate and personal property)
Flora Beny	Washerwoman	$25
Kesiah Boyd	—	$5,300
Charlotte Branch	Washerwoman	$20
Mary Brock	Washerwoman	$20
Caroline Brook	Washerwoman	$25
Tann Buckner	Washerwoman	$40
Mary Burbage	—	$60
Anne Burton	Washerwoman	$40
Abby Can	Cook	$30
Eliza Chism	Washerwoman	$20
Mary Clark	Washerwoman	$150
Julia Cole	Chambermaid	$20
Harriet Cook	Washerwoman	$20
Sarah Cousins	Seamstress	$40
Delphy Cox	Washerwoman	$75
Rachael Cross	Seamstress	$25
Mary Curtis	Coffeehouse worker	$200
Cynthia Davis	—	$700
Flora Ellis	—	$800
Lucy Erskine	Saloon keeper	$200
Caroline Evans	Chambermaid	$75
Sarah Ford	Chambermaid	$75
Caroline Franklin	—	$60
Louisa Gaines	—	$5,204
Susan Gough	Washerwoman	$60
Mary Graham	Cook	$25
Hannah Gregory	Washerwoman	$60
Hester Griffin	Cook	$20
Eliza Harley	Hairdresser	$50
Mary E. Henson	Mantuamaker	$25
Mary Hill	Cook	$25
Maria Huchings	Washerwoman	$300
Rebecca Hunter	Washerwoman	$60
Dice Ishman	—	$630
Susan Johnson	Cook	$20
Sarah Johnston	Washerwoman	$20
Jenny Jones	Chambermaid	$40
Priscillia Jones	Coffeehouse worker	$900
Mary J. Kane	Chambermaid	$50
Rachael A. King	Washerwoman	$40
Jemima Kinston	Washerwoman	$50

Table App.19. (cont.)

Sarah Mack	Chambermaid	$20
Caroline Mason	Chambermaid	$100
Mary McClure	Laundress	$25
Rachel McMillen	Washerwoman	$300
Caroline Miller	Washerwoman	$20
Sarah J. Morgan	Washerwoman and ironer	$25
Caroline Mukes	Laundress	$40
Ellen Norris	Chambermaid	$60
Margaret Page	Washerwoman	$30
Anne A. Phillips	Boarding house keeper	$9,300
Harriet Phillips	Washerwoman	$60
Arabella Pullman	Seamstress	$40
Judy Qualls	Washerwoman	$20
Matilda Robinson	Laundress	$7
Agnes Ross	Grocer	$100
Margaret Ross	Laundress	$75
Harriet E. Sale	Washerwoman	$50
Elsie Scott	Washerwoman	$75
Mary Silk	Washerwoman	$20
Agnes Smith	Chambermaid	$25
Mary Talbolt	—	$40
Jane True	Porter	$200
Louisa Watson	Washerwoman	$60
Eliza J. Weaver	Washerwoman	$20
Sarah Wells	Washerwoman	$100
Nancy Williams	Washerwoman	$40
Matilda Wright	Washerwoman	$40
Total		**$26,786**

FOURTEENTH WARD

Mary Bird	Washerwoman	$100
Eliza Essex	Washerwoman	$100
Mary J. Grelding	—	$1,000
Grace Jackson	Washerwoman	$30
Harriet Kennedy	Washerwoman	$20
Lucy Loving	Washerwoman	$30
Betsy Mulligan	Washerwoman	$25
Eliza Potter	Hairdresser	$2,400
Martha Sanders	Washerwoman	$50
Melissa Sledge	Peddler	$20
Georgiana Spriggs	Washerwoman	$50
Elizabeth Thompson	Washerwoman	$50
Matilda Toliver	Washerwoman	$30
Total		**$3,905**

Table App.19. (cont.)

Name	Occupation	Property value (real estate and personal property)
FIFTEENTH WARD		
Eliza Cousins	—	$50
Jane Davis	Washerwoman	$25
Mary J. Davis	Seamstress	$25
Catharine Dorham	—	$10,000
Darcus Flowers	—	$3,150
Lucy Henry	Washerwoman	$25
Keziah Jackson	Washerwoman	$50
Milla Johnson	—	$25
Lydia A. Jones	Cook	$25
Elizabeth Masby	Washerwoman	$30
Celia Sims	Washerwoman	$25
Eliza Tompkins	Washerwoman	$25
Total		**$13,455**
GRAND TOTAL		**$115,161**

NOTES

INTRODUCTION

1. John Malvin, *Autobiography of John Malvin: A Narrative* (Cleveland: Leader Printing, 1879), 39.

2. Ibid., 40.

3. B. Drake and E. D. Mansfield, *Cincinnati in 1826* (Cincinnati: Morgan, Lodge, and Fisher, 1827), 67. For contemporary references to Cincinnati as "Queen City of the West," see Isabella Lucy Bird Bishop, *The Englishwoman in America* (London: John Murray, 1856), 116; John Mercer Langston, *From the Virginia Plantation to the National Capitol; or, The First and Only Negro Representative in Congress from the Old Dominion* (Hartford, CT: American Publishing, 1894), 62; *Harper's Weekly*, June 30, 1888.

4. Henry Louis Taylor Jr., "Spatial Organization and the Residential Experience: Black Cincinnati in 1850," *Social Science History* 10 (Spring 1986): 49.

5. Leonard P. Curry, *The Free Black in Urban America, 1800–1850: The Shadow of the Dream* (Chicago: University of Chicago Press, 1981), 245.

6. Patrick Folk, "'The Queen City of Mobs': Riots and Community Reactions in Cincinnati, 1788–1848" (Ph.D. diss., University of Toledo, 1978).

7. Eric Foner, *The Story of American Freedom* (New York: W. W. Norton, 1998), xv–xvi.

8. Henry Louis Taylor Jr., ed., preface to *Race and the City: Work, Community, and Protest in Cincinnati, 1820–1970* (Urbana: University of Illinois Press, 1993), xiv.

9. In 1825, 60 percent of Cincinnati's heads of household had been born in the Northeast. According to the 1841 city directory, 56 percent of the 6,534 heads of household were from northeastern states. Harvey Hall, *The Cincinnati Directory for 1825* (Cincinnati: Samuel Browne, 1825); Charles Cist, *Cincinnati in 1841: Its Early Annals and Future Prospects* (Cincinnati: Charles Cist, 1841), 39.

10. John O. Wattles, *Annual Report of the Educational Condition of the Colored People of Cincinnati, Including the Sentiment in Mercer County, Ohio: Presented at the Exhibition of the Cincinnati High School* (Cincinnati: John White, 1847), 7.

11. Frederick Jackson Turner, *The Frontier in American History* (New York: Henry Holt, 1921), 212.

12. James Hall, *The West: Its Commerce and Navigation* (New York: H. W. Derby, 1848), 37.

13. Ibid., 265.

14. Harriet Martineau, *Retrospect of Western Travel* (London: Saunders and Otley, 1838), 230.

15. According to Henry Louis Taylor Jr., "These warring souls produced constant tension while simultaneously providing Cincinnati with a unique culture and way of life." See Taylor, preface to *Race and the City*, xiv.

16. C. Vann Woodward contends that segregation as an institution was born in the North and was fully developed before it moved to the South. See C. Vann Woodward, *The Strange Career of Jim Crow*, 3rd rev. ed. (New York: Oxford University Press, 1974), 17.

17. Frederick Jackson Turner indirectly explained how and why mob violence was sanctioned in the West: "[Extralegal associations] were usually not so much evidences of a disrespect for law and order as the only means by which real law and order were possible in a region where settlement and society had gone in advance of the institutions and instrumentalities of organized society." Turner, *Frontier in American History*, 344. For more discussion of western frontier justice, see John Caughey, *The American West: Frontier and Region* (Los Angeles: Ward Ritchie Press, 1969), 167–91. According to Caughey, western frontier vigilantism emerged when people moved west more quickly than government.

18. *Proceedings of the Semi-centenary Celebration of the African Methodist Episcopal Church* is essentially oral history told from a collective community memory and passed from one generation to the next. Benjamin W. Arnett, *Proceedings of the Semi-centenary Celebration of the African Methodist Episcopal Church of Cincinnati, Held in Allen Temple, February 8th, 9th, and 10th, 1874* (Cincinnati: H. Watkin, 1874).

19. Despite the presumption of literacy, many free blacks were only functionally literate in this era. While the system of slavery had denied African Americans the right to an education, freedom did not necessarily throw open the school doors. Ohio denied blacks the right to a public education until 1849. Consequently, few African Americans left traditional historical records. For example, it is rare to find travel journals or diaries written by African Americans before the Civil War. Researching black Cincinnati in the nineteenth century has been further complicated by fires that have destroyed many municipal records. All of these problems make it incumbent upon any serious historian to mine all sources—not just those left by blacks—looking for ways to amplify the black voices that are in the historical record. Newspapers, census data, and city directories have been indispensable sources. Added to those sources are three autobiographies, the institutional records of the AME Church, Black School Board, orphanage, mutual aid societies, and the proceedings from the state conventions of colored men.

CHAPTER 1

1. Writers' Program of the Works Projects Administration in the State of Ohio, *The Beautiful River* (Cincinnati: Wiesen-Hart Press, 1940), 9,10; Alexis de

Tocqueville, *Democracy in America*, ed. Harvey Mansfield and Delba Winthrop (Chicago: University of Chicago Press, 2000), 331; George Washington, "Extract from the Journal of Colonel Washington on His Oyo Expedition" (March 31, 1754), in *George Washington in the Ohio Valley*, ed. Hugh Cleland (Pittsburgh: University of Pittsburgh Press, 1955), 67.

2. Joe William Trotter Jr., *River Jordan: African American Urban Life in the Ohio Valley* (Lexington: University Press of Kentucky, 1998), 6; Leland D. Baldwin, *The Keelboat Age on Western Waters* (Pittsburgh: University of Pittsburgh Press, 1941), 68.

3. Tocqueville, *Democracy in America*, 331.

4. During an expedition to the Ohio valley in 1770, a young George Washington remarked upon the fertility of the soil: "the Hills are the richest Land; the soil upon the Side and the Summits of them, being as black as Coal and the Growth, Walnut, Cherry, Spice Bushes, etca." George Washington, "Remarks and Occurs," (October 15, 1770), in Cleland, *George Washington in the Ohio Valley*, 244.

5. Writers' Program of the WPA, *Beautiful River*, 8–9; Eric Hinderaker, *Elusive Empires: Constructing Colonialism in the Ohio Valley, 1673–1800* (Cambridge: Cambridge University Press, 1997), 3.

6. Darrel Bigham, *Towns and Villages of the Lower Ohio* (Lexington: University Press of Kentucky, 1998), 13–14; Hinderaker, *Elusive Empires*, 137.

7. Hinderaker, *Elusive Empires*, 135–44.

8. George Washington, "The Journal of George Washington," (October 31, 1753), in Cleland, *George Washington in the Ohio Valley*, 10.

9. Patrick Folk, "'Queen City of Mobs': Riots and Community Reactions in Cincinnati, 1788–1848" (Ph.D. diss., University of Toledo, 1978), 29.

10. Richard Wade, *The Urban Frontier: The Rise of Western Cities, 1790–1830* (Cambridge, MA.: Harvard University Press, 1959), 22.

11. David Gerber, *Black Ohio and the Color Line, 1860–1915* (Urbana: University of Illinois Press, 1976), 9; Folk, "Queen City of Mobs," 29–30; Wade, *Urban Frontier*, 22–23. According to Wade, the name Losantiville was derived from a combination of Greek, Latin, and French words meaning "village opposite the mouth," referring to its location opposite the Licking River.

12. Wade, *Urban Frontier*, 23.

13. Hinderaker, *Elusive Empires*, 243.

14. Folk, "Queen City of Mobs," 30. For a discussion of other Shawnee attacks on Cincinnati white settlers, see *Cincinnati Miscellany*, September 1845, 132–33.

15. Folk, "Queen City of Mobs," 31; Wade, *Urban Frontier*, 25.

16. Folk, "Queen City of Mobs," 31–33.

17. Hinderaker, *Elusive Empires*, 244; Wade, *Urban Frontier*, 23; Folk, "Queen City of Mobs," 6–7.

18. Gerber, *Black Ohio and the Color Line*, 9.

19. Isabella Lucy Bird Bishop, *The Englishwoman in America* (London: John Murray, 1856), 116–17.

20. Wade, *Urban Frontier,* 24.

21. Ibid.

22. Bishop, *Englishwoman in America,* 117–19.

23. Ibid., 118.

24. Frances Trollope, *Domestic Manners of the Americans* (London: Whittaker, Treacher, 1832), 51.

25. Harriet Martineau, *Retrospect of Western Travel* (London: Saunders and Otley, 1838), 233; Trollope, *Domestic Manners of the Americans,* 85.

26. Trollope, *Domestic Manners of the Americans,* 85.

27. John Wattles, *Annual Report of the Educational Condition of the Colored People of Cincinnati, Including the Sentiment in Mercer County, Ohio: Presented at the Exhibition of the Cincinnati High School* (Cincinnati: John White, 1847), 7.

28. Wade, *Urban Frontier,* 39.

29. Glenn Miller, "Transportation and Urban Growth in Cincinnati, Ohio and Vicinity, 1788–1980" (Ph.D. diss., University of Cincinnati, 1983), 91.

30. James Hall, *The West: Its Commerce and Navigation* (New York: H. W. Derby, 1848), 10. Hall comparatively surveys aspects of commerce in various western cities in this volume. Ultimately, he makes an argument that Cincinnati was the premier western city in manufacturing, commerce, and business.

31. Wade, *Urban Frontier,* 39–40.

32. Ibid., 40.

33. Ibid., 41.

34. Ibid., 40.

35. Hall, *West,* 13.

36. Ibid., 11.

37. Daniel Drake, *Natural and Statistical View, or Picture of Cincinnati and the Miami Country* (Cincinnati: Looker and Wallace, 1815), 148.

38. B. Drake and E. D. Mansfield, *Cincinnati in 1826* (Cincinnati: Morgan, Lodge, and Fisher, 1827), 77.

39. Ibid.

40. Ibid., 71.

41. Hall, *West,* 313.

42. Drake and Mansfield, *Cincinnati in 1826,* 78.

43. Harry N. Scheiber, *Ohio Canal Era: A Case Study of Government and the Economy, 1820–1861* (Athens: Ohio University Press, 1969), 205–6.

44. Drake and Mansfield, *Cincinnati in 1826,* 78.

45. Scheiber, *Ohio Canal Era,* 205.

46. Drake and Mansfield, *Cincinnati in 1826,* 72.

47. Ibid., 59.

48. Ibid., 73.

49. Despite the momentum, most of the manufactories mentioned in the 1826 city directory were not yet operating to full capacity. Upon close analysis, much of the data is only a *projection* for future success. For example, by the time that directory was issued, "but a small amount of sugar [had been] refined in

[the sugar refinery] during the . . . year." However, Drake and Mansfield optimistically projected that the sugar refinery, "when in full operation . . . [would be] capable of refining about 180,000 pounds per annum." Similarly, they projected that the white lead factory would "hereafter manufacture 1,500 kegs of white lead per annum." Drake and Mansfield, *Cincinnati in 1826*, 59–66.

50. Steven J. Ross, *Workers on the Edge: Work, Leisure, and Politics in Industrializing Cincinnati, 1788–1890* (New York: Columbia University Press, 1985), 7.

51. Oliver Farnsworth, *The Cincinnati Directory* (Cincinnati: Morgan, Lodge, 1819), 49–50.

52. Drake and Mansfield, *Cincinnati in 1826*, 59.

53. Charles Cist, *Cincinnati in 1841: Its Early Annals and Future Aspects* (Cincinnati: Charles Cist, 1841), 236.

54. Kim M. Gruenwald, *River of Enterprise: The Commercial Origins of Regional Identity in the Ohio Valley, 1790–1850* (Bloomington: Indiana University Press, 2002), 124.

55. Scheiber, *Ohio Canal Era*, 3–4.

56. Drake and Mansfield, *Cincinnati in 1826*, 16.

57. Scheiber, *Ohio Canal Era*, 127.

58. Ibid., 221, 258.

59. Raymond Boryczka and Lorin Lee Cary, *No Strength without Union: An Illustrated History of Ohio Workers, 1803–1980* (Columbus: Ohio Historical Society, 1982), 4.

60. Wade, *Urban Frontier*, 68.

61. *Western Spy*, May 9, 1817.

62. Boryczka and Cary, *No Strength without Union*, 10.

63. Ibid.

64. Trollope, *Domestic Manners of the Americans*, 54.

65. Farnsworth, *Cincinnati Directory* [1819], 151; Fairbank and Robinson, *The Cincinnati Directory for the Year 1829* (Cincinnati: Whetstone and Buxton, 1829), 155.

66. U.S. Census Bureau, *The Sixth Census of the United States, 1840*, vol. 1, ser. no. 8 (New York: Norman Ross Publishing, 1990), 306; U.S. Census Bureau, *The Seventh Census of the United States, 1850*, vol. 1, (New York: Norman Ross Publishing, 1990). There are several reasons for this significant increase in Cincinnati's total population in this decade. First, the 1840s were the most critical years for German and Irish immigration. Other considerations which may have contributed to the population boom in that decade were transportation innovations, which facilitated relocation. Steamboats, canal systems, railroads, and the National Road provided greater mobility, allowing people to move greater distances.

67. U.S. Census Bureau, *Sixth Census of the United States, 1840* ; U.S. Census Bureau, *Seventh Census of the United States, 1850*; William Cheek and Aimee Lee Cheek, "John Mercer Langston and the Cincinnati Riot of 1841," in Taylor, *Race and the City*, 30.

68. Harvey Hall, *The Cincinnati Directory for 1825* (Cincinnati: Samuel Browne, 1825), 4.

69. Cist, *Cincinnati in 1841*, 39. There is a slight discrepancy in Cist's totals for "Natives of the United States." The total recorded there is 6,594; the correct number is 6,534.

70. Gerber, *Black Ohio and the Color Line*, 4; U.S. Census Bureau, *The Second Census of the United States, 1800* (Washington, DC: n.p., 1801).

71. Gerber, *Black Ohio and the Color Line*, 14.

72. In 1840, 43.9 percent of the 317 black heads of household in the city directory hailed from Virginia, and another 14.3 percent were from Kentucky. Altogether, more than 58 percent of the city's black heads of household were from these two states. Henry D. Shaffer, *The Cincinnati, Covington, Newport, and Fulton Directory for 1840* (Cincinnati: Donogh, 1840), 467–75; Edward Abdy, *Journal of a Residence and Tour in the United States of North America from April 1833 to October 1834* (London: n.p., 1835), 383; Ohio Anti-Slavery Society, *Proceedings of the Ohio Anti-Slavery Society Convention Held at Putnam, Ohio* (Putnam: Ohio Anti-Slavery Society, 1835), 31. The 1840 census does not indicate place of origin.

73. Ross, *Workers on the Edge*, 74.

74. William Bullock, *Sketch of a Journey through the Western States of North America* (London: John Miller, 1827).

75. To Mrs. Trollope's disappointment, the bazaar she opened in Cincinnati was not lucrative. Her dreams shattered, she left Cincinnati a poor woman.

76. Ross, *Workers on the Edge*, 74; Charles Cist, compiler of the 1841 city directory, found that 46 percent of the city's 12,232 heads of household were foreign-born. Sixty percent of those were from Germany. Thus, Germans accounted for 28 percent of all of Cincinnati's heads of household in 1841. See Cist, *Cincinnati in 1841*, 39.

77. Stanley Nadel, *Little Germany: Ethnicity, Religion, and Class in New York City, 1845–1880* (Urbana: University of Illinois Press, 1990), 22.

78. Bishop, *Englishwoman in America*, 120.

79. The 1836 city council included Ebenezer Hulse, Septimus Hazen, George Nefell, and Ebenezer Hinman.

80. Boryczka and Cary, *No Strength without Union*, 12; Bishop, *Englishwoman in America*, 120.

81. Charles Cist, *Sketches and Statistics of Cincinnati in 1859* (Cincinnati: n.p., 1859), 166.

82. Cist, *Cincinnati in 1841*, 39; Ross, *Workers on the Edge*, 173.

83. Ross, *Workers on the Edge*, 173; Moses King, *King's Pocket-Book of Cincinnati* (Cincinnati: John Shillito, 1879), 61.

84. David H. Bennett, *The Party of Fear: From Nativist Movements to the New Right in American History* (Chapel Hill: University of North Carolina Press, 1988), 64.

85. Charles Cist, *Sketches and Statistics of Cincinnati in 1851* (Cincinnati: William H. Moore, 1851), 47. This figure is derived from Cist's reports that there were 13,616 Irish in Cincinnati in 1851. The total population of Cincinnati was 115,434 in 1850.

86. The Second Great Awakening (1795–1835), sparked a wave of Protestant zeal in camp meetings around the nation. For a lengthier discussion of this

Great Awakening and the conflict between Catholics and Protestants in this age, see Bennett, *Party of Fear,* 36–37.

87. In his seminal work on Irish assimilation in antebellum Philadelphia, historian Noel Ignatiev cites several origins for anti-Irish hostility: 1) class snobbery: upper-class native whites believed the poor Irish immigrants to be inferior, 2) partisan antagonisms between the Irish, who were Democrats, and upper-class Americans, who were Whigs, 3) native Protestant suspicion and fear of Catholicism, 4) concerns that Irish workers would degrade labor and force wages down, and 5) Irish intemperance. Noel Ignatiev, *How the Irish Became White* (New York: Routledge, 1995), 148–49.

88. Bishop, *Englishwoman in America,* 120.

89. Drake, *Natural and Statistical View,* 172.

90. Ibid.

91. Bishop, *Englishwoman in America,* 119–20.

92. Trollope, *Domestic Manners of the Americans,* 61. Trollope indicated that "it is more than petty treason to the republic to call a free citizen a servant."

93. Drake, *Natural and Statistical View,* 172.

94. The city directories fail to specify what these jobs entailed.

95. J. H. Woodruff, *The Cincinnati Directory and Advertiser for the Years 1836–1837* (Cincinnati: J. H. Woodruff, 1836). This was the earliest city directory that distinguished African American residents. It is also the first directory to list the occupations of African Americans. For these reasons, I have used it to make analyses about the period before 1830.

96. John Warren, quoted in Benjamin Drew, *The Refugee: Or the Narratives of Fugitive Slaves in Canada; Related by Themselves, with an Account of the History and Condition of the Colored Population in Upper Canada* (Boston: John P. Jewett, 1856), 185.

97. Drake, *Natural and Statistical View,* 170.

98. Trollope, *Domestic Manners of the Americans,* 49. Frances Trollope asserted that she had great difficulty finding a vacant house.

99. Henry Louis Taylor Jr. and Vicky Dula, "The Black Residential Experience and Community Formation in Antebellum Cincinnati," in Taylor, *Race and the City,* 99.

100. Ibid., 115.

101. Ibid., 102.

102. The earliest historical record that refers to this neighborhood as Little Africa was Trollope, *Domestic Manners of the Americans,* 52.

103. Cist, *Sketches and Statistics of Cincinnati in 1859,* 166.

104. Nancy Bertaux, "Structural Economic Change and Occupational Decline among Black Workers in Nineteenth-Century Cincinnati," in Taylor, *Race and the City,* 127.

105. Ignatiev, *How the Irish Became White,* 41.

106. Ibid., 100.

107. Antialienism is a term used by historian David Bennett to describe nativist sentiments in the colonial, revolutionary, and early national periods.

Antialienism eventually gave way to full-blown nativism in the 1840s. Responding to the wave of foreign immigration from Ireland and Germany, branches of the Native American Party sprang up in major cities in the 1840s. Local nativist parties like the American Republican Club in Philadelphia were established largely to lobby for a twenty-one year waiting period on naturalization and exclusion of foreign-born people from holding office. In the mid-1850s the Know-Nothing movement added energy to the movement against the further incursion of foreigners on American politics. Among other things, the Know-Nothings blamed political corruption that had become commonplace in American politics on immigrants. Know-Nothings wanted to prohibit immigrants from participation in the political process. Ignatiev, *How the Irish Became White*, 149. Historian David Grimsted posits that Know-Nothings were at once "anti-anti-slavery and anti-proslavery" and opposed any other political issue that threatened disunion. See David Grimsted, *American Mobbing, 1828–1861: Toward Civil War* (New York: Oxford University Press, 1998), 219.

108. Grimsted, *American Mobbing*, 219.

109. David Bennett's premise in *Party of Fear* is that nativists were those people who felt that America was a paradise that needed to be protected from foreigners threatening to destroy it. They saw themselves as the protectors of that dream. See Bennett, *Party of Fear*, 3, 9, 103. Nativism was a social movement of like-minded people who used the political process, the press, and even violence to achieve their objectives.

110. Ignatiev, *How the Irish Became White*, 149; Bennett, *Party of Fear*, 54.

CHAPTER 2

1. Paul Finkelman, *Slavery and the Founders: Race and Liberty in the Age of Jefferson* (Armonk, NY: M. E. Sharpe, 1996), 34; David Gerber, *Black Ohio and the Color Line, 1860–1915* (Urbana: University of Illinois Press, 1976), 3.

2. Raymond Boryczka and Lorin Lee Cary, *No Strength without Union: An Illustrated History of Ohio Workers, 1803–1980* (Columbus: Ohio Historical Society, 1982), 15; Frank U. Quillin, *The Color Line in Ohio: A History of Race Prejudice in a Typical Northern State* (Ann Arbor, MI: George Wahr, 1913), 25; Gerber, *Black Ohio and the Color Line*, 10. Gerber estimates that the black population in some counties was as high as 8 percent in 1860.

3. For a discussion of Cincinnati free blacks who worked and saved money to purchase enslaved loved ones see, Ohio Anti-Slavery Society, *Proceedings of the Ohio Anti-Slavery Society Convention Held at Putnam, Ohio* (Putnam: Ohio Anti-Slavery Society, 1835), 25, 29, 30.

4. U.S. Census Bureau, *The Seventh Census of the United States, 1850* (Washington, DC: Robert Armstrong, 1853); Henry Louis Gates Jr., preface to *A Hairdresser's Experience in High Life* by Eliza Potter (New York: Oxford University Press, 1991), xxxvi.

5. Eugene H. Berwanger, *The Frontier against Slavery: Western Anti-Negro Prejudice and*

the *Slavery Extension Controversy* (Urbana: University of Illinois Press, 1967), 18–19; Gerber, *Black Ohio and the Color Line*, 9.

6. U.S. Census Bureau, *The Second Census of the United States, 1800* (Washington, DC: n.p., 1801); Gerber, *Black Ohio and the Color Line*, 4.

7. Helen M. Thurston, "The 1802 Constitutional Convention and the Status of the Negro," *Ohio History* 81 (Winter 1972): 16–17. Thirty-five delegates, representing nine counties, were selected to draft the constitution. Counties with higher populations sent more delegates. Hamilton County, where Cincinnati was located, sent ten delegates. The Cincinnati delegation was composed exclusively of privileged white men. According to Thurston, they were, by profession, legislators, teachers, physicians, attorneys, land developers, clergy, and farmers.

8. Ibid., 22.

9. Ibid. Although Thurston concludes that no generalizations can be made about the delegates' voting patterns vis à vis their geographical residence, delegates from Hamilton County were generally more supportive of voting rights and other civil rights for blacks than were delegates from other counties. A majority of Hamilton County delegates, for example, voted for suffrage and against the denial of citizenship rights to African Americans.

10. *Journal of the Convention of the Territory of the United States North-West of the Ohio*, (Chillicothe, OH: N. Willis, 1802), 30.

11. Thurston, "1802 Constitutional Convention and the Status of the Negro," 22.

12. *Journal of the Convention of the Territory of the United States North-West of the Ohio*, 30.

13. James Grubb of Ross County and David Abbott of Trumbull County were the delegates who changed their votes from favoring black suffrage to denying it. Helen Thurston argues that Grubb may have changed his vote to be in accord with other delegates from his county, while Abbot may have been trying to counter the pro-Negro vote of the other delegate from his county. If her analysis is correct, these men were thinking more about politics than about the rights of African Americans. See Thurston, "The 1802 Constitutional Convention and the Status of the Negro," 24. Although these men simply may have been persuaded by antiblack delegates who raised the specter of how suffrage would confer equality, there is no way to know why these men changed their minds because the transcript of this convention is not detailed.

14. *Journal of the Convention of the Territory of the United States North-West of the Ohio*, 32.

15. Berwanger, *Frontier against Slavery*, 22.

16. For a discussion of the motivations of those who espoused universal white male suffrage, See Leon F. Litwack, *North of Slavery: The Negro in the Free States, 1790–1860* (Chicago: University of Chicago Press, 1961), 76.

17. Ibid., 72–84; Berwanger, *Frontier against Slavery*, 21.

18. Thurston, "1802 Constitutional Convention and the Status of the Negro," 35.

19. Quillin, *Color Line in Ohio*, 21. Eugene Berwanger defines "Black Laws" as "a term applied to any legislative measure passed by a free state restricting the

civil rights or immigration of free [African Americans]." Berwanger, *Frontier against Slavery*, 22.

20. "An Act to Regulate Black and Mulatto Persons" and "An Act to Amend the Last Named Act 'An Act to Regulate Black and Mulatto Persons,'" in Stephen Middleton, *The Black Laws in the Old Northwest: A Documentary History* (Westport, CT: Greenwood, 1993), 15–18.

21. Quillin, *Color Line in Ohio*, 21–22.

22. "An Act to Regulate Black and Mulatto Persons," in Middleton, *Black Laws in the Old Northwest*, 16.

23. Ibid.

24. Daniel Drake, *Natural and Statistical View, or Picture of Cincinnati and the Miami Country* (Cincinnati: Looker and Wallace, 1815), 172.

25. This legislation was not strictly classist, that is, intended to deter all indigents. White settlers did not have to pay bonds to settle in Ohio, nor were there any prejudgments about their ability to care for themselves. If white persons proved unable to care for themselves, they were usually sent back to their place of birth, in the custom of the Poor Law.

26. Fires at the Cincinnati Courthouse in 1884 burned court records of individuals who posted the bond.

27. "An Act to Amend the Last Named Act 'An Act to Regulate Black and Mulatto Persons,'" in Middleton, *Black Laws in the Old Northwest*, 17; Quillin, *Color Line in Ohio*, 22.

28. The average daily wage of laborers in Philadelphia between 1825 and 1830 was $1.00 per day. The wage for common laborers on the Erie Canal between 1828 and 1830 was between $.71 and $.75 per day. U.S. Department of Commerce, *Historical Statistics of the United States: Colonial Times to 1970* (Washington, DC: Bureau of the U.S. Census, 1975), 1:163–64.

29. David Grier, quoted in Benjamin Drew, *The Refugee: Or the Narratives of Fugitive Slaves in Canada; Related by Themselves, with an Account of the History and Condition of the Colored Population in Upper Canada* (Boston: John P. Jewett, 1856), 372.

30. *Liberty Hall and Cincinnati Gazette*, August 31, 1819; Lyle Koehler, *Cincinnati's Black Peoples: A Chronology and Bibliography, 1787–1982* (Cincinnati: Cincinnati Arts Consortium, 1986), 5; *Liberty Hall*, September 3, 1819.

31. "An Act to Amend the Last Named Act 'An Act to Regulate Black and Mulatto Persons,'" in Middleton, *Black Laws in the Old Northwest*, 17.

32. Henry Louis Taylor Jr., preface to *Race and the City: Work, Community, and Protest in Cincinnati, 1820–1970* (Urbana: University of Illinois Press, 1993), xiii; Gerber, *Black Ohio and the Color Line*, 4.

33. Carter G. Woodson, *The Education of the Negro Prior to 1861* (New York: Arno, 1968), 327.

34. Koehler, *Cincinnati's Black Peoples*, 2.

35. *Philanthropist*, July 23, 1839; *Ohio State Journal*, January 22, 1839, and January 25, 1839; Carter G. Woodson, "Race Hate in Early Ohio," *Negro History Bulletin* 10 (June 1947): 206.

36. *Ohio State Journal,* January 25, 1839.

37. Kenneth L. Kusmer, *A Ghetto Takes Shape: Black Cleveland, 1870–1930* (Urbana: University of Illinois Press, 1976), 7.

38. Ibid., 7–8. State legislators ultimately denied suffrage for African Americans. It was not until the Fifteenth Amendment was ratified in 1870 that African Americans received the right to vote in Ohio.

39. Ibid., 5–7; Gerber, *Black Ohio and the Color Line,* 11–13.

40. Kusmer, *Ghetto Takes Shape,* 16.

41. John Malvin, *Autobiography of John Malvin: A Narrative* (Cleveland: Leader Printing, 1879), 50; John Mercer Langston, *From the Virginia Plantation to the National Capitol; or, The First and Only Negro Representative in Congress from the Old Dominion* (Hartford, CT.: American Publishing, 1894), 77.

42. Malvin, *Autobiography of John Malvin,* 64–66; William Cheek and Aimee Lee Cheek, *John Mercer Langston and the Fight for Black Freedom, 1829–1865* (Urbana: University of Illinois Press, 1989), 147–48; Langston, *From the Virginia Plantation to the National Capitol,* 77.

43. Some establishments in Cleveland refused to admit African American patrons. Gerber, *Black Ohio and the Color Line,* 13. During his stay there, Malvin was locked out of his trade as a carpenter, prevented from getting a boating license, and subjected to segregated seating in his church. Malvin, *Autobiography of John Malvin,* 50, 55, 57.

44. Koehler, *Cincinnati's Black Peoples,* 2.

45. Ibid., 3; Richard Wade, "The Negro in Cincinnati, 1800–1830," *Journal of Negro History* 39 (January 1954): 46.

46. William Cheek and Aimee Lee Cheek, "John Mercer Langston and the Cincinnati Riot of 1841," in Taylor, *Race and the City,* 32; Gerber, *Black Ohio and the Color Line,* 6; Carter G. Woodson, "The Negroes of Cincinnati Prior to the Civil War," *Journal of Negro History* 1 (January 1916): 17. The poor houses were shelters for those who were "incapable of taking care of themselves." See City of Cincinnati, *First Annual Report of the Board of Directors of the City Infirmary to the City Council of the City of Cincinnati* (Cincinnati: Cincinnati Gazette, 1853), 47.

47. *Western Globe,* September 13, 1839.

48. Cincinnati Lane Seminary, "Statement of the Faculty Concerning the Late Difficulties in the Lane Seminary," *Fifth Annual Report of the Trustees of the Cincinnati Lane Seminary: Together with the Laws of the Institution and a Catalogue of the Officers and Students* (Cincinnati: Corey and Fairbank, 1834), 36–37.

49. Transiency of the community is measured here by the frequency with which black families move in and out of the historical record. African American families rarely remained from one city directory or census to the next.

50. Roughly 282 African Americans lived in independent households. U.S. Census Bureau, *The Fourth Census of the United States, 1820* (Washington, DC: Gales and Seaton, 1821). As late as 1835, the Ohio Anti-Slavery Society reported that large numbers of African Americans were servants in white families. See Ohio Anti-Slavery Society, *Proceedings,* 28.

51. For a discussion of the work and personal lives of house servants, see Whittington B. Johnson, *The Promising Years, 1750–1830: The Emergence of Black Labor and Business* (New York: Garland, 1993), 151; and Tera W. Hunter, *To 'Joy My Freedom: Southern Black Women's Lives and Labors after the Civil War* (Cambridge, MA: Harvard University Press, 1997), 54.

52. An examination of the census data for 1820 reveals that many black children lived in white households by themselves. Although indentures were illegal in Ohio, these data clearly suggest that children were informally indentured.

53. In that year, 876 of the 1,090 black residents lived in independent households. U.S. Census Bureau, *The Fifth Census of the United States, 1830* (Washington, DC: Duff Green, 1832).

54. Wade, "Negro in Cincinnati," 45.

55. Koehler, *Cincinnati's Black Peoples*, 6.

56. Wade, "Negro in Cincinnati," 45.

57. Frances Trollope, *Domestic Manners of the Americans* (London: Whittaker, Treacher, 1832), 52; *Cincinnati Advertiser*, August 18, 1830.

58. Koehler, *Cincinnati's Black Peoples*, 6.

59. *Liberty Hall*, August 25, 1825.

60. Only a few primary sources dated prior to 1829 even mention African Americans in Cincinnati. Most of the extant sources merely enumerate the black population in the city or make disparaging comments about black residents. Even fewer sources document the presence of a self-conscious black community in Cincinnati before 1829. The mere presence of blacks in Cincinnati is not evidence that they formed a self-conscious, functioning community.

61. James Oliver Horton and Lois E. Horton, introduction to *In Hope of Liberty: Culture, Community, and Protest among Northern Free Blacks, 1700–1860* (New York: Oxford University Press, 1997), xi.

62. Malvin, *Autobiography of John Malvin*, 39.

63. Ibid.

64. Koehler, *Cincinnati's Black Peoples*, 3.

65. Ibid. There is no extant evidence about who burned the church.

66. Litwack, *North of Slavery*, 196.

67. Carol V. R. George, *Segregated Sabbaths: Richard Allen and the Rise of the Independent Black Churches, 1760–1840* (New York: Oxford University Press, 1973), 54.

68. Ibid.; Horton and Horton, *In Hope of Liberty*, 138.

69. Gary Nash, *Forging Freedom: The Formation of Philadelphia's Black Community, 1720–1840* (Cambridge, MA: Harvard University Press, 1988), 118.

70. Ibid., 112.

71. Ibid., 103–4.

72. Ibid., 112.

73. For more information on the history of the AME Church see George, *Segregated Sabbaths;* and Nash, *Forging Freedom*, 100–133.

74. Benjamin W. Arnett, *Proceedings of the Semi-centenary Celebration of the African Methodist Episcopal Church of Cincinnati, Held in Allen Temple, February 8th, 9th, and 10th, 1874* (Cincinnati: H. Watkin, 1874).

75. Ibid., 13–14.

76. Peter Clark, "The Developing Power of African Methodism," in Arnett, *Proceedings of the Semi-centenary Celebration*, 100.

77. Arnett, *Proceedings of the Semi-centenary Celebration*, 14.

78. As the story was passed down over the years, it may have been exaggerated and even made legendary. The burst blood vessel, for example, seems legendary. Arnett wrote this history for the church's fiftieth anniversary and, in order to dramatize the church's beginnings, he may have embellished some of the anecdotes. It cannot be dismissed as a source for the history of the black church: Arnett's account is *some* version of the truth. In fact, it is the collective history of a generation that witnessed it.

79. Arnett, *Proceedings of the Semi-centenary Celebration*, 14. J. H. Piatt cannot be found in either the 1829 or 1831 city directories. However, a Jacob W. Piatt is listed in both as an attorney. Possible explanations for this discrepancy are that Arnett got the middle initial wrong or that J. H. Piatt is actually the son, father, or brother of Jacob W. Piatt. See Robinson and Fairbank, *The Cincinnati Directory for the Year 1829* (Cincinnati: Whetstone and Buxton, 1829), 98; Robinson and Fairbank, *The Cincinnati Directory for the Year 1831* (Cincinnati: Robinson and Fairbank, 1831), 124.

80. The Gradual Abolition Act of Pennsylvania applied to children born after March 1, 1780. Females could be indentured until age eighteen and males until twenty-one, after which they were to be emancipated. For a lengthier discussion of this law and its effect see, Nash, *Forging Freedom*, 60.

81. Arnett, *Proceedings of the Semi-centenary Celebration*, 14.

82. Ibid.,13. No other information can be obtained about Joseph Dorcas or William Buck. Neither man is listed in any of the city directories or the 1820 or 1830 censuses.

83. Ibid., 14.

84. Ibid., 15.

85. Ibid.

86. Ibid., 15–16. There is very little information about this case because there are no extant court records. See *Ohio State Journal*, May 28, 1841; *Cincinnati Daily Gazette*, May 21, 1841, and June 1, 1841; and *Colored American*, May 22, 1841. For a complete narrative of the case, see Paul Finkelman, *An Imperfect Union: Slavery, Federalism, and Comity* (Chapel Hill: University of North Carolina Press, 1981), 165.

87. Ibid., 16. This dramatic moment is remarkably similar to one in the history of the AME Church in Philadelphia, suggesting that black churches in Cincinnati were established under similar circumstances.

88. Ibid.

89. Ibid.

90. Ibid., 17. No further data can be found on Phillip Brodie. He does not appear in any of the census data or city directories.

91. Ibid., 18.

92. Ibid.

93. Ibid.

94. Eddie Glaude Jr., *Exodus!: Religion, Race, and Nation in Early Nineteenth-Century Black America* (Chicago: University of Chicago Press, 2000), 22.

95. Arnett, *Proceedings of the Semi-centenary Celebration*, 18–19.

96. Clark, "Developing Power of African Methodism," in Arnett, *Proceedings of the Semi-centenary Celebration*, 100.

97. Ibid., 19.

98. Glaude, *Exodus!* 4–5.

99. *Cincinnati Daily Gazette*, July 4, 1829.

100. Malvin, *Autobiography of John Malvin*, 41–42nn4, 5. J. W. Piatt and Longworth were both attorneys. Longworth was arguably "one of the richest men in Cincinnati" and had earned his wealth mainly through land ownership. John Clingman was a local hatter. See Robinson and Fairbank, *Cincinnati Directory for the Year 1829*, 31, 77, 98.

101. Malvin, *Autobiography of John Malvin*, 40.

102. Arnett, *Proceedings of the Semi-centenary Celebration*, 16.

103. Ibid. Again, it is unclear which Piatt helped with the church.

104. Malvin, *Autobiography of John Malvin*, 42n4.

105. Ibid., 42.

106. Arnett, *Proceedings of the Semi-centenary Celebration*, 19.

107. *Ohio State Journal*, August 24, 1826; Woodson, *Education of the Negro Prior to 1861*, 327.

108. Drake, *Natural and Statistical View*, 157; Wade, "Negro in Cincinnati,," 47.

109. Oliver Farnsworth, *The Cincinnati Directory* [1819] (Cincinnati: Morgan, Lodge, 1819), 42.

110. Wade, "Negro in Cincinnati," 47.

111. Ohio Anti-Slavery Society, *Report on the Condition of the People of Color in the State of Ohio* (Putnam, OH: Beaumont and Wallace [ca. 1835]), 4.

112. Abdy, *Journal of a Residence and Tour in the United States*, 401.

113. Farnsworth, *Cincinnati Directory* [1819], 42.

114. Woodson, *Education of the Negro Prior to 1861*, 124.

115. Samuel Matthews, "The Black Educational Experience in Nineteenth-Century Cincinnati, 1817–1874" (Ph.D. diss., University of Cincinnati, 1985), 33.

116. Cincinnati Colored Public Schools, *Eighth Annual Report of the Board of Trustees for the Colored Public Schools of Cincinnati for the School Year Ending June 30, 1857* (Cincinnati: Moore, Wilstach, Keys, 1857), 9.

117. Arnett, *Proceedings of the Semi-centenary Celebration*, 62. It was reported that Mr. Cooly was "a trifling drunken fellow, not fit for a school teacher." He reportedly "drank whisky all day and night, play[ed] cards, [and] bet on horse races [and] chicken fights." Cincinnati Colored Public Schools, *Eighth Annual Report*, 9.

118. Ohio Anti-Slavery Society, *Report on the Condition of the People of Color in the State of Ohio*, 4.

119. Ibid.

120. Arnett, *Proceedings of the Semi-centenary Celebration*, 62.

121. None of the teachers listed here appear in any of the city directories or censuses, suggesting that they were in Cincinnati only briefly.

122. Abdy, *Journal of a Residence and Tour in the United States*, 394.

123. John O. Wattles, *Annual Report of the Educational Condition of the Colored People of Cincinnati, Including the Sentiment in Mercer County, Ohio: Presented at the Exhibition of the Cincinnati High School* (Cincinnati: John White, 1847), 4.

CHAPTER 3

1. For a discussion of African American "acts of self-determination," see Vincent P. Franklin, *Black Self-Determination: A Cultural History of the Faith of the Fathers* (New York: Lawrence Hill Books, 1992), 194.

2. Early historians of the 1829 African American exodus from Cincinnati, such as Frank Quillin and David Gerber, argue that decades of social persecution and economic and political repression against African Americans were eclipsed by the mob violence of 1829. This interpretation posits that it was violence that precipitated the exodus. Only *some* African Americans who left, however, did so because of the violence; many voluntarily participated in an organized scheme of emigration to Wilberforce. Historian Carter G. Woodson argues that the violence was "only incidental to the exodus" and that the African Americans left "to escape enforcement of the black laws." A narrow focus on either the violence or the enforcement of the black laws as the cause of the out-migration obscures the emigrationist impulse among Cincinnati's black community. Although this exodus *was* fueled by oppressive social and economic conditions, including mob violence, it was also driven by the collective goals of a community desiring self-determination. African Americans were agents of their own destinies rather than reactionaries or refugees. Carter G. Woodson, "The Negroes of Cincinnati Prior to the Civil War," *Journal of Negro History* 1 (January 1916): 6–7; Frank U. Quillin, *The Color Line in Ohio: A History of Race Prejudice in a Typical Northern State* (Ann Arbor, MI.: George Wahr, 1913), 32; Leon F. Litwack, *North of Slavery: The Negro in Free States, 1790–1860* (Chicago: University of Chicago Press, 1961), 73; James Oliver Horton, *Free People of Color: Inside the African American Community* (Washington, DC: Smithsonian Institution Press, 1993), 141; William Cheek and Aimee Lee Cheek, *John Mercer Langston and the Fight for Black Freedom, 1829–1865* (Urbana: University of Illinois Press, 1989), 49; Patrick Rael, *Black Identity and Black Protest in the Antebellum North* (Chapel Hill: University of North Carolina Press, 2002), 121; Joe William Trotter Jr., *River Jordan: African American Urban Life in the Ohio Valley* (Lexington: University Press of Kentucky, 1998), 35; David Gerber, *Black Ohio and the Color Line, 1860–1915* (Urbana: University of Illinois Press, 1976), 14.

Even those historians who acknowledge an organized emigration scheme depict Wilberforce as a hastily and poorly planned colony established in response to the violence in Cincinnati. In his seminal work on emigration and colonization, historian Floyd J. Miller fails to acknowledge Wilberforce as a legitimate emigrationist colony. Scholars of black Canadian history have also been reluctant to concede the significance of either Wilberforce or the emigration scheme that gave birth to it. These critics use the colony's short life and the questionable integrity of its leadership as the yardstick of the colony's success. Robin Winks, Daniel Hill, Jason Silverman, and Donald George Simpson have all concluded that by the mid-1830s, its leadership divided and its internal organization broken, Wilberforce was a failure. Jane Pease and William H. Pease labeled it a "total failure" and "a forlorn dream."

Contemporary sources drew similar conclusions about Wilberforce's success. Hiram Wilson, who worked extensively with other black colonies in Canada, concluded in 1839 that the colony was a failure. Wilson believed the colony would have been "much more prosperous . . . had it not been for the agency of Israel Lewis." *Friend of Man*, May 1, 1839; Robin Winks, *The Blacks in Canada: A History* (New Haven, CT: Yale University Press, 1971), 162; Daniel Hill, *The Freedom-Seekers: Blacks in Early Canada* (Agincourt, Ontario: Book Society of Canada, 1981), 71; Donald George Simpson, "Negroes in Ontario from Early Times to 1870" (Ph.D. diss., University of Western Ontario, 1971), 370; William H. Pease and Jane H. Pease, *Black Utopia: Negro Communal Experiments in America* (Madison: State Historical Society of Wisconsin, 1963), 52; Jason Silverman, *Unwelcome Guests: Canada West's Response to American Fugitive Slaves, 1800–1865* (Millwood, NY: National University Publications, 1985), 34.

3. U.S. Census Bureau, *The Fourth Census of the United States, 1820* (Washington, DC: Gales and Seaton, 1821).

4. Ibid.; Robinson and Fairbank, *The Cincinnati Directory for the Year 1829* (Cincinnati: Whetstone and Buxton, 1829), 155. These numbers grossly underestimate the number of fugitive slaves residing in the city. Fugitive slaves would have been unwilling to allow themselves to be enumerated by either census takers or city directory compilers. Even free blacks who housed fugitive slaves would have underreported the number of people in their households, making it difficult to assess a more accurate number of blacks in Cincinnati in these years.

5. Per annum rate of increase = $2(p2-p1)/n(p1 + p2)$. Formula provided by Dr. Michael Kay, University of Toledo.

6. The city directories record 690 African Americans in 1826 and 2,258 in 1829. B. Drake and E. D. Mansfield, *Cincinnati in 1826* (Cincinnati: Morgan, Lodge, and Fisher, 1827); Robinson and Fairbank, *Cincinnati Directory for the Year 1829*, 155.

7. Robinson and Fairbank, *Cincinnati Directory for the Year 1829*, 155.

8. *Cincinnati Chronicle and Literary Gazette*, August 31, 1833, cited in Daniel Aaron, *Cincinnati, Queen City of the West, 1819–1838* (Columbus: Ohio State University Press, 1992), 20.

9. Eugene H. Berwanger, *The Frontier against Slavery: Western Anti-Negro Prejudice and the Slavery Extension Controversy* (Urbana: University of Illinois Press, 1967), 36.

10. *Cincinnati Daily Gazette*, July 24, 1829, cited in Richard Wade, *The Urban Frontier: The Rise of Western Cities, 1790–1830* (Cambridge, MA: Harvard University Press, 1959), 225.

11. *Liberty Hall*, August 25, 1825, cited in Wade, "The Negro in Cincinnati, 1800–1830," *Journal of Negro History* 39 (January 1954): 46.

12. *Ohio State Journal*, December 22, 1827, cited in Frank U. Quillin, *The Color Line in Ohio: A History of Race Prejudice in a Typical Northern State* (Ann Arbor, MI: George Wahr, 1913), 56.

13. Sean Wilentz, "Society, Politics, and the Market Revolution, 1815–1848," in *The New American History*, ed. Eric Foner (Philadelphia: Temple University Press, 1990), 52–53.

14. Bruce Laurie, *Artisans into Workers: Labor in Nineteenth-Century America* (New York: Hill and Wang, 1989), 35.

15. Ibid., 35–36.

16. Ibid., 42.

17. James C. Brown, quoted in Benjamin Drew, *The Refugee: Or the Narratives of Fugitive Slaves in Canada; Related by Themselves, with an Account of the History and Condition of the Colored Population in Upper Canada* (Boston: John P. Jewett, 1856), 240–41.

18. Ohio Anti-Slavery Society, *Report on the Condition of the People of Color in the State of Ohio* (Putnam, OH: Beaumont and Wallace, 1835), 3.

19. Cincinnati City Council Minutes, August 29, 1827, 4:72–73. Held at the Cincinnati City Hall vault. The names of the petitioners are not listed.

20. Ibid.

21. Leonard P. Curry, *The Free Black in Urban America, 1800–1850: The Shadow of the Dream* (Chicago: University of Chicago Press, 1981), 51.

22. Drake and Mansfield, *Cincinnati in 1826*, 35.

23. Ibid. The African Church was located just one block from the area targeted in the complaint, suggesting that the neighborhood was the heart of the black community.

24. Wade, *Urban Frontier*, 91–92; Curry, *Free Black in Urban America*, 51.

25. Cincinnati City Council Minutes, August 29, 1827, 4:72–73.

26. Patrick A. Folk, "'The Queen City of Mobs': Riots and Community Reactions in Cincinnati, 1788–1848" (Ph.D. diss., University of Toledo, 1978), 13–14.

27. Wade, *Urban Frontier*, 78. The 1827 city council members were Lewis Howell (merchant), Septimus Hazen (grocer), James McIntyre (grocer), William Noble (merchant), William Stephenson (tanner), Samuel Newell (tanner), Oliver Lovell (painter), Charles Tatem (iron founderer), Ebenezer Hulse (merchant), Henry Gassaway (wholesale grocer), Steven Burrows (tobacconist), and J. Whetstone (lumber merchant). Many of these 1827 councilmen retained their positions on the city council for years. Hazen, Tatem, Burrows, Newell, Lovell, and Hulse were all reelected for another term in 1829. The professional and economic profile of the 1829 city council differed little from that of the 1827 council. The 1829 city council included two tanners and curriers, an iron dealer, the owners of an iron foundry and an oil mill, an attorney, a carpenter, a tobacconist, a painter, a merchant and tavern keeper, a U.S. Army paymaster, and a man whose occupation is listed only as "city hotel." Robinson

and Fairbank, *Cincinnati Directory for the Year 1829*; Drake and Mansfield, *Cincinnati in 1826*.

28. U.S. Census Bureau, *The Fifth Census for the United States, 1830* (Washington, DC: Duff Green, 1832).

29. Drake and Mansfield, *Cincinnati in 1826*, 37; Wade, *Urban Frontier*, 227. Wade's footnotes cite the Cincinnati Colonization Society's *Proceedings* (1833). I have been unable to locate such a document. The Cincinnati Historical Society admits that the document may have been lost.

30. *African Repository*, October 1832; James Oliver Horton and Lois E. Horton, *In Hope of Liberty: Culture, Community, and Protest among Northern Free Blacks* (New York: Oxford University Press, 1997), 187.

31. David Smith, *The First Annual Report of the Ohio State Society for Colonizing the Free People of Colour of the United States* (Columbus: Ohio State Society for Colonizing Free People of Colour, 1827), 3. The Ohio branch of the ACS had its first meeting on December 19, 1827.

32. Ohio State Colonization Society, *Brief Exposition of the Views of the Society for the Colonization of Free Persons of Colour in Africa* (Columbus: Office of the Ohio Monitor, 1827), 7.

33. *Ohio State Journal*, July 12, 1827.

34. *Rights of All*, August 14, 1829.

35. Smith, *First Annual Report of the Ohio State Society for Colonizing the Free People of Colour of the United States*, 7.

36. Horton and Horton, *In Hope of Liberty*, 188; Floyd J. Miller, *The Search for a Black Nationality: Black Emigration and Colonization, 1787–1863* (Urbana: University of Illinois Press, 1975), 54.

37. *Ohio State Journal*, July 12, 1829.

38. Cincinnati City Council Minutes, November 19, 1828, cited in Wade, *Urban Frontier*, 225.

39. Folk, "Queen City of Mobs," 45.

40. *Cincinnati Daily Gazette*, March 27, 1829.

41. "An Act to Amend the Last Named Act 'An Act to Regulate Black and Mulatto Persons,'" in Stephen Middleton, *The Black Laws in the Old Northwest: A Documentary History* (Westport, CT: Greenwood, 1993), 17–18.

42. Folk, "Queen City of Mobs," 47. The winning candidates were George Lee (Fifth Ward), Benjamin Hopkins (Second Ward), and William Mills (Sixth Ward). Two of the newly elected trustees were skilled craftsmen: Benjamin Hopkins was a carpenter, and George Lee was a wagonmaker. The only occupation listed for Mills in the city directory is township trustee; Robinson and Fairbank, *Cincinnati Directory for the Year 1829*.

43. It is unclear who brought these suits in the lower courts. Contemporary sources mention the suits only in passing. *Cincinnati Daily Gazette*, July 20, 1829; *Ohio State Journal*, July 16, 1829; *African Repository*, August 1829: 185; *Rights of All*, August 14, 1829. According to the *Rights of All*, the plaintiff's argument stated that these laws denied African Americans the right to life, liberty, and the pursuit of happiness.

44. *Cincinnati Daily Gazette*, March 27, 1829.

45. In the March 27, 1829, issue of the *Cincinnati Daily Gazette*, one African American wrote, "We once had a favorable opinion, that we had many gentlemen who respected us in this part of the world. If that Act is enforced, we, the poor sons of Aethiopia, must take shelter where we can find it. In a multitude of counsellors [sic] there is a safety, and if we cannot find it in America, where we were born and have spent all our days, we must beg it elsewhere, but where Heaven only knows."

46. Miller, *Search for a Black Nationality*, 100.

47. Franklin, *Black Self-determination*, 87.

48. Ibid., 1–9, 101.

49. Ibid., 87; Miller, *Search for a Black Nationality*, 3–20.

50. Miller, *Search for a Black Nationality*, 3–4.

51. Ibid., 16–17.

52. The Newport society attempted to win support for emigration from the Free African Society of Philadelphia. However, the Free African Society was not receptive to emigration.

53. Paul Cuffe, a merchant captain and owner of several vessels, believed that a black migration to Africa would spread Christianity, "civilization," and commercial development to the continent. In 1815, Cuffe carried a group of thirty-eight African Americans to Sierra Leone. Miller, *Search for a Black Nationality*, 40.

54. *Genius of Universal Emancipation*, January 1825, 51–52; Miller, *Search for a Black Nationality*, 79; Wade, "Negro in Cincinnati, 1800–1830," 47.

55. *African Repository*, August 1829, 185.

56. Miller, *Search for a Black Nationality*, 76–79; Wade, "Negro in Cincinnati, 1800–1830," 47.

57. Taken from a letter written by Lewis Woodson, a resident of Chillicothe, Ohio. *Freedom's Journal*, January 31, 1829.

58. James C. Brown, quoted in Benjamin Drew, *Refugee*, 241; C. Peter Ripley, ed., *The Black Abolitionist Papers*, vol. 2, *Canada, 1830–1865* (Chapel Hill: University of North Carolina Press, 1986), 73n17.

59. *Cincinnati Daily Gazette*, July 1, 1829.

60. U.S. Census Bureau, *Fourth Census of the United States, 1820*.

61. Austin Steward, *Twenty-two Years a Slave, and Forty Years a Free Man; Embracing a Correspondence of Several Years, While President of Wilberforce Colony, London, Canada West* (New York: Negro Universities Press, 1968), 238.

62. Hill, *Freedom-Seekers*, 67; Drew, *Refugee*, 244–45.

63. *Cincinnati Daily Gazette*, August 22–29, 1829; Drew, *Refugee*, 245–46; Winks, *Blacks in Canada*, 156; Silverman, *Unwelcome Guests*, 27.

64. Patrick Shirreff, *A Tour through North America Together with a Comprehensive View of the Canadas and United States as Adapted for Agricultural Emigration* (Edinburgh: Oliver and Boyd, 1835), 178; Benjamin Lundy, *Genius of Universal Emancipation*, March 1832; *Cincinnati Daily Gazette*, August 22–29, 1829.

65. Steward, *Twenty-two Years a Slave, and Forty Years a Free Man*, 167.

66. Cited in Miller, *Search for a Black Nationality*, 98–99.

67. *Cincinnati Daily Gazette*, June 30, 1829.

68. *Liberty Hall and Cincinnati Gazette*, August 31, 1819, and September 3, 1819.

69. *Cincinnati Daily Gazette*, July 1, 1829. This is the only reference to such a meeting; there is no list of the leaders or topics discussed.

70. The term "emigrant" implies a proactive move to another city or country. The emigrant chooses to leave and chooses the direction in which he or she is headed. This person leaves with a sense of dignity. The term "refugee," on the other hand, implies a flight from persecution. The refugee simply seeks asylum and has little choice where that place of refuge is.

71. *Cincinnati Daily Gazette*, July 30–August 10, 1829.

72. *Rights of All*, September 18, 1829. Curiously, news of the riots was suppressed in the Cincinnati papers. Most local papers carried no news of this riot. Much of the narrative can be obtained only from other Ohio papers or from the black press. One possible explanation for this is that Cincinnati white officials, embarrassed by the riots, caused a news blackout to minimize their impact.

73. *Lebanon (Ohio) Western Star*, August 29, 1829. The papers reported that one white man, Eli Herricks, was killed in the riots. However, none of the local papers reported the number of injuries and fatalities among African Americans. Edward Abdy posited that a true accounting of the white fatalities was not reported because several of the persons "belonged to respectable families" who concealed their fates. Furthermore, he adds, "It was agreed . . . to throw over the circumstances of the defeat that veil, which could not be found for those of the attack." Edward Abdy, *Journal of a Residence and Tour in the United States of North America from April 1833 to October 1834* (London: n.p., 1835), 383.

74. *Portsmouth (Ohio) Western Times*, August 22, 1829.

75. Leonard L. Richards, *Gentlemen of Property and Standing: Anti-abolition Mobs in Jacksonian America* (New York: Oxford University Press, 1970), 83, 133.

76. Folk, "Queen City of Mobs," 55.

77. According to the 1829 directory, there were 2,258 blacks in the city. A year later, in the 1830 census, there were only 1,090 African Americans in the city, suggesting that—at the least—1,100 left. See U.S. Census Bureau, *Fifth Census of the United States, 1830*; Robinson and Fairbank, *Cincinnati Directory for the Year 1829*.

Between 1820 and 1829, there was a 15 percent per annum increase in the black population. If the black population had continued to increase at that rate without molestation, the 1829 population of 2,258 would have naturally grown to 2,597 by 1830. Instead, there were only 1,090 blacks counted in the 1830 census. The difference between projected and actual numbers suggests that 1,507 African Americans left the city. These numbers may be grossly underestimated because of the number of fugitive slaves in Cincinnati who did not allow themselves to be enumerated in the city directory or census. In addition, those who compiled the city directories admitted to undercounting many blacks because of living situations that made it difficult to carry out an accurate count.

Many families may have left only temporarily and returned in time to be counted in the census the next year.

78. According to Benjamin Lundy, some black Cincinnatians were "frightened into exile." See Fred Landon, ed., *The Diary of Benjamin Lundy Written during His Journey through Upper Canada, January 1832* (Ontario: Ontario Historical Society, n.d.), 5n2.

79. Benjamin Lundy claimed that despite the fact that some African Americans were exiled "not one has actually been forced to go out of the state." This suggests that they settled in other areas within Ohio. Ibid.

80. James C. Brown, quoted in Drew, *Refugee,* 239–48; John Malvin, *Autobiography of John Malvin: A Narrative* (Cleveland: Leader Printing, 1879), 38–41.

81. Malvin, *Autobiography of John Malvin,* 40. A closer analysis shows that both men were skilled workers, mulattoes, and leaders in the black community. Perhaps they traveled in the same social circle, the one out of which the emigration society was born.

82. James C. Brown, quoted in Drew, *Refugee,* 245. In his statement, Brown incorrectly identified the mayor as Elisha Hotchkiss.

83. Ibid. James C. Brown claims that he "sent three wagon loads [of emigrants] to Sandusky."

84. Sources that cite 2,000 settlers are *Minutes and Proceedings of the First Annual Convention of the People of Colour* (Philadelphia: Committee of Arrangements, 1831), 13, in *Minutes of the Proceedings of the National Negro Conventions, 1830–1864,* ed. Howard Holman Bell (New York: Arno, 1969); Landon, *Diary of Benjamin Lundy,* 115. Benjamin Drew asserts that the number was 460. See Drew, *Refugee,* 246.

85. Steward, *Twenty-two Years a Slave, and Forty Years a Free Man,* 180.

86. Ibid.

87. Ibid., 192.

88. Drew, *Refugee,* 246; Population returns for the township indicate that its population was only ninety-five in 1833. House of Assembly, Canada, *Aggregate Statement of the Population of the London District, as Taken from the Returns of Assessors of Townships for the Year 1832* (Ontario: n.p., 1832), n.p. Held at the University of Western Ontario.

89. Landon, *Diary of Benjamin Lundy,* 6; Charles Stuart, *Remarks on the Colony of Liberia and the American Colonization Society with Some Account of the Settlement of Coloured People at Wilberforce, Upper Canada* (London: J. Messender, 1832), 9.

90. *Journal of the House of Assembly of Upper Canada, 8 January–6 March 1830* (York: William Lyon McKenzie, 1830), 180. This figure could be exaggerated. It is highly likely that these petitioners were motivated by the desire to rid Colchester of blacks. There is no way to determine exactly how many Cincinnati blacks settled in the township. Also, no definitive analysis can be made about why the migrants settled in Colchester Township because the only record of the settlement is a petition filed by the white inhabitants. Colchester may have appealed to some black settlers because of the availability of work in its tobacco fields. For more on this, see Winks, *Blacks in Canada,* 145.

91. The petition also prayed that white immigrants be required to produce documents of their character from their home countries. *Journal of the House of Assembly of Upper Canada, 8 January–6 March 1830,* 180.

92. Landon, *Diary of Benjamin Lundy,* 5; *London Free Press,* August 27, 1966.

93. Pease and Pease, *Black Utopia,* 47; Winks, *Blacks in Canada,* 156.

94. Malvin, *Autobiography of John Malvin,* 42.

95. Pease and Pease, *Black Utopia,* 47–48; Winks, *Blacks in Canada,* 156; Silverman, *Unwelcome Guests,* 27–28; Stan Shantz, "Ontario Refuge for Slaves, Wilberforce Remembered," *London (Ontario) Free Press,* August 27, 1966. The land "included most of the farms on both sides of the present highway No. 4, between St. Patrick's Roman Catholic Church and the Au Sable River." S. Garret, "Few Traces Left of Clandeboye Settlement Where Busy Centre Established along River," *London (Ontario) Free Press,* March 7, 1942. This article is based on oral sources from the time of publication.

96. Steward, *Twenty-two Years a Slave, and Forty Years a Free Man,* 180.

97. Ibid., 181.

98. Landon, *Diary of Benjamin Lundy,* 6.

99. Ibid. Also see Garret, "Few Traces Left of Clandeboye Settlement."

100. Shirreff, *Tour through North America,* 178.

101. Stuart, *Remarks on the Colony of Liberia,* 15; *Liberator,* November 5, 1831.

102. *Liberator,* November 5, 1831.

103. Landon, *Diary of Benjamin Lundy,* 68.

104. Ibid., 6.

105. Austin Steward claimed that although Israel Lewis was somewhat educated, his wife was illiterate. Steward, *Twenty-two Years a Slave, and Forty Years a Free Man,* 238.

106. See, for example, the *Minutes and Proceedings of the First Annual Convention of the People of Colour,* in Bell, *Minutes of the Proceedings of the National Negro Conventions, 1830–1864,* n.p. The committee of inquiry stated that "education, temperance, and economy are best calculated to promote the elevation of mankind to a proper rank and standing among men" (5).

107. Landon, *Diary of Benjamin Lundy,* 6.

108. Ripley, *Black Abolitionist Papers,* 2:51n3.

109. Stuart, *Remarks on the Colony of Liberia,* 11.

110. "Contributions Received by the Rev. N. Paul to July 20, 1832," in Stuart, *Remarks on the Colony of Liberia,* 16.

111. Landon, *Diary of Benjamin Lundy,* 6.

112. Ripley, *Black Abolitionist Papers,* 2:51n4.

113. Simpson, "Negroes in Ontario from Early Times to 1870," 367.

114. Austin Steward was elected to the office of clerk for Biddulph Township. Although Steward did not specify what the other commissioner positions entailed, his duties as clerk were to "hold and keep all moneys, books, and papers belonging to said town" and "to administer oaths." Steward, *Twenty-two Years a Slave, and Forty Years a Free Man,* 260–61.

115. Ibid.

116. Elizabeth Rauh Bethel, *The Roots of African-American Identity: Memory and History in Antebellum Free Communities* (New York: St. Martin's Press, 1999), 120.

117. *Rights of All*, August 14, 1829.

118. American Society of Free Persons of Colour, *Constitution of the American Society of Free Persons of Colour*, in Bell, *Minutes of the Proceedings of the National Negro Conventions, 1830–1864*, v.

119. Ibid., 11.

120. Ibid., 10–11.

121. Ibid., 11.

122. *Minutes and Proceedings of the First Annual Convention of the Free People of Colour*, in Bell, *Minutes of the Proceedings of the National Conventions 1830–1864* [5].

123. *Liberator*, November 23, 1833.

124. Steward, *Twenty-two Years a Slave, and Forty Years a Free Man*, 182.

125. *Liberator*, November 23, 1833.

126. Stuart, *Remarks on the Colony of Liberia*, 10.

127. Simpson, "Negroes in Ontario from Early Times to 1870," 360.

128. Horton and Horton, *In Hope of Liberty*, 209.

129. Stan Shantz, "Wilberforce Remembered," *London (Ontario) Free Press*, August 27, 1966.

130. If each family had, on average, four members, then the initial settlement may have had between sixteen and twenty members. In 1831, the colony may have had between fifty-six and sixty residents.

131. The following year, the population was eighty-three. The official record ceases to name the colony after 1833. By 1834, the colony's population totals are included with the figures for Biddulph Township. Ironically, the 1836 population returns fail even to list Biddulph Township: it seems that the population returns for Biddulph were added to those for Tucker Smith—a bordering community. Thus, Wilberforce's identity was subsumed under Biddulph, and Biddulph's under Tucker Smith, making it difficult to draw any conclusions about population growth. House of Assembly, *Aggregate Statement of the Population of the District of London . . . for the Year 1832*, n.p.; Shantz, "Wilberforce Remembered," *London (Ontario) Free Press*, August 27, 1966.

132. General Return of the Population of the Western District for the Year 1835 in Biddulph Township: Ontario, Canada: n.p.

133. Steward, *Twenty-two Years a Slave, and Forty Years a Free Man*, 179.

134. Horton and Horton, *In Hope of Liberty*, 143; Ripley, *Black Abolitionist Papers*, 2:42–43n11.

135. Steward, *Twenty-two Years a Slave, and Forty Years a Free Man*, 180.

136. The board of managers for Wilberforce was not a legislative body. Their main function was managing the financial affairs of the colony.

137. Steward, *Twenty-two Years a Slave, and Forty Years a Free Man*, 348. None of the managers can be traced to Cincinnati through the 1820 census or the 1829 city directory. Some, like Steward and Butler, were admittedly not from Cincinnati.

138. Ibid., 287.

139. Stuart, *Remarks on the Colony of Liberia*, 15–16.

140. See the *Liberator*, March 14, 1835, for information about Paul's lecture at the Trades Hall in Glasgow in December 1834. Although Paul's lecture was supposed to be about the Wilberforce colony, the content was more about southern slavery. Also see the *Liberator*, June 22, 1833, for a letter from Paul about his activities in England.

141. *Liberator*, June 22, 1833.

142. Steward, *Twenty-two Years a Slave, and Forty Years a Free Man*, 264.

143. *Liberator*, December 25, 1832, February 9, 1833.

144. Steward to J. Budd, June 1833, in Steward, *Twenty-two Years a Slave, and Forty Years a Free Man*, 351.

145. *Liberator*, March 9, 1833.

146. *Friend of Man*, August 14, 1839; *Colored American*, August 24, 1839. This caution was signed by Simon Wyatt, Lisbon Wine, William Smith, Henry Shaw, William Bell, Samuel Wallace, John Thompson, Peter Butler, Phillip Harris, Joseph Taylor, John Whitehead, Ephraim Taylor, Daniel A. Turner, Solomon Brown, and Cesar King.

147. Samuel E. Cornish to Austin Steward, n.d., in Carter G. Woodson, *The Mind of the Negro as Reflected in Letters Written during the Crisis, 1800–1860* (New York: Negro Universities Press, 1969), 626.

148. *Friend of Man*, May 1, 1839.

149. Ibid.

150. *Liberator*, February 23, 1833.

151. Ibid.

152. *Liberator*, April 13, 1833.

153. *Liberator*, March 9, 1833.

154. Steward, *Twenty-two Years a Slave, and Forty Years a Free Man*, 235.

155. Israel Lewis to William Lloyd Garrison, February 11, 1833, in Woodson, *Mind of the Negro*, 183; *Liberator*, February 23, 1833.

156. *Liberator*, February 23, 1833.

157. *Liberator*, March 8, 1834.

158. *Friend of Man*, May 1, 1839.

159. *Liberator*, February 23, 1833.

160. *Liberator*, April 13, 1833.

161. *Cazenovia*, January 26, 1833, cited in Woodson, *Mind of the Negro*, 182. Israel Lewis wrote, "There is one thing that gives me some satisfaction; that is, discerning men know that in all great undertakings like this, those engaged in them must be more or less persecuted; more especially when they stand in the midst of an ignorant people, coming from different sections of the country, under different views, and with different habits."

162. Hill, *Freedom-Seekers*, 68.

163. Winks, *Blacks in Canada*, 180, 202.

164. Pease and Pease, *Black Utopia*, 60.

165. *London Times*, April 27, 1849.

CHAPTER 4

1. In his study of black life in Cincinnati prior to 1830, historian Richard Wade discredits those who did not emigrate. By his account, the stronger, more talented population emigrated, leaving a weaker, less determined one. "Among these displaced persons were many of the most industrious, stable and prosperous members of the Negro community. They had the financial resources and social energy needed for movement, while the less successful and weaker stayed behind. Some leadership remained in the city, but the cream was skimmed off." Richard Wade, "The Negro in Cincinnati, 1800–1830," *Journal of Negro History* 39 (January 1954): 56. A disproportionate number of African Americans with resources did leave Cincinnati, but history does not support the claim that those who remained were less successful or weaker than those who left.

2. "Emerging from fire" is a double entendre referring to African Americans' survival of the 1829 mob action and the racism and discrimination they endured.

3. Lyle Koehler, *Cincinnati's Black Peoples: A Chronology and Bibliography, 1787–1982* (Cincinnati: Cincinnati Arts Consortium, 1986), 11.

4. Koehler, *Cincinnati's Black Peoples*, 11.

5. *Cincinnati Daily Gazette*, August 22–29, 1829.

6. Ibid., August 17, 1829.

7. Ibid.

8. Ohio Anti-Slavery Society, *Proceedings of the Ohio Anti-Slavery Society Convention Held at Putnam, Ohio* (Putnam: Ohio Anti-Slavery Society, 1835), 30. According to the organization, the average price these people had paid for themselves was $452.77. The society surveyed only two "small districts" in Cincinnati. It is not clear whether each "district" was an entire ward or a portion thereof.

9. Ibid., 25, 29, 30; Edward Abdy, *Journal of a Residence and Tour in the United States of North America from April 1833 to October 1834* (London: n.p., 1835), 384.

10. Ohio Anti-Slavery Society, *Proceedings*, 26.

11. Ibid., 35.

12. Ibid., 25.

13. U.S. Census Bureau, *The Fourth Census of the United States, 1820* (Washington, DC: Gales and Seaton, 1821); U.S. Census Bureau, *The Fifth Census of the United States, 1830* (Washington, DC: Duff Green, 1832).

14. U.S. Census Bureau, *Fourth Census of the United States, 1820*; U.S. Census Bureau, *Fifth Census of the United States, 1830*.

15. Robinson and Fairbank, *The Cincinnati Directory for the Year 1829* (Cincinnati: Whetstone and Buxton, 1829); U.S. Census Bureau, *Fifth Census of the United States, 1830*.

16. U.S. Census Bureau, *Fourth Census of the United States, 1820*; U.S. Census Bureau, *Fifth Census of the United States, 1830*.

17. Abdy, *Journal of a Residence and Tour in the United States*, 390.

18. There are no extant records indicating which African Americans posted bond in Hamilton County.

19. U.S. Census Bureau, *Fifth Census of the United States, 1830*.

20. Benjamin W. Arnett, *Proceedings of the Semi-centenary Celebration of the African Methodist Episcopal Church of Cincinnati, Held in Allen Temple February 8th, 9th, and 10th, 1874* (Cincinnati: H. Watkin, 1874), 31–34.

21. U.S. Census Bureau, *Fifth Census of the United States, 1830*.

22. Many of those African Americans who remained in the city were active members of one of the black churches. George Jones, Thomas Arnold, and Joseph Kyte belonged to the Deer Creek Methodist Episcopal Church. Several members of the AME body also remained in the city. Phillip Tolliver, for example, joined the Deer Creek Church after settling in Cincinnati in 1817. Several years later, he joined the AME church, where he worshipped for the rest of his life. Elizabeth Jones joined the AME church in 1824, and Charlotte McDonald joined in 1825; both women enjoyed lifelong memberships in the church. Arnett, *Proceedings of the Semi-centenary Celebration*, 32–36.

23. Rev. James King led the congregation until the early 1830s, when Wyle Reynolds succeeded him. Although many more members were added to the body under Reynolds, his true legacy was the construction of Bethel. He served until 1839, when Henry Adcrisson succeeded him. Church historian Arnett summarized Adcrisson's contributions : "[He] was a man of God, and he did much good, and many souls were added to the church, while the members were strengthened in their hope of conquering when done with the trials of life." Adcrisson served for two years and was succeeded by Rev. Charles Peters. Ibid., 20–21. No further information could be found about any of these ministers.

24. Ibid., 31–34. Fowler does not appear in the 1830 census.

25. Ibid., 63.

26. Ibid., 31.

27. *Liberator*, July 30, 1831.

28. William Cheek and Aimee Lee Cheek, "John Mercer Langston and the Cincinnati Riot of 1841," in *Race and the City: Work, Community, and Protest in Cincinnati, 1820–1970*, ed. Henry Louis Taylor Jr. (Urbana: University of Illinois Press, 1993), 61n27; Amzi Barber, "Of the Present Condition of the Colored People in Cincinnati," in Ohio Anti-Slavery Society, *Report of the Second Anniversary of the Ohio Anti-Slavery Society, Held in Mount Pleasant on the Twenty-seventh of April 1837* (Cincinnati: Ohio Anti-Slavery Society, 1837), 63–64.

29. James Oliver Horton, *Free People of Color: Inside the African American Community* (Washington, DC: Smithsonian Institution Press, 1993), 43.

30. Arnett, *Proceedings of the Semi-centenary Celebration*, 20.

31. Ibid.

32. *The Holy Bible* (Nashville: Thomas Nelson Publishers, 1990), concordance at 75.

33. Arnett, *Proceedings of the Semi-centenary Celebration*, 20.

34. Wendell P. Dabney, *Cincinnati's Colored Citizens: Historical, Sociological, and Biographical* (Cincinnati: Dabney Publishing, 1926), 370. Taken from a report made by G. W. Hays Sr. in 1879. Those present at the meeting were George Jones, Eli-

jah Forte, Reuben Hawkins, Prince Austin, Thomas Arnold, Robert Lawson, Henry Williams, Richard Lunsford, Joseph Moore, John Webb, Hannah Moore, Ann Fleming, Mila Banks, and Polly Geist.

35. It is ironic that these men led this move for independence from Enon Baptist; after all, just two years earlier, they had asserted their commitment not to offend their white "friends" at Deer Creek.

36. Dabney, *Cincinnati's Colored Citizens*, 370.

37. Ibid.

38. Ibid. Benjamin Arnett also discusses the emergence of the Union Baptist Church in his sketch of the AME church. There are some discrepancies between these two accounts, however. Arnett posits that, before 1835, most black churchgoers had attended one of the two black Methodist churches even if they did not wholly subscribe to the Methodist doctrine. According to him, the African Union Baptist Church emerged from the AME body: Baptists who worshipped at the AME church had become numerous enough to establish their own church. This pattern is inconsistent with the pattern of the establishment of other independent black churches. Black churches were usually established in response to discrimination within white churches and blacks' desire for religious autonomy. Arnett also claims that David Nickens organized the African Union Baptist Church, apparently on the basis of his having been the church's first minister. Although Arnett provides a detailed glimpse of the institutional life of black Cincinnati's antebellum community, he was the church historian for the AME church, not the Baptist church: some of his facts on the history of Union Baptist may not be precise. See Arnett, *Proceedings of the Semicentenary Celebration*, 59.

39. James Oliver Horton and Lois E. Horton, *In Hope of Liberty: Culture, Community, and Protest among Northern Free Blacks, 1700–1860* (New York: Oxford University Press, 1997), 143.

40. Ibid.

41. Ibid., 142–43. African Union Baptist Church was part of a national black Baptist church movement. The first independent black Baptist church in the North was organized in Philadelphia in 1805. By 1812, black Baptist churches were located in Boston and New York City, as well.

42. Christopher Phillips, *Freedom's Port: The African American Community of Baltimore, 1790–1860* (Urbana: University of Illinois Press, 1997), 134.

43. Dabney, *Cincinnati's Colored Citizens*, 370.

44. Arnett, *Proceedings of the Semi-centenary Celebration*, 59.

45. David Nickens was an ordained minister—the first ordained black minister in the state—although it is not clear where he received his religious training. Cheek and Cheek, "John Mercer Langston and the Cincinnati Riot of 1841," 31.

46. These were black celebrations of freedom and protest held on July 5 to underscore the hypocrisy of Independence Day and to emphasize African American protest against it.

47. David Nickens, "Address to the People of Color in Chillicothe," *Liberator*, August 11, 1832.

48. Ibid.

49. Cheek and Cheek, "John Mercer Langston and the Cincinnati Riot of 1841," 61.

50. Dabney, *Cincinnati's Colored Citizens*, 371.

51. John Mercer Langston, *From the Plantation to the National Capitol; or, The First and Only Negro Representative in Congress from the Old Dominion* (Hartford, CT.: American Publishing, 1894), 62.

52. Frederika Bremer, *The Homes of the New World: Impressions of America* (London: Arthur Hall, Virtue, 1853), 2:417.

53. Ibid., 418–19.

54. Ibid., 419.

55. Ohio Anti-Slavery Society, *Report on the Condition of the People of Color in the State of Ohio* (Putnam, OH: Beaumont and Wallace, 1835), 11.

56. Patrick Rael, *Black Identity and Black Protest in the Antebellum North* (Chapel Hill: University of North Carolina Press, 2002), 133.

57. Phillips, *Freedom's Port*, 170; Patrick Rael defines respectability as "a particular form of public regard for individual attainments," yet he also insists that it encompasses adherence to the will of God. For further discussion, see Rael, *Black Identity and Black Protest in the Antebellum North*, 130, 133.

58. Rael, *Black Identity and Black Protest in the Antebellum North*, 188–89.

59. Ibid., 200.

60. Ohio Anti-Slavery Society, *Report on the Condition of the People of Color in the State of Ohio*, 11; Ohio Anti-Slavery Society, *Proceedings of the Ohio Anti-Slavery Society Convention Held at Putnam, Ohio*, 33.

61. Prov. 20:1; Prov. 23:21; Isa. 5:22, 23; Isa. 28:7; Rom. 13:13; Matt. 24:48–51 (KJV).

62. Jane H. Pease and William H. Pease, *They Who Would Be Free: Blacks' Search for Freedom, 1830–1861* (Urbana: University of Illinois Press, 1990), 124.

63. Barber, "Of the Present Condition of the Colored People in Cincinnati," 63; Pease and Pease, *They Who Would Be Free*, 125.

64. Barber, "Of the Present Condition of the Colored People in Cincinnati," 63–64. This society was in no way affiliated with the American Reform Society, which opposed to names that made color distinctions. Although comprised of free blacks, the American Reform Society admonished against the use of terms like "colored" or "African." The society in Cincinnati, the Moral Reform Society of the Colored Citizens of Ohio, was clearly a different organization.

65. Barber, "Of the Present Condition of the Colored People in Cincinnati," 64.

66. Ibid.

67. Ibid.

68. Ohio Anti-Slavery Society, *Report on the Condition of the People of Color in the State of Ohio*, 11; Ohio Anti-Slavery Society, *Proceedings of the Ohio Anti-Slavery Society Con-*

vention Held at Putnam, Ohio, 33; There are no extant records or membership rolls of the Female Benevolent Society.

69. Horton and Horton, *In Hope of Liberty,* 128.

70. *Colored American,* August 25, 1838, cited in C. Peter Ripley, ed., *The Black Abolitionist Papers* (Chapel Hill: University of North Carolina Press, 1986), microfilm, 12468.

71. Ohio Anti-Slavery Society, *Proceedings of the Ohio Anti-Slavery Society Convention Held at Putnam, Ohio,* 33; Carter G. Woodson, *The Education of the Negro Prior to 1861* (New York: Arno, 1968), 11. There are no extant records or membership rolls of the Cincinnati Union Society, and therefore no concrete way to determine what class of blacks joined.

72. Rael, *Black Identity and Black Protest in the Antebellum North,* 127.

73. John O. Wattles, *Annual Report of the Educational Condition of the Colored People of Cincinnati, Including the Sentiment in Mercer County, Ohio: Presented at the Exhibition of the Cincinnati High School* (Cincinnati: John White, 1847), 4.

74. Vicky Y. Dula, "The Wolf and the Pack: Black Residence and Social Organization in Antebellum Cincinnati" (master's thesis, Ohio State University, 1984), 11.

75. John B. Shotwell, *A History of the Schools of Cincinnati* (Cincinnati: School Life, 1902), quoted in Dabney, *Cincinnati's Colored Citizens,* 100; Abdy, *Journal of a Residence and Tour in the United States,* 394. The common school system fell under the auspices of the Board of Trustees and Visitors of Common Schools. Common schools were to be financed by property taxes equivalent to two mills per dollar of the property's value. The fund was to provide for the construction of building and operating costs.

76. Abdy, *Journal of a Residence and Tour in the United States,* 394.

77. Shotwell, *History of the Schools of Cincinnati,* quoted in Dabney, *Cincinnati's Colored Citizens,* 101; Koehler, *Cincinnati's Black Peoples,* 11.

78. Shotwell, *History of the Schools of Cincinnati,* quoted in Dabney, *Cincinnati's Colored Citizens,* 11. Shotwell discusses "Ohio in Africa" only parenthetically. No further information about this scheme exists. A secondary source that mentions this colony (also parenthetically) is Floyd J. Miller, *The Search for a Black Nationality: Black Emigration and Colonization, 1787–1863* (Urbana: University of Illinois Press, 1975), 166.

79. Ohio Anti-Slavery Society, *Report on the Condition of the People of Color in the State of Ohio,* 4.

80. Ibid.; Koehler, *Cincinnati's Black Peoples,* 14.

81. Ohio Anti-Slavery Society, *Report on the Condition of the People of Color in the State of Ohio.*

82. Miss Matthews, Miss Bishop, Miss Lowe, Miss Rakestraw, and Miss Merrill. Shotwell, *History of the Schools of Cincinnati,* quoted in Dabney, *Cincinnati's Colored Citizens,* 101; Barber, "Of the Present Condition of the Colored People in Cincinnati," in Ohio Anti-Slavery Society, *Report of the Second Anniversary of the Ohio Anti-Slavery Society,* 59.

83. Abdy, *Journal of a Residence and Tour in the United States*, 400–401; Ohio Anti-Slavery Society, *Report on the Condition of the People of Color in the State of Ohio*, 4–9; *Philanthropist*, November 26, 1839, and December 19, 1836.

84. *Philanthropist*, November 26, 1839.

85. Ibid.

86. Ibid.

87. Arnett, *Proceedings of the Semi-centenary Celebration*, 63.

88. Ibid.

89. *Philanthropist*, November 26, 1839.

90. One teacher wrote, "God has placed a few of them [blacks] in our midst, and he is by his Providence saying unto us, 'Lovest thou me?' then 'Feed my lambs.' . . . In an intellectual and moral sense, they [African Americans] are *starved, cold and naked*, and will perish in this condition unless we hear and obey the voice of our Father and their Father." *Philanthropist*, November 26, 1839.

91. Cincinnati Lane Seminary, "Statement of the Faculty Concerning the Late Difficulties in the Lane Seminary," in *Fifth Annual Report of the Trustees of the Cincinnati Lane Seminary: Together with the Laws of the Institution and a Catalogue of the Officers and Students* (Cincinnati: Corey and Fairbank, 1834), 36–37.

92. Cheek and Cheek, "John Mercer Langston and the Cincinnati Riot of 1841," 61.

93. Shotwell, *History of the Schools of Cincinnati*, quoted in Dabney, *Cincinnati's Colored Citizens*, 100.

94. Ibid., 102. Baker Jones is noted as a man of "considerable wealth for that day." No further biographical data can be found about him. This source does not list the date these schools opened. The best approximation is that they opened sometime between 1834 and 1841.

95. Ibid., 100.

96. Wattles, *Annual Report of the Educational Condition of the Colored People of Cincinnati*, 4; Arnett, *Proceedings of the Semi-centenary Celebration*, 63.

97. Shotwell, *History of the Schools of Cincinnati*, quoted in Dabney, *Cincinnati's Colored Citizens*, 101.

98. Ohio Anti-Slavery Society, *Report on the Condition of the People of Color in the State of Ohio*, 4.

99. Shotwell, *History of the Schools of Cincinnati*, quoted in Dabney, *Cincinnati's Colored Citizens*, 103.

100. Ohio Anti-Slavery Society, *Report on the Condition of the People of Color in the State of Ohio*, 4.

101. Ibid.

102. Ibid.

103. Barber, "Of the Present Condition of the Colored People in Cincinnati," 60.

104. Abdy, *Journal of a Residence and Tour in the United States*, 401; *Philanthropist*, November 26, 1839.

105. Ohio Anti-Slavery Society, *Report on the Condition of the People of Color in the State of Ohio*, 4.

106. Barber, "Of the Present Condition of the Colored People in Cincinnati," 59.

107. Ibid., 62.

108. Ibid.

109. *Philanthropist*, December 19, 1836.

110. Ibid.

111. Cheek and Cheek, "John Mercer Langston and the Cincinnati Riot of 1841," 39.

112. Barber, "Of the Present Condition of the Colored People in Cincinnati," 57–65. See also *Philanthropist*, October 22, 1839.

113. Barber, "Of the Present Condition of the Colored People in Cincinnati," 62; Woodson, *Education of the Negro Prior to 1861*, 245.

114. "An Act Relating to Juries," in Stephen Middleton, *The Black Laws in the Old Northwest: A Documentary History* (Westport, CT: Greenwood, 1993), 47–48.

115. Gray v. State, 4 Ohio 353 (1831).

116. Kenneth Stampp, *The Peculiar Institution: Slavery in the Ante-bellum South* (New York: Vintage Books, 1956), 195.

117. Gray v. State, 4 Ohio 353 (1831).

118. Ibid.

119. Thacker v. Hawk, 11 Ohio 376 (1842).

120. Jeffries v. Ankeny, 11 Ohio 372 (1842).

121. Koehler, *Cincinnati's Black Peoples*, 17.

122. *Morning Herald*, January, 20, 1844, quoted in James Oliver Horton and Stacy Flaherty, "Black Leadership in Antebellum Cincinnati," in Taylor, *Race and the City*, 90.

123. Ohio Anti-Slavery Society, *Report on the Condition of the People of Color in the State of Ohio*, 3.

124. J. H. Woodruff, *The Cincinnati Directory and Advertiser for 1836–7* (Cincinnati: J. H. Woodruff, 1836).

125. Ira Berlin, *Slaves without Masters: The Free Negro in the Antebellum South* (New York: Vintage Books, 1974), 230.

126. James C. Brown, quoted in Benjamin Drew, *The Refugee: Or the Narratives of Fugitive Slaves in Canada; Related by Themselves, with an Account of the History and Condition of the Colored Population in Upper Canada* (Boston: John P. Jewett, 1856), 241.

127. Abdy, *Journal of a Residence and Tour in the United States*, 384–85.

128. Whittington B. Johnson, *The Promising Years, 1750–1830: The Emergence of Black Labor and Business* (New York: Garland, 1993), 105. According to Johnson, carpentry was the trade blacks most commonly practiced, although he provides no hard data or statistics to substantiate this point.

129. Woodruff, *Cincinnati Directory and Advertiser for 1836–7*.

130. Johnson, *Promising Years*, 100. Johnson described the skills that are used in masonry.

131. That person was John Mercer Langston. John Mercer Langston, *From the Virginia Plantation to the National Capitol; or, The First and Only Negro Representative in Congress from the Old Dominion* (Hartford, CT: American Publishing, 1894), 117, 123; Paul

Finkelman, "Not Only the Judges' Robes Were Black: African-American Lawyers as Social Engineers," *Stanford Law Review* 47 (November 1994): 161–209.

132. Johnson, *Promising Years*, 160.

133. *Philanthropist*, October 8, 1839. In 1839, a mob of twenty to thirty masked men attacked the home of a black physician. The physician was accused of quackery—namely benefiting from the "gullibility of our citizens." The mob action did not occur until after the doctor had "erected a splendid edifice," so it is possible that the accusations of quackery were a manifestation of jealousy of this doctor's success. The mob ran him out of town.

134. Woodruff, *Cincinnati Directory and Advertiser for 1836–7*.

135. Menial labor jobs translated to low wages, making basic survival difficult. To supplement the family income, many black children were forced to work as soon as they were able and had to forgo an education. Some of these working youngsters assisted their parents in their jobs. Young girls, for example, might do washing with their mothers. Sometimes these children might earn extra money as hucksters on street corners or as extra hands at the river. These children were very vulnerable to exploitation—often overworked and underpaid. Yet even with the extra income, black families found it difficult to make ends meet. Denied benefits from the Poor Fund, indigent blacks could seek refuge neither in the county's Poor House nor the Cincinnati Orphan Asylum. The black community's benevolent and mutual aid societies were a crucial resource in times of need.

136. Woodruff, *Cincinnati Directory and Advertiser for 1836–7*. This city directory actually has a separate category for African Americans. These figures, were obtained by extracting entries for all black female heads of household and counting the actual number who were washers. This is not an exact representation of black female washers because city directories, by nature, exclude many people.

137. Woodruff, *Cincinnati Directory and Advertiser for the Year 1836–7*.

138. Ibid. The 1836 city directory lists 163 black heads of household. Of that number, twenty were barbers. City directory compilers were not consistent in recording black residents. If those 163 names are a representative sample, they amount to about 12 percent of the heads of household.

139. Langston, *From the Virginia Plantation to the National Capitol*, 61; Charles Cist, *The Cincinnati Directory for the Year 1842* (Cincinnati: E. Morgan, 1842).

140. Carter G. Woodson, "The Negroes of Cincinnati Prior to the Civil War," *Journal of Negro History* 1 (January 1916): 9; Richard Pih, "Negro Self-Improvement Efforts in Ante-bellum Cincinnati, 1836–1850," *Ohio History* 78 (Summer 1969): 182; William Cheek and Aimee Lee Cheek, *John Mercer Langston and the Fight for Black Freedom, 1829–1865* (Urbana: University of Illinois Press, 1989), 53.

141. Pih, "Negro Self-Improvement Efforts in Ante-bellum Cincinnati," 182. According to Pih, the bedstead company's success was short-lived after a series of fires in the late 1840s made it uninsurable. Boyd may have been the victim of arsonists who resented his unparalleled success. U.S. Census Bureau, *The Seventh Census of the United States, 1850* (Washington, DC: Robert Armstrong, 1853).

142. Woodson, "Negroes of Cincinnati Prior to the Civil War," 9; U.S. Census Bureau, *Seventh Census of the United States, 1850*.

143. Langston, *From the Virginia Plantation to the National Capitol,* 62.

144. Ibid., 61.

CHAPTER 5

1. American Society of Free Persons of Colour, *Constitution of the American Society of Free Persons of Colour,* in *Minutes of the Proceedings of the National Negro Conventions, 1830–1864,* ed. Howard Holman Bell (New York: Arno, 1969), 9.

2. Note the name of the First Convention for the American Society of Free Persons of Colour. The name of the next convention was Second Annual Convention for the American Society of the Free People of Colour. For clarification, I use black convention movement.

3. *Minutes and Proceedings of the First Annual Convention of the People of Colour . . . from the Sixth to the Eleventh of June, Inclusive, 1831,* in *Minutes of the Proceedings of the National Negro Conventions, 1830–1864,* ed. Howard Holman Bell (New York: Arno, 1969), 9. Neither Hatfield nor Liverpool was a leader of any organization. Charles Hatfield appears in none of the city directories, suggesting he was not a head of household at this time. He may have resided with one of his relatives—Joseph or John Hatfield. The 1830 census indicates that John Liverpool was in the 55–100 age category in 1830. U.S. Census Bureau, *The Fifth Census of the United States, 1830* (Washington, DC: Duff Green, 1832).

4. *Minutes and Proceedings of the First Annual Convention of the People of Colour,* in Bell, *Minutes of the Proceedings of the National Negro Conventions 1830–1864,* 5–6. Black leaders first met on September 20–24, 1830, in Philadelphia to discuss emigration and the general condition of African Americans. The American Society of Free Persons of Colour was born from that meeting, which elected Richard Allen as the society's president and Austin Steward and Dr. Belfast Burton as its vice-presidents. Black leaders returned the following year for the First Annual Convention of the People of Colour, held June 6–11, 1831—also in Philadelphia. This time, the convention focused not on emigration but on racial uplift and improving the condition of African Americans. Education was one of its main focuses, along with temperance and moral reform.

5. James Oliver Horton and Lois E. Horton, *In Hope of Liberty: Culture, Community, and Protest among Northern Free Blacks, 1700–1860* (New York: Oxford University Press, 1997), 208. After 1835, the conventions were suspended due to low attendance.

6. Before adjourning, the convention appointed officers for the year. A vice-president and corresponding secretary were appointed for each state represented. Charles Hatfield and John Liverpool were chosen as Ohio's vice-president and corresponding secretary, respectively. The duties of the state vice-president and secretary were to organize state auxiliaries, collect dues, and remit monies to the national treasurer. The corresponding secretary was charged with communicating

the convention's views on the Canadian settlement to the constituency and with maintaining correspondence related to the proposed college in New Haven. These officers were expected to be actively involved with the convention throughout the year. See *Minutes and Proceedings of the First Annual Convention of the People of Colour,* in Bell, *Minutes of the Proceedings of the National Negro Conventions, 1830–1864,* 9–10.

7. John Malvin, *Autobiography of John Malvin: A Narrative* (Cleveland: Leader Printing, 1879), 65. Malvin claims that he "called a meeting of colored men and suggested to them the propriety of calling a State convention of colored men, which was done." Only with great skepticism should Malvin be trusted about his role in organizing this convention because he tended to embellish his own importance. It is more likely that those who attended the Convention of the Free People of Colour in Philadelphia brought the idea of a state convention back to Ohio. Malvin went on to add, "[A]s far as I know it was the first colored convention ever known in the United States; at least I never heard of one before." As an educated black man who was both well traveled and active in civic affairs, Malvin was aware of the black conventions that had been held annually in Philadelphia since 1830. With this statement, he seems to be attempting to take credit for having started the state black convention movement. Despite his self-conscious attempts to inflate his contributions to the struggle for civil rights in Ohio, Malvin may have been instrumental in the organizing stages of this convention.

8. David Gerber, *Black Ohio and the Color Line, 1860–1915* (Urbana: University of Illinois Press, 1976), 22.

9. *Philanthropist,* October 22, 1839; Malvin, *Autobiography of John Malvin,* 65.

10. Malvin, *Autobiography of John Malvin,* 65; *Philanthropist,* September 24, 1839.

11. Lane Seminary, *Fifth Annual Report of the Trustees of Lane Seminary: Together with the Laws of the Institution and a Catalogue of the Officers and Students* (Cincinnati: Corey and Fairbank, 1834), 34–39.

12. Edward Abdy, *Journal of a Residence and Tour in the United States of North America from April 1833 to October 1834* (London: n.p., 1835), 402. William Cheek and Aimee Cheek, "John Mercer Langston and the Cincinnati Riot of 1841," in *Race and the City: Work, Community, and Protest in Cincinnati, 1820–1970,* ed. Henry Louis Taylor Jr. (Urbana: University of Illinois Press, 1993), 61.

13. Lane Seminary, *Fifth Annual Report,* 42–47.

14. Lane Seminary's total enrollment in the theological class and the preparatory department shrank from one hundred in January 1834 to only thirty-seven the following fall. Among those who left the school but remained active in CAS activities in Cincinnati were H. Lyman and Marcus Robinson, who also had participated in the antislavery society at the school. They were two of four men who signed a letter to Lane faculty in June 1834 in defense of their actions at Lane Seminary.

15. *Philanthropist,* February 5, 1836.

16. Reprinted in the *Philanthropist,* January 8, 1836.

17. "A threatening letter from Kentucky," quoted in David Grimsted, *American Mobbing, 1828–1861: Toward Civil War* (New York: Oxford University Press, 1998), 59.

18. *Cincinnati Daily Gazette,* January 22, 1836; *Philanthropist,* January 29, 1836. Also in attendance were hardware merchant and city councilman William Neff; rolling mill owner and city councilman Joseph McCandless: Surveyor General Lt. Robert Lytle: Deputy Postmaster Elam P. Langdon: Port Warden Joseph Pierce: the president of Lafayette Bank, Josiah Lawrence; and the president of the Ohio Insurance Company, David Loring.

19. *Philanthropist,* April 22, 1836.

20. Ohio Anti-Slavery Society, *Narrative of the Late Riotous Proceeding against the Liberty of the Press in Cincinnati with Remarks and Historical Notices Relating to Emancipation* (Cincinnati: Ohio Anti-Slavery Society, 1836), 13.

21. Ibid., 12–13. According to David Grimsted, the mob participants included a manufacturer, three skilled mechanics—two of whom owned their shops—and three sons of prominent merchants and politicians.

22. Ibid., 14–15; *Philanthropist,* July 15, 1836.

23. Consequently, "mob" is an imprecise and even misleading term to describe this violence because it implies an element of disorganization. Historian Leonard L. Richards defines a mob as a situation in which "dozens, hundreds, or even thousands of persons temporarily assisted one another and in a violent or turbulent manner broke up meetings, assaulted abolitionists, damaged or destroyed property." He also distinguishes between mobs that had no prior organization and those that "involved explicit planning and organization." See Leonard L. Richards, *Gentlemen of Property and Standing: Anti-abolition Mobs in Jacksonian America* (New York: Oxford University Press, 1970), 3, 84.

24. Ohio Anti-Slavery Society, *Narrative of the Late Riotous Proceeding against the Liberty of the Press,* 39–40; Grimsted, *American Mobbing,* 61.

25. Ohio Anti-Slavery Society, *Narrative of the Late Riotous Proceeding against the Liberty of the Press,* 45. The only biographical data on Dennis Hill indicate that he was originally from Maryland. In 1840, he resided on Race Street between Court and Canal streets. See Henry D. Shaffer, *The Cincinnati, Covington, Newport, and Fulton Directory for 1840* (Cincinnati: Donogh, 1840), 472.

26. Ohio Anti-Slavery Society, *Narrative of the Late Riotous Proceeding against the Liberty of the Press in Cincinnati,* 45.

27. Ibid.

28. Ibid.

29. Amzi Barber, "Of the Present Condition of the Colored People in Cincinnati," in Ohio Anti-Slavery Society, *Report of the Second Anniversary of the Ohio Anti-Slavery Society, Held in Mount Pleasant on the Twenty-seventh of April 1837* (Cincinnati: Ohio Anti-Slavery Society, 1837), 58.

30. *Philanthropist,* March 1, 1839.

31. *Philanthropist,* February 21, 1837, February 20, 1838, February 19, 1839, and July 23, 1839. In response to such memorials, the legislature, in 1837, appointed a judiciary committee to deliberate whether it was advisable to repeal the laws. Not ashamed of its own racism, the committee submitted a vehement objection to the repeal of the laws: "The repeal would encourage blacks and mulattoes to flock to Ohio, in expectation of meeting a favorable reception, and materially

elevating their condition. Such expectation ought not to be encouraged, as it would not be realized. All attempts to elevate blacks to a happy political equality with the whites, must prove unavailing. There never can be a happy political equality, whilst there is a social inequality between the two races; and the committee do not understand that the petitioners and memorialists propose to place the blacks on a social equality with the whites—and certainly the people of Ohio would not tolerate any such proposition." Ohio General Assembly, "Report of the Majority of the Judiciary Committee on Questions Concerning Slavery, and Black and Mulatto Persons," *Journal of the Ohio House of Representatives,* February 7, 1837. Two years later, the Black Laws resurfaced on the floor of the legislature. Again, legislators voted to uphold them: "That in the opinion of this General Assembly, it is unwise, impolitic and inexpedient, to repeal any law now in force, imposing disabilities upon black or mulatto persons, thus placing them upon an equality with the whites, so far as the Legislature can do, and indirectly inviting the black population of other states to emigrate to this state, to manifest injury of the public interest." Frank U. Quillin, *The Color Line in Ohio: A History of Race Prejudice in a Typical Northern State* (Ann Arbor, MI: George Wahr, 1913), 23.

32. *Philanthropist,* February 19, 1839, July 23, 1839, February 21, 1837, February 20, 1838.

33. Frederick J. Blue, *Salmon P. Chase: A Life in Politics* (Kent, OH: Kent State University Press, 1987), 28.

34. Blue, *Salmon P. Chase,* 30; Stephen Middleton, "Antislavery Litigation in Ohio: The Chase-Trowbridge Letters," *Mid-America: An Historical Review* 70 (October 1988): 106–7.

35. Blue, *Salmon P. Chase,* 33; *Philanthropist,* March 17, 1837; *Philanthropist,* March 24, 1837. Matilda's master had willingly brought her to Cincinnati in 1836. Chase argued the case, which was decided in favor of Matilda's owner. Birney was acquitted of any wrongdoing. *Lawrence v. Lawrence* was reported only in local papers. For details of the circumstances see *Birney v. State,* 8 Ohio 230 (1837).

36. Middleton, "Antislavery Litigation in Ohio," 107.

37. Colored Citizens of Cincinnati, *The Address and Reply on the Presentation of a Testimonial to Salmon Portland Chase by the Colored People of Cincinnati* (Cincinnati: Henry Derby, 1845).

38. *Philanthropist,* March 5, 1839.

39. Ibid.

40. Ibid.

41. Gary Nash, *Forging Freedom: The Formation of Philadelphia's Black Community, 1720–1840* (Cambridge, MA: Harvard University Press, 1988), 239–40; Julie Winch, *Philadelphia's Black Elite: Activism, Accommodation, and the Struggle for Autonomy, 1787–1848* (Philadelphia: Temple University Press, 1988), 37–38; James Oliver Horton and Lois E. Horton, *Black Bostonians: Family Life and Community Struggle in the Antebellum North* (New York: Holmes and Meier, 1979), 98; Floyd J. Miller, *The Search for a Black Nationality: Black Emigration and Colonization, 1787–1863* (Urbana: University of Illinois Press, 1975), 48–49, 83–84.

CHAPTER 6

1. *Cincinnati Enquirer,* September 9, 1841.

2. Patrick A. Folk, "'The Queen City of Mobs': Riots and Community Reactions in Cincinnati, 1788–1848" (Ph.D. diss., University of Toledo, 1978), 207.

3. *Cincinnati Enquirer,* September 9, 1841.

4. Ibid., September 10, 1841.

5. Ibid.

6. Ibid., August 10, 1841.

7. John Mercer Langston, *From the Virginia Plantation to the National Capitol; or, The First and Only Negro Representative in Congress from the Old Dominion* (Hartford, CT: American Publishing, 1894), 63; *Cincinnati Daily Gazette,* September 6, 1841.

8. Langston, *From the Virginia Plantation to the National Capitol,* 63; *Cincinnati Daily Gazette,* September 6, 1841; *Cincinnati Enquirer,* September 4, 1841.

9. Langston, *From the Virginia Plantation to the National Capitol,* 63.

10. William Cheek and Aimee Lee Cheek, "John Mercer Langston and the Cincinnati Riot of 1841," in *Race and the City: Work, Community, and Protest in Cincinnati, 1820–1970,* ed. Henry Louis Taylor Jr. (Urbana: University of Illinois Press), 30.

11. Langston, *From the Virginia Plantation to the National Capitol,* 59, 61, 65.

12. Ibid., 64.

13. Cheek and Cheek, "John Mercer Langston and the Cincinnati Riot of 1841," 46; William and Aimee Lee Cheek and Cheek, *John Mercer Langston and the Fight for Black Freedom, 1829–1865* (Urbana: University of Illinois Press, 1989), 80.

14. Langston, *From the Virginia Plantation to the National Capitol,* 64.

15. *Cincinnati Enquirer,* September 9, 1841.

16. *Cincinnati Daily Gazette,* September 6, 1841; Cheek and Cheek, "John Mercer Langston and the Cincinnati Riot of 1841," 63. Most contemporary newspapers asserted that the mob was comprised of outsiders—Kentuckians; however, the theory that so many outsiders would have a vested interest in driving blacks from a city not their own is dubious. Outsiders would not have known even where the black section of town was located. The papers may have placed the blame on outsiders because it was easier to accept that strangers were the culprits of such horrendous atrocities and lawlessness.

17. Lyle Koehler, *Cincinnati's Black Peoples: A Chronology and Bibliography, 1787–1982* (Cincinnati: Cincinnati Arts Consortium, 1986), 23.

18. *Cincinnati Enquirer,* September 2, 1841.

19. *Cincinnati Daily Gazette,* September 6, 1841.

20. Langston, *From the Virginia Plantation to the National Capitol,* 64; *Cincinnati Enquirer,* September 4, 1841.

21. *Cincinnati Daily Gazette,* September 6, 1841.

22. Ibid.

23. *Cincinnati Daily Chronicle,* September 4, 1841. There is no way to determine or even speculate about who attended this meeting because there are no other extant records.

24. Ibid.

25. Ibid.

26. Ibid.

27. *Cincinnati Daily Chronicle*, September 4, 1841; *Cincinnati Enquirer*, September 6, 1841.

28. Langston, *From the Virginia Plantation to the National Capitol*, 64, 65–66.

29. *Cincinnati Daily Gazette*, September 6, 1841.

30. Ibid.

31. *Cincinnati Daily Gazette*, September 7, 1841.

32. Langston, *From the Virginia Plantation to the National Capitol*, 66.

33. *Cincinnati Daily Gazette*, September 6, 1841. For rape allegations, see *Cincinnati Daily Chronicle*, September 7, 1841.

34. *Cincinnati Enquirer*, September 6, 1841; *Cincinnati Daily Gazette*, September 6, 1841; *Cincinnati Daily Gazette*, September 8, 1841; Langston, *From the Virginia Plantation to the National Capitol*, 67.

35. *Cincinnati Daily Gazette*, September 8, 1841.

36. Langston, *From the Virginia Plantation to the National Capitol*, 66.

37. David Grimsted, *American Mobbing, 1828–1861: Toward Civil War* (New York: Oxford University Press, 1998), 86, 101.

38. *Cincinnati Daily Gazette*, September 6, 1841.

39. Ibid.

40. The terms of black self-defense were played out in the Cincinnati press. For some whites, self-defense was only acceptable to defend oneself, family, or property. Many felt that once African Americans had gone beyond the thresholds of their own homes or a "full one hundred yards from their houses" they became the aggressors. See the *Cincinnati Enquirer*, September 9, 1841.

41. John Malvin, *Autobiography of John Malvin: A Narrative* (Cleveland: Leader Printing, 1879), 39–40.

42. Rev. Benjamin Arnett provides the only extant information we have on these associations in his program for the Semi-centenary Celebration of the AME church in 1874. Benjamin W. Arnett, *Proceedings of the Semi-centenary Celebration of the African Methodist Episcopal Church of Cincinnati, Held in the Allen Temple February 8th, 9th, and 10th, 1874* (Cincinnati: H. Watkin, 1874), appendix.

43. Ibid., 123–24.

44. Union Association of the Colored Men of New Richmond, Ohio, *Constitution, By-Laws, and Records of the Union Association of New Richmond, Ohio* (Columbus: n.p., 1851), 8–9.

45. Arnett, *Proceedings of the Semi-centenary Celebration*, 130. Charter Members of the Daughters of Samaria were Rebecca Darnes, Jane Taverns, Priscilla Ware, Martha Johnson, Ann Smith, Catherine Brown, Mary Ann Butler, and Minerva Butler.

46. Arnett, *Proceedings of the Semi-centenary Celebration*, 36.

47. Elsa Barkley Brown, "Womanist Consciousness: Maggie Lena Walker and the Independent Order of Saint Luke," in *Unequal Sisters: A Multicultural Reader in U.S.*

Women's History, ed. Vicki Ruiz and Ellen Carol DuBois (New York: Routledge, 1994), 271.

48. Brown, "Womanist Consciousness," 272.

49. New Orphan Asylum, *Constitution and By-Laws of the Association and Board of Trustees of the New Orphan Asylum* (Cincinnati: Dumas and Lawyer, 1853), 3. Many of the African Americans who helped establish this orphanage were among the black elite. The founders included Rev. Charles Satchell, pastor of the Union Baptist Church. Satchell owned a drying and scouring establishment and served as an agent for the Columbus *Palladium of Liberty*. The other founders of the asylum were mostly barbers like Michael Clark, who owned a barbershop and bath house, as well as Wilson Bates, William Darnes, and Louis Brux.

50. Moses King, *King's Pocket-Book of Cincinnati* (Cincinnati: John Shillito, 1879), 24.

51. Some churches that donated money to the asylum were Vine Street Church, Ninth Street Baptist, Broadway Presbyterian, Disciples Church, Wesley Chapel, and Zion Baptist Church. See Colored Orphan Asylum, *Eleventh Annual Report of the Managers of the Colored Orphan Asylum for 1855–1856* (Cincinnati: Henry Watkin, 1856), 4. Held at the Cincinnati Historical Society. Black churches like the Zion Baptist Church and the Union Baptist Church made yearly contributions. In 1856, African American barber and bathhouse owner William Watson raised eighty-eight dollars for the asylum.

52. Ibid., 4; Colored Orphan Asylum, *Twenty-first Annual Report of the Board of Trustees of the Colored Orphan Asylum of Cincinnati for 1864–1865* (Cincinnati: A. Moore, 1865), 4. Held at the Cincinnati Historical Society.

53. For the initial decade, whites dominated the board of managers. In 1855, its officers included Ruth E. Watson [white], president; Margaret Bowler [white], vice-president; Sarah Ernst [white], treasurer. The board of managers included Catherine Coffin [white], wife of Levi Coffin; Eliza Potter [black]; Mary Brown; Louisa Nelson; Martha Draper; and Hannah McDaniel. By the 1860s, blacks had assumed greater control of this institution. Rufus Conrad served as president; William Parham acted as clerk; and Peter H. Clark was the treasurer. Colored Orphan Asylum, *Eleventh Annual Report*, 1. Colored Orphan Asylum, *Twenty-first Annual Report*.

54. Arnett, *Proceedings of the Semi-centenary Celebration*, 130.

55. James Oliver Horton and Lois E. Horton, *In Hope of Liberty: Culture, Community, and Protest Among Northern Free Blacks, 1700–1860* (New York: Oxford University Press, 1997), 125–26.

56. Gary B. Nash, *Forging Freedom: The Formation of Philadelphia's Black Community 1720–1840* (Cambridge, MA: Harvard University Press, 1988), 218.

57. Much of the early history of the black Masonic order in Cincinnati is sketchy, largely because the organization is steeped in secrecy. William Hartwell Parham discovered there were no printed records of their proceedings before 1855; the organization's history to that point had been passed on orally by its

members and the grand secretary. At best, Parham's history is only pieces of a larger enigma. William Hartwell Parham, *An Official History of the Most Worshipful Grand Lodge, Free and Accepted Masons for the State of Ohio* (n.p., 1906). Held at the Cincinnati Historical Society.

58. Ibid., 30.

59. Ibid., 22–24.

60. Ibid., 26.

61. Ibid., 30–31.

62. Ibid; Henry D. Shaffer, *The Cincinnati, Covington, Newport, and Fulton Directory for 1840* (Cincinnati: Donogh, 1840); Robinson and Jones, *Robinson and Jones' Cincinnati Directory for 1846* (Cincinnati: Robinson and Jones, 1846); U.S. Census Bureau, *The Seventh Census of the United States, 1850* (Washington, DC: Robert Armstrong, 1853).

63. Parham, *Official History of the Most Worshipful Grand Lodge*, 31; Wendell P. Dabney, *Cincinnati's Colored Citizens: Historical, Sociological, and Biographical* (Cincinnati: Dabney Publishing, 1926), 370; Arnett, *Proceedings of the Semi-centenary Celebration*, 38.

64. Union Association of the Colored Men of New Richmond, Ohio, *Constitution, By-Laws, and Records of the Union Association of the Colored Men of New Richmond, Ohio*, 8–9.

65. Ibid., 1.

66. Cheek and Cheek, "John Mercer Langston and the Cincinnati Riot of 1841," 39; Jane H. Pease and William H. Pease, *They Who Would Be Free: Blacks' Search for Freedom, 1830–1861* (Urbana: University of Illinois Press, 1990), 116; *Colored Citizen*, May 19, 1866. Biographical data for Woodson and Yancy taken from Robinson and Jones, *Robinson and Jones' Cincinnati Directory for 1846* (Cincinnati: Robinson and Jones, 1846).

67. *Colored Citizen*, November 7, 1863. The editors between 1863 and 1869 were Joseph Corbin, John Sampson, Charles Bell, H. F. Leonard, and Rev. George Williams.

68. *Colored Citizen*, November 7, 1863; *Colored Citizen*, May 19, 1866.

69. Pease and Pease, *They Who Would Be Free*, 117n62.

70. *Colored Citizen*, November 7, 1863.

71. John Mercer Langston, *From the Virginia Plantation to the National Capitol*, 61.

72. Richard Pih, "Negro Self-Improvement Efforts in Ante-bellum Cincinnati, 1836–1850," *Ohio History* 78 (Summer 1969): 182.

73. U.S. Census Bureau, *Seventh Census of the United States, 1850*.

74. *Colored American*, October 17, 1840.

75. A daguerreotype is the earliest type of photograph. Images were made on copper plates with polished silver treated with mercury. The process made photos affordable to all. Daguerreotypes were wildly popular around the time Ball was trained. James Ball, *Ball's Splendid Mammoth Pictorial Tour of the United States Comprising Views of the African Slave Trade; of Northern and Southern Cities; of Cotton and Sugar Planta-*

tions; of the Mississippi, Ohio and Susquehanna Rivers, Niagara Falls, &c. (Cincinnati: Achilles Pugh, 1855), 7, 8.

76. A number of his images portrayed traditional African life before slavery. In one description, Ball wrote, "The natives of Africa, before they are unmanned and imbruted, by slavery, are far from being the indolent and ignorant savages that many suppose them to be." Ball, *Splendid Mammoth Pictorial Tour of the United States*, 11.

77. U.S. Census Bureau, *Population of the United States in 1860* (Washington, DC: Government Printing Office, 1864).

78. Langston, *From the Virginia Plantation to the National Capitol*, 61.

79. The earliest record of barber William Watson is in the 1834 city directory. E. Deming, *The Cincinnati Directory for 1834* (Cincinnati: E. Deming, 1834), 196; J. H. Woodruff, *The Cincinnati Directory Advertiser for the Years 1836–1837* (Cincinnati: J. H. Woodruff, 1836); Henry D. Shaffer, *Cincinnati Directory for 1840*; Charles Cist, *The Cincinnati Directory for the Year 1842* (Cincinnati: E. Morgan, 1842); Robinson and Jones, *Robinson and Jones' Cincinnati Directory for 1846*.

80. Langston, *From the Virginia Plantation to the National Capitol*, 61; Cheek and Cheek, *John Mercer Langston and the Fight for Black Freedom 1829–1865*, 52.

81. U.S. Census Bureau, *Seventh Census of the United States, 1850*.

82. Langston, *From the Virginia Plantation to the National Capitol*, 61. In 1850, William Watson owned $5,500 worth of real estate. U.S. Census Bureau, *Seventh Census of the United States, 1850*.

83. James Oliver Horton and Stacy Flaherty, "Black Leadership in Antebellum Cincinnati," in Taylor, *Race and the City*, 77, 79.

84. U.S. Census Bureau, *Seventh Census of the United States, 1850*.

85. Woodruff, *Cincinnati Directory and Advertiser for the Year 1836–1837*; U.S. Census Bureau, *Seventh Census of the United States, 1850*.

86. This high occurrence of black barbers was not as common in any other free black community. In Baltimore, for the same period, more than half of the free black population was employed as "laborers" and just over 3 percent were barbers. Christopher Phillips, *Freedom's Port: The African American Community of Baltimore, 1790–1860* (Urbana: University of Illinois Press, 1997), 109.

87. Among them was Eliza Clark, the mother of Peter Clark—who would become one of the most important black leaders in Cincinnati. In 1850, Eliza owned real estate valued at $15,000. U.S. Census Bureau, *Seventh Census of the United States, 1850*.

88. At first glance, the historical record suggests that these were women of leisure; a closer look reveals that census takers did not consistently record the occupations of black female heads of households. Some of the women with no occupation listed may have been employed.

89. James C. Brown, quoted in Benjamin Drew, *The Refugee: Or the Narratives of Fugitive Slaves in Canada; Related by Themselves, with an Account of the History and Condition of the Colored Population in Upper Canada* (Boston: John P. Jewett, 1856), 245; James Oliver Horton and Stacy Flaherty, "Black Leadership in Antebellum Cincinnati," in

Race and the City: Work, Community, and Protest in Cincinnati, 1820–1970, ed. Henry Louis Taylor Jr. (Urbana: University of Illinois Press, 1993), 81.

90. The customary distinction between black and mulatto was not based on parentage, but on skin color. Census takers classified African Americans as "M" for mulatto or "B" for black by looking at their features. This method of classification was faulty and inconsistent. Because there were many different census takers for one city, there many different perceptions on how dark one had to be to be classified as black or how light one had to be to be designated a mulatto. Frustrating this classification even more was "Q"—occasionally used for "quadroon."

91. James Oliver Horton, *Free People of Color: Inside the African American Community* (Washington, DC: Smithsonian Institution Press, 1993), 137.

92. Sharon G. Dean, introduction to *A Hairdresser's Experience in High Life* by Eliza Potter (New York: Oxford University Press, 1991), xl.

93. In 1860, a nineteen-year-old hairdressing apprentice, Louisa Taylor, lived with Eliza Potter. U.S. Census Bureau, *Population of the United States in 1860.*

94. Ibid.

95. Potter, *Hairdresser's Experience in High Life,* 12.

96. Ibid., xlviii. Although she may have joined the Episcopal Church as a theological decision, it may have been partly a business decision. Worshiping in a white church provided access to white clientele.

97. Ibid., 16–18, 142.

98. Horton, *Free People of Color,* 135, 136. Although skin color is a subjective category, Horton tried to make it as much of a science as he could. He compared names from the 1850 and 1860 censuses to determine whether African Americans had been designated the same way in both censuses. However, he found that only 5 to 8 percent of African American men listed in the 1850 census could be found in the 1860 one, leaving no real way to definitively say which African Americans were, indeed, light complexioned.

99. Horton, *Free People of Color,* 137.

100. Horton and Flaherty, "Black Leadership in Antebellum Leadership," 82.

101. Langston, *From the Virginia Plantation to the National Capitol,* 66.

CHAPTER 7

1. One contemporary estimate says forty thousand fugitive slaves were in Canada as of 1862. *Anti-Slavery Advocate,* June 2, 1862.

2. Wilbur H. Siebert, *The Mysteries of Ohio's Underground Railroads* (Columbus: Long's College Book Company, 1951), 26–27.

3. N. L. Van Zandt to Wilbur H. Siebert, March 12, 1893, Wilbur H. Siebert Collection, MSS 116, "Underground Railroad" in Ohio: Hamilton County, boxes 106 and 107, Ohio Historical Society.

4. Curiously, this pivotal case was not reported in any state law journals. However, it was reported in several newspapers. See *Ohio State Journal,* May 28, 1841;

Cincinnati Daily Gazette, May 21, 1841, and June 1, 1841; and *Colored American,* May 22, 1841. For a complete narrative of the case, see Paul Finkelman, *An Imperfect Union: Slavery, Federalism, and Comity* (Chapel Hill: University of North Carolina Press, 1981), 165.

5. *Ohio State Journal,* May 28, 1841, June 2, 1841, and June 9, 1841.

6. Alexis de Tocqueville, *Democracy in America,* ed. Harvey C. Mansfield and Delba Winthrop (Chicago: University of Chicago Press, 2000), 332.

7. The phrase is taken from John O. Wattles, *Annual Report of the Educational Condition of the Colored People of Cincinnati, Including the Sentiment in Mercer County, Ohio: Presented at the Exhibition of the Cincinnati High School* (Cincinnati: John White, 1847), 7.

8. John Hope Franklin and Loren Schweninger, *Runaway Slaves: Rebels on the Plantation* (New York: Oxford University Press, 1999), 116–17.

9. Levi Coffin, *Reminiscences of Levi Coffin: The Reputed President of the Underground Railroad* (New York: AMS Press, 1876), 207.

10. Ibid., 162; Siebert, *Mysteries of Ohio's Underground Railroads,* 29.

11. Coffin, *Reminiscences of Levi Coffin,* 393.

12. Although it is extremely rare occurrence now, the Ohio River frequently froze over in the nineteenth century. Rutherford B. Hayes claimed that the river froze over in the winters of 1850, 1851, 1852, 1853, 1855, and 1856, which facilitated crossing on foot. R. B. Hayes to Wilbur H. Siebert, spring 1893, Siebert Collection, "Underground Railroad" in Ohio: Hamilton County; Coffin, *Reminiscences of Levi Coffin,* 147, 471–72; Harriet Beecher Stowe, *Uncle Tom's Cabin: Or, Life among the Lowly* (Boston: John P. Jewett, 1852), also available at http://xroads.virginia.edu/~HYPER/STOWE/stowe.html.

13. Margaret Garner, the infamous mother who committed infanticide, had relatives in Cincinnati.

14. Coffin, *Reminiscences of Levi Coffin,* 345–51.

15. *Western Globe,* September 13, 1839.

16. Henry Bibb, "Narrative of the Life and Adventures of Henry Bibb, an American Slave, Written by Himself," in *Puttin' on Ole Massa: The Slave Narratives of Henry Bibb, William Wells Brown, and Solomon Northup,* ed. Gilbert Osofsky (New York: Harper and Row, 1969), 83–44, 89; *Colored American,* June 20, 1840.

17. Siebert, *Mysteries of Ohio's Underground Railroads,* 19, 56.

18. In the novel written by fugitive slave William Wells Brown, *Clotelle: A Tale of the Southern States* (Philadelphia: Albert Saifer, 1955), the fictional characters Isabella and William escaped from slavery by posing as a free white man and his servant, respectively, taking passage aboard a steamer headed to Cincinnati. Siebert, *Mysteries of Ohio's Underground Railroads,* 28; Coffin, *Reminiscences of Levi Coffin,* 333.

19. Bibb, "Narrative of the Life and Adventures of Henry Bibb," 151.

20. Amy Clark to Wilbur Siebert, n.d., Siebert Collection, "Underground Railroad" in Ohio: Hamilton County. Well-known Ripley Underground Railroad conductor John P. Parker recounted how, during his escape from slavery, a black deckhand on a steamer gave him a plate of food and cup of coffee. John

P. Parker, *His Promised Land: The Autobiography of John P. Parker, Former Slave and Conductor on the Underground Railroad* (New York: W. W. Norton, 1996), 43; For a broader perspective on the role black sailors played as "angels of liberty," see W. Jeffrey Bolster, *Black Jacks: African American Seamen in the Age of Sail* (Cambridge, MA: Harvard University Press, 1997), 190–214; Coffin, *Reminiscences of Levi Coffin*, 333, 375, 458; Laura Haviland, *A Woman's Life-Work: Including Thirty Years' Service on the Underground Railroad and in the War* (Grand Rapids, MI: S. B. Shaw, 1881), 133; Siebert, *Mysteries of Ohio's Underground Railroads*, 56.

21. Bolster, *Black Jacks*, 212–13.

22. Ibid., 194; Bernard E. Powers Jr., *Black Charlestonians: A Social History, 1822–1885* (Fayetteville: University of Arkansas Press, 1994), 32; Douglas Egerton, *He Shall Go out Free: The Lives of Denmark Vesey* (Madison, WI: Madison House, 1999), 217.

23. Andrew J. Gordon, "Address by Andrew J. Gordon on May 6, 1845 at Union Baptist Church," in *The Address and Reply on the Presentation of a Testimonial to Salmon Portland Chase by the Colored People of Cincinnati* (Cincinnati: Henry Derby, 1845), 14.

24. It was not uncommon for slaves traveling with their owners to stop in northern port cities. Finkelman, *Imperfect Union*, 296.

25. Benjamin W. Arnett, *Proceedings of the Semi-centenary Celebration of the African Methodist Episcopal Church of Cincinnati, Held in Allen Temple February 8th, 9th, and 10th, 1874* (Cincinnati: H. Watkin, 1874), 15–16; Coffin, *Reminiscences of Levi Coffin*, 312, 360.

26. Allen Sydney, "Perils of Escape," Siebert Collection, "Underground Railroad" in Ohio: Hamilton County.

27. *Colored American*, May 22, 1841; Stephen Middleton, *The Black Laws in the Old Northwest: A Documentary History* (Westport, CT: Greenwood, 1993), 144, 149; Coffin, *Reminiscences of Levi Coffin*, 549, 555, 560; Finkelman, *Imperfect Union*, 164–65.

28. Haviland, *Woman's Life-Work*, 122.

29. State v. Hoppess, 10 Ohio Dec. Reprint 279 (1845); Ex parte Robinson, 20 F. Cas. 969 (C.C.S.D. Ohio 1855) (No. 11,935).

30. State v. Hoppess, 10 Ohio Dec. Reprint 279 (1845); Finkelman, *Imperfect Union*, 167–71.

31. Rosetta Armstead's case was never reported, although it was a major factor in the case against U.S. Marshal H. H. Robinson in *Ex parte Robinson*, 20 F. Cas. 969 (C.C.S.D. Ohio 1855) (No. 11,935). Levi Coffin also discussed this case: Coffin, *Reminiscences of Levi Coffin*, 554–57. Also see Finkelman, *Imperfect Union*, 174–77.

32. Franklin and Schweninger, *Runaway Slaves*, 109.

33. Coffin, *Reminiscences of Levi Coffin*, 114.

34. According to John P. Parker, an Underground Railroad conductor in Ripley, Ohio, "The fugitive depended entirely on his own race for assistance." Parker, *His Promised Land*, 137.

35. Bibb, "Narrative of the Life and Adventures of Henry Bibb," 84–85.

36. The phrase "nigger stealing" can be found in many primary sources, including Siebert, *Mysteries of Ohio's Underground Railroads*, 16; and "Glorious Old Thief," *Chicago Tribune*, June 29, 1893, Siebert Collection, "Underground Railroad" in Ohio: Hamilton County; Haviland, *Woman's Life-Work*, 82.

37. Bibb, "Narrative of the Life and Adventures of Henry Bibb," 90.

38. Coffin, *Reminiscences of Levi Coffin*, 298. For a brief discussion of white conductors in the 1820s, see Siebert, *Mysteries of Ohio's Underground Railroads*, 32.

39. Coffin, *Reminiscences of Levi Coffin*, 461.

40. Ibid., 297. Coffin was very critical of black UR operators in Cincinnati: "[T]here were a few wise and careful managers among the colored people, but it was not safe to trust all of them with the affairs of our work. Most of them were too careless, and a few unworthy—they could be bribed by the slave-hunters to betray the hiding places of the fugitives." Such comments reflect the general lack of respect Coffin had for African Americans, but also suggest that he felt compelled to demean them so that he could take full credit for the Underground Railroad in Cincinnati. Ibid., 298.

41. John Malvin, *Autobiography of John Malvin: A Narrative* (Cleveland: Leader Printing, 1879), 44.

42. Ibid., 44–45.

43. Arnett, *Proceedings of the Semi-centenary Celebration*, 19.

44. Birney to Lewis Tappan, February 27, 1837, in *Letters of James Gillespie Birney, 1831–1857*, ed. Dwight Dumond (Gloucester, MA: Peter Smith, 1966), 1:376–77. Also see Keith Griffler, *Front Line of Freedom: African Americans and the Forging of the Underground Railroad in the Ohio Valley* (Lexington: University Press of Kentucky, 2004), 48.

45. "Henry Young interviewed by W. H. Siebert," August 3, 1895, Siebert Collection, "Underground Railroad" in Ohio: Hamilton County. Young must have mistakenly named John Hatfield, James. There was no James Hatfield in Cincinnati.

46. Coffin, *Reminiscences of Levi Coffin*, 298.

47. "Perils of Escape Told by Allen Sidney," *Detroit Sunday News Tribune*, August 12, 1894, Siebert Collection, "Underground Railroad" in Ohio: Hamilton County.

48. U.S. Census Bureau, *Seventh Census of the United States, 1850*.

49. Coffin, *Reminiscences of Levi Coffin*, 335; Siebert Collection, "Underground Railroad" in Ohio: Hamilton County.

50. Carter G. Woodson, *Free Negro Heads of Families in the United States in 1830: Together with a Brief Treatment of the Free Negro* (Washington, DC: Association for the Study of Negro Life and History, 1925), 126; J. H. Woodruff, *The Cincinnati Directory and Advertiser for the Years 1836–1837* (Cincinnati: J. H. Woodruff, 1836); Charles Cist, *The Cincinnati Directory for the Year 1842* (Cincinnati: E. Morgan, 1842); Robinson and Jones, *Robinson and Jones' Cincinnati Directory for 1846* (Cincinnati: Robinson and Jones, 1846); Henry D. Shaffer, *The Cincinnati, Covington, Newport, and Fulton Directory for 1840* (Cincinnati: Donogh, 1840); U.S. Census Bureau,

Seventh Census of the United States, 1850; Siebert Collection, "Underground Railroad" in Ohio: Hamilton County.

51. Siebert, *Mysteries of Ohio's Underground Railroads,* 31.

52. Woodruff, *Cincinnati Directory and Advertiser for the Years 1836–1837;* Cist, *Cincinnati Directory for the Year 184;* Robinson and Jones, *Robinson and Jones' Cincinnati Directory for 1846;* Shaffer, *Cincinnati Directory for 1840;* U.S. Census Bureau, *Seventh Census of the United States, 1850.*

53. Coffin, *Reminiscences of Levi Coffin,* 330, 347; "Glorious Old Thief."

54. Among the white abolitionists who went into Kentucky to rescue slaves from bondage were Calvin Fairbank and Laura Haviland. For a discussion of the arrest of Haviland and Fairbank, see Calvin Fairbank, *Rev. Calvin Fairbank during Slavery Times: How He "Fought the Good Fight" to Prepare "The Way"* (New York: Negro Universities Press, 1969), 45–53. For a discussion of Fairbanks's trial and conviction, see pages 93–103.

55. The earliest record of the Hatfields was in the 1829 city directory. Robinson and Fairbank, *The Cincinnati Directory for the Year 1829, also, the Annual Advertiser* (Cincinnati: Whetstone and Buxton, 1829),138; Woodson, *Free Negro Heads of Families in the United States in 1830,* 126; Shaffer, *Cincinnati Directory for 1840,* 471; Robinson and Jones, *Robinson and Jones' Cincinnati Directory for 1846;* Woodruff, *Cincinnati Directory Advertiser for the Years 1836–1937.* Joseph Hatfield disappears from all city directories and census data after 1830.

56. U.S. Census Bureau, *Seventh Census of the United States, 1850.*

57. "Testimony of Henry Young," Siebert Collection, "Underground Railroad" in Ohio: Hamilton County; Haviland, *Woman's Life-Work,* 166; Coffin, *Reminiscences of Levi Coffin,* 308–9.

58. Coffin, *Reminiscences of Levi Coffin,* 330–32, 347; Robinson and Jones, *Robinson and Jones' Cincinnati Directory for 1846* (Cincinnati: Robinson and Jones, 1846); Siebert, *Mysteries of Ohio's Underground Railroads,* 32; Haviland, *Woman's Life-Work,* 167.

59. Rev. Calvin Fairbank acknowledges these two men as operators on the underground system. Fairbank, *Rev. Calvin Fairbank during Slavery Times,* 35, 60; "Glorious Old Thief."

60. Very little biographical data remain about Augustus R. Green. He appears in none of the city directories. Mention of him can be found in Arnett, *Proceedings of the Semi-centenary Celebration,* 22; and Coffin, *Reminiscences of Levi Coffin,* 324. Levi Coffin erroneously states that Green was the preacher at Allen AME. A cross-check against the records of the Allen AME Church proves that the new church was constructed *after* Green's tenure as pastor. He actually initiated that endeavor. Green was a delegate to the National Emigration Convention of Colored People in 1854.

61. For a discussion of Green's Underground Railroad activities, see Coffin, *Reminiscences of Levi Coffin,* 324–25, 326, 378.

62. Ibid., 343; Arnett, *Proceedings of the Semi-centenary Celebration,* 19; Siebert, *Mysteries of Ohio's Underground Railroads,* 31.

63. Arnett, *Proceedings of the Semi-centenary Celebration*, 60; Wendell P. Dabney, *Cincinnati's Colored Citizens: Historical, Sociological, and Biographical* (Cincinnati: Dabney Publishing, 1926), 374; Haviland, *Woman's Life-Work*, 112, 135. The Zion Baptist Church was founded by Wallace Shelton in 1845. An ordained minister, Shelton earned his living as a barber. After arriving in the city in the 1830s Shelton joined the African Union Baptist Church. He orchestrated the break from Union Baptist Church after he and a group of other members "became dissatisfied with that church on its position on the question of slavery." At the 1849 State Convention of the Colored Citizens of Ohio, Shelton explained that he had been "silenced by the [Union Baptist] church because of his anti-slavery views." Shelton favored excluding slaveholders from church. He had no tolerance for those who might "fellowship with slaveholders or their abettors." Shelton clearly believed that the black Baptist church had a moral obligation to distance itself publicly from the institution of slavery. Anything less than that was unacceptable to him. See also *Minutes and Address of the State Convention of the Colored Citizens of Ohio, Convened at Columbus, January 10th, 11th, 12th, 13th, 1849*, in *Proceedings of the Black State Convention, 1840–1865*, ed. Philip S. Foner and George Walker (Philadelphia: Temple University Press, 1980), 1:224.

64. Siebert, *Mysteries of Ohio's Underground Railroads*, 31; Coffin, *Reminiscences of Levi Coffin*, 314.

65. Arnett, *Proceedings of the Semi-centenary Celebration*, 19.

66. A party of twenty-eight Kentucky slaves planned to escape at once. As plans were being made to accommodate them in Cincinnati, an Underground Railroad worker purportedly dropped to his knees in prayer, asking the protection of the "God of Abraham, Isaac, and Jacob, who led the children of Israel out of Egyptian bondage through the waters of the Red Sea and the dangers of the wilderness, into the Promised Land, that he would likewise give the helping [sic] ones then assembled, keep them safe from the dangers and the detention by the way and bring them into the land where they would be free." "Members of the Wilson Family in Underground Work, College Hill, April 14, 1892," Siebert Collection, "Underground Railroad" in Ohio: Hamilton County.

67. Dabney, *Cincinnati's Colored Citizens*, 129.

68. Coffin, *Reminiscences of Levi Coffin*, 339, 342, 377.

69. Fairbank, *Rev. Calvin Fairbank during Slavery Times*, 21, 60.

70. Transcript of interview of "Ex-Pres R. B. Hayes," spring 1893, Siebert Collection, "Underground Railroad" in Ohio: Hamilton County.

71. Letter from H. N. Wilson, April 14, 1892, ibid.

72. Haviland, *Woman's Life-Work*, 29, 32 34–35.

73. Ibid., 111–32.

74. Ibid., 121.

75. Coffin, *Reminiscences of Levi Coffin*, 428–58.

76. Ibid., 431, 304–5.

77. Ibid., passim.

78. Coffin left North Carolina to settle in Newport in 1826. According to his autobiography, many whites in the neighborhood were "aloof from the work,

fearful of the penalty of the law." Initially, most of them helped fund the endeavor but refused to shelter slaves in their homes. Ibid.,108, 111.

79. Siebert, *Mysteries of Ohio's Underground Railroads*, 37.

80. Jane H. Pease and William H. Pease, *They Who Would Be Free: Blacks' Search for Freedom, 1830–1861* (Urbana: University of Illinois Press, 1990), 336; Robinson and Jones, *Robinson and Jones' Cincinnati Directory for 1846.*

81. Coffin, *Reminiscences of Levi Coffin*, 307–12.

82. Haviland, *Woman's Life-Work*, 161. Coffin, *Reminiscences of Levi Coffin*, 113, 299; Pease and Pease, *They Who Would Be Free*, 207–8.

83. He received between fifty cents and one dollar from each of these neighbors. Coffin, *Reminiscences of Levi Coffin*, 320–22.

84. Ibid., 301.

85. "Reply of Hon. D. W. H. Howard of Wauseon, Ohio," August 22, 1894, Siebert Collection, "Underground Railroad" in Ohio: Hamilton County; Coffin, *Reminiscences of Levi Coffin*, 300–301, 302, 308–9; Haviland, *Woman's Life-Work*, 112; Pease and Pease, *They Who Would Be Free*, 300–301. Women who were in the Anti-Slavery Sewing Circle were Mrs. Sarah Ernst, Miss Sarah O. Ernst, Mrs. Henry Miller, Dr. Aydelott's wife, Mrs. Julia Harwood, Mrs. Amanda Foster, Mrs. Elizabeth Coleman, Mrs. Mary Mann, Mrs. Mary Guild, and Miss K. Emery.

86. See, for example, Coffin, *Reminiscences of Levi Coffin*, 459.

87. Thomas D. Morris, *Free Men All: The Personal Liberty Laws of the North, 1780–1861* (Baltimore: Johns Hopkins University Press, 1974), 130–47.

88. Alvin Harlow, *The Serene Cincinnatians* (New York: E. P. Dutton, 1950), 216, 217. There is no information regarding what become of these men after they were taken from Cincinnati.

89. National Emigration Convention of Colored People, *Proceedings of the National Emigration Convention of Colored People Held at Cleveland, Ohio, on Thursday, Friday, and Saturday, the 24th, 25th, and 26th of August 1854* (Pittsburgh: A. Anderson, 1854), 25.

90. James Oliver Horton and Lois E. Horton, *In Hope of Liberty: Culture, Community and Protest among Northern Free Blacks, 1700–1860* (New York: Oxford University Press, 1998), 253.

91. Middleton, "The Fugitive Slave Crisis in Cincinnati, 1850–1860: Resistance, Enforcement, and Black Refugees," *Journal of Negro History* 72 (Winter–Spring, 1987): 21.

92. Horton and Horton, *In Hope of Liberty*, 256.

93. Ibid., 255–56; James Oliver Horton and Lois E. Horton, *Black Bostonians: Family Life and Community Struggle in the Antebellum North* (New York: Holmes and Meier, 1979), 113.

94. Horton and Horton, *Black Bostonians*, 114.

95. Ibid., 116–18.

96. Haviland, *Woman's Life-Work*, 134.

97. Eliza Potter, *A Hairdresser's Experience in High Life* (New York: Oxford University Press, 1991), 16, 17. It was probably no coincidence that two enslaved sib-

lings escaped from the same owner only one week after their first encounter with Eliza Potter. It is more likely that she helped both siblings escape or directed them to Underground Railroad agents.

98. Ibid., 18.

99. Ibid., 17–19. Potter provides the only account of the public spectacle of her arrest.

100. Miller v. McQuerry, 17 F. Cas. 335 (C.C.D. Ohio 1853) (No. 9,583); Coffin, *Reminiscences of Levi Coffin*, 542–48.

101. Coffin, *Reminiscences of Levi Coffin*, 543.

102. Miller v. McQuerry, 17 F. Cas. 335 (C.C.D. Ohio 1853) (No. 9,583).

103. Coffin, *Reminiscences of Levi Coffin*, 549–51.

104. Ibid., 557–67; "Margaret Garner Case, January 1856," Siebert Collection, "Underground Railroad" in Ohio: Hamilton County; Middleton, "Fugitive Slave Crisis in Cincinnati," 28; Many of the details of the murder can be found in Steven Weisenburger, *Modern Medea: A Family Story of Slavery and Child-Murder from the Old South* (New York: Hill and Wang, 1998), 62–75. Weisenburger reconstructed the narrative of the murder using newspaper accounts and Levi Coffin's autobiography. A summary of the events, taken directly from contemporary newspaper sources is included in his book on page 73.

105. *Cincinnati Daily Gazette*, January 30, 1856; Siebert Collection, "Underground Railroad" in Ohio: Hamilton County.

106. Coffin, *Reminiscences of Levi Coffin*, 560–61, 566; Middleton, "Fugitive Slave Crisis in Cincinnati," 28.

107. "Margaret Garner Case, January 1856," Siebert Collection, "Underground Railroad" in Ohio: Hamilton County.

108. Weisenburger, *Modern Medea*, 220–32. Contemporary accounts of Priscilla's death leave some question about whether Margaret finished the deed she had attempted two months earlier or whether the collision knocked her and the baby from the steamer. According to the eyewitnesses, she "exhibited no other feeling than joy at the loss of her child." See Siebert Collection, "Underground Railroad" in Ohio: Hamilton County.

CHAPTER 8

1. Stephen Middleton, *The Black Laws in the Old Northwest: A Documentary History* (Westport, CT: Greenwood, 1993), 38–40.

2. Henry Allen Bullock, *A History of Negro Education in the South: From 1619 to the Present* (Cambridge, MA: Harvard University Press, 1967); David Freedman, "African-American Schooling in the South Prior to 1861," *Journal of Negro History* 84 (Winter 1999): 1–47; Leon F. Litwack, *North of Slavery: The Negro in the Free States, 1790–1860* (Chicago: University of Chicago Press, 1961). Much of the existing scholarship on the African American struggle for education centers on the twentieth century. All too often, that work emphasizes the detrimental effects of segregation on African American children. The nineteenth century—especially

the period before the Civil War—has not received adequate attention, and even the scholarship that does examine black education in the nineteenth century context focuses on the South; the most notable of these works is James D. Anderson, *The Education of Blacks in the South, 1860–1935* (Chapel Hill: University of North Carolina Press, 1988). This seminal piece is a meticulously researched and comprehensive overview of black education in the South from primary school through higher education. It illuminates the critical role that churches and associations played in funding and supporting southern black schools. Similarly, Henry Bullock's work on black education covers the period from 1619 through the twentieth-century freedom struggle; Bullock's work and David Freedman's article focus on the South. Carter G. Woodson's *The Education of the Negro Prior to 1861,* and to a lesser extent, Leon F. Litwack's *North of Slavery,* are the most important of an even smaller pool of work that critically examines Northern black schools in the nineteenth century. Cincinnati is an important site because of its exceptionality; few nineteenth-century African American communities could boast of the resources this community had at its disposal.

3. David Gerber, *Black Ohio and the Color Line, 1860–1915* (Urbana: University of Illinois Press, 1976), 192.

4. This analysis of segregated schools being better than the "forgotten alternative" of exclusion is attributed to Howard Rabinowitz, *Race Relations in the Urban South, 1865–1890* (New York: Oxford University Press, 1978), 331–32.

5. "An Act to Amend an Act Entitled 'An Act to Amend the Act to Provide for the Maintenance and Better Regulation of Common Schools in the City of Cincinnati, Passed January 27, 1853, and April 18, 1854,'" in Stephen Middleton, *The Black Laws in the Old Northwest: A Documentary History* (Westport, CT: Greenwood, 1993), 43.

6. Samuel Matthews, "John Isom Gaines: The Architect of Black Public Education," *Queen City Heritage: The Journal of the Cincinnati Historical Society* 45 (Spring 1987): 44. Gilmore left in protest of the church's neutral position on slavery.

7. John O. Wattles, *Annual Report of the Educational Condition of the Colored People of Cincinnati, Including the Sentiment in Mercer County, Ohio: Presented at the Exhibition of the Cincinnati High School* (Cincinnati: John White, 1847), 8.

8. Benjamin W. Arnett, *Proceedings of the Semi-centenary Celebration of the African Methodist Episcopal Church of Cincinnati, Held in Allen Temple February 8th, 9th, and 10th, 1874* (Cincinnati: H. Watkin, 1874), 63; John B. Shotwell, *A History of the Schools of Cincinnati* (Cincinnati: School Life, 1902), 453; Carter G. Woodson, *The Education of the Negro Prior to 1861* (New York: G. P. Putnam, 1915), 124–29.

9. Wattles, *Annual Report of the Educational Condition of the Colored People of Cincinnati,* 8; Shotwell, *History of the Schools of Cincinnati,* 455; Matthews, "John Isom Gaines," 44.

10. Some speculated that it was due to Hiram Gilmore's relocation to a utopian community. Cincinnati Colored Public Schools, *Eighth Annual Report of the Board of Trustees for the Colored Public Schools of Cincinnati for the School Year Ending June 30, 1857* (Cincinnati: Moore, Wilstach, Keys, 1857), 11.

11. "An Act to Provide for the Support and Better Regulation of Common Schools," in Middleton, *Black Laws in the Old Northwest*, 34.

12. Ibid., 34–35.

13. *Colored American*, January 16, 1841.

14. Matthews, "John Isom Gaines," 41, 44.

15. C. S. Williams, *Williams' City Directory and Business Advertiser for 1849–1850* (Cincinnati: C. S. Williams, 1849); William and Aimee Cheek and Cheek, "John Mercer Langston and the Cincinnati Riot of 1841," in *Race and the City: Work, Community, and Protest in Cincinnati, 1820–1970*, ed. Henry Louis Taylor Jr. (Urbana: University of Illinois Press, 1993), 58–59.

16. John Mercer Langston, *From the Virginia Plantation to the National Capitol* (New York: Arno, 1969), 66–67.

17. John Isom Gaines, *Oration, Delivered on the First of August 1849 before the Colored Citizens of Columbus, Ohio* (Columbus: n.p., 1849), 11.

18. James Oliver Horton and Lois E. Horton, *In Hope of Liberty: Culture, Community and Protest among Northern Free Blacks, 1700–1860* (New York: Oxford University Press, 1997), 121–22.

19. A stereotypist was a person who set printing type.

20. Wendell P. Dabney, *Cincinnati's Colored Citizens: Historical, Sociological, and Biographical* (Cincinnati: Dabney Publishing, 1926), 114.

21. Samuel Matthews, "The Black Educational Experience in Nineteenth-Century Cincinnati, 1817–1874" (Ph.D. diss., University of Cincinnati, 1985), 69.

22. William Simmons, *Men of Mark: Eminent, Progressive, and Rising* (New York: Arno, 1968), 374–75.

23. Ibid., 376; Matthews, "Black Educational Experience," 70.

24. Ohio State Auxiliary Equal Rights League, "Constitution of the Ohio State Auxiliary Equal Rights League" in *Proceedings of a Convention of the Colored Men of Ohio Held in Xenia on the 10th, 11th, and 12th Days of January 1865* (Cincinnati: A. Moore, 1865), 17.

25. Gerber, *Black Ohio and the Color Line*, 175. See also Herbert G. Gutman's seminal article on Clark's socialist activities, "Peter H. Clark: Pioneer Negro Socialist, 1877," *Journal of Negro Education* 34 (September 1965), 413–18.

26. Matthews, "Black Educational Experience," 83; Frank Quillin, *The Color Line in Ohio: A History of Race Prejudice in a Typical Northern State* (Ann Arbor, MI: George Wahr, 1913), 38–39.

27. Blacks were again denied the right to vote at the 1850–51 state constitutional convention.

28. "An Act to Authorize the Establishment of Separate Schools for the Education of Colored Children, and for other Purposes," in Middleton, *Black Laws in the Old Northwest*, 39; Matthews, "Black Educational Experience," 86.

29. Cincinnati Common Schools, *Twenty-second Annual Report of the Trustees and Visitors of Common Schools* (Cincinnati: Nonpareil Office, 1852), 12; Cincinnati Colored Public Schools, *Eleventh Annual Report of the Board of Trustees for the Colored*

Public Schools of Cincinnati for the School Year Ending June 30, 1860 (Newport: Free South Office, 1860), 24; State ex. rel. Directors of the Eastern and Western School Districts of Cincinnati v. City of Cincinnati, 19 Ohio 178 (1850).

30. Matthews, "Black Educational Experience," 83.

31. Cincinnati Colored Public Schools, *Eleventh Annual Report of the Board of Trustees,* 24.

32. State ex. rel. Directors of the Eastern and Western School Districts of Cincinnati v. City of Cincinnati, 19 Ohio 178 (1850).

33. "An Act to Provide for the Maintenance and Better Regulation of the Common Schools in the City of Cincinnati," "An Act to Provide for the Reorganization, Supervision, and Maintenance of Common Schools," and "An Act to Amend the 'Act to Provide for the Maintenance and Better Regulation of Common Schools, in the City of Cincinnati, Passed January 27, 1853," in Middleton, *Black Laws in the Old Northwest,* 40–42.

34. The members of the board of trustees for 1854–55 were Rufus King (president), George Rice, and Josephus Fowler. For 1855–56, the board consisted of James Johnson (president), Peter Harbinson, Lovell Flewellen, Henry Boyd, Daniel Gibson, and Joseph Fowler. See Cincinnati Colored Public Schools, *Second Annual Report of the Board of Trustees for the Colored Public Schools of Cincinnati for the School Year Ending June 30, 1856* (Cincinnati: Jacob Ernst, 1856), 30.

35. Cincinnati Colored Public Schools, *First Annual Report of the Board of Trustees for the Colored Public Schools of Cincinnati for the School Year Ending June 30, 1855* (Cincinnati: Moore, Wilstach, Keys, 1855), 5–6.

36. Cincinnati Colored Public Schools, *Second Annual Report of the Board of Trustees,* 13.

37. Ibid., 7.

38. State Convention of the Colored Freemen of Ohio, *Proceedings of the State Convention of the Colored Freemen of Ohio Held in Cincinnati, January 14–18, 1852* (Cincinnati: Dumas and Lawyer, 1852), 8.

39. Cincinnati Common Schools, *Twenty-fourth Annual Report of the Trustees and Visitors of Common Schools* (Cincinnati: Cincinnati Gazette, 1853), 17.

40. "An Act to Amend an Act Entitled 'An Act to Amend the Act to Provide for the Maintenance and Better Regulation of Common Schools in the City of Cincinnati, Passed January 27, 1853, and April 18, 1854,'" in Middleton, *Black Laws in the Old Northwest,* 42–43; Matthews, "Black Educational Experience," 90–91.

41. Cincinnati Colored Public Schools, *Eighth Annual Report of the Board of Trustees,* 29. John Gaines was reelected to the board along with Phillip Ferguson, Lovell Flewellen, George Peterson, Wallace Shelton, and Peter Fossett.

42. Cincinnati Colored Public Schools, *Eighteenth Annual Report of the Board of Directors for the Colored Public Schools of Cincinnati for the Year Ending June 30, 1867* (Cincinnati: Moore and McGrew, 1868), 4–5.

43. Cincinnati Colored Public Schools, *Second Annual Report of the Board of Trustees,* 5; Cincinnati Colored Public Schools, *Twelfth Annual Report of the Board of Trustees for the Colored Public Schools of Cincinnati for the School Year Ending June 30, 1861* (Cincinnati: Moore, Wilstach, Keys, 1861), 4.

44. Cincinnati Common Schools, *Twenty-fifth Annual Report of the Trustees and Visitors of the Common Schools of Cincinnati for the School Year Ending June 30, 1854* (Cincinnati: Benjamin Franklin Mammoth Steam Printing, 1854), 9.

45. Cincinnati Colored Public Schools, *Eighteenth Annual Report of the Board of Directors*, 4.

46. U.S. Census Bureau, *Population of the United States in 1860* (Washington, DC: Government Printing Office, 1864).

47. Cincinnati Colored Public Schools, *Tenth Annual Report of the Board of Trustees for the Colored Schools of Cincinnati for the Year Ending June 30, 1859* (Cincinnati: Wrightson, 1859), 1.

48. Cincinnati Colored Public Schools, *Ninth Annual Report of the Board of Trustees for the Colored Public Schools of Cincinnati for the School Year Ending June 30, 1858* (Cincinnati: Wrightson, 1858), 8.

49. Barber, "Of the Present Condition of the Colored People in Cincinnati," in Ohio Anti-Slavery Society, *Report of the Second Anniversary of the Ohio Anti-Slavery Society, Held in Mount Pleasant on the Twenty-seventh of April 1837* (Cincinnati: Ohio Anti-Slavery Society, 1837), 59.

50. Cincinnati Common Schools, *Twenty-second Annual Report of the Trustees and Visitors*, 31; Cincinnati Colored Public Schools, *Eighteenth Annual Report of the Board of Directors*, 5.

51. Cincinnati Colored Public Schools, *Twelfth Annual Report of the Board of Trustees*, 8.

52. Cincinnati Colored Public Schools, *Eighth Annual Report of the Board of Trustees*, 26–27.

53. Cincinnati Colored Public Schools, *Seventeenth Annual Report of the Board Directors for the Colored Public Schools of Cincinnati for the Year Ending June 30, 1866* (Cincinnati: A. Moore, 1866), 29.

54. Colored Schools of Cincinnati, *Nineteenth Annual Report of the Board of Directors for the Colored Public Schools of Cincinnati for the School Year Ending June 30, 1868* (Cincinnati: Gazette Steam Book and Job Printing, 1868), 18.

55. Cincinnati Colored Public Schools, *Eleventh Annual Report of the Board of Trustees*, 18.

56. Female teachers earned twenty-three dollars per month, whereas the males earned thirty-five dollars per month. Cincinnati Colored Public Schools, *Fifteenth Annual Report of the Board of Directors for the Colored Public Schools of Cincinnati for the School Year Ending June 30, 1864* (Cincinnati: A. Moore, 1864), 25.

57. John Gaines, "What is the Duty of the Colored American Parent?" in Cincinnati Colored Public Schools, *Ninth Annual Report of the Board of Trustees*, 7.

58. Ibid., 8–9.

59. Ibid., 6.

60. For more information regarding black private schools, see chapter 4.

61. The Female School in the Eastern District was located in a room on Sixth Street. The other female school was on Union Street, near Elm. Cincinnati Colored Public Schools, *Eighth Annual Report of the Board of Trustees*, 79–80.

62. Ibid., 7.

63. Cincinnati Colored Public Schools, *First Annual Report of the Board of Trustees*, 16; Cincinnati Colored Public Schools, *Second Annual Report of the Board of Trustees*, 10.

64. Rufus King, *Report to the State Commissioner of Schools on the History and Condition of the Public Schools in Cincinnati* (Cincinnati: n.p., 1859), 14.

65. Cincinnati Colored Public Schools, *Tenth Annual Report of the Board of Trustees*, 6.

66. John P. Foote, *The Schools of Cincinnati and Its Vicinity* (Cincinnati: C. F. Bradley, 1855), 92–93.

67. "An Act to Amend 'An Act for the Reorganization and Maintenance of Common Schools . . . ,'" in Middleton, *Black Laws in the Old Northwest*, 44–45; Gerber, *Black Ohio and the Color Line*, 206.

68. David L. Calkins, "Black Education and the Nineteenth-Century City: An Institutional Analysis of Cincinnati's Colored Schools, 1850–1887," *Cincinnati Historical Society Bulletin* 33 (Spring 1975), 167.

69. King, *Report to the State Commissioner of Schools*, 15.

70. Cincinnati Colored Public Schools, *Eighteenth Annual Report of the Board of Directors*, 5.

71. Cincinnati Colored Public Schools, *Eighth Annual Report of the Board of Trustees*, 4.

72. Cincinnati Colored Public Schools, *Second Annual Report of the Board of Trustees*, 9; Cincinnati Colored Public Schools, *Ninth Annual Report of the Board of Trustees*, 4.

73. Cincinnati Colored Public Schools, *Tenth Annual Report of the Board of Trustees*, 8.

74. Gerber, *Black Ohio and the Color Line*, 205–6.

75. *Colored American*, August 4, 1838.

76. *Cincinnati Commercial*, April 2, 1872, April 12, 1872, and April 16, 1872, cited in Lyle Koehler, *Cincinnati's Black Peoples: A Chronology and Bibliography, 1787–1982* (Cincinnati: Cincinnati Arts Consortium, 1986), 71.

77. Gerber, *Black Ohio and the Color Line*, 199–205.

78. Ibid.

79. Middleton, *Black Laws in the Old Northwest*, 44–45.

CHAPTER 9

1. Scott v. Sandford, 60 U.S. 393 (1857).

2. James Oliver Horton and Lois E. Horton, *In Hope of Liberty: Culture, Community, and Protest among Northern Free Blacks, 1700–1860* (New York: Oxford University Press, 1997), 259.

3. The state conventions assumed different names. In 1843, it was called the "Convention of the Colored People of Ohio"; in 1849, it was the "Convention of the Colored Citizens of Ohio." By 1851, the name of the organization had changed again—this time to "State Convention of Colored Men"; the following year, the name was the "Convention of the Colored Freemen of Ohio." In 1856, the convention went by "State Convention of Colored Men"; two years later, it was "Convention of the Colored Men of Ohio." I have used "Convention of the Colored Men of Ohio" throughout for consistency.

4. Convention of the Colored Men of Ohio, *Proceedings of a Convention of the Colored Men of Ohio Held in the City of Cincinnati on the 23rd, 24th, 25th, and 26th Days of November 1858* (Cincinnati: Moore, Wilstach, Keys, 1858), 15–16.

5. Ohio [State] Anti-Slavery Society, *Proceedings of the First Annual Meeting* (n.p., 1860), 1. Held at the Cincinnati Historical Society. After decades of struggle, this was the first annual meeting of this organization. The Ohio State Anti-Slavery Society was a newly-established, all-black organization that had been born in the state conventions of the Colored Men of Ohio. The Ohio State Anti-Slavery Society linked the struggle for abolition with the struggle for citizenship rights for free blacks in Ohio. This is the only extant record of this organization.

5. Ibid.

6. Colored Men of Ohio, *Proceedings . . . 1858*, 7–8.

7. "An Act to Authorize the Establishment of Separate Schools for the Education of Colored Children, and for Other Purposes," in Stephen Middleton, *The Black Laws in the Old Northwest: A Documentary History* (Westport, CT: Greenwood, 1993), 38–40.

8. There were several cases that affirmed the rights of quadroon and octoroon— or very fair-skinned biracial—men to vote in Ohio. Although *Jeffries v. Ankeny* (1842) centered on whether a person of mixed Native American and white ancestry could vote, it had implications for those who were of mixed African and white ancestry. The state supreme court ruled that those people of mixed ancestry who were "nearer white than black, or of the grade between the mulattoes and the whites, were entitled to enjoy every political and social privilege of the white citizen." See *Jeffries v. Ankeny*, 11 Ohio 372 (1842). In *Thacker v. Hawk*, the Ohio Supreme Court upheld the *Jeffries v. Ankeny* decision and reversed the lower court's decision to deny a biracial man the right to vote. See *Thacker v. Hawk*, 11 Ohio 376 (1842). Finally, in the *Anderson v. Millikin* case, Alfred Anderson attempted to vote in the 1856 election for president of the United States but was denied that right by the board of electors in Butler County because he was one-eighth black. Citing the Polly Gray case, the court held that if a biracial person "held a larger portion of the blood of the white race, he was to be regarded as white." Hence, Anderson was granted suffrage rights. See *Anderson v. Millikin*, 9 Ohio St. 568 (1859).

10. The last of Ohio's antikidnapping legislation was passed in 1857. "An Act to Prevent Kidnapping," in Middleton, *Black Laws in the Old Northwest*, 31–32.

11. "An Act to Prescribe the Duties of Judges of Election's [sic]in Certain Cases, and Preserve the Purity of Elections," in Middleton, *Black Laws in the Old Northwest*, 12.

12. "An Act Supplementary to the Act Entitled 'An Act to Preserve the Purity of Elections,' Passed March 20th 1841, and to Protect the Judges of Elections in the Discharge of Their Duties, Passed April 16, 1858," 65 Ohio Laws 97 (1858).

13. Ibid.

14. Monroe v. Collins, 17 Ohio St. 665 (1867).

15. Ibid.

16. John Mercer Langston, "Memorial of John Mercer Langston for Colored People of Ohio to General Assembly of the State of Ohio, June 1854," in *Proceedings of the Black National and State Conventions, 1865–1900*, ed. Philip S. Foner and George E. Walker (Philadelphia: Temple University Press, 1986), 298; State Convention of Colored Men, *Address to the Constitutional Convention of Ohio* (Columbus: E. Glover, 1851), 6–7.

17. Langston, "Memorial," 299, 302.

18. Ibid., 302.

19. Colored Men of Ohio, *Proceedings . . . 1858*, 7–8.

20. Ibid., 15.

21. Peter H. Clark, *The Black Brigade of Cincinnati* (New York: Arno, 1969), 4.

22. Benjamin Quarles, *The Negro in the Civil War* (New York: Little, Brown, 1953), 27.

23. Ibid., 28.

24. William A. Jones to Simon Cameron, November 27, 1861, in *Free At Last: A Documentary History of Slavery, Freedom, and the Civil War*, ed. Ira Berlin et al. (New York: New Press, 1992), 18–19.

25. Quarles, *Negro in the Civil War*, 29.

26. Clark, *Black Brigade of Cincinnati*, 4–5.

27. Quarles, *Negro in the Civil War*, 29.

28. Clark, *Black Brigade of Cincinnati*, 5; *Colored Citizen*, November 7, 1863.

29. Clark, *Black Brigade of Cincinnati*, 5.

30. Cincinnati City Council, Minutes of the Cincinnati City Council, September 11, 1862; *Cincinnati Commercial*, September 2, 1862.

31. Clark, *Black Brigade of Cincinnati*, 5–6.

32. Ohio const., art. V, § 1.

33. Clark, *Black Brigade of Cincinnati*, 7.

34. Wallace, in turn, had probably acted in accordance with a piece of federal wartime legislation passed that summer. The Militia Act repealed the federal ban on black military service and permitted free blacks to be used in the war effort, although it was generally understood that that did not include as soldiers. Ohio retained its ban on black military service, meaning that in all likelihood, the use of black men in Cincinnati had been carried out and justified under the Militia Act. James M. McPherson, *The Negro's Civil War: How American Negroes Felt and Acted during the War for the Union* (Urbana: University of Illinois Press, 1982), 165.

35. The War Department had apparently given permission for military officers in Norfolk, Virginia, to use "forcible persuasion" to recruit black laborers there. Asa Prescott to Edwin M. Stanton, July 11, 1863, in Berlin et al., *Free At Last*, 200.

36. Leon F. Litwack, *Been in the Storm So Long: The Aftermath of Slavery* (New York: Knopf, 1979), 38; Quarles, *Negro in the Civil War*, 47.

37. In 1864 in Richmond, free blacks and slaves were seized from their homes and from the market to act as laborers for the Confederacy.

38. Clark, *Black Brigade of Cincinnati*, 8, 17. They were not allowed to march on paved roads but were forced to walk on dusty roads. These men were also forced to squat at gunpoint.

39. Ibid., 9.

40. Ibid., 13.

41. Ibid., 20. They received $1.00 per day for the first week and $1.50 per day for the second week.

42. Ibid., 13.

43. Ibid., 15. The source indicates that one thousand black men served. The total black population in 1860 was roughly thirty-seven hundred.

44. Ibid.

45. David Gerber, *Black Ohio and the Color Line, 1860–1915* (Urbana: University of Illinois Press, 1976), 34.

46. Clark, *Black Brigade of Cincinnati*, 3.

47. Ohio State Auxiliary Equal Rights League, "Constitution of the Ohio State Auxiliary Equal Rights League," in *Proceedings of a Convention of the Colored Men of Ohio Held in Xenia on the 10th, 11th, and 12th days of January 1865 with the Constitution of the Ohio Equal Rights League* (Cincinnati: A. Moore, 1865), 17, 19.

48. National Convention of Colored Men, "Preamble and Constitution of the National Equal Rights League," in *Proceedings of the National Convention of Colored Men Held in the City of Syracuse, New York, October 4, 5, 6, and 7, 1864, with the Bill of Wrongs and Rights and the Address to American People*, in *Minutes of the Proceedings of the National Negro Conventions, 1830–1864*, ed. Howard Holman Bell, 36; National Equal Rights League, *Proceedings of the First Annual Meeting of the National Equal Rights League, Held in Cleveland, Ohio October 19, 20, and 21, 1865*, in Foner and Walker, *Proceedings of the Black National and State Conventions, 1865–1900*, 64.

49. Gerber, *Black Ohio and the Color Line*, 40.

CHAPTER 10

1. Nancy Bertaux, "Structural Economic Change and Occupational Decline among Black Workers in Nineteenth-Century Cincinnati," in *Race and the City: Work, Community, and Protest in Cincinnati, 1802–1970*, ed. Henry Louis Taylor Jr. (Urbana: University of Illinois Press, 1993), 127.

2. Lafcadio Hearn, *Children of the Levee*, ed. O. W. Frost (Lexington: University Press of Kentucky, 1957), 34.

3. Wendell P. Dabney, *Cincinnati's Colored Citizens: Historical, Sociological, and Biographical* (Cincinnati: Dabney Publishing, 1926), 153.

4. Henry Louis Taylor Jr. and Vicky Dula argue that the black residential pattern in nineteenth-century Cincinnati was clustering, which they define as two or more families that live in the same building, next door, or a few doors away from other African American households. Taylor and Dula also assert that black neighborhoods like Bucktown and Little Africa were significant because black institutions were concentrated there. They state that the concentration of black

institutions "created a 'commons' for black Cincinnati during the pre-ghetto era." See Henry Louis Taylor Jr. and Vicky Dula, "Black Residential Experience," in *Race and the City: Work, Community, and Protest in Cincinnati, 1820–1970*, ed. Henry Louis Taylor Jr. (Chicago: University of Illinois Press, 1993), 102, 115.

5. Dabney, *Cincinnati's Colored Citizens*, 156.

6. Hearn, *Children of the Levee*, 5, 34.

7. Often times, they only emerge from the shadows of history when they are arrested or appear in court. Although jail and court records are extremely problematic sources, they do provide a small glimpse into some of the activities of the shadow community.

8. For biographical information on Hearn see Simon J. Bronner, ed., *Lafcadio Hearn's America: Ethnographic Sketches and Editorials* (Lexington: University Press of Kentucky, 2002), 3–9, 12, 18.

9. Hearn, *Children of the Levee*, 5.

10. Ibid., 36.

11. In 1850, 196 of the 1,962 heads of household worked in the river industry. In 1860, 508 of the 1,894 heads of household worked as river workers. U.S. Census Bureau, *The Seventh Census of the United States, 1850* (Washington, DC: Robert Armstrong, 1853); U.S. Census Bureau, *Population of the United States in 1860* (Washington, DC: Government Printing Office, 1864).

12. The census takers used several different designations for boat hand, including river hand, boatman, steamboat man, deckhand, and steamboat laborer. These designations include the wide range of unskilled and menial labor that these persons did aboard vessels.

13. W. Jeffrey Bolster, "'To Feel Like a Man': Black Seamen in the Northern States, 1800–1860," in *A Question of Manhood: A Reader in U.S. Black Men's History and Masculinity*, ed. Darlene Clark Hine and Earnestine Jenkins (Bloomington: Indiana University Press, 1999), 1:369–70.

14. Bertaux, "Structural Economic Change and Occupational Decline," 137.

15. Louis C. Hunter, *Steamboats on the Western Rivers: An Economic and Technological History* (Cambridge, MA: Harvard University Press, 1949), 451.

16. Ohio Anti-Slavery Society, *Proceedings of the Ohio Anti-Slavery Society Convention Held in Putnam in 1835* (Putnam: Ohio Anti-Slavery Society, 1835), 27.

17. James Hall, *The West: Its Commerce and Navigation* (New York: Burt Franklin, 1970), 134.

18. Ibid., 141.

19. Ibid., 180–82.

20. Hearn, *Children of the Levee*, 63.

21. Hunter, *Steamboats on the Western Rivers*, 453.

22. U.S. Census Bureau, *Population of the United States in 1860*.

23. Hearn, *Children of the Levee*, 62.

24. U.S. Census Bureau, *Seventh Census of the United States, 1850*; U.S. Census Bureau, *Population of the United States in 1860*.

25. Lyle Koehler, *Cincinnati's Black Peoples: A Chronology and Bibliography, 1787–1982* (Cincinnati: Cincinnati Arts Consortium, 1986), 57.

26. Regarding the "Negro Seamen Acts," see chapter 7.

27. Bolster, "To Feel Like a Man," 1:368–69.

28. W. Jeffrey Bolster argues that "overtly racist actions by other sailors were often subordinated to the requirements of shipboard order, and the unprecedented toleration that existed at sea afforded black men a virtually unknown degree of equality with white coworkers." Ibid., 360. Although there was a degree of interracial cooperation aboard these vessels, segregation and racist occupational hierarchies and pay scales hardly paint a picture of equality.

29. Hearn, *Children of the Levee*, 67.

30. Bolster, "To Feel Like a Man," 1:368. Many historians argue that seamen were "a class without customs, roots or social ties." Black rivermen in Cincinnati were not absolutely without roots or ties, although, admittedly, those ties were weak. See W. J. Rorabaugh, *The Alcoholic Republic: An American Tradition* (New York: Oxford University Press, 1979), 140.

31. Hearn, *Children of the Levee*, 69.

32. Ibid., 82.

33. Ibid., 17.

34. Ohio Anti-Slavery Society, *Proceedings of the Ohio Anti-Slavery Society Convention*, 27.

35. Ibid., 28.

36. Hearn, *Children of the Levee*, 65.

37. Most of the women employed in this industry in 1860 were chambermaids on the vessels. U.S. Census Bureau, *Population of the United States in 1860*.

38. Marcus Rediker, *Between the Devil and the Deep Blue Sea: Merchant Seamen, Pirates, and the Anglo-American Maritime World, 1700–1750* (Cambridge: Cambridge University Press, 1987), 203.

39. Ibid., 189.

40. Hearn, *Children of the Levee*, 71. "Patting juba" was a "rhythmic, stamping, clapping, patting type of dance" that was derived from the dance crafted by William Henry Lane, also known as Master Juba. In the 1840s, Master Juba was considered the greatest dancer of his time and toured the country performing for white audiences. Lynne Fauley Emery, *Black Dance in the United States from 1619 to 1970* (Palo Alto, CA: National Press Books, 1972), 187–88.

41. Hearn, *Children of the Levee*, 24.

42. Ibid., 69.

43. Ibid., 50, 52–53.

44. Ibid., 59.

45. His wife and child died shortly thereafter. Biographical data is provided by Lafcadio Hearn in *Children of the Levee*, 57–58.

46. Ibid., 59.

47. Ibid., 55, 84–85.

48. Ibid., 54.

49. Ibid., 77.

50. Ibid., 84–90.

51. Ibid., 85.

52. Ibid., 55. More than likely, these women were only girlfriends: Ohio had banned intermarriage in 1861.

53. Ibid., 79.

54. Although black taverns were almost exclusively social spaces, white taverns and saloons were also political spaces—sites for raising and rallying mobs. In 1843, Scanlan, a slave owner, visited the Alhambra, a tavern on Third Street, to rally support for his effort to reclaim an enslaved child from the abolitionist he suspected of harboring her. At the tavern Scanlan "gave orders for an open bar, and, after dispensing liquor freely to all, made a speech to them relating his grievances." After buying support and sympathy with liquor, Scanlan implored the patrons to "help obtain his slave and to see the fun." In drunken animation, a mob formed and set out to help reclaim Scanlan's slave. One man is reported to have exclaimed, "If my property was in there, I'd have it or I'd have those villains' blood." Although the mob was unsuccessful, Scanlan's ease in mobilizing a mob from a tavern suggests that the culture inside fostered such lawlessness. Levi Coffin, *Reminiscences of Levi Coffin, the Reputed President of the Underground Railroad* (New York: AMS Press, 1876), 538.

55. Rediker, *Between the Devil and the Deep Blue Sea,* 192; *Cincinnati Enquirer,* August 21, 1873.

56. The 1860 census lists the residence of these boatmen on steamboats. Blacks listed in the Second Ward, almost without exception, lived on steamboats. The Fourth Ward also had a very high number of residents living on steamboats. These men did not appear in the 1850 census, which means that, by 1860, Cincinnati officials had recognized their presence in the city and recognized steamboats as a valid place of residence.

57. Twenty-eight black men resided at the Broadway Hotel in 1860. U.S. Census Bureau, *Population of the United States in 1860.*

58. Dabney, *Cincinnati's Colored Citizens,* 180.

59. U.S. Census Bureau, *Population of the United States in 1860.*

60. According to Louis Hunter, sixty percent of all maritime workers in 1850 were under the age of thirty. Hunter, *Steamboats on the Western Rivers,* 448.

61. Dabney, *Cincinnati's Colored Citizens,* 180–81.

62. Ibid., 179.

63. Hamilton County, Hamilton County Jail Registers, November 1834–October 1841, vol. 1. This is one of the few volumes of nineteenth-century jail records that survived fires. It is also one of the few volumes that list the race of the arrested suspects. Even then, race is recorded only haphazardly. Because there were so many officers who logged in their own prisoners, there is also a great deal of inconsistency. Because of handwriting, it is difficult to distinguish a "M" (mulatto) from a "W" (white) in the jail log. In addition to those difficulties, the officers had inconsistent designations for the color of African Americans. Some used a "C" (colored) to designate a category that sometimes in-

cluded light-skinned African Americans and Choctaw Indians, while others used "M." In addition, a particular person might be designated two different ways from one entry to the next—being listed as a mulatto in one entry and black in another. Such inconsistencies make the data difficult to analyze; Hearn, *Children of the Levee*, 45, 46.

64. A brothel in the Fourteenth Ward appears in the 1860 census as a house of prostitution and even includes a list of employees (without names of prostitutes).

65. Hearn, *Children of the Levee*, 43, 46, 80.

66. Ibid., 80.

67. "An Act to Prevent the Amalgamation of the White and Colored Races," in Middleton, *Black Laws in the Old Northwest*, 135–36.

68. Dabney claimed that Coville was sentenced to six months in jail, but the legislation mandated a sentence not exceeding three months in jail. Dabney, *Cincinnati's Colored Citizens*, 165–66.

69. Koehler, *Cincinnati's Black Peoples*, 57.

70. Hearn, *Children of the Levee*, 44.

71. Ibid., 39, 73.

72. Ibid., 34.

73. Ibid.; Hamilton County, Hamilton County Jail Registers, November 1842–December 1848, vol. 2. In August 1848, African Americans Peter Winston and Miles Wilson were arrested for counterfeiting, along with three white men.

74. Dabney, *Cincinnati's Colored Citizens*, 164.

75. Writers' Program of the Works Projects Administration in the State of Ohio, *The Beautiful River* (Cincinnati: Wiesen-Hart Press, 1940), 36.

76. Leonard Harding, "The Cincinnati Riots of 1862," *Bulletin of the Cincinnati Historical Society* 25 (October 1967): 237.

77. *Cincinnati Daily Commercial*, July 11, 1862.

78. Hearn, *Children of the Levee*, 57; Harding, "Cincinnati Riots of 1862," 232.

79. Hearn, *Children of the Levee*, 57; *Colored Citizen*, November 7, 1863; Harding, "Cincinnati Riots of 1862," 229–33.

80. Hearn, *Children of the Levee*, 56.

81. Koehler, *Cincinnati's Black Peoples*, 67; Harding, "Cincinnati Riots of 1862," 239.

82. Koehler, *Cincinnati's Black Peoples*, 63. In 1860, the city's black population was 3,731. Although the 5,900 African Americans who resided in Cincinnati in 1870 comprised only 2.7 percent of the city's population of 216,239, whites were, nonetheless, alarmed. So frightening was the black migration into the state that one member of the House of Representatives lamented, "If the rush of free negroes to this paradise continues . . . you will have no one here but Congressmen and negroes, and that will be punishment enough." Samuel S. Cox, "Emancipation and Its Results—Is Ohio to Be Africanized?" Speech of Hon. Samuel S. Cox of Ohio Delivered in the House of Representatives, June 6, 1862 (n.p.: 1862), 7.

83. Hamilton County, *Hamilton County Jail Registers*, vol.1, November 1834–October 1841.

84. Hearn, *Children of the Levee*, 32.

85. Ibid., 36.

86. Ibid., 37.

87. U.S. Census Bureau, *Population of the United States in 1860*. Also see Ellen Brown's household in the Fifth Ward.

88. Children and elderly people lived in homes with families with different surnames.

89. Hearn, *Children of the Levee*, 80.

90. Ibid., 97. It is impossible to determine either Auntie Porter's first name or any other biographical data about her.

91. Hearn, *Children of the Levee*, 57.

92. Cincinnati Colored Public Schools, *Ninth Annual Report of the Board of Trustees for the Colored Public Schools of Cincinnati for the School Year Ending June 30, 1858* (Cincinnati: Wrightson, 1858), 8.

93. Dabney, *Cincinnati's Colored Citizens*, 155; Hearn, *Children of the Levee*, 40.

94. Dabney, *Cincinnati's Colored Citizens*, 153.

95. Hearn, *Children of the Levee*, 59.

96. David Gerber, *Black Ohio and the Color Line, 1860–1915* (Urbana: University of Illinois Press, 1976), 110.

BIBLIOGRAPHY

ARCHIVAL SOURCES

Cincinnati Historical Society, Cincinnati

Arnett, Benjamin W. *Proceedings of the Semi-centenary Celebration of the African Methodist Episcopal Church of Cincinnati Held in Allen Temple, February 8th, 9th, and 10th, 1874*. Cincinnati: H. Watkin, 1874.

Board of Trustees for Colored Public Schools. *Annual Reports of the Board of Trustees for the Colored Public Schools of Cincinnati*. Cincinnati: Various publishers, 1855–1872.

Bullock, William. *Sketch of a Journey through the Western States of North America*. London: John Miller, 1827.

Cincinnati City Infirmary. *Annual Reports of the Board of Directors of the City Infirmary to the City Council of the City of Cincinnati*. Cincinnati: Various publishers, 1853–1865.

Cincinnati Common Schools. *Annual Reports of the Trustees and Visitors of Common Schools*. Cincinnati: Various publishers, 1854–1871.

Colored Citizens of Cincinnati. *The Address and Reply on the Presentation of a Testimonial to Salmon Portland Chase by the Colored People of Cincinnati*. Cincinnati: Henry Derby, 1845.

———. *Minutes and Address of the State Convention of the Colored Citizens of Ohio, Convened at Columbus January 10th, 11th, 12th, and 13th, 1849*. Oberlin: J. M. Fitch's Power Press, 1849.

Colored Men of Ohio. *Proceedings of a Convention of the Colored Men of Ohio Held in Cincinnati on the 23rd, 24th, 25th, and 26th Days of November 1858*. Cincinnati: Moore, Wilstach, Keys, 1858.

———. *Proceedings of a Convention of the Colored Men of Ohio Held in Xenia on the 10th, 11th, and 12th Days of January 1865*. Cincinnati: A. Moore, 1865.

Convention of the Colored Freemen of Ohio. *Proceedings of the State Convention of the Colored Freemen of Ohio Held in Cincinnati, January 14–18, 1852*. Cincinnati: Dumas and Lawyer, 1852.

King, Rufus. *Report to the State Commissioner of Schools on the History and Condition of the Public Schools in Cincinnati*. Cincinnati: n.p., 1859.

Perkins, J. H. *Oration Delivered on the First of August 1849 before the Colored Citizens of Cincinnati*. Cincinnati: J. H. Perkins, 1849.

Wattles, John O. *Annual Report of the Educational Condition of the Colored People of Cincinnati, Including the Sentiment in Mercer County, Ohio: Presented at the Exhibition of the Cincinnati High School.* Cincinnati: John White, 1847.

Ohio Historical Society, Columbus

Cincinnati Lane Seminary. "Statement of the Faculty Concerning the Late Difficulties in the Lane Seminary." In *Fifth Annual Report of the Trustees of the Cincinnati Lane Seminary: Together with the Laws of the Institution and a Catalogue of the Officers and Students.* Cincinnati: Corey and Fairbank, 1834.

Colored Citizens of Cincinnati. *Minutes of the State Convention of the Colored Citizens of Ohio Convened at Columbus January 15th, 16th, 17th, and 18th, 1851.* Columbus: E. Glover, 1851.

Cox, Samuel S. "Emancipation and Its Results—Is Ohio to Be Africanized?" Speech of Hon. S. S. Cox, of Ohio, Delivered in the House of Representatives, June 6, 1862. n.p.,n.d.

Foote, John P. *The Schools of Cincinnati and Its Vicinity.* Cincinnati: C. F. Bradley, 1855.

Gaines, John Isom. *Oration Delivered on the First of August 1849 before the Colored Citizens of Columbus, Ohio.* Columbus: n.p., 1849.

Landon, Fred, ed. *The Diary of Benjamin Lundy Written during His Journey through Upper Canada, January 1832.* Ontario: Ontario Historical Society, n.d.

Lundy, Benjamin. Benjamin Lundy Papers, MSS 112.

National Emigration Convention of Colored People. *Proceedings of the National Emigration Convention of Colored People Held at Cleveland, Ohio, on Thursday, Friday, and Saturday, the 24th, 25th, and 26th of August 1854.* Pittsburgh: A. Anderson, 1854.

Ohio Anti-Slavery Society. *Memorial of the Ohio Anti-Slavery Society to the General Assembly of the State of Ohio.* Cincinnati: Pugh and Dodd, 1838.

———. *Narrative of the Late Riotous Proceedings against the Liberty of the Press in Cincinnati with Remarks and Historical Notices Relating to Emancipation.* Cincinnati: Ohio Anti-Slavery Society, 1836.

———. *Proceedings of the Ohio Anti-Slavery Society Convention Held at Putnam, Ohio.* Putnam: Ohio Anti-Slavery Society, 1835.

———. *Report of the Second Anniversary of the Ohio Anti-Slavery Society, Held in Mount Pleasant, Jefferson County, Ohio, on the Twenty-seventh of April 1837.* Cincinnati: Ohio Anti-Slavery Society, 1837.

———. *Report of the Third Anniversary of the Ohio Anti-Slavery Society Held in Granville County, Ohio, on the 30th of May 1838.* Cincinnati: Ohio Anti-Slavery Society, 1838.

———. *Report on the Condition of the People of Color in the State of Ohio.* Putnam, OH: Beaumont and Wallace [ca. 1835].

Ohio General Assembly. "Report of the Majority of the Select Committee Proposing to Repeal All Laws Creating Distinctions on the Account of Color, Commonly Called the Black Laws." *Journal of the Ohio House of Representatives,* January 18, 1845.

——. "Report of the Majority of the Judiciary Committee on Questions Concerning Slavery, and Black and Mulatto Persons." *Journal of the Ohio House of Representatives,* February 7, 1837.

——. "Report of the Minority of the Select Committee upon the Subject of the
Laws Relative to People of Color." *Journal of the Ohio House of Representatives,* January 18, 1845.

Ohio State Anti-Slavery Society. *Proceedings of the First Annual Meeting.* n.p., 1860.

Ohio State Colonization Society. *A Brief Exposition of the Views of the Society for the Colonization of Free Persons of Colour in Africa.* Columbus: Office of the Ohio Monitor,
1827.

Parham, William Hartwell. *An Official History of the Most Worshipful Grand Lodge, Free and
Accepted Masons for the State of Ohio.* n.p., 1906.

Siebert, Wilbur H. Wilbur H. Siebert Collection, MSS 116, The "Underground
Railroad" in Ohio: Hamilton County, boxes 106 and 107.

——. The "Underground Railroad" in Ohio: Lucas to Morrow Counties, box 109.

Smith, David. *The First Annual Report of the Ohio State Society for Colonizing the Free People of
Colour of the United States.* Columbus: Ohio State Society for Colonizing Free
People of Colour, 1827.

State Convention of Colored Men. *Minutes of the State Convention of the Colored Citizens
of Ohio Convened at Columbus, Jan. 15th, 16th, 17th, and 18th, 1851.* Columbus: E.
Glover, 1851.

——. *Address to the Constitutional Convention of Ohio.* Columbus: E. Glover, 1851.

——. *Proceedings of the State Convention of Colored Men Held in the City of Columbus, Ohio, Jan.
15th, 16th, 17th, and 18th, 1856.* [Columbus?]: n.p., [1856?].

Union Association of the Colored Men of New Richmond, Ohio. *Constitution,
By-Laws, and Records of the Union Association of the Colored Men of New Richmond, Ohio.*
Columbus: n.p., 1851.

University of Western Ontario, London

House of Assembly of Canada, *Journal of the House of Assembly of Upper Canada, 8 January–6
March 1830.* York, Canada: William Lyon McKenzie, 1830.

——. *Aggregate Census and Assessments Returns for Upper Canada, 1824–1850* (Ontario:
n.p., 1832).

PUBLISHED PRIMARY SOURCES

Abdy, Edward. *Journal of a Residence and Tour in the United States of North America from April
1833 to October 1834.* London: n.p., 1835.

Ball, James. *Ball's Splendid Mammoth Pictorial Tour of the United States Comprising Views of the
African Slave Trade; of Northern and Southern Cities; of Cotton and Sugar Plantations; of the
Mississippi, Ohio and Susquehanna Rivers, Niagara Falls, &c.* Cincinnati: Achilles Pugh,
1855.

Berlin, Ira, ed. *Free At Last: A Documentary History of Slavery, Freedom, and the Civil War.* (New York: New Press, 1992).

Bishop, Isabella Lucy Bird. *The Englishwoman in America.* London: John Murray, 1856.

Bremer, Frederika. *The Homes of the New World: Impressions of America.* London: Arthur Hall, Virtue, 1853.

Bronner, Simon J., ed. *Lafcadio Hearn's America: Ethnographic Sketches and Editorials.* Lexington: University Press of Kentucky, 2002.

Brown, William Wells. *Clotelle: A Tale of the Southern States.* Philadelphia: Albert Saifer, 1955.

Chase, Salmon P. "Speech of Salmon P. Chase in the Case of the Colored Woman, Matilda, Who Was Brought before the Court of Common Pleas of Hamilton County, Ohio." In *Southern Slaves in Free State Courts: The Pamphlet Literature,* edited by Paul Finkelman. New York: Garland Publishing, 1988.

Cist, Charles. *Cincinnati Directory for the Year 1842.* Cincinnati: E. Morgan, 1842.

———. *Cincinnati in 1841: Its Early Annals and Future Aspects.* Cincinnati: Charles Cist, 1841.

———. *Sketches and Statistics of Cincinnati in 1851.* Cincinnati: William H. Moore, 1851.

———. *Sketches and Statistics of Cincinnati in 1859.* Cincinnati: n.p., 1859.

Clark, Peter. *The Black Brigade of Cincinnati.* New York: Arno, 1969.

Cleland, Hugh, ed. *George Washington in the Ohio Valley.* Pittsburgh: University of Pittsburgh Press, 1955.

Coffin, Levi. *Reminiscences of Levi Coffin: The Reputed President of the Underground Railroad.* Cincinnati: Western Tract Society, 1876.

Convention of the Territory of the United States North-West of the Ohio. *Journal of the Convention of the Territory of the United States North-West of the Ohio.* Chillicothe, OH: N. Willis, 1802.

Deming, E. *The Cincinnati Directory for 1834.* Cincinnati: Deming, 1834.

Drake, B., and E. D. Mansfield. *Cincinnati in 1826.* Cincinnati: Morgan, Lodge, and Fisher, 1827.

Drake, Daniel. *Natural and Statistical View, or Picture of Cincinnati and the Miami Country.* Cincinnati: Looker and Wallace, 1815.

Drew, Benjamin. *The Refugee: Or the Narratives of Fugitive Slaves in Canada; Related by Themselves, with an Account of the History and Condition of the Colored Population in Upper Canada.* Boston: John P. Jewett, 1856.

Dumond, Dwight, ed. *Letters of James Gillespie Birney, 1831–1857.* 2 vols. Gloucester, MA: Peter Smith, 1966.

Fairbank, Calvin. *Rev. Calvin Fairbank during Slavery Times: How He "Fought the Good Fight" to Prepare "The Way."* New York: Negro Universities Press, 1969.

Farnsworth, Oliver. *The Cincinnati Directory.* Cincinnati: Morgan, Lodge, 1819.

Finkelman, Paul, ed. *Southern Slaves in Free State Courts: The Pamphlet Literature.* New York: Garland Publishing, 1988.

Foner, Philip S., and George E. Walker, eds. *Proceedings of the Black National and State Conventions, 1865–1900*. Philadelphia: Temple University Press, 1986.

———. *Proceedings of the Black State Conventions, 1840–1865*. Philadelphia: Temple University Press, 1980.

Hall, Harvey. *The Cincinnati Directory for 1825*. Cincinnati: Samuel Browne, 1825.

Hall, James. *The West: Its Commerce and Navigation*. New York: H. W. Derby, 1848.

Haviland, Laura. *A Woman's Life-Work: Including Thirty Years' Service on the Underground Railroad and in the War*. Grand Rapids. MI: S. B. Shaw, 1881.

Hearn, Lafcadio. *Children of the Levee*. Edited by O. W. Frost. Lexington: University Press of Kentucky, 1957.

Henson, Josiah. *Life of Josiah Henson, Formerly a Slave*. Boston: Arthur D. Phelps, 1849.

King, Moses. *King's Pocket-Book of Cincinnati*. Cincinnati: John Shillito, 1879.

Langston, John Mercer. *From the Virginia Plantation to the National Capitol; or, The First and Only Negro Representative in Congress from the Old Dominion* (Hartford, CT: American Publishing, 1894).

Malvin, John. *Autobiography of John Malvin: A Narrative*. Cleveland: Leader Printing, 1879.

Martineau, Harriet. *Retrospect of Western Travel*. London: Saunders and Otley, 1838.

Middleton, Stephen. *The Black Laws in the Old Northwest: A Documentary History*. Westport, CT: Greenwood, 1993.

Osofsky, Gilbert, ed. *Puttin' on Ole Massa: The Slave Narratives of Henry Bibb, William Wells Brown, and Solomon Northup*. New York: Harper and Row, 1969.

Parker, John P. *His Promised Land: The Autobiography of John P. Parker, Former Slave and Conductor on the Underground Railroad*. New York: W.W. Norton, 1996.

Potter, Eliza. *A Hairdresser's Experience in High Life*. New York: Oxford University Press, 1991.

Ripley, C. Peter. *The Black Abolitionist Papers*. Vol. 2, *Canada, 1830–1865*. Chapel Hill: University of North Carolina Press, 1986.

Robinson and Fairbank. *The Cincinnati Directory for the Year 1829*. Cincinnati: Whetstone and Buxton, 1829.

———. *The Cincinnati Directory for the Year 1831*. Cincinnati: Robinson and Fairbank, 1831.

Robinson and Jones. *Robinson and Jones' Cincinnati Directory for 1846*. Cincinnati: Robinson and Jones, 1846.

Shaffer, Henry D. *The Cincinnati, Covington, Newport, and Fulton Directory for 1840*. Cincinnati: Donogh, 1840.

———. *Shaffer's Advertising Directory for 1839–40*. Cincinnati, n.p., n.d.

Shirreff, Patrick. *A Tour through North America Together with a Comprehensive View of the Canadas and United States as Adapted for Agricultural Emigration*. Edinburgh: Oliver and Boyd, 1835.

Sprague, Stuart Seely. *His Promised Land*. New York: W. W. Norton, 1996.

Steward, Austin. *Twenty-two Years a Slave, and Forty Years A Free Man*. New York: Negro Universities Press, 1968.

Stowe, Harriet Beecher. *Uncle Tom's Cabin: or, Life among the Lowly.* Boston: John P. Jewett, 1852.

Stuart, Charles. *Remarks on the Colony of Liberia and the American Colonization Society with Some Account of the Settlement of Coloured People at Wilberforce, Upper Canada.* London: J. Messender, 1832.

Tocqueville, Alexis de. *Democracy in America.* Edited by Harvey Mansfield and Delba Winthrop. Chicago: University of Chicago Press, 2000.

Trollope, Frances. *Domestic Manners of the Americans.* London: Whittaker, Treacher, 1832.

Webster, Delia. *Kentucky Jurisprudence: A History of the Trial of Miss Delia Webster at Lexington, Kentucky, Dec'r 17–21, 1844, before the Hon. Richard Buckner on a Charge of Aiding Slaves to Escape from that Commonwealth, with Miscellaneous Remarks, Including Her Views on American Slavery.* Vergennes: R. W. Blaisdell, 1845.

Williams, C. S. *Williams' Cincinnati Guide and General Business Directory.* Cincinnati: C. S. Williams, 1848–1868.

Woodruff, J. H. *The Cincinnati Directory and Advertiser for the Years 1836–1837.* Cincinnati: J. H. Woodruff, 1836.

Woodson, Carter G. *The Education of the Negro Prior to 1861.* New York: Arno, 1968.

——. *Free Negro Heads of Families in the United States in 1830: Together with a Brief Treatment of the Free Negro.* Washington, DC: Association for the Study of Negro Life and History, 1925.

——. *The Mind of the Negro as Reflected in Letters Written during the Crisis, 1800–1860.* New York: Negro Universities Press, 1969.

——. "The Negroes of Cincinnati Prior to the Civil War." *Journal of Negro History* 1 (January 1916): 1–22.

——. "Race Hate in Early Ohio." *Negro History Bulletin* 10 (June 1947): 203–11.

GOVERNMENT DOCUMENTS

Cincinnati City Council. Minutes. Vols. 3–35. July 28, 1824–June 19, 1863. Held in the Cincinnati City Hall Vault.

Hamilton County, Ohio. Hamilton County Jail Registers. Vols. 1–8. November 1834–February 1866. Held at the University of Cincinnati Archives, Blegan Hall.

London District. Assessment Rolls for 1835. Held at the University of Western Ontario.

London District. *Aggregate Statement of the Population of the London District, as Taken From the Returns of Assessors of Townships for the Year 1832.* Held at the University of Western Ontario.

U.S. Census Bureau. United States Census Returns for the Years 1800–1870. Hamilton County, Ohio.

U.S. Department of Commerce. *Historical Statistics of the United States, Colonial Times to 1970.* Washington, DC: U.S. Census Bureau, 1975.

NEWSPAPERS

Anglo-African. Held at the University of Detroit Mercy, Detroit.

Chatham (Ontario) Journal. Held at the London Public Library, London, Ontario.

Cincinnati Catholic Telegraph. Held at the Ohio Historical Society, Columbus.

Cincinnati Daily Chronicle. Held at the Cincinnati Historical Society, Cincinnati, Ohio.

Cincinnati Daily Gazette. Held at the Cincinnati Historical Society, Cincinnati.

Cincinnati Enquirer. Held at the Cincinnati Historical Society, Cincinnati.

Cincinnati Miscellany. Held at the Ohio Historical Society, Columbus.

Cist's Weekly Advertiser. Held at the Ohio Historical Society, Columbus.

Colored American. Held at the Schomburg Library, New York City.

Colored Citizen. Held at the University of Cincinnati, Blegan Hall.

Courier and Western District Advertiser. Held at the London Public Library, London, Ontario.

Freedom's Journal

Friend of Man. Held at the Schomburg Library, New York City.

Liberator. Held at the Schomburg Library, New York City.

London (Ontario) Free Press. Held at the London Public Library, London, Ontario.

National Republican and Ohio Political Register. Held at the Cincinnati Historical Society, Cincinnati.

Ohio Journal. Held at the Ohio State University, Columbus.

Philanthropist

Rights of All

Saturday Evening Chronicle. Held at the Cincinnati Historical Society, Cincinnati.

Week: Illustrated. Held at the Cincinnati Public Library, Cincinnati.

Weekly Advocate

Wesleyan Advocate. Held at the London Public Library, London, Ontario.

Western Spy. Held at the Cincinnati Historical Society, Cincinnati.

SECONDARY SOURCES

Aaron, Daniel. *Cincinnati, Queen City of the West, 1819–1838.* Columbus: Ohio State University Press, 1992.

Anderson, James D. *The Education of Blacks in the South, 1860–1935.* Chapel Hill: University of North Carolina Press, 1988.

Baldwin, Leland D. *The Keelboat Age on Western Waters.* Pittsburgh: University of Pittsburgh Press, 1941.

Bell, Howard Holman, ed. *Minutes of the Proceedings of the National Negro Conventions, 1830–1864.* New York: Arno, 1969.

Bennett, David H. *The Party of Fear: From Nativist Movements to the New Right in American History.* Chapel Hill: University of North Carolina Press, 1988.

Berlin, Ira. *Slaves without Masters: The Free Negro in the Antebellum South.* New York: Vintage Books, 1974.

Bertaux, Nancy. "Structural Economic Change and Occupational Decline among Black Workers in Nineteenth-Century Cincinnati." In *Race and the City: Work, Community, and Protest in Cincinnati, 1820–1970*, edited by Henry Louis Taylor Jr., 126–55. Urbana: University of Illinois Press, 1993.

Berwanger, Eugene H. *The Frontier against Slavery: Western Anti-Negro Prejudice and the Slavery Extension Controversy*. Urbana: University of Illinois Press, 1967.

Bethel, Elizabeth Rauh. *The Roots of African-American Identity: Memory and History in Antebellum Free Communities*. New York: St. Martin's Press, 1999.

Bigham, Darrel. *Towns and Villages of the Lower Ohio*. Lexington: University Press of Kentucky, 1998.

Blight, David W., ed. *Passages to Freedom: The Underground Railroad in History and Memory*. Washington, DC: Smithsonian Books, 2004.

Blue, Frederick. *Salmon P. Chase: A Life in Politics*. Kent, OH: Kent State University Press, 1987.

Bolster, W. Jeffrey. *Black Jacks: African American Seamen in the Age of Sail*. Cambridge, MA: Harvard University Press, 1997.

———. "'To Feel Like a Man': Black Seamen in the Northern States, 1800–1860." In *A Question of Manhood: A Reader in U.S. Black Men's History and Masculinity*, edited by Darlene Clark Hine and Earnestine Jenkins, 354–81. Bloomington: Indiana University Press, 1999.

Boryczka, Raymond and Lorin Lee Cary. *No Strength without Union: An Illustrated History of Ohio Workers, 1803–1980*. Columbus: Ohio Historical Society, 1982.

Brown, Elsa Barkley. "Womanist Consciousness: Maggie Lena Walker and the Independent Order of Saint Luke." In *Unequal Sisters: A Multicultural Reader in U.S. Women's History*, edited by Vicki Ruiz and Ellen Carol DuBois. New York: Routledge, 1994.

Bullock, Henry Allen. *A History of Negro Education in the South: From 1619 to the Present*. Cambridge, MA: Harvard University Press, 1967.

Calkins, David L. *A Bibliography of the Nineteenth Century Cincinnati Negro Community*. Unpublished manuscript. Held at the Ohio Historical Society.

———. "Black Education and the Nineteenth-Century City: An Institutional Analysis of Cincinnati's Colored Schools, 1850–1887." *Cincinnati Historical Society Bulletin* 33 (Spring 1975): 161–73.

Caughey, John Walton. *The American West: Frontier and Region*. Los Angeles: Ward Ritchie Press, 1969.

Cheek, William and Aimee Lee Cheek. "John Mercer Langston and the Cincinnati Riot of 1841." In *Race and the City: Work, Community, and Protest in Cincinnati, 1820–1970*, edited by Henry Louis Taylor Jr., 29–69 Urbana: University of Illinois Press, 1993.

———. *John Mercer Langston and the Fight for Black Freedom, 1829–1865*. Urbana: University of Illinois Press, 1989.

Curry, Leonard P. *The Free Black in Urban America, 1800–1850: The Shadow of the Dream*. Chicago: University of Chicago Press, 1981.

Dabney, Wendell P. *Cincinnati's Colored Citizens: Historical, Sociological, and Biographical*. Cincinnati: Dabney Publishing, 1926.

Dula, Vicky Y. "The Wolf and the Pack: Black Residence and Social Organization in Antebellum Cincinnati." Master's thesis, Ohio State University, 1984.

Egerton, Douglas. *He Shall Go out Free: The Lives of Denmark Vesey*. Madison, WI: Madison House, 1999.

Emery, Lynne Fauley. *Black Dance in the United States from 1619 to 1970*. Palo Alto, CA: National Press Books, 1972.

Finkelman, Paul. *An Imperfect Union: Slavery, Federalism, and Comity*. Chapel Hill: University of North Carolina Press, 1981.

———. "Not Only the Judges' Robes Were Black: African-American Lawyers as Social Engineers." *Stanford Law Review* 47 (November 1994): 161–209.

———. *Slavery and the Founders: Race and Liberty in the Age of Jefferson*. Armonk, NY: M. E. Sharpe, 1996.

Folk, Patrick. "'Queen City of Mobs'": Riots and Community Reactions in Cincinnati, 1788–1848." Ph.D. diss., University of Toledo, 1978.

Foner, Eric, ed. *The New American History*. Philadelphia: Temple University Press, 1990.

———. *The Story of American Freedom*. New York: W. W. Norton, 1998.

Franklin, John Hope, and Loren Schweninger. *Runaway Slaves: Rebels on the Plantation*. New York: Oxford University Press, 1999.

Franklin, Vincent P. *Black Self-Determination: A Cultural History of the Faith of the Fathers*. New York: Lawrence Hill Books, 1992.

Freedman, David. "African-American Schooling in the South Prior to 1861." *Journal of Negro History* 84 (Winter 1999): 1–47.

George, Carol V. R. *Segregated Sabbaths: Richard Allen and the Rise of the Independent Black Churches, 1760–1840*. New York: Oxford University Press, 1973.

Gerber, David. *Black Ohio and the Color Line, 1860–1915*. Urbana: University of Illinois Press, 1976.

Glaude, Eddie S., Jr. *Exodus!: Religion, Race, and Nation in Early Nineteenth-Century Black America*. Chicago: University of Chicago Press, 2000.

Griffler, Keith. *Front Line of Freedom: African Americans and the Forging of the Underground Railroad in the Ohio Valley*. Lexington: University Press of Kentucky, 2004.

Grimsted, David. *American Mobbing, 1828–1861: Toward Civil War*. New York: Oxford University Press, 1998.

Gruenwald, Kim M. *River of Enterprise: The Commercial Origins of Regional Identity in the Ohio Valley, 1790–1850*. Bloomington: Indiana University Press, 2002.

Gutman, Herbert G. "Peter H. Clark: Pioneer Negro Socialist, 1877." *Journal of Negro Education* 34 (September 1965), 413–18.

Harding, Leonard. "The Cincinnati Riots of 1862." *Cincinnati Historical Society Bulletin* 25 (October 1977): 229–39.

Harlow, Alvin. *The Serene Cincinnatians*. New York: E. P. Dutton, 1950.

Hill, Daniel. *The Freedom-Seekers: Blacks in Early Canada*. Agincourt, Ontario: Book Society of Canada Limited, 1981.

Hinderaker, Eric. *Elusive Empires: Constructing Colonialism in the Ohio Valley, 1673–1800.* Cambridge: Cambridge University Press, 1997.

Hine, Darlene Clark, and Earnestine Jenkins, eds. *A Question of Manhood: A Reader in U.S. Black Men's History and Masculinity.* Bloomington: Indiana University Press, 1999.

Horton, James Oliver. *Free People of Color: Inside the African American Community* Washington, DC: Smithsonian Institution Press, 1993.

Horton, James Oliver, and Lois E. Horton. *Black Bostonians: Family Life and Community Struggle in the Antebellum North.* New York: Holmes and Meier, 1979.

——. *In Hope of Liberty: Culture, Community, and Protest among Northern Free Blacks, 1700–1860.* New York: Oxford University Press, 1997.

Hunter, Louis C. Steamboats on the Western Rivers: An Economic and Technological History. Cambridge, MA: Harvard University Press, 1949.

Hunter, Tera W. *To 'Joy My Freedom: Southern Black Women's Lives and Labors after the Civil War.* Cambridge, MA: Harvard University Press, 1997.

Ignatiev, Noel. *How the Irish Became White.* New York: Routledge, 1995.

Johnson, Whittington B. *The Promising Years, 1750–1830: The Emergence of Black Labor and Business.* New York: Garland, 1993.

Koehler, Lyle. *Cincinnati's Black Peoples: A Chronology and Bibliography, 1787–1982.* Cincinnati: Cincinnati Arts Consortium, 1986.

Kusmer, Kenneth L. *A Ghetto Takes Shape: Black Cleveland, 1870–1930.* Urbana: University of Illinois Press, 1976.

Laurie, Bruce. *Artisans into Workers: Labor in Nineteenth-Century America.* New York: Hill and Wang, 1989.

Litwack, Leon F. *Been in the Storm So Long: The Aftermath of Slavery.* New York: Knopf, 1979.

——. *North of Slavery: The Negro in the Free States, 1790–1860.* Chicago: University of Chicago Press, 1961.

Matthews, Samuel. "The Black Educational Experience in Nineteenth-Century Cincinnati, 1817–1874." Ph.D. diss., University of Cincinnati, 1985.

——. "John Isom Gaines: The Architect of Black Public Education." *Queen City Heritage: The Journal of the Cincinnati Historical Society* 45 (Spring 1987): 41–48.

McPherson, James M. *The Negro's Civil War: How American Negroes Felt and Acted during the War for the Union.* Urbana: University of Illinois Press, 1982.

Middleton, Stephen. "Antislavery Litigation in Ohio: The Chase-Trowbridge Letters." *Mid-America: An Historical Review* 70 (October 1988): 106–7.

——. "The Fugitive Slave Crisis in Cincinnati, 1850–1860: Resistance, Enforcement, and Black Refugees." *Journal of Negro History* 72 (Winter–Spring, 1987): 20–32.

Miller, Floyd J. *The Search for a Black Nationality: Black Emigration and Colonization, 1787–1863.* Urbana: University of Illinois Press, 1975.

Miller, Glenn. "Transportation and Urban Growth in Cincinnati, Ohio and Vicinity, 1788–1980. Ph.D. diss., University of Cincinnati, 1983.

Morris, Thomas D. *Free Men All: The Personal Liberty Laws of the North, 1780–1861.* Baltimore: Johns Hopkins University Press, 1974.

Nadel, Stanley. *Little Germany: Ethnicity, Religion, and Class in New York City, 1845–1880.* Urbana: University of Illinois Press, 1990.

Nash, Gary. *Forging Freedom: The Formation of Philadelphia's Black Community, 1720–1840.* Cambridge, MA: Harvard University Press, 1988.

Quarles, Benjamin. *The Negro in the Civil War.* New York: Da Capo, 1953.

Quillin, Frank U. *The Color Line in Ohio: A History of Race Prejudice in a Typical Northern State.* Ann Arbor, MI: George Wahr, 1913.

Parham, William Hartwell. *An Official History of the Most Worshipful Grand Lodge, Free and Accepted Masons for the State of Ohio.* n.p., 1906.

Pease, Jane H., and William H. Pease. *They Who Would Be Free: Blacks' Search For Freedom, 1830–1861.* Urbana: University of Illinois Press, 1990.

Pease, William H., and Jane H. Pease. *Black Utopia: Negro Communal Experiments in America.* Madison: State Historical Society of Wisconsin, 1963.

Phillips, Christopher. *Freedom's Port: The African American Community of Baltimore, 1790–1860.* Urbana: University of Illinois Press, 1997.

Pih, Richard. "Negro Self-Improvement Efforts in Ante-bellum Cincinnati, 1836–1850." *Ohio History* 78 (Summer 1969): 179–87.

Powers, Bernard E., Jr. *Black Charlestonians: A Social History, 1822–1885.* Fayetteville: University of Arkansas Press, 1994.

Rabinowitz, Howard N. *Race Relations in the Urban South, 1865–1890.* New York: Oxford University Press, 1978.

Rael, Patrick. *Black Identity and Black Protest in the Antebellum North.* Chapel Hill: University of North Carolina Press, 2002.

Rediker, Marcus. *Between the Devil and the Deep Blue Sea: Merchant Seamen, Pirates, and the Anglo-American Maritime World, 1700–1750.* Cambridge: Cambridge University Press, 1987.

Richards, Leonard L. *Gentlemen of Property and Standing: Anti-abolition Mobs in Jacksonian America.* New York: Oxford University Press, 1970.

Ruiz, Vicky and Ellen Carol Dubois, eds. *Unequal Sisters: A Multicultural Reader in U.S. Women's History.* New York: Routledge, 1994.

Rorabaugh, W. J. *The Alcoholic Republic: An American Tradition.* New York: Oxford University Press, 1979.

Ross, Steven J. *Workers on the Edge: Work, Leisure, and Politics in Industrializing Cincinnati, 1788–1890.* New York: Columbia University Press, 1985.

Scheiber, Harry N. *Ohio Canal Era: A Case Study of Government and the Economy, 1820–1861.* Athens: Ohio University Press, 1969.

Shotwell, John B. *A History of the Schools of Cincinnati.* Cincinnati: School Life, 1902.

Siebert, Wilbur H. *The Mysteries of Ohio's Underground Railroads.* Columbus: Long's College Book Company, 1951.

Silverman, Jason. *Unwelcome Guests: Canada West's Response to American Fugitive Slaves, 1800–1865.* Millwood, NY: National University Publications, 1985.

Simmons, William. *Men of Mark: Eminent, Progressive, and Rising.* New York: Arno, 1968.

Simpson, Donald George. "Negroes in Ontario from Early Times to 1870." Ph.D. diss., University of Western Ontario, 1971.

Stampp, Kenneth. *The Peculiar Institution: Slavery in the Ante-bellum South.* New York: Vintage Books, 1956.

Taylor, Henry Louis, Jr., ed. *Race and the City: Work, Community, and Protest in Cincinnati, 1820–1970.* Urbana: University of Illinois Press, 1993.

———. "Spatial Organization and the Residential Experience: Black Cincinnati in 1850." *Social Science History* 10 (Spring 1986) 45–69.

Taylor, Henry Louis Jr. and Vicky Dula. "The Black Residential Experience and Community Formation in Antebellum Cincinnati." In *Race and the City: Work, Community, and Protest in Cincinnati, 1820–1970,* edited by Henry Louis Taylor Jr., 96–125. Urbana: University of Illinois Press, 1993.

Thurston, Helen M. "The 1802 Constitutional Convention and Status of the Negro." *Ohio History* 81 (Winter 1972): 15–37.

Trotter, Joe William, Jr. *River Jordan: African American Urban Life in the Ohio Valley.* Lexington: University Press of Kentucky, 1998.

Turner, Frederick Jackson. *The Frontier in American History.* New York: Henry Holt, 1921.

Wade, Richard. "The Negro in Cincinnati, 1800–1830." *Journal of Negro History* 39 (January 1954): 43–57.

———. *The Urban Frontier: The Rise of Western Cities, 1790–1830.* Cambridge, MA: Harvard University Press, 1959.

Weisenburger, Steven. *Modern Medea: A Family Story of Slavery and Child-Murder from the Old South.* New York: Hill and Wang, 1998.

Winch, Julie. *Philadelphia's Black Elite: Activism, Accommodation, and the Struggle For Autonomy, 1787–1848.* Philadelphia: Temple University Press, 1988.

Winks, Robin. *The Blacks in Canada: A History.* New Haven, CT: Yale University Press, 1971.

Woodward, C. Vann. *The Strange Career of Jim Crow.* 3rd rev. ed. New York: Oxford University Press, 1974.

Works Projects Administration in the State of Ohio. *The Beautiful River.* Cincinnati: Wiesen-Hart Press, 1940.

———. *Cincinnati: A Guide to the Queen City and its Neighbors.* Cincinnati: Wiesen-Hart Press, 1943.

INDEX

Abdy, Edward, 97
abolitionists
    legacy of, in Cincinnati, 29
    in Western Reserve, 36
    colonization, opposition to, 72
    emigration, support for, 72
    Wilberforce, endorsement of, 72
    schools for African Americans,
        founding of, 109
    abolitionist journalism, birth of,
        109–12
    Philanthropist, threats against, 110
    Philanthropist, attack by mob, 111–12
    targeting by mob, 111–12, 123
    attorneys, 114–15, 158, 160
    and *State v. Farr*, 118
    souring economic relationship with
        the South, accusations of, 118
    scarcity of jobs, blame for, 119
    "nigger stealing," accusations of, 146
    and Underground Railroad, 138–60
    Fugitive Slave Act, protest against,
        155–60
activism and resistance, African Americans
    education, 46
    Canada, search for new home in, 51
    colonization, resistance to, 57
    emigrationist scheme, initiation of,
        58–63
    emigrationist position of, 59
    1829 exodus of, 64–65
    racial codes, breaking of, 119
    and insolence, 119
    Irish, fight with, 119
    and armed self-defense, 120–21,
        125–26, 159–60
    See also African Americans
"Act to preserve the purity of elections,"
    177
Adams, Enos, 70

Adcrissan, Henry, 121, 252n23
Africa, 55, 59, 60, 88, 93, 109, 164
African Americans
    population in Ohio, 1, 30, 31
    neighborhoods of, 3, 26, 38, 148,
        186, 187, 198, 199, 200, 283n4
    elite, 8, 104, 122, 128, 130, 131, 132,
        133, 134, 137, 167, 187
    population in Cincinnati, 20, 28–29,
        51, 63, 81, 91, 246n77, 283n43,
        287n82
    origins of those living in Cincinnati,
        21
    reasons for settling in Cincinnati, 21,
        28–29
    settlement in counties along Ohio
        River, 28
    migration from Cincinnati, 50, 80
    and color, 98–100, 135, 136–37,
        268n90, 281n8
    See also activism and resistance, African
        Americans; black community;
        economic conditions, African
        Americans; legal disabilities, Afri-
        can Americans; political activism,
        African Americans; racial uplift,
        African Americans; social limita-
        tions, African Americans
Africania, 60
African Lodge of Pennsylvania, 129
African Methodist Episcopal Church
        (AME), 49, 130
    birth of, 7
    history of, 7, 43–44
    affiliation with national AME, 43
    nicknamed "Little Red Church on the
        Green," 43
    location of, 43, 54, 85
    political action and discourse, site for,
        43, 48

Clarke, Molliston Madison (M. M.), 108, 112, 113
Clarkson, Thomas, 75
Clay, Henry, 55
Cleveland (OH), 35, 36, 179
Clingman, John, 45
Coffin, Catherine, 151, 152, 265n53
Coffin, Levi
autobiography of, 7
criticism of black Underground Railroad operators, 146–47, 271n40
Underground Railroad activities of, 151–54
narrative of Louis, the fugitive slave, 158
encounter with whites who refuse to help with Underground Railroad, 273n78
and Margaret Garner case, 275n104
Colbourne, John, 61, 75
Colchester (Ontario), 34, 66, 67, 247n90
Collins, Henry, 47
colonization, 56–57, 59, 164. *See also* American Colonization Society (ACS); Ohio Colonization Society (OCS)
Colored American, 163
Colored Branch of Enon Baptist Church, 87
Colored Citizen, 131–32
Colored Orphan Asylum, 130
philanthropy, funding through, 128
as racial uplift organization, 131
officers of, 136, 265n51
alternative to, 200–201
founders of, 265n49
Colored School Board, 166–69, 171, 278n34
Compromise of 1850, 154
Convention of the Colored Freemen of Ohio, 167, 280n3
Convention of the Colored Men of Ohio, 176, 179, 280n3
Convention of the People of Colour, 69, 70–72, 260n7
Corinthian Lodge, 129
Cornish, Samuel, 70, 77
Covington (KY)
ordinances regulating movement of free blacks, 36–37
link to Underground Railroad in Cincinnati, 141–42

escape from, 144, 148
fortifications in, 182
ceremony in, 183
Craft, William and Ellen, 156
crime, 185–87, 193, 196–97, 199
Crissup, Thomas, 61, 67, 78, 84
Cuffe, Paul, 60
Cuyahoga County (Cleveland, OH), 35

Dabney, Wendell, 164, 196
daguerreotyping, 133, 266n75
Darnes, Rebecca, 130
Darnes, William, 29, 130
Daughters of Samaria, 127, 264n45
Daughters of Union, 127
Davies, Samuel, 122
Dawn (Ontario), 78
Deer Creek, 12, 13, 42, 47
Deer Creek Methodist Episcopal Church, 86
construction of, 42
affiliation with white church, desire to end, 42, 43
Wesley Chapel, dependence on, 42, 44
political stand, unwillingness to take, 44–45, 88
patrons of, 45
conciliatory compliance, 122
See also New Street Chapel
Delaware Indians, 11
Democratic Party, 118, 202
Dickinson, William, 182
Disfranchised American, 131, 132
Disney, William, 65
domestic workers, 37–38
Dorcas Relief Society, 127
Dorcas, Joseph, 42
Dorum, Jane, 148, 149, 152–53
Dorum, Thomas, 143, 148, 149, 152–53
Drake, Daniel, 24, 25, 33
Dred Scott decision, 175–76
Dumas House
attack by mob, 119
station on Underground Railroad, 150–51, 196
steamboat workers, boarding of, 195
fraternity, center of, 196
gambling spot, 196
Dutton, Stephen, 8

economic conditions, African Americans oppression of, 5

Hill, Dennis, 17, 26, 112–14, 261n25
Hiram Grand Lodge, 129
Home Guards, 179–80, 182
Hoppess, State v., 144
Horton, James Oliver, 38, 135, 136
Horton, Lois E., 38
Hudson River (NY), 17
Huron, Lake, 62

indentured servitude, 30, 238n52
Independent Daughters of Hope, 127
interracial sex, 196–97
Irish, 21
    Cincinnati, settlement in, 23,
        231n66
    stereotypes of, 24
    competition with African Americans
        for jobs, 24–25, 119, 197, 198
    occupations of, 24
    neighborhoods, 24, 26
    social status of, 26
    Wilberforce, settlement in vicinity, 78
    attack by African Americans, alleged,
        119
    antiblack mobs, participation in, 124,
        197–98
    culture of, on levee, 197
    attack on black stevedores, 197
    as steamboat workers, 190
Iron Chest Company, 103, 132–33
Iroquois Council of Pennsylvania, 11

Jackson, Andrew, 55
Jeffries v. Ankeny, 281n8
John Gaines High School, 69, 172
Johnson, John, 129, 130
Jolliffe, John, 115, 158, 159–60
Jones, Absalom, 40
Jones, George, 86, 252n34
Juvenile Daughters of Samaria, 127

Keelboat Era, 15
Kentucky, 29, 101
kidnapping, 5, 32, 37, 155
King, James, 42, 43, 45, 84, 252n23
Kite, Joseph and Elijah, 159

Ladies' Benevolent Association, 128
Lane Seminary
    boarding of students with black fami-
        lies, 37
    public lectures at, 47

education of African Americans by
    students, 47, 94, 95, 164
exclusion of African Americans, 93
as catalyst for formal antislavery
    movement in Cincinnati, 108–9
debates over slavery, 109
Lane Rebels, 109, 260n14
Langston, Charles, 36
Langston, John Mercer
    autobiography of, 7
    life in Cincinnati, 36
    African Union Baptist Church, com-
        ments on, 89
    black elite, description of, 104
    witness to 1841 mob, 120, 123, 124
    and William Watson, 133, 134
    black community, comments on, 137
    Gilmore High, attendance at, 163
    taxation without representation, me-
        morial on, 179
legal cases. *See* names of specific cases
legal disabilities, African Americans
    immigration to Ohio, proscription
        of, 2
    jury service, prohibition against, 2,
        31, 35, 98
    legislative assault against, 2
    privileges of citizenship, exclusion
        from, 2, 27, 31, 177
    testifying against whites, prohibition
        against, 2, 98
    military service, exclusion from, 31,
        32, 94
    suffrage, denial of, 31, 177–78
    civil status of, 32
    intermarriage, prohibition against, 177
    taxation without representation, 177
    1851 Constitutional Convention re-
        fusal to extend rights to, 177
    See also African Americans; Black Laws
        of 1804 and 1807
Lewis, Israel, 69, 74–78
    as land agent for emigration scheme,
        61, 67
    as fundraising agent for Wilberforce,
        75–78, 250n161
    embezzlement, accusations of, 76–77
    death of, 78
    blame for "failure" of Wilberforce,
        242n2
Lexington (KY), 4
Liberator, 73, 74, 76, 77, 78

Disenfranchised American, publisher of, 131
  as teacher, 169
  and taverns, 193
North Star, 165
Northwest Ordinance, 28
Northwest Territory, 32

Oberlin (OH), 36
Oberlin College, 6, 109, 164
occupations
  of Irish, 24
  of Germans, 24
  of African Americans, 25, 101–3,
    133–34, 185–86, 188–90,
    258n135
Ohio
  black population of, 21, 30, 31
  refuge for fugitive slaves, perception
    as, 32, 33
  settlement requirements for African
    Americans, 32–35
  Black Laws of 1804 and 1807, 32–35
Ohio Anti-Slavery Society
  records of, 6
  reports of, 47, 53, 82, 97, 100,
    237n50
  temperance message of, 91
  Lane Seminary students and, 109
  Philanthropist, assumption of control of,
    111
  steamboat workers, attempt to edu-
    cate, 191
Ohio Canal
  construction of, 17
  direction of, 17
  and commerce, 18
Ohio Colonization Society (OCS), 56,
  115
Ohio constitution, 2, 3, 30, 31
Ohio constitutional conventions
  1802 convention, 30–32, 235n7,
    235n9, 235n13
  1851 convention, 177, 181, 277n27
Ohio Female Anti-Slavery Association,
  94
Ohio General Assembly
  military service, exclusion of blacks
    from, 32
  Black Laws, enactment of, 32
  petition, debate over right to, 35, 114
  fugitive slaves, fear of, 33
  repeal of Black Laws, consideration

of, 261n31
Ohio in Africa, 4, 255n78
Ohio Indians, 11, 12
Ohio Mechanics' Institute, 8, 100
Ohio River, 13, 51, 157, 160, 182, 188
  access to West, 4, 14
  names of, 10
  directions of, 10
  Alexis de Tocqueville, observations of,
    10
  origins of, 10
  descriptions of, 10
  canal system, links to, 17
  Irish settlement near, 26
  slavery, prohibition north of, 28
  African American settlement near, 28
  Promised Land, north of, 29
  workers on, 83
  Philanthropist press thrown into, 112,
    123
  fugitive slaves, transport across, 139,
    140–41, 153
  as frontier of freedom and frontier of
    slavery, 140
  as bridge between free blacks and en-
    slaved communities, 141–42
  ice on, 141, 144
  and shaping of community, 185–88
  decline of, 185, 189, 197, 198
  river workers face job dislocation,
    185–86
  steamboat workers on, 188–93
  flows on, 201
Ohio State Anti-Slavery Society, 176,
  281n5
Ohio State Auxiliary Equal Rights
  League, 165, 184
Ohio State Journal, 52
Ohio Supreme Court, 58, 99, 151,
  281n8
Ohio Territory, 28, 30
Ohio valley
  description of, 10
  early societies of, 11
Over-the-Rhine, 23

Palladium of Liberty (Columbus), 131,
  265n49
Parham, William Hartwell, 7, 129,
  265n53, 265n57
Parker, John, 269n20, 270n34
Paul, Benjamin, 70, 73, 74

Paul, Nathaniel
    manual labor college, fund-raising
        for, 69, 74
    First African Baptist Church, pastor
        of, 70
    migration from Albany, 73
    leadership of, 74
    as fund-raising agent, 75
    lectures in Glasgow, 250n140
Paul, Thomas, Jr., 74
Pearl, Mary, 196
Pennsylvania Gradual Abolition Act
    (1780), 1
Peterson, George, 129, 130, 278n41
Philadelphia (PA), 39, 40, 57, 71, 107,
    129, 139, 259n4, 260n7
Philanthropist, 109–12, 116, 112–13, 123
Piatt, J. H., 41, 42, 45, 239n79
Piatt, Jacob Wykoff, 45, 125, 239n79,
    240n100
Pickett, Henry, 194, 201, 202
Pickett's Tavern, 193–95
Pittsburgh (PA), 4, 15, 19
Plessy v. Ferguson, 162
political activism, African Americans
    petitioning, 35, 48, 93, 114, 176
    voting rights, lawsuit for, 281n8
    Fugitive Slave Act, protest against,
        155–60
    habeas corpus, 158, 176
    school board, election of, 165
    school funds, lawsuit for, 165–66
    Black Laws, repeal of, 165–66, 176
    management of own public schools
        166–74
    control of own schools, demand for,
        166–67
    rights of, 176–77
    suffrage, 177–78, 281n8
    Democratic Party, recruitment for,
        202
    See also African Americans; black com-
        munity
population
    of African Americans in Ohio, 1, 30,
        31
    of Cincinnati, 2, 19, 20, 82, 231n66,
        287n82
    of African Americans in Cincinnati,
        20, 28–29, 51, 63, 91, 246n77,
        283n43, 287n82
    of Germans in Cincinnati, 22

of Irish in Cincinnati, 22, 23–24
of Wilberforce, 74, 249n130, 249n131
Porter, Auntie, 200
Port Stanley (Ontario), 66, 74
Potter, Eliza, 7, 125, 135–36, 157,
    274n97
prostitution, 186, 187, 193, 196–97, 198,
    199
Pugh, Achilles, 111, 112, 115

racial uplift, African Americans, 90–93,
    94, 96, 104, 105, 107, 201, 131,
    258n106, 259n4
    education and progress of, 7
    school taxes, payment of, 63
    purchase of enslaved loved ones, 82
    and white philanthropic efforts,
        90–93
    temperance, 91
    education, 94, 95, 96, 174
    school attendance, 96
    and respectability, 104
    strategies of, 105
    and black convention movement, 107
    mutual aid, 127–28, 201
    and black elite, 131
    and mutuality, 131
    and literacy, 132
    Underground Railroad activities of,
        138–54
    fugitive slaves, risks of aiding, 146
    Fugitive Slave Act, resistance to,
        157–60
    orphans, care for, 200
    education, temperance, and economy,
        248n106
    platform of black convention, 259n4
    See also African Americans
racial violence. *See* mob violence; riot of
    1829; riot of 1836; riot of 1841;
    riot of 1862
railroads, 18, 185
Raisin Institute, 151
Ramsay, Charles, 110
Rights of All, 70
riot of 1829, 7, 50, 63–64, 80, 81, 105,
    106, 241n2
    class composition of mob, 64
    discussion of, during black conven-
        tion, 70–71
riot of 1836, 109–12
    Philanthropist, attacks against, 109–12

class composition of mob, III
black community, attacks against, 112
riot of 1841, 7, 117, 118–26
    black armed self-defense, 117,
        120–21, 125–26, 264n40
    composition of mob, 124, 263n16
    analysis of, 124–25
    recapture of fugitive slaves during,
        146, 286n53
riot of 1862, 197–98
    ethnic composition of mob, 198
    sanction of, in West, 228n17
    black physician, attack on home of,
        258n133
    mob, definition of, 261n23
Rochester Inquirer, 77
Ross County (OH), 31

Sandusky (OH), 65
Satchell, Charles, 88
School Fund Institute, 108, 112–13
schools, private
    Lane students, classes held by, 47
    white philanthropists, established by,
        47, 93
    African Americans, established by,
        47
    and Sunday Schools, 47
    secularization of, 47
    impermanence of, 47, 48
    white opposition to, 48
    in Wilberforce, 68–69
    underground operation of, 93
    teachers at, 94–95
    tuition, 94, 95
    locations of, 95–96
    curriculum of, 96
    financing of, 97
    challenges of, 97
    Gilmore High School, 162–63, 164
    black leaders, grooming of, 164
    See also education; schools, public
schools, public
    as centers of protest, 5
    as civil rights issue, 161
    attendance at, 167–68
    and educational capital, 168–69
    teachers at, 169
    parental involvement in, 169–70
    quality of, 170
    Colored School Board as educational
        broker of, 171–72

limited course of study, 172
school census, 172
Gaines High School, 172
as social and cultural spaces, 173
value of, 174
See also education; schools, private
Scioto River, 10
Seven Years' War, 11
shadow community, 185–202
    definition of, 186
    and steamboat workers, 188–93
    culture of, 192–93
    nightlife of, 193–95
    living arrangements of, 195–97
    interracial sex in, 196–97
    mob violence against, 197–98
    survival in, 198–200
    mutuality in, 200
    respectability of, 201–2
    political activism in, 202
Shawnee Indians, 11
Shelton, Wallace, 273n63, 278n41
Shirreff, Patrick, 8
Siebert, Wilbur, 8
Simpson, Donald, 70, 242n2
slaves
    Cincinnati ordinances regarding, 36
    impoverishment of, 51
    in transit through Ohio, 118, 139,
        143–45
    presence in Cincinnati, 143
    purchase of freedom by, 251n8
    See also fugitive slaves
social limitations, African Americans
    limited freedom of in Cincinnati, 2
    and segregation, 5, 37
    stereotypes of, 24
    antithesis of citizenship, 27
    requirements for their settlement in
        Ohio, 32–35
    public schools, exclusion from, 35,
        46, 93
    Poor Fund, denial of benefits from,
        36
    hospitals, orphanages, and house of
        refuge, denial of admission to, 36
    kidnapping of, 37, 155
    white anxiety about, 51
    white perceptions of, 52, 56
    arrest of, 122, 124
    impressment into military duty,
        180–82

Index — 313

Virginia, 29, 84
Virginia Military District, 11
voodoo, 193

wages, 18, 53, 64
Wallace, Lewis, 181
Walnut Hills, 123, 139, 151
Watson, William, 133–34, 149, 265n51, 267n79
Wattles, Augustus, 94, 109
Wayne, Anthony, 12
Webster, Daniel, 55
Webster, Delia, 151
Weld, Theodore Dwight, 109
Wesley Chapel, 41, 42
Western Baptist Association, 70
Western Emigration Society, 18
Western Reserve, 35–36
white, legal definition in Ohio, 99
Wilberforce, 50
   location of, 62
   and self-sufficiency, 62
   journey to, 65–66
   planting crops in, 66, 68
   abandonment by original settlers, 66, 78
   land, inability of settlers to purchase, 67–68
   schools, establishment of, 68–69
   manual labor college, fund-raising for, 69
   churches, establishment of, 70
   political participation in, 70

endorsement by black convention movement, 72
   as ornament of abolitionist movement, 73
   publicity about, 73
   population of, 74
   tensions between old and new leadership, 74–75
   fund-raising agents, 75–76
   Irish community, supplantation by, 78–79
   settlers, intimidation of, 78
   success of, 241n2
Wilberforce Colonization Company, 77
Wilkerson, James, 120–21
Wilson, Hiram, 77, 242n2
women (African American)
   absence from historical records, 8, 9
   as heads of household, 9
   occupations of, 102–3
   as washerwomen, 102–3
   mutual aid societies of, 127–28
   financial independence of, 134–35
   and shadow community, 201
   and middle-class womanhood, 201
Woodson, John, 120
Woodson, Lewis, 59, 60, 62, 131

Yancy, Willian. H., 131
Young, Henry, 148
Young Ladies' Orphan Aid Society, 128

Zion Baptist Church, 150, 273n63